BECOMING A POET IN ANGLO-SAXON ENGLAND

Combining historical, literary and linguistic evidence from Old English and Latin, *Becoming a Poet in Anglo-Saxon England* creates a new, more complete picture of who and what pre-Conquest English poets really were. It includes a study of Anglo-Saxon words for 'poet' and the first list of named poets in Anglo-Saxon England. Its survey of known poets identifies four social roles that poets often held – teachers, scribes, musicians and courtiers – and explores the kinds of poetry created by these individuals. The book also offers a new model for understanding the role of social groups in poets' experience: it argues that the presence or absence of a poetic community affected the work of Anglo-Saxon poets at all levels, from minute technical detail to the portrayal of character. This focus on poetic communities provides a new way to understand the intersection of history and literature in the Middle Ages.

EMILY V. THORNBURY is an Assistant Professor in the Department of English at the University of California, Berkeley.

D0885682

CAMBRIDGE STUDIES IN MEDIEVAL LITERATURE

General Editor
Alastair Minnis, *Yale University*

Editorial Board
Zygmunt G. Barański, *University of Cambridge*
Christopher C. Baswell, *Barnard College and Columbia University*
John Burrow, *University of Bristol*
Mary Carruthers, *New York University*
Rita Copeland, *University of Pennsylvania*
Roberta Frank, *Yale University*
Simon Gaunt, *King's College, London*
Steven Kruger, *City University of New York*
Nigel Palmer, *University of Oxford*
Winthrop Wetherbee, *Cornell University*
Jocelyn Wogan-Browne, *Fordham University*

This series of critical books seeks to cover the whole area of literature written in the major medieval languages – the main European vernaculars, and medieval Latin and Greek – during the period c. 1100–1500. Its chief aim is to publish and stimulate fresh scholarship and criticism on medieval literature, special emphasis being placed on understanding major works of poetry, prose, and drama in relation to the contemporary culture and learning which fostered them.

A complete list of titles in the series can be found at the end of the volume.

BECOMING A POET IN ANGLO-SAXON ENGLAND

EMILY V. THORNBURY

CAMBRIDGE
UNIVERSITY PRESS

CAMBRIDGE
UNIVERSITY PRESS

University Printing House, Cambridge CB2 8BS, United Kingdom

Cambridge University Press is part of the University of Cambridge.

It furthers the University's mission by disseminating knowledge in the pursuit of education, learning and research at the highest international levels of excellence.

www.cambridge.org
Information on this title: www.cambridge.org/9781107643079

© Emily V. Thornbury 2014

First published 2014
First paperback edition 2016

A catalogue record for this publication is available from the British Library

Library of Congress Cataloguing in Publication data
Thornbury, Emily Victoria, 1977–
Becoming a poet in Anglo-Saxon England / Emily Victoria Thornbury.
    pages   cm. – (Cambridge studies in medieval literature)
        ISBN 978-1-107-05198-0 (hardback)
 1. English poetry – Old English, ca. 450–1100 – History and criticism.
 2. Literature and society – England – History – To 1500.   I. Title.
                PR203.T46   2013
                829'.1009–dc23
                2013026730

        ISBN 978-1-107-05198-0 Hardback
        ISBN 978-1-107-64307-9 Paperback

Contents

Figures and tables

Figures

Tables

Acknowledgements

Without the support (and judgment) of a number of communities, this would have been an infinitely poorer book. The idea and research for *Becoming a Poet* began at the University of Cambridge, and I would like first to thank Rosalind Love, who supervised my doctoral work, and Andy Orchard, under whose auspices I was admitted as a postgraduate student. Given that I turned up knowing nothing whatever about Anglo-Latin, I have continual reason to be grateful to their generosity and insight. I would also like to thank the other members of the Department of Anglo-Saxon, Norse and Celtic – especially Richard Dance – for their support during my time at Cambridge. Much of the primary research for Chapters 2 and 4 of this book was undertaken while I was a Junior Research Fellow at Churchill College, Cambridge: my thanks to the Master and Fellows of the College for the opportunity to pursue my work in such a vibrant setting. And while the litany of friends, colleagues, co-conspirators, etc. that shaped my time in Cambridge is too long for a full transcription, I'd particularly like to acknowledge two sets. First, my fellow ASNCs: especially including Aaron Kleist, Chris Abram, Claudia Di Sciacca, Flora Spiegel, Leslie Lockett (ASNC *honoris causa*), Manish Sharma, Rebecca Rushforth, and the many undergraduates who survived my tutelage (and went on to great things despite it), especially Erik Nibleus. Likewise, I'd like to thank Paul Szarmach for the opportunity to work at successive NEH Summer Seminars: it was a wonderful (if occasionally perilous) experience, and gave me the chance to get to know many great colleagues, including Jacqueline Stodnick, Martin Foys, Rebecca Stephenson, Renée Trilling, Robin Norris, and Samantha Zacher. The Kalamazoo/Notre Dame nexus also put me in touch with Miranda Wilcox, who has been exceptionally generous in sharing her unpublished work.

Berkeley's English Department is a truly extraordinary place to pursue any kind of intellectual project – but especially a first book. I should like to thank the university for its generous support of my research via a Fellowship at the Townsend Center for the Humanities; a Regents Junior Faculty Fellowship; a Humanities Research Fellowship; and several conference grants. The advice and enthusiasm of my colleagues in the English Department has buoyed up this project during the years I've been working on it. Especially constant in their moral support and brilliant critique have been the junior faculty reading group, for which I have Catherine Flynn, David Landreth, David Marno, Kathleen Donegan, Nadia Ellis, Namwali Serpell, Steven Lee, Todd Carmody, and especially Eric Falci to thank. Even before I was hired, my medievalist colleagues provided both extraordinary encouragement and bracing insight: I'm a better scholar and teacher (and, no doubt, person) for working with Jennifer Miller, Maura Nolan, and Steven Justice. My thanks also to Frank Bezner for timely advice on matters Latinate, and to the Medieval Studies graduate students (especially Benjamin Saltzman and Marcos Garcia) for valuable discussion. To Katherine O'Brien O'Keeffe, I owe more than I can really express, and not just for her tireless generosity in reading repeated drafts of this book and helping me solve its problems large and small. Her friendship, wisdom, and insight into the (occasionally pitch-dark) comedy of academic life have been constant since the first, hideously early hour of new-faculty orientation here, and I'm deeply grateful.

Finally, my gratitude to Linda Bree for her advice and work on transforming a stack of paper into a Cambridge book; to the other press editors, especially Anna Bond; to the extremely helpful anonymous reviewers; and to the series editors: thanks especially to Roberta Frank for her vote of confidence. I'd also like to offer thanks to my friends and family, who have endured many complaints about The Book: the especially long-suffering include Flora Spiegel, Mairi McLaughlin, Mellody Hayes, Natalia Cecire, Sean Curran, and Yolanda Ho; and my parents, Donald and Susan Thornbury, and my sister Erin. This wouldn't have been possible without you.

Abbreviations

Abbreviations for Old English texts are those of the *Dictionary of Old English*.

ACMRS	Arizona Center for Medieval and Renaissance Studies
AH	Dreves and Blume (ed.), *Analecta hymnica*
ASC	*Anglo-Saxon Chronicle*
ASE	*Anglo-Saxon England*
ASPR	Krapp and Dobbie (eds.), *Anglo-Saxon Poetic Records*
BL	London, British Library
BN	Paris, Bibliothèque nationale
Bodleian	Oxford, Bodleian Library
CCCC	Cambridge, Corpus Christi College
CCSL	Corpus Christianorum Series Latina. Turnhout: Brepols
CSASE	Cambridge Studies in Anglo-Saxon England. Cambridge University Press
CUL	Cambridge, University Library
DAM	Bede, *De arte metrica*, ed. Kendall
DDI	Bede, *De die iudicii*, in CCSL 122, ed. Fraipont
Dümmler	Dümmler (ed.), MGH PLAC 1
EEMF	Early English Manuscripts in Facsimile. Copenhagen: Rosenkilde & Bagger
EETS	Early English Text Society. Oxford University Press
	OS Original Series
	SS Supplementary Series
Ehwald	Ehwald (ed.), *Aldhelmi Opera*
	CdV Carmen de virginitate
	CE Carmina ecclesiastica
	Enig Enigmata
ES	Wulfstan Cantor, *Epistola specialis*. In Lapidge, *Cult*
G	Gneuss, *Handlist of Anglo-Saxon Manuscripts* (references by catalogue number)

HE	Bede, *Historia ecclesiastica*, ed. Colgrave and Mynors.
JEGP	*Journal of English and Germanic Philology*
JML	*Journal of Medieval Latin*
Ker	Ker, *Catalogue of Manuscripts Containing Anglo-Saxon*
MGH	Monumenta Germaniae Historica. Berlin: Weidmann
	AA: Auctores antiquissimi
	Ep: Epistolarum
	PLAC: Poetae Latini aevi Carolini
OEB	Godden and Irvine (eds.), *Old English Boethius*
PL	*Patrologia Latina*
Tangl	Tangl (ed.), *Briefe des heiligen Bonifatius*
Vatican	Rome, Vatican City, Biblioteca Apostolica Vaticana
VC	Bede, *Vita metrica S. Cuthberti*, ed. Jaager
VW	Stephen of Ripon, *Vita S. Wilfridi*, ed. Colgrave

Introduction
How can we know about Anglo-Saxon poets?

In the nineteenth century – the Heroic Age of medieval scholarship – the distant past changed quickly. Each new edition, archaeological dig, or phonological law had the power to transform the way the premodern world appeared in the minds of the reading public. Sometimes these metamorphoses were very startling indeed, as instanced by Thomas Wright's discoveries in the Old English illustrated Hexateuch (Cotton Claudius B.iv): 'The costume of the Anglo-Saxon ladies and Anglo-Saxon boys is here very well shown; but there is one peculiarity which is deserving of special notice, the colour of the hair – sky blue.' Such an effect, Wright concluded, could only be produced by art: 'We trace in other pictorial manuscripts this taste of the Anglo-Saxons for blue hair. It must, of course, have been coloured artificially, either by a dye or by powder.' The silence of Anglo-Saxon writers on this matter suggests that they 'seem to have overlooked a little what was going on at home . . . or, perhaps, they had a taste for blue hair.'[1]

Metaphorically speaking, the Anglo-Saxons' blue hair is the terror of anyone who sets out to say something new about the past. Though Wright was not the greatest of scholars (his teacher, John Mitchell Kemble, declared him incapable of original thought), he still *was* a scholar, and he founded his conclusions on research. He looked at Cotton Claudius B.iv, in other words, saw blue hair on the painted figures, and made a straightforward deduction. Given the illustrations, Wright's idea that the Anglo-Saxons might have dyed their hair blue was rational; but once he had conceived this bold notion, he was wrong not to test it against other alternatives. If the Anglo-Saxons *had* dyed their hair blue, we would indeed expect to see pictures of people with blue hair. Yet – as Wright knew, but chose to explain away – one would also expect Anglo-Saxon writers to have mentioned the practice, and that there would be remarks on this (undoubtedly remarkable) custom in the writings of travellers to Britain or those who had dealings with the English. We would also look to encounter recipes for dye, and evidence of woad-works on a scale necessary to supply the cosmetic needs of a blue-haired nation. And yet we find none of these things.

But as Anglo-Saxonists well know, a historical situation can have widely pertained and yet have left little or no trace. When one's subjects of inquiry mainly built in perishable materials in an often damp homeland that has been continuously inhabited since, it is easy to have only a few shreds of physical evidence for practices that must have been widespread for centuries – or *may* have been widespread for a while – or may have been unique. In such circumstances, any hypothesis involves intellectual risk. To be sure, problems of epistemology are not unique to the study of Anglo-Saxon England (or indeed to the study of the past), and more evidence does not always make for more knowledge. But for scholars of cultures whose remnants are broken and effaced, the questions 'How can we know?' and – more disturbing – 'Is what we think we know true?' are naggingly constant. When there are so few traces to follow, some will almost inevitably prove to be blue herrings.

All we can do to correct our course is ask ourselves *why* we think we know what we do: to re-examine our evidence, and the principles that guide our reasoning from that evidence. In Wright's case, his problem was not ignorance of the manuscripts, or colourblindness, but his assumption that the painter of the illustrated Hexateuch's miniatures used a mimetic colour scheme, and dismissal of the most likely meaning of the lack of corroborating textual evidence. It was easier, it seems, for Wright to postulate a world of blue-haired people than one in which art did not literally represent the artists' world.

By falling headfirst into this particular intellectual ditch, Wright (and, somewhat less dramatically, many of his contemporaries) provided a valuable object lesson for scholars of the twentieth century, who perceived all too clearly how even our best efforts to shed our preconceptions and see the past through its inhabitants' eyes are bound to be imperfect. Our access to the Anglo-Saxons' world is mediated not only by an incomplete and damaged set of artifacts, but by our own presuppositions about how to interpret those artifacts. As a result, we can never fully comprehend the true otherness of the past. Contemplating the problem of how to imagine a genuinely alien consciousness, the philosopher Thomas Nagel observed that 'Our own experience provides the basic material for our imagination, whose range is therefore limited.'[2] Though the Anglo-Saxons were surely more like us than Nagel's Martians or bats, we are still constantly hampered by the temptation – perhaps the necessity – to interpret their thoughts as analogous to our own. Imaginative sympathy is so dangerous precisely because it prevents us from seeing the extent to which we have created the past in our own image.

And yet without imaginative sympathy, our capacity for discovering anything new in the past is foreclosed. Among the great accomplishments of twentieth-century scholarship has been to reject pre-existing models that were based on prejudice or naïvely anachronistic assumptions. One result of this has been a tendency towards small-scale, particularized studies rather than grand syntheses. In their acute awareness of how their predecessors went wrong, scholars in the last half-century have mainly preferred stripping away false tableaux to constructing new ones. But in the absence of a better model, the old assumptions tend to reassert themselves, like a painted image gradually showing through a layer of whitewash: for medievalists, this too often takes the form of long-refuted absurdities appearing over and over in popular culture. We need new, more accurate accounts of the culture of the past, therefore, even though this exposes us to the old dangers of misapprehension. As the inheritors of a fragmentary legacy, we are like eavesdroppers hearing only one side of a conversation. We can either resign ourselves to understanding almost nothing of what we hear, or attempt to reconstruct the other side, knowing at the same time that some of our guesses will be wrong. But by continually returning to the evidence, and by thinking through the principles on which our methodology is based, we can construct a few nets before making our *salto mortale*.

For in the twenty-first century we do in fact know a great deal more about the Anglo-Saxons' world than did our predecessors in the nineteenth. Especially in the course of the last decades, scholars have advanced to an extraordinary degree both our knowledge of the early Middle Ages, and our capacity for increasing that knowledge even further. Studies of important but neglected authors, genres, and stylistic modes have joined new editions and new tools like searchable electronic corpora of texts and manuscripts, so that it is now possible to accomplish in days what a century ago would have taken decades. With unprecedented access to primary evidence, and well-tested methodological models for interpreting that evidence, we are ideally positioned to create new synthetic accounts of the early medieval world.

This book is intended to create a new way of understanding Anglo-Saxon poets and their work by drawing upon this great wealth of scholarship. I begin my study by re-examining the bases of our knowledge. The questions I ask in the first two chapters are simple but fundamental: in Anglo-Saxon England, what was a poet, and who actually became poets? Early scholarship often evaded these questions, conflated legendary and historiographical material, or too readily assumed that the practices of other cultures (whether in Ireland, central Europe, Africa, or elsewhere) could serve as stand-ins when evidence from early England was difficult or lacking. The result has all too often been confusion or (at best) resigned agnosticism. But now that more recent studies have cleared away many of the more egregious false constructs, we can survey the entirety of the Old English corpus and a very large proportion of Anglo-Latin and, finally, answer these questions with reasonable certainty.

Chapter 1 brings together all the words for 'poet' in Anglo-Latin and Old English in order to discover what Anglo-Saxons meant when they used these words. Strikingly, we find that it was very rare indeed to refer to oneself as a poet in this period, and almost unheard-of to call contemporaries poets. This is a very different situation than we find in Ireland, say, or Scandinavia, and it points out the absolute necessity of recognizing variation among early medieval cultures. The distribution of referents for 'poet' in the Anglo-Saxon corpus also highlights another important epistemological issue: how to read blank spaces. Absence of evidence is not *necessarily* evidence of absence. But when there is no evidence of a practice – such as a formal status for poets in historical Anglo-Saxon England – and no strong reason to believe that there ever *was* such evidence, then it is best to conclude that the practice did not widely pertain.

The data presented in Chapter 1 suggest that for most of the Anglo-Saxon period, poets were not special, chosen beings, but people who, among other things, composed verse.[3] Chapter 2 sets out to discover all we still can about who those makers of verse actually were. The core prosopographical material is presented in Appendix I, as a new handlist of named poets in Anglo-Saxon England. This handlist indicates that people whom we know were poets were very likely to also be teachers, scribes, musicians, or courtiers: some were more than one of these. In Chapter 2, I examine in depth the evidence for the kinds of poetry composed by people belonging to these four groups, in order to understand what value poetry had for them and why it was worthwhile for them to become poets. This method of correlating poets with their work uncovers some striking correspondences – musicians, for instance, seem almost invariably to have also been hagiographers. By studying the social roles of known poets, we can also perceive how often Anglo-Saxon poetry was instrumental in its makers' society. Becoming a poet was useful, though sometimes indirectly so.

Once we know that most Anglo-Saxon poets practised their art as one aspect of their duties, we have a variety of new ways to understand what particular poems were for in particular times and places. But to understand the experience of the poets themselves, we must take a step back and think about poetry as a social and linguistic phenomenon. Verse is a continual negotiation between the individual and the group: between someone who presents words as poetry, and others who accept or reject them. This dynamic has consequences both for poets and for their work.

Let us take as an example the most famous story about a poet that any Anglo-Saxon has left us: Bede's account of Cædmon in *Historia ecclesiastica* iv.24. Now Cædmon emphatically was *not* a poet. Bede tells us that

> Siquidem in habitu saeculari usque ad tempora prouectioris aetatis consti-
> tutus, nil carminum aliquando didicerat. Vnde nonnumquam in conuiuio,
> cum esset laetitiae causa decretum ut omnes per ordinem cantare deberent,
> ille, ubi adpropinquare sibi citharam cernebat, surgebat a media caena et
> egressus ad suam domum repedabat.[4]

> For though he had remained in the state of a layman to a fairly advanced age,
> he had never learned any songs. And so quite often in social gatherings, when
> it had been decided that for the entertainment everyone should sing in turn,
> he would get up as soon as he saw the harp approaching him, and, leaving in
> the middle of the party, would return to his own home.

When a mysterious figure comes to him in a dream and requests a song, Cædmon apologizes:

> 'Nescio,' inquit, 'cantare; nam et ideo de conuiuio egressus huc secessi, quia
> cantare non poteram.'[5]

> 'I don't know how to sing,' he said. 'That's why I withdrew to this place after
> leaving the party, because I couldn't sing.'

As we have the story, Cædmon's actions are not those of someone who hates secular song, but of someone ashamed of his incompetence in it. He does not leave parties when the singing begins, but when he is in danger of having to produce something. Though it was his turn to take care of the cows on the fateful night he spent in the byre, Cædmon's reply to the dream-figure suggests that he thought of it mainly as a convenient refuge: *huc secessi*, he says, not *stabulam petiui*.

Why did Cædmon run away? His actions indicate actual terror at the idea of his comrades hearing him try and fail to sing something. It seems, in other words, to be the prospect of judgmental listeners that sends him back to the company of the cattle. Only when his supernatural auditor leaves him no escape – and provides him with a new subject – is he willing to make an attempt. Cædmon is made to submit to several more rounds of judgment: from his overseer, and then from the monks and the abbess of Whitby. But listeners no longer hold any terror for him, now that he is able to produce at will 'carmen dulcissimum ... suauiusque resonando doctores suos uicissim auditores sui faciebat' ('an exceedingly lovely song ... his delightful recitation of which transformed his teachers into his audience').

Cædmon's story is still an inexhaustible source of reflection, as no doubt it was meant to be.[6] For the present study, it beautifully exemplifies several aspects of what it might mean to be a poet. First, the production of poetry could simultaneously be an occasion for entertainment, collective bonding, and immense anxiety. Even when singing or reciting the words of others, a performer evidently could not expect unconditional support. It likewise seems there were rules. Apparently Cædmon's companions at the feast would not have been satisfied if he had just pretended to sing, or told a funny story instead; and when after his revelation he is brought before Abbess Hild and her more learned monks, they test him by reading a sacred text aloud, 'praecipientes eum, si posset, hunc in modulationem carminis transferre' ('bidding him to translate it into poetic metre if he could'). Only when the resulting poem is indeed found to be *optimum* is Cædmon adjudged to have been favoured by God, and invited to join the monastery. Both Hild and her monks and the laymen in the *convivium* must therefore have had a strong sense of what counted as a poem, and what made such a poem good. These communities may not have had identical standards – indeed, they probably didn't – but a poet who wanted to succeed with either audience would have to reckon with the opinions of the group.

Seventh-century Whitby is such a useful paradigm because it was not unique. Though Cædmon's flight to the cowshed was perhaps excessive, poems in both Old English and Latin reveal that their creators were likewise deeply concerned with anticipating and managing the reaction of hearers and readers. Poetry provides a very specific, rule-governed venue for judging others' words, but the impulse to police language is a universal feature of human societies. As I show in Chapter 3, tools developed to help us understand how communities interact with language allow us to perceive something of what it was like to be an Anglo-Saxon poet in a community. Sociolinguistics, in particular, is an immensely useful resource: by reverse-engineering models of the behaviour of modern speech communities, we can see the imprint of the Anglo-Saxons' vanished social groups on their work.

The expectation of judgment is the most telling sign of poets' experience in communities. As the mechanism by which individuals are kept within the bounds of group norms, judgment is a pervasive feature of linguistic behaviour, especially in communities where dialect is a major part of the group's identity. In poetic communities – groups, that is, that will receive and judge a poem – judgment is a constant. We see reflections of this throughout Anglo-Saxon literature, together with canny strategies for turning that judgment to the poets' advantage. Voice is one simple but powerful method. Just as Cædmon coaxed his audience to share his burden in the opening phrase of his poem, *Nu sculon herigean* ('Now *we* must praise'), subtle shifts in person reveal how Anglo-Saxon poets worked to bring their audience into solidarity with their aims. Skilled poets, however, had many tactics to rely on. In Chapter 3 I show how the author of *The Battle of Maldon* uses evaluation – a notable feature of oral narrative – to redirect the audience's judgment from the poem to the behaviour of the characters within it. The result is a triumph of verisimilitude, one that still persuades modern readers as it likely also persuaded audiences at the end of the tenth century.

Though we usually cannot know who Anglo-Saxon poets' audiences were, we can often tell a good deal about what the poets thought they were. Cynewulf, for instance, includes books and readers in the circle of those whom he expects to judge him (and who, he gently suggests, will also themselves be judged). Cynewulf's seamless, apparently untroubled incorporation of written media into his imagined poetic community indicates that the transition between oral and literate modes of thinking about poetry was not always difficult or traumatic. By thinking of books as people – or as a straightforward means of speaking to people – Cynewulf could envision a community unbound by time that nevertheless acted and judged just as any other community. The writings of Aldhelm, too, imply a world in which written poetry was a useful means of maintaining social ties, rather than an alternative system of existence. Aldhelm is almost unique in the extent of the available material for documenting his real-world social system. By mapping his overlapping commitments (to students, teachers, ecclesiastical colleagues, and royal kindred) we can see how literature worked to create and reinforce bonds between people. Reconstructing Aldhelm's connections also helps us understand how his writings – and his style – spread so quickly across Britain. The breadth and complexity of his social network is an important reason that his work became paradigmatic: he knew his audience.

Cædmon seems to have spent his later life as a respected figure in Whitby monastery, enjoying, Bede tells us, the reputation of a moral instructor.[7] If his later poems had survived, they would doubtless tell us a good deal about what it was like to be a poet in that community. But one of the most interesting features of the story as Bede tells it is the way Cædmon is presented as innocent of worldly corruption. *He* seems deeply ashamed of his inability to remember or produce secular songs, but Bede leaves us in no doubt that this was a Good Thing:

> Namque ipse non ab hominibus neque per hominem institutus canendi artem didicit, sed diuinitus adiutus gratis canendi donum accepit. Vnde nil umquam friuoli et superuacui poematis facere potuit, sed ea tantummodo, quae ad religionem pertinent, religiosam eius linguam decebant.[8]

> For he, taught 'not of men, nor by man,' did not so learn the art of singing, but as one divinely aided received by grace the gift of singing. He could therefore never make any frivolous and inane poem; only those that pertained to religion were worthy of his religious voice.

Though Cædmon had heard worldly poems for years, he remained a blank slate, ready for the inscription of heavenly words. He was able to 'start from scratch' and to be the first and greatest of the creators of English religious verse. Whether or not Cædmon's poetry was really devoid of influence from the secular poetry he had heard but not made (a point modern scholars doubt), the idea of beginning from first principles was very much in line with *Bede's* philosophy of verse.

As I discuss in Chapter 4, Bede's own poetry is indeed that of one who has tried to reject immediate influences and start afresh. He depends not on the standards of a knowledgeable community, but instead on standards he has deduced for himself from his own reading. This remarkable, apparently self-imposed poetic isolation gives Bede's poetry a unique stylistic signature, along with many of the peculiarities common to autodidacts. While Cynewulf's work shows us that literacy was wholly compatible with a living poetic community, nevertheless only the advent of writing could make it possible to become a poet alone. In such authors, as I show through a close study of the Old English *Christ and Satan*, we see how isolated poets read earlier works in order to extrapolate rules for their own verse. But without a wider community to determine what was right or wrong, these autodidacts tended to generate rules that (though logical) were strange, and which a better-connected poet would often have considered incorrect. Many of the metrical oddities of *Christ and Satan* as it stands in Junius XI can be traced back to its redactor's use of a flawed manuscript of earlier verse, in much the same way that Bede's idiosyncratic use of archaisms stems from his determination to derive stylistic rules from first principles.

There was no single, universal way of becoming an Anglo-Saxon poet, then, and from the diversity of poets' experiences – and the diversity of the communities within which they worked (or didn't) – we have received such a diverse corpus of poetry. In the final chapter of this book, I explore three case studies representing intermediate modes of community and isolation. The isolation of a small community, for example, made the verse produced by St Boniface and his English colleagues in Germany increasingly self-similar, as the Aldhelmian style the missionaries favoured became a touchstone for their group identity: this is a phenomenon seen also in isolated dialects. Conversely, isolation *within* a community – as experienced by Wulfstan Cantor, an extraordinarily gifted poet and musician who became precentor of Winchester Cathedral in the late tenth century – also produced a drive towards self-similarity. Wulfstan's responsibility to speak for the community (or perhaps, rather, to produce words through which it might choose to speak) seems to have resulted in some characteristic stylistic tics. As a kind of poetic intercessor, Wulfstan developed a signature style that helped him fulfil his duties to the Winchester community.

In the late tenth and eleventh centuries we also see the development of a new form of Old English verse that gives us insight into the formation of new poetic communities. The rise to hegemony of the Wessex kings coincided with the rise of English as a language of administration and of intellectual inquiry in England. We see this reflected in a new strain in the poetry of the period: though peculiar by the standards of Cynewulf or the *Beowulf*-poet, late Southern verse is remarkable for the way it presents readers with a simulacrum of the experience of reading Latin texts. Alienation from the style of earlier vernacular poetry enabled poets to create in their readers, at least some of whom were probably laypeople, a sense of participating directly in high ecclesiastical and philosophical culture. The ascension of the Southern mode shows us how Anglo-Saxon poets could create new forms to serve new goals and new communities.

Chapter 5's case studies do not exhaust the possibilities for studying the interaction between Anglo-Saxon poets and their communities. The texts and poets that appear in this study do so because they exemplify particularly clear or interesting ways of becoming a poet, and therefore tend to be those about whose circumstances something concrete is known. But I believe that works of more ambiguous origin – including much of the Old English corpus – are also amenable to this approach. The value of my model, as I see it, is that it lets us recognize how poetry is both a sociolinguistic phenomenon and a particular rule-governed art. My hope is that *Becoming a Poet* will help us develop a richer, more finely grained understanding of how poetry worked in the communities that helped give it birth. Each region was different, and so was each town, monastery, book, and time-period: further study of these local environments will help us see their reflections in the poems produced within them. But each poet, too, was different. An individual's art was not an inevitable consequence of his or her environment, but rather a negotiation with and reaction to it. Anglo-Saxons, on the whole, became poets in order to live more fully within their world, and by studying the social environment of their poetry we can understand more fully how they thought it was best to live.

CHAPTER I

What was a poet?

Like 'love,' the word 'poet' has connotations so far-reaching and deeply established that its use brings some danger of misunderstanding into even the driest and most technical discussion. Any two discussants may intend something altogether different by the same word, and may never discover it because to each the meaning seems wholly transparent, although the ideas meant by 'poet' – again, like 'love' – have long been recognized as subject to cultural and historical variation. The difficulty lies in the temptation to interpret such variations as failures or deviation from the 'universal truth' of one's own assumptions. This was a continual pitfall for early historians of Anglo-Saxon culture. Sharon Turner, for instance, introduced poetry into his *History of the Anglo-Saxons* with these remarks:

> In no country can the progress of the poetical genius and taste be more satisfactorily traced than in our own. During that period which this work attempts to commemorate, we find it in its earliest state. It could, indeed, have scarcely been more rude, to have been at all discernible. But though its dress was homely, and its features coarse, yet it was preparing to assume the style, the measures, and the subjects, which in subsequent ages were so happily displayed as to deserve the notice of the latest posterity . . .

> In the mind of poetry we look for its imagination, its feeling, and its force of thought; but these in all ages obey and display the tastes, sentiment, and habits of the passing day. In the Anglo-Saxon times, though women were highly respected and valued, yet that cultivated feeling which we call love, in its intellectual tenderness and finer sympathies, was neither predominant nor probably known. The stern and active passions were the rulers of society, and all the amusements were gross or severe. Women were reverenced, but not loved; and hence, except in the little effusions which have been noticed of our self-cultivated Alfred, there is no affectionate allusion to the fair sex in any Anglo-Saxon poem.[1]

For Turner, difference is unidirectional: the past's strangeness deviates from the normality of the present. His images present this in a variety of ways: the past as infancy ('earliest state'); as peasantry ('its dress was homely, and its features coarse'); as emotional wilderness ('yet that cultivated feeling'). But one of the odder corollaries of this equation requires difference to be multiplied: because Anglo-Saxon literature is unlike the modern, therefore the inner experience and actual nature of its producers must also radically differ.

I have quoted Turner because he is not a straw man: his work was historically important to the development of Anglo-Saxon scholarship, and the immense breadth of his reading means that, after more than two hundred years, it can still occasionally be useful.[2] He also, however, stands at the head of a long train of assumptions about the makers of Anglo-Saxon verse based on hypothetical reconstructions of a prehistoric era. Witness his summary of the development of Old English poetry:

> Thus humbly, it is conceived, the Anglo-Saxon poetry arose: at first the rude exclamations of a rude people, with a rude language, greeting their chieftains; soon repeated or imitated by some men, from the profit derived from it. When, from the improvement of the manners and state of the people, a more cultivated style, or that we call prose, became general, because better fitted to the uses of life, then the old rude style dropped out of common use. The bards, however, retained and appropriated this, because more instrumental to their professional advantages. To enjoy these more exclusively, to secure their monopoly of credit and gifts, they added more difficulties to the style they adopted, to make it more remote from the vulgar attainment; till at length their poetical style became for ever separated from prose.[3]

Several crucial themes conjoin here: the primitivism of Old English poetry; its essential connection to a tribal system of power; the poet as part of a class removed from normal society, enjoying special privileges through the exercise of his art, and manipulating a language whose esoteric purpose brings it closer to a thieves' argot than to an elevated register. Turner's choice to refer to these composers of verse as *bards* is also important, for it avoids the modern word 'poet' – with all the connotations it would have held for a reader of English at the beginning of the nineteenth century – in favour of a term equally freighted, but with rather different meanings. The bard was closely connected with a Celtic past newly reimagined by Turner's contemporaries.

In her learned and amusing lecture 'The Search for the Anglo-Saxon Oral Poet', Roberta Frank conducted a tour of 'an oral-poet theme park, a Bard-World' to demonstrate that many common ideas about what genuine (and therefore oral) Anglo-Saxon poets must have been were derived from Romantic notions of Celtic bards or Norse skalds – which in turn owed as much to imagination as to scholarship.[4] Her thesis – that 'each age gets the Anglo-Saxon oral poet it deserves' – is illustrated with examples from both early and recent scholarship, demonstrating that what we see in the past is as much a function of 'the tastes, sentiment, and habits of the passing day' as contemporary literature.[5] This leaves us with something of a dilemma, for seeing with eyes other than our own is a great difficulty: we can only hope that, once we have cleared away some illusions, what remains is actually in some sense *there* – remnants of a past that was not expecting or foretelling us, but would exist whether we were here or not.[6]

Though Frank's demolition programme revealed how many scholarly constructs were without foundations, it did not eradicate all trace of such longstanding assumptions. The ghost of the Anglo-Saxon bard persists, and must be addressed before it can be dismissed. The main tenet of this 'bardic' view of Anglo-Saxon poetry as developed in the nineteenth and twentieth centuries is that poets held a separate, exalted, and semi-sacral place in society, one that was essential to the proper conduct of secular life. In the section on Old English in *A Literary History of England* (1967), the authors stated that

> At an early date Germanic kings began to keep professional poets, with functions not wholly unlike those of the poet laureate or official poet of later times. Among the English a court poet was called a *scop* or *gleeman* ... We conclude that the scop had the important function of immortalizing his patron by singing his praises. These poems of praise, handed down by word of mouth, and making part of the repertory of many a gleeman, were meant to keep the prince's name and deeds alive in the minds of men forever.[7]

More recently, Charles Dunn wrote that the Old English 'poet is trusted as the potential savior of the tribe, for he has acquired traditional wisdom and can be expected to utter his potent judgments whenever he is called upon to do so'.[8] (It is worth noting that in Dunn's discussion of the Old English poet, he provides five lines of inset quotations from Old English poems, and five from Welsh.) In his study of Anglo-Saxon oral poets, Jeff Opland concluded that

> The scop uttered eulogies in praise of the chief or king and his ancestors, and in so doing ensured the sympathetic attention of the dynasty to the concerns of the present ruler. Since that ruler was sacral ... the scop was in effect establishing the well-being of the people through his eulogies of the ruler: he was the king's poet as well as the tribal poet.[9]

Frank provides a chain of similar appearances of the Anglo-Saxon bard and his royal patrons, some from the 1990s.[10] Like earlier studies such as

Anderson's *The Anglo-Saxon Scop*, all three of the discussions just cited rely heavily on three Old English texts: *Beowulf*, *Widsith*, and *Deor*.

On the whole, most recent scholarship has not rejected the vatic image of the Anglo-Saxon poet so much as it has declined to take a position on the matter. For instance, the influential *New Critical History of Old English Literature* uses 'poet' strictly with a logical meaning of 'author of a particular poem'.[11] The eighth edition of the *Norton Anthology of English Literature* frequently resorts to the passive voice – e.g., 'Germanic heroic poetry continued to be performed orally in alliterative verse and was at times used to describe current events.'[12] Silence on the identity of Anglo-Saxon poets has strategic merit. Close reading – still perhaps the most versatile weapon in the modern critical arsenal – is originally based on a philosophy of literature that explicitly repudiates the relevance of external factors, including authorial identity. Even more contextualized modes of reading, such as those that examine poems in relation to their presumed sources, manuscripts, or reception and use, do not necessarily require knowledge of the author's identity or circumstances. Indeed, since almost all Old English poetry has been transmitted anonymously, Anglo-Saxonists have worked to develop modes of reading which do not demand assumptions or conclusions about authorship, date, or even relative chronology.

Yet the fossilized traces of older views remain. The *Norton Anthology*, for instance, refers to the 'Germanic *scop*, or bard', and its notes on *Beowulf* prefer the term 'bard' for performers of oral compositions.[13] In the absence of a new conception of who and what an Anglo-Saxon poet was, it seems those who wish to speak about the creators of verse are forced to rely on the old vocabulary – and thus, in part, on old assumptions. The purpose of this chapter, therefore, is to re-examine the evidence for the Anglo-Saxons' own conceptions of what poets were. By clarifying the implications of calling someone a *scop* or *poeta*, we can draw firmer conclusions about what the category of 'poet' contained, and construct a more accurate critical vocabulary. In other words, my goal here is to establish what we talk about when we talk about Anglo-Saxon poets.

The literary *scop*

The trouble with the bardic idea of the *scop* is that it is built on assertions about the social status of poets in the *historical* period derived mainly from literary works set in a fictionalized Heroic Age. As John Niles has pointed out, the Anglo-Saxons' own vision of Germanic poets, as seen in the poems *Deor*, *Widsith*, and *Beowulf*, was as romantic in its own way as that of eighteenth-century antiquarians. The picturesquely named Deor and Widsith were creatures mainly of legend, born perhaps, as Niles persuasively suggests, partly out of longing for the imagined Heroic Age's 'simplicity of master/man relations in a world where the actual workings of power were becoming ever more remote and impersonal'.[14] Thus poetry and power enjoy a happy union in Widsith's description:

> Ond ic wæs mid Eormanrice ealle þrage,
> þær me Gotena cyning gode dohte.
> Se me beag forgeaf, burgwarena fruma,
> on þam siex hund wæs smætes goldes,
> gescyred sceatta scillingrime.
> Þone ic Eadgilse on æht sealde,
> minum hleodryhtne, þa ic to ham bicwom,
> leofum to leane, þæs þe he me lond forgeaf,
> mines fæder eþel, frea Myrginga.
> Ond me þa Ealhhild oþerne forgeaf,
> dryhtcwen duguþe, dohtor Eadwines;
> hyre lof lengde geond londa fela
> þonne ic be songe secgan sceolde,
> hwær ic under swegle selast wisse
> goldhrodene cwen giefe bryttian.[15]

And I was with Eormanric for a long time, where the king of the Goths treated me well. He, lord of the city-dwellers, gave me a ring, whose value in money was reckoned at six hundred gold coins. This I gave to Eadgils, into the possession of my gracious lord once I had arrived home, as recompense to my dear lord, since he, lord of the Myrgings, gave me land, my father's homestead. And then Ealhhild, Eadwine's daughter, noble queen among the host, gave me another [ring]; her glory extended through many lands when I would recount in song where I knew the best gold-adorned queen under the skies was sharing out gifts.

Ealhhild's generosity to the poet and her immortalization in song are part of the same process of reciprocal gift-giving rather than commercial exchange. Widsith is the ideal retainer: he has travelled the world and received vast wealth, but the relationship he values most is that with his own lord, Eadgils. To him Widsith gladly gives the treasures he acquired abroad, in return for receiving 'mines fæder eþel' (96a: 'my father's homestead'). Interestingly, poetry has no direct role in this, the poem's most significant exchange: Widsith is a loyal retainer returning from profitable service abroad, like Beowulf returning to Hygelac's court. What seems to matter is the intimacy of the gift-giving, rather than how the gifts were acquired.

In *Deor*, we also see a lord–retainer relation between a secular leader and a poet, albeit one gone wrong:

> Þæt ic bi me sylfum   secgan wille,
> þæt ic hwile wæs   Heodeninga scop,
> dryhtne dyre –   me wæs Deor noma.
> Ahte ic fela wintra   folgað tilne,
> holdne hlaford,   oþþæt Heorrenda nu,
> leoðcræftig monn   londryht geþah
> þæt me eorla hleo   ær gesealde.
> Þæs ofereode,   þisses swa mæg.[16]

> What I will say about myself is that I once was a poet of Heoden's folk, dear to my lord: my name was Deor. For many years I had a good place, a loyal lord, until now Heorrenda, a man clever in his poems, has received the land-right that the protector of warriors formerly gave me. That passed over; so may this.

This is one of only two instances in Old English in which a speaker describes himself as a *scop* (the other self-proclaimed *scop*, in Exeter *Riddle* 8, is a nightingale). Like Widsith, Deor received land for his service, although Heorrenda has now been rewarded in the same way.[17] It has generally been assumed that Deor held some sort of official post:[18] Heorrenda's advent has seemingly displaced his predecessor, which suggests there could be only one poet at a time, rather in the style of the Poet Laureate invoked by Baugh and Malone above. It is possible that Deor's position at court was never imagined as a formal one, however, and that Heorrenda, apparently renowned as a singer in heroic legend, has received attention and favour, but not an office or title.[19] Probably, though, it is misguided to interrogate the details of Deor's status too closely, for the famous names with which he associates himself – Heoden and Heorrenda – proclaim the fictionality of his lament in a gesture that cleverly reorients both the catalogue of legendary episodes and the poem's refrain. As Niles explains it,

> the fictive speaker Deor uses the rhetoric of first-person address to insert himself into the same legendary world that he evokes in the earlier parts of the poem through his allusions to Weland the smith, Theodoric the Goth, Eormanric the Goth, and other legendary figures of the Germanic past. At the end of the poem we therefore make a discovery . . . Not only have we been hearing about heroes of the Germanic Heroic Age, those larger-than-life inhabitants of the Continental homeland of the English. In a bold conceit, we are to imagine ourselves in the presence of one of them.[20]

Deor's poem, then, tells us something about what an Anglo-Saxon poet imagined it was like to live in the Heroic Age: as with Rosencrantz and

Guildenstern in Tom Stoppard's skewed take on *Hamlet*, being a support-
ing character required a stiff dose of philosophy.

The poets in *Beowulf* are more ambiguous figures, less immediately
present than either Widsith or Deor. No *scop* speaks directly in *Beowulf*,
and it is not always clear when one is speaking indirectly. For instance, when
Heorot is first built, we hear that

> þær wæs hearpan sweg,
> swutol sang scopes.   Sægde se þe cuþe
> frumsceaft fira   feorran reccan,
> cwæð þæt se ælmihtiga   eorðan worhte . . .[21]

there was the sound of the harp, the sweet song of the poet. He spoke who
knew how to recount from afar the first creation of men: he said that the
Almighty made the earth . . .

While the *scop* and *se þe cuþe* might be the same man – the paratactic
connection is consistent with the *Beowulf*-poet's style – it is possible that the
Creation was retold in normal speech, not verse, and that as many as three
different performers are enumerated here. Likewise, the man who tells the
story of Sigemund and the dragon on the journey back from Grendel's mere
is usually presumed to be reciting (or improvising) poems:

> Hwilum cyninges þegn,
> guma gilphlæden,   gidda gemyndig,
> se ðe eal fela   ealdgesegena
> worn gemunde,   word oþer fand
> soðe gebunden;   secg eft ongan
> sið Beowulfes   snyttrum styrian
> ond on sped wrecan   spel gerade,
> wordum wrixlan;   welhwylc gecwæð
> þæt he fram Sigemundes   secgan hyrde
> ellendædum . . .[22]

Other times, the king's retainer, a man laden with brave words, mindful of
sayings, he who remembered an immense number of old stories, forged other
words bound truly together; the man again began skilfully to recount
Beowulf's journey and cleverly to make a story well, varying his words; he
told almost everything that he had heard tell from Sigemund's brave deeds . . .

This passage is often analysed as an example of oral performance and, possibly,
improvisation of verse.[23] We should note, though, that poetry is not actually
specified, and some of the vocabulary – especially *spel* and *saga* – is more
usually associated with non-verse discourse. Like most scholars, I do think
that the style of both these passages indicates that the *Beowulf*-poet is

describing the performance of verse; but it is important to remember that this is a matter of interpretation. One could also consider the 'Last Survivor' and the old man mourning his hanged son to be poets. The former is possibly lamenting in verse (we are simply told that he *fea worda cwæð*, 'spoke a few words': 2246b); if so, his is *Beowulf*'s only directly inset poem. The old man does seem to be described as composing verse – we are told *he gyd wrece, / sarigne sang*, 'he might make a poem, an anguished song' (2446b–7a) – but he exists only as Beowulf's extended simile for King Hrethel's grief at his own son's death.

So the only indisputable instance of performed verse in *Beowulf* is the 'Finnsburh episode', sung during the feast in Heorot after Grendel's defeat. We are told:

> Þær wæs sang ond sweg   samod ætgædere
> fore Healfdenes   hildewisan,
> gomenwudu greted,   gid oft wrecen,
> ðonne healgamen   Hroþgares scop
> æfter medobence   mænan scolde
> be Finnes eaferum . . .[24]

> There was song and music both together in the presence of Healfdene's battle-leader: the harp touched, a story often made, when along the mead-bench Hrothgar's poet related the hall-entertainment about Finn's children . . .

The *Beowulf*-poet proceeds to relate the story in his own words, and when the episode concludes it is described as a *leoð* and *gleomannes gyd*, 'poem' and 'gleeman's tale' (1159b, 1160a). But the identity of *Hroþgares scop* is left uncertain. Curiously, when Beowulf later describes the feast for Hygelac, he seems to imply that Hrothgar himself told the story:

> Þær wæs gidd ond gleo;   gomela Scilding,
> felafricgende   feorran rehte;
> hwilum hildedeor   hearpan wynne,
> gomenwudu grette,   hwilum gyd awræc
> soð ond sarlic,   hwilum syllic spell
> rehte æfter rihte   rumheort cyning. . .[25]

> There was conversation and rejoicing; the aged descendant of Scyld, having learned many things, recounted from far back; sometimes the battle-brave man for the harp's joy touched the instrument, sometimes made a true and sorrowful poem, sometimes the magnanimous king accurately recounted a marvellous tale. . .

It is quite possible that the *gomela Scilding*, *hildedeor*, and *rumheort cyning* are three different people; the passage is very ambiguous.[26] However, *gamela*

Scylding is only used once elsewhere in *Beowulf*: at 1792a, where it unambiguously describes Hrothgar. The word *hildedeor* occurs several times, but
elsewhere it only describes Beowulf or (after his death) his chief thegns: it is
not, therefore, a standard epithet for a warrior.[27] This makes it perhaps
more likely that Hrothgar is intended by all three phrases, but not beyond
doubt. If Hrothgar *is* meant as the reciter of the 'Finnsburh episode', then
Hroþgares scop (1066b) must be read as a metaphor meaning 'Hrothgar's
poetic skill', perhaps akin to *widcuþes wig* ('the battle-prowess of the far-
renowned man': literally, 'the battle of the far-renowned one', 1042a). Such
an interpretation seems strained, but not impossible.

On the whole, the evidence from *Beowulf* seems to indicate that its poet
believed one did not need to be called a *scop* to compose poetry. Beowulf
imagines the unfortunate father composing poems on his son's death; the
king's thegn seems to perform verse on the way back from Grendel's mere;
and Hrothgar himself may be making or reciting poems. However, Deor
and Widsith seem to be solely or mainly poets: their skill in making or
performing poems is apparently integral both to their identities and to their
livelihoods. These latter in turn are bound up with the deeply personal
lord–retainer relations of Heroic Age society as commonly envisioned in
Old English literature. It is also possible that Hrothgar was imagined to
retain one or more poets whose sole function was to make and perform verse
in Heorot, although this is much less clear.

In Old English poems set in the Heroic Age, then, the Anglo-Saxons
seemed to share an idea of a world in which there were poets at court, even if
these were not quite the same as later scholarly conceptions of court poets.
The traveller rewarded by rulers for his songs should be viewed as a vital part
of the Anglo-Saxons' own 'mental modeling of their ancestral past', as Niles
puts it.[28] Characters like Widsith, Deor, and the unnamed poets in *Beowulf*
surely affected the self-conception of real Anglo-Saxon poets – by contrast,
if nothing else. But the mythic dimension cannot have been the only
component of Anglo-Saxon ideas of the poet, and one way of glimpsing
more workaday notions of what being a poet would have meant can be
found in the way the word 'poet' itself was used.

Words for the poet: Old English

In *Anglo-Saxon Oral Poetry*, Opland provides a detailed consideration of
Old English words for poets and poetry in an attempt to discern nuances of
genre and practice. Opland's main concern was to demonstrate that, contrary to the assumption that the 'Anglo-Saxon oral poet [was] a harper who

entertained the guests in his lord's hall, a scop who could also be called a gleoman', the true poet – the *scop* – unlike the *gleoman*, was not an itinerant performer and did not accompany himself with an instrument when presenting his compositions.[29] Although Opland's study was published the year before the complete corpus of Old English was made available in machine-searchable form,[30] his conclusions are still in part tenable. It certainly does seem there was a sense-distinction between the *scop*, a poet, and the *gleoman*, a more general sort of entertainer. Ælfric's *Glossary* gives a good instance of this distinction:

> *poeta.* sceop oððe leoðwyrhta.
> *mimus* oððe *scurra.* gligmann.[31]

> *Poet.* Scop or leoðwyrhta.
> *Mime* or *clown.* Gleoman.

These two glosses are consecutive; perhaps significantly, they also follow a batch of glosses on musical instruments and their players, although I think this is not necessarily damaging to Opland's argument. He may be correct in his contention that there was never an instrumental component to the performance of Old English epic verse: this would have significant implications for some theories of Old English metre.

Opland's focus, however, was purely on the *oral* poet. A broader examination of the way poets of all sorts were discussed in Anglo-Saxon texts, however, would be of greater use in establishing whom contemporaries or successors identified as poets; how (or whether) poets self-identified as such; and the general tenor of references to poets. It is difficult to establish words' associations for their users from limited and ambiguous evidence, but often one can determine whether particular terms had positive, negative, or neutral connotations. Accordingly, I have examined all uses of words for 'poet' in Old English, and as many as I have been able to gather for Anglo-Latin. Thanks to the work of the *Dictionary of Old English* and the *Thesaurus of Old English*, it is possible to speak with considerable confidence about such vernacular literature as survives. The situation of Anglo-Latin is more difficult. Latin was never a 'mother tongue' during the historical Anglo-Saxon period, and it is not always clear what models of Latinity the Anglo-Saxons themselves regarded as authoritative, though generally they seem to have conformed to expected usage – which is to say, that of the patristic, Late Antique, or (later in the period) Carolingian texts they seem mainly to have read. Moreover, although that part of the corpus edited to date in the *Monumenta Germaniae Historica*, *Patrologia Latina*, *Acta Sanctorum*, and *Corpus Christianorum – Series Latina* is now searchable

Table 1.1 *Anglo-Saxon words for 'poet'*

Old English	Latin
Group 1	poeta
scop	uates
leoðwyrhta	uersificus
meterwyrhta	*In genres*
Group 2	comicus
woðbora	lyricus
gleoman	tragicus
sangere	satiricus

Table 1.2 *Old English words for 'poet'*

Word	Total	Incidence		
		A	B	C
scop	115	115	-	-
leoðwyrhta	6	6	-	-
meterwyrhta	1	1	-	-
woðbora	7	-	4	3
gleoman	24	-	10	14
sangere	30	-	5	25
Total	183	122	19	42

A: Certainly or almost certainly referred to someone who composed in verse
B: Possibly refers to composer of verse
C: Probably or certainly *does not* refer to composer of verse

electronically, many important texts are not online, and much lexical evidence, such as occasional glossing, remains unedited. The discussion of Anglo-Latin usage presented here is based entirely on published texts, and must therefore be regarded as somewhat incomplete.

Table 1.1 lists and groups the Old English and Latin words used to designate poets; Table 1.2 shows the incidence of the vernacular words. Three Old English words unambiguously mean *poet*: *scop* (and its compounds), *leoðwyrhta*, and *meterwyrhta*. Of these, *scop* is by far the most common; it occurs in all forms of text, and should be considered the 'normal' Old English term for a poet. *Meterwyrhta* is found only in the Cleopatra Glossary under the lemma *metricus*, and is probably a loan-formation.[32] The distribution of *leoðwyrhta* is more interesting. While two thirds of its occurrences are in glossaries (where it renders *poeta*, *uates*, or the very rare word *melopius*),[33] it also turns up twice in the Old English versions of Boethius: in the prose, where it loosely translates the Latin *tragoediarum clamor* (II, pr. ii);[34] and in the verse preface to the prosimetrical text in BL, Cotton Otho A.vi:

> Ðus Ælfred us   ealdspell reahte,
> cyning Westsexna,   cræft meldode,
> leoðwyrhta list.   Him wæs lust micel
> ðæt he ðiossum leodum   leoð spellode,
> monnum myrgen,   mislice cwidas,
> þy læs ælinge   ut adrife
> selflicne secg,   þonne he swelces lyt
> gymð for his gilpe.   Ic sceal giet sprecan,
> fon on fitte,   folccuðne ræd
> hæleðum secgean.   Hliste se þe wille.[35]

Thus Alfred recounted us old stories: the king of the West Saxons, a versifier, revealed his skill and wit. He had a great desire to retell poems for these people, various sayings as amusement for men, lest weariness drive away the proud man, heeding for his arrogance few things of this sort. I shall speak further, making into episodes the counsel known to the people [which] I shall tell to warriors. Let him listen who will.

Here, *leoðwyrhta* (3a) is in apposition with *Ælfred* (1a) and *cyning Westsexna* (2a), explicitly identifying King Alfred as the poet. But it is not clear who is calling Alfred a *leoðwyrhta*: the preface's voice is ambiguous, since *us* (1a) could be either dative or accusative. If the former, it is probably in apposition with *ðiossum leodum* (4a); otherwise, it agrees with *ealdspell*, as Earl has argued.[36] Earl's contention – that this metrical proem, like the metrical proem and epilogue to Alfred's Old English version of the *Cura Pastoralis*, is voiced by the book itself and the texts it contains – is in many respects appealing. But elsewhere in the *Metres of Boethius*, finite forms of *reccean* are always preceded by a pronominal indirect object, making it more likely that *us* denotes those hearing the *ealdspell*.[37] This still does not altogether resolve the question of the poem's voice, for the shift to the first person singular in 8b seems to imply the speaker is the poet. This would render *us* (1a) a feint, part of the third person humility topos seen in the prose preface of the Cotton version of the Boethius, and would make it likely, as Godden argued in 1990, that the speaker is Alfred himself.[38] But O'Brien O'Keeffe raises an alternative possibility that the first person channels the voice of the lector, not the author: *us* would then include the lector and his auditors, who might be envisioned as far removed in time or space from Alfred himself.[39] The prefatory material could, thus, be a later addition unconnected to the prosimetrical *Boethius* itself, as Frantzen has contended.[40] It would be valuable to know which of the various scenarios is the true one – whether Alfred is designating himself a *leoðwyrhta*, or (a subtle but significant difference) prompting readers to call him a *leoðwyrhta*, or whether a later versifier identified Alfred as a *leoðwyrhta*. If the last, it would be equally helpful to know if the preface's author were writing during Alfred's life. But certainty now seems impossible, partly because of the notorious instability of the voice of Alfredian writings, and partly because of our lack of evidence for the textual history of this passage.[41] One final point is also unclear: whether *leoðwyrhta*, like *meterwyrhta*, is a loan-formation from the Latin *uersificus*. The word's relative rarity is probably in favour of its origin as a loan-formation, but since *leoð* is a native simplex, and the formation as a whole was widely used (e.g., *scowyrhta* 'shoemaker', *scipwyrhta* 'shipwright'), it could have originated independently of any Latin influence.

Scop and its various compounds trace a more nuanced picture of Old English usage. Table 1.3 summarizes the referents of all forms of *scop* in the vernacular corpus. This data has several striking features; first, that the people most likely to be called a *scop* in the surviving texts were psalmists, most commonly in the compound *sealmscop*. This emphasizes that the

Table 1.3 *Referents of* scop *and its compounds*

	Word forms	Referent	Number of occurrences
Person	(p)s(e)almsc(e)op; sealmscopwirhta (Schaefer/Palm Sunday)	Psalmist	62
	sc(e)op; ealascop (*Canons of Edgar, Institutes of Polity*)	General (any poet)	26
	scop	Fictional character	4
	æfensceop (*Riddle* 8: 5a)	An animal (figurative use)	1
	sc(e/i)op	Historical figure (non-Anglo-Saxon)	13
	sceop	Historical figure (Anglo-Saxon)	1
Poem	scopleoð; sceopcræft (*Ælfric Gramm.*); scoplic (adj.; Aldhelm glosses)	Any poem; poetic art	4
	scopleoð; scopgereord (*HE* iv.25.342.4)	A particular person's poem	4

Anglo-Saxons accepted the Book of Psalms as poetry – not necessarily an inevitable position, given that none of their standard Latin versions were metrical – and that the word *scop* cannot have had negative connotations in itself. Another very interesting aspect of this word's usage is the fact that no historical Anglo-Saxon identifies himself as a *scop*. This is strikingly different from the situation in Scandinavia, where many people were known as *skáld*.[42] The sole instance of a self-identified *scop*, as we saw above, was the fictitious Heroic Age poet Deor, while the only known Anglo-Saxon called a *scop* by a later English poet is Aldhelm, bishop of Sherborne, in the macaronic poem inserted between the contents list and opening salutation of Aldhelm's *Prosa de uirginitate* in CCCC 326:[43]

> Þus me gesette   sanctus et iustus
> beorn boca gleaw,   bonus auctor,
> Ealdelm, æþele sceop,   etiam fuit
> ipselos on æðele   Angolsexna,
> byscop on Bretene.[44]

Thus he arranged me, the holy and just man learned in books, the excellent author Aldhelm, the noble poet: likewise he was distinguished in the noble kindred of the Anglo-Saxons, a bishop in Britain.

The flamboyance of the poet's praise finds a counterpart in the exuberant combination of Old English, Latin, and Greek. The poet – perhaps also the scribe of these lines, since this verse is paralleled nowhere else among the numerous manuscripts of the *Prosa de uirginitate* – clearly knew more of Aldhelm's writings than the treatise in CCCC 326, since he describes him as an *æðele sceop*. Unfortunately, I do not think we can conclude from the poet's use of Old English that he thought of Aldhelm as a vernacular as well as a Latin author. We *can* be sure that he thought highly of the early bishop as a scholar and author, and was proud to connect him with Anglo-Saxon England: *sceop* here is certainly a term of praise.

In general, being identified as a *scop* seems to have been positive, and, among named individuals, reserved for those known mainly for their poetry. Virgil, Homer, and Terence are all identified as *scopas*.[45] So are less respectable characters, especially in the Old English version of Orosius' *Historia aduersus paganos*: there we find Nero composing a *scopleoð* about the burning of Rome, and the *scop* chosen as king of the Lacedaemonians leading his people to a hollow victory.[46] These figures, however, are also in the Latin source text; in general, when a *scop* or his poetry is to be understood as bad or immoral, the word is qualified with an adjective like *unwurð*.[47] Often, though, the usage of *scop* is entirely neutral; for instance,

Ælfric habitually uses it to gloss Latin *poeta* throughout his bilingual *Grammar*, and *scop* is made equivalent to *uates* as well as *comicus, tragedus,* and *lyricus* in the corpus of glossaries and glossed texts.[48]

As Table 1.2 indicates, three other Old English words were sometimes used in ways that suggest 'poet' might have been part of their field of meaning. Of these, *sangere* was mainly a technical term equivalent to 'singer': often, it glossed or translated Latin *cantor*.[49] In a few instances, it might also conceivably mean 'poet'. The description of King David in the metrical *Psalm 50* – *Sangere he wæs soðfæstest,* 'he was the truest of singers' – implies David was responsible for his songs' content as well as their music.[50] The text called *Grið* contains a list in which *sangere* could mean 'poet':

> We witan, þæt þurh Godes gyfe þræl wearð to ðegene 7 ceorl wearð to eorle, sangere to sacerde 7 bocere to biscpe.[51]

> We know, that through God's gift a slave has become a soldier, a farmer has become a nobleman, a singer a priest and a scribe a bishop.

The ecclesiastical context of this word-pair makes it more likely, though, that *sangere* means *cantor*. And while a cantor might be responsible for writing verse, as we shall see in the next chapter, this was not a requirement for either the official cantor of a cathedral or monastery, or the person acting as cantor during the Divine Office.[52]

The *woðbora* seems more securely associated with the production of words, but it is not clear that these words were necessarily poetic. The one occurrence of *woðbora* outside verse texts is in the Cleopatra Glossary:

rethoribus: woðborum

The identification of the prophet Isaiah[53] and astronomers[54] as *woðboran* should probably also qualify our interpretation of the other instances of this word, especially where it is associated with *word* and *gied*.[55] I think Opland is right that 'a meaning such as "bearer of eloquence" seems to be suggested for *woþbora*', although I doubt the Old English users of this term as we find it in the surviving corpus associated it with the pagan god Woden, despite the etymological connection.[56] However, Latin *uates*, as Opland, Hollowell, and others have noted, is a reflex of the same root as OE *woð*, and the connection of the Latin word with both poetry and prophecy may indeed help our understanding of *woðbora*'s semantic field. A *uates* might speak in verse, but need not necessarily do so; the same was probably considered true of a *woðbora*.

Finally, the *gleoman* seems to be associated with the production of verse within the poetic corpus, but prose usage mainly indicates that (as Opland argued) *gleoman* denoted a performer or entertainer, perhaps especially a mimic actor.[57] Like the *woðbora*, the *gleoman* is connected with *gied* in Old English poems; all three poetic occurrences link the two words.[58] Only the instance in *Beowulf* makes clear that verse is intended:

> Leoð wæs asungen,
> gleomannes gyd.[59]
> The poem was sung, the gleeman's tale.

These words mark the conclusion of the 'Finnsburh episode', which, as discussed above, the poet seems to envision as a public performance of verse.

For this study, the most striking aspect of Old English terms for 'poet' is how infrequently they were applied to living individuals or to Anglo-Saxons: self-identification with any of these terms is even rarer, and (with the possible exception of the metrical preface to the prosimetrical *Old English Boethius*) confined to fictional characters. This is reflected in the historical record; the only one of these six vernacular words known to have been used as a cognomen is *sangere*, where it clearly means *cantor* (here, a monastic official in charge of music).[60]

Words for the poet: Anglo-Latin

We would expect that the Old English usage of terms for 'poet' would differ considerably from the Latin. In both Classical and Late Antique literature, poets often called themselves *poeta* or *uates*, and in Roman society the composition of verse was socially recognized as a vocation, if not exactly a profession in the modern sense.[61] With a few noteworthy exceptions, however, Anglo-Latin poets do not describe themselves as poets, even when they were keenly conscious of themselves as makers of verse. Among those with a substantial verse corpus who never speak of themselves as *poeta, uates*, or *uersificus* are Bede, Boniface, Frithegod, Lantfred,[62] and Wulfstan Cantor. As Table 1.4 shows, the most common Anglo-Latin usages of these terms for 'poet' either speak generally of a composer of verse, or introduce quotations. *Vates* (the only term among these three whose meaning can encompass non-poets) is most commonly used to describe saints or biblical prophets.[63]

Yet unlike their counterparts in Old English, some historical Anglo-Latin poets did describe themselves as such. The mode of these references differed substantially, for reasons apparently to do both with these poets' reading and with contemporary influences. Of these self-proclaimed *poetae*, Alcuin was the most direct. His status as *poeta* and *uates* formed part of his literary

Table 1.4 *Referents of words for 'poet' in Anglo-Latin*

Referent	poeta	uates	uersificus	lyricus	comicus	satiricus
Self	16	12	0	0	0	0
Contemporary	0	4	0	0	0	0
Historical poet:	64	14	5	0	5	2
With quote	60	9	2		5	2
Without quote	4	5	3		0	0
Psalmist	0	5	0	0	0	0
Nonspecific (a poet in general)	71	13	2	1	1	1
A non-poet	0	80	0	0	0	0
Total	151	128	7	1	6	3

Texts searched: All Anglo-Latin texts edited in the MGH and CCSL; Wulfstan Cantor, *Narratio metrica* . . .; Frithegod, *Breuiloquium*; 'Three Latin Poems from Winchester', ed. Lapidge; 'Metrical Calendar of Winchcombe', ed. Lapidge; *Chronicle of Æthelweard*, ed. Campbell

persona: in this respect, he resembled – and doubtless influenced – his contemporaries at Charlemagne's court.[64] While at court, Alcuin adopted the Classical by-name 'Flaccus', and his students and associates took on similarly grand literary aliases: so, for instance, in one epanaleptic verse epistle we find

> Dulcis Homere, precor, Flacci memor esto poetae,
> Sis memor ut Samuel, dulcis Homere, precor.[65]

Sweet Homer, I pray you, be mindful of Flaccus the poet: be mindful like Samuel, sweet Homer, I pray.

'Homer' was the Frankish priest Angilbert. Charlemagne himself was 'David', the poet-king: thus Angilbert wrote in his praise-poem,

> Dauid amat uates, uatorum est gloria Dauid.
> Dulcis amor Dauid inspiret corda canentum,
> Cordibus in nostris faciat amor ipsius odas.
> Vatis Homerus amat Dauid, fac, fistula, uersus.
> Dauid amat uates, uatorum est gloria Dauid.[66]

David loves poets, David is the poets' glory. May sweet love of David inspire the singers' hearts: may love of him form poems in our hearts. The poet Homer loves David: make verses, flute. David loves poets, David is the poets' glory.

While this passage does not altogether clarify how Angilbert merited his exalted nickname, it does demonstrate how Charlemagne's court poets

figured themselves: as vatic bards led by a king also infused with the spirit of
divine poetry.

The tone of these panegyrics, circular epistles, and pastorals, with their
elaborate biblically tinged Classical masquerade, is exceedingly slippery. When
directed towards other court poets, they are frequently playful and occasionally
satirical, and it is not always clear how serious these poets were in describing
themselves and others as *uates* or *poeta*. Theodulf of Orleans'

> Sit praesto et Flaccus, nostrorum gloria uatum,
> Qui potis est lyrico multa boare pede[67]

> And let Flaccus be near at hand, the glory of our bards, who is capable of
> bellowing out most things in lyric measure

is tinctured with contempt, but Angilbert's poem for 'King David', excerpted above, seems earnest and indeed soon turns to religious admonition.
Alcuin's usage varies. Certainly his description of himself in his poem to the
princess 'Delia' has a self-dramatizing air:

> Nec tu quippe tuum curasti, filia, Flaccum:
> Vester abit toto tremulus, heu, corpore uatis,
> Vergilii resonans tacito uix carmine uersum:
> Me circum ualidus uentus, nix, undique nimbus.[68]

> Since you cared no more for your Flaccus, daughter, your poet departed
> trembling (alas) through his whole body, near-silently murmuring in song
> Virgil's verse: all around me are strong wind, snow, and cloud everywhere.

But elsewhere Alcuin's self-appellations sound serious and authoritative.
His *titulus* for a reliquary is one such example:

> Haec, tu quam cernis, praeparua domuncula, lector,
> Reliquias propter sacras iam condita constat,
> Ut locus hic mundus suffragia sancta teneret:
> Seruulus ut Christi ueniens oraret in isto.
> Iusserat Albinus uates haec tecta parare,
> Pro quo, qui titulum uideas, orare memento.[69]

> This very small house which you see, reader, exists to keep safe holy relics,
> so that a fitting place here might hold the holy favours, and that a servant
> of Christ, approaching, might pray upon it. That this shrine be made, the
> poet Albinus commanded: for whom, you who may see this verse,
> remember to pray.

The concluding request for prayers indicates that Alcuin was not merely the
composer of the *titulus*, but the commissioner of the reliquary on which it

was engraved, and the address to the reader indicates that he envisions the shrine and its verses remaining to be seen after its origin has been forgotten. While his choice of *uates* as a cognomen was doubtless partly metrically conditioned (*abbas*, for instance, would not have lengthened the final syllable of *Albinus*), it still indicates how Alcuin intended posterity to perceive him. A hyperbolical joke, such as 'Flaccus' sometimes made of himself in his occasional verse, would have been thoroughly inappropriate in an inscription for a reliquary.

Alcuin must have genuinely considered himself a *uates* and *poeta*, then, as did many of his contemporaries in Charlemagne's court. But it would probably be mistaken to interpret these terms as markers of a formal position or even a primary vocation. As Mary Garrison pointed out, most of the poems produced by the circle of poets at the Carolingian court have disappeared because their authors or disciples never bothered to collect and preserve them:

> Judging from the features of textual transmission . . . many early Carolingian writers were apparently relatively unconcerned with transmitting a literary legacy to posterity. For the intellectuals at the Carolingian court did not consider themselves to be poets primarily, but rather, agents of a wide-ranging movement of religious and cultural reform and renewal.[70]

While Charlemagne's poets may have modelled their self-descriptions on those of Venantius Fortunatus – one of the last professional poets of Latin Antiquity – their production of verse was only one, and probably not the most important, aspect of their service to the king.[71]

Only one other Anglo-Saxon poet identified himself as a *uates* or *poeta* as openly as Alcuin did, and he seems to have been strongly influenced by Alcuin's work. Æthilwulf, author of the early ninth-century historical poem *De abbatibus* and monk in a small Yorkshire monastery,[72] refers to himself twice as *poeta* and five times as *uates* within his 819-line work. Perhaps the most interesting of these references occur in the (authorial) section headings. The title to xxII, *Somnium quod uidit poeta dominica nocte* ('The dream which the poet saw on a Sunday night'), lends concreteness to the strange vision of a colonnaded tower in the fields of paradise inhabited by some of Æthilwulf's dead teachers. This autobiographical specificity in turn conditions readers to accept the final section as personal, not merely conventional:

> XXIII. *Salutatio et precatio uatis ad sanctos et ad dominum*
> haec Lupus, alte pater, stolido de pectore Clarus
>   carmina conposuit, corpore, mente rogans,
> quatinus indigno sancti sua munera prestent,
>   et poscant ueniam cum pauido precibus.[73]

XXIII. *The poet's salutation and prayer to the saints and to the Lord.* Exalted father, Clarus Lupus [=Æthilwulf] arranged these songs from out of his dull heart, seeking with his body and mind that the saints might bestow on him (though unworthy) their gifts, and with their prayers seek pardon for him in his fear.

Æthilwulf's incorporation of the Latinized elements of his own name, as Aldhelm had done for the addressee of his *Carmen rhythmicum*,[74] renders his self-identification as *uates* and *poeta* all the more insistent. But it is less clear what he thought this entailed. The vision he relates is consistent with ancient conceptions of the *uates* as a person connected directly with the unseen world of divine powers and capable of expressing such revelations in verse. But it is difficult to be sure that Æthilwulf connected his dream with his poetic abilities per se; it may be that when he called himself a *uates*, he meant not 'a visionary' but simply 'the author of this poem'. This latter interpretation becomes more likely when we compare Æthilwulf's probable sources. In the invocation to his poem on 'the bishops, kings, and saints of York', Alcuin wrote:

> Christe deus, summi uirtus sapientia patris,
> uita, salus, hominum factor, renouator, amator,
> unica lingua Dei, donorum tu dator alme,
> munera da mentis, fragili da uerba poetae
> irrorans stolidum uiuaci flumine pectus,
> ut mea lingua queat de te tua dicere dona . . .[75]

O Christ God, power and wisdom of the high Father: of men the life, salvation, maker, restorer, and lover: sole voice of God, holy giver of gifts, give the gifts of the mind, give words to the frail poet, flooding the dull heart with the living waters, so that my tongue through you might strive to speak of your gifts . . .

This passage – a confection of various Christian Latin authors, as Godman's notes indicate – shares phrases and images with Æthilwald's prayer (the *stolidum pectus* and the *munera* sought from heaven, as well as the self-designation as *poeta*) but differs strikingly in the association of the *poeta* with divine inspiration. Neither in Æthilwulf's various introductory addresses nor in his concluding *precatio* does he seek heavenly assistance for his verse: rather, he asks for the reader's pardon and prayers. This seems consistent with earlier Anglo-Latin authors' attitudes towards the divine inspiration of poetry.[76] It is possible, however, that Alcuin and other Carolingian writers helped re-legitimize the poetic invocation, since Æthelweard uses one in his curious poem on Edgar:

Tingite nunc calamo, Musae, propriumque uocate
Carmen, et ignoto uentis properate secundis.
Cum placido steterint fontes, aperite poetam.[77]

Dip your pens [in ink], O Muses, and call up your own song, and with following winds hasten to a stranger [*or*, an ignorant man]. Disclose your springs to the poet while they remain in stillness.

Æthelweard's Delphic vocabulary and syntax make his meaning difficult to parse, but I read the self-designation as *ignoto*, and the request that the Muses' springs *placido steterint*, as an acknowledgement of inexperience as a *poeta* – an acknowledgement that his use of the Classical invocation was doubtless intended to mitigate.[78]

The author whose practice seems closest to that of Æthilwulf (rather than Æthelweard) in using *poeta* as self-description is Tætwine, an eighth-century archbishop of Canterbury whose set of forty *enigmata*, linked by a complex acrostic, ends with a titled quatrain:

> *Conclusio poetae de supra dictis enigmatibus*
> Versibus intextis uatem nunc iure salutat,
> litterulas summa capitum hortans iungere primas,
> uersibus extremas hisdem, ex minio coloratas;
> conuersus gradiens rursum perscandat ab imo.[79]

The poet's conclusion to the riddles given above. Now he properly greets the ?solver with interwoven verses, urging him to join the first little letters at the very beginnings, and the last ones in those same verses, coloured in red; turning round and proceeding backward, may he rise from the bottom.

As Æthilwulf did in *De abbatibus*, Tætwine uses a prose heading to identify the voice of these lines as that of the poet – a necessary clarification, since each of Tætwine's riddles is spoken by its personified solution and his readers would thus be hypersensitized to voice. Curiously, though, the *poeta* – unlike any of the riddle-creatures – makes his address only in third person. This makes the referent of *uatem* in line 1 somewhat puzzling, for if the subject of *salutat* is the *poeta* of the heading, the object must be the reader, not the poet. *Vates* thus would mean something like 'seer [of hidden solutions]': Erika von Erhardt-Siebold, who translated Tætwine's riddles for the Corpus Christianorum Series Latina, rendered it as 'the wise reader'.[80] Such a meaning would be unparalleled elsewhere in Anglo-Latin literature, and it may be that the best way of reading the *uatem* is as a mistake for *uates* – and, thus, synonymous with the *poeta*.[81]

Tætwine's brief, oblique self-reference as a *poeta* had some precedence in Aldhelm's writings. In his treatise on metre, Aldhelm cited many lines of verse as examples, sometimes by name and sometimes anonymously; as, for instance:

> D. Quae est caesura trititrochaici uel tritus trocheus?
> M. Cum tertio loco pes dactilo terminatur, sicut poeta prompsit, dicens 'Hoc uolo, ne breuiter mihi sillaba prima legatur' . . .; item epigramma Prosperi triton trocheon protulit: 'At bona, quae uere bona sunt nec fine tenentur'.[82]

> *Discipulus.* What is the worn trochaic caesura, or the worn trochee?
> *Magister.* That is when the foot in the third position ends with a dactyl, as the poet demonstrated, saying 'I would prefer my first syllable not be read as short' . . .; and also the epigram of Prosper shows the worn trochee: 'But those things are good which are truly good and have no ending.'

The first example is from Symphosius, whom Aldhelm often quotes; he also cites Sedulius and Virgil simply as *poeta*. It seems reasonable to infer that the latter two poets were so well known that naming them was unnecessary. Such a context makes the following passage all the more interesting:

> D. Facilius ratione flector, si exempla praebueris.
> M. Vergilius libro .IV.: 'At regina graui iamdudum saucia cura' . . . et Sibilla profetissa ait 'Denumerat tacitis tot crimina conscius ultor' et alibi poeta dicit 'Petrus apostolicae qui culmina praesidet arcis', scanditur ita: Petrusa. postoli. caequi: ecce pars districti; culmina. praesidet. arcis: ecce pars diuisi![83]

> D. I would understand more easily if you would give examples.
> M. Virgil in Book IV [. . .]; and Sybilla, the prophetess, said [. . .], and elsewhere a poet says 'Peter, who commands the summits of the apostolic citadel', which is scanned thus: Petrusa. postoli. caequi. (see, a section of divided words); culmina. praesidet. arcis (here, a section of separated words).

The *poeta* who speaks *alibi* is Aldhelm himself, who apparently devised this example for the occasion. Elsewhere, Aldhelm cites himself as a nameless *poeta* in the *Epistle to Geraint, Prosa de uirginitate,* and the treatise on the number seven that opens his metrical textbook.[84] In these three latter instances, he always quotes the same verse: 'Clauiger aethereus, portam qui pandit in aethra' ('Heavenly key-holder, who opens the gate in the heavens'), which is found in his *titulus* for a church dedicated to SS. Peter and Paul, and (slightly altered) for an altar to St Peter.[85] This obscure mode of self-citation could perhaps be interpreted as a humility topos, but it is difficult to be sure how humble Aldhelm is really being: our interpretation must depend on understanding the circulation of his *Carmina ecclesiastica.* If Aldhelm expected his verses to be widely known and recognized as his, then these self-references were perhaps intended to reinforce his audience's respect for his *auctoritas*. But if the church *tituli* were intended only for local consumption – or anonymous circulation – then while the *line* might become authoritative, Aldhelm's own status would remain unaffected. But there is one final possibility: since this line was formed from two conflated verses from Book I of Arator's *De actibus apostolorum*, it is not altogether impossible that, in these instances, by *poeta* Aldhelm meant his model, Arator.[86]

Uncommon as it generally was for Anglo-Saxons to describe themselves as *poeta* or *uates*, it was seemingly even less common to describe their contemporaries as such. As with their modes of self-representation, Alcuin and his circle at Charlemagne's court are anomalous in this respect. Alcuin writes of or to other *uates* three times, and as the quotations above from Angilbert and Theodulf exemplify, portraying other members of the court circle as collaborating or rival poets was integral to the way this group constructed its own identity.[87]

In one interesting and ambiguous case, the author of the *Carmen de libero arbitrio* – a student effort preserved only in CUL Kk.5.34 – addresses as 'uates clariuidens' an unnamed bishop, who, as Lapidge argues, was probably Æthelwold of Winchester.[88] In his edition, Lapidge translates this as 'far-seeing poet', which is certainly a plausible interpretation. Although no surviving verse has been attributed to Æthelwold, Wulfstan Cantor describes him as having learned the rules of metre at Glastonbury, and as teaching metrics to his own students, several of whom became very accomplished poets.[89] Yet the epithet *clariuidens* ('clear-seeing') seems more appropriate to a prophet; and Æthelwold's prophetic dream, as reported by Wulfstan in chapter 39 of his *Vita S. Æthelwoldi*, might be the allusion here. Moreover, the connection of the word *uates* with saints was well established in Anglo-Latin at least since Bede's use of it in his metrical *Vita S. Cuthberti*. While the addressee of the *Carmen de libero arbitrio* was apparently still living – his actions are described in the present tense – the couplet

> claret hoc a domino quod celsa talenta benigno
> sint tibi, summe pater: te decus omne decet[90]

> This shows that heavenly rewards from the loving Lord will be yours, greatest father: all glory is fitting for you

suggests an anticipated cult, as do many parts of Wulfstan's *vita*. So while *uates* here may mean 'poet', it may also mean 'prophet' – or perhaps both at once.

As Table 1.4 shows, terms for the authors of particular genres – *comici*, *lyrici*, *satyrici*, *tragoeci* – were known to the Anglo-Saxons, but seem to have been rarely used except as tags for quotations or in glossaries. Unexpectedly, the same was apparently true of *uersificus*. *Psalmista*, on the other hand, was exceedingly common, but remained essentially a technical term for the historical figures to whom the Psalms were attributed.

Speaking of Anglo-Saxon poets

While it is impossible to determine how precisely the surviving corpus of Anglo-Latin and Old English writings reflected the entirety of written and spoken discourse in the Anglo-Saxon period, the patterns of word-use described above must at least give probabilistic force to our conclusions. There are, I think, three chief characteristics of the way words for 'poet' were used in Old English and Latin.

First, the overall pattern of usage in both languages is broadly similar, so that the ways in which Anglo-Latin authors used *poeta* seem much closer to Old English usage of *scop* than to Classical habits of speaking about *poetae*.[91] The chief exception is found in the circle of poets associated with Charlemagne's court, a self-conscious 'revival' or re-creation of the ancient status of *poeta* or *uates*, which had some, albeit limited, impact among Northumbrians in the years after Alcuin's departure for the Continent. Overall, though, it seems that the Anglo-Saxons had a relatively consistent idea of what a poet was.

It likewise seems clear that both *scop* and *poeta* – to focus on the words for which the most abundant and relevant information is available – were terms of relative prestige. Both were used to designate authorities, and *scop* formed part of a compound used for the psalmists, as an English equivalent for *psalmista*. While it was certainly possible to speak negatively of poets, to do so it usually seems to have been necessary to qualify the term, and so we have *unwurð scop*, *ealuscop*, and *poetae gentilium*.

Finally, there is no solid evidence that a professional class of poets existed in Anglo-Saxon England. It was uncommon to speak of oneself as a poet at all, and even more uncommon to designate one's contemporaries as poets. One must repeat the qualifier that our evidence is incomplete; but the balance of probability suggests that had *scop* or *poeta* been available as identifiers for a particular social or professional status, these terms would have sometimes designated particular individuals. But this does not seem to have been the case. Even those historical individuals who called themselves *uates* or *poetae* (and perhaps *leoðwyrhtan*) had other primary social signifiers for determining their status: Aldhelm, for instance, did not address his letters as *poeta*, but as abbot of Malmesbury or bishop of Sherborne.

What I think this evidence indicates is that in Anglo-Saxon England, words meaning 'poet' functioned something like the modern category of 'statesman'. The term is not really a professional category, but rather a word for those who have excelled in the professions of politics or diplomacy. 'Statesman' is so commonly reserved for those retiring from public life – or, preferably, safely dead – because of the force it carries; and while one can aspire to be a statesman, declaring oneself actually to be one would smack of hubris. A similar situation, I think, held true of *scop* or *poeta* in early England: it was something one could hope to be called after death. Anglo-Saxons like Cynewulf or Wulfstan Cantor, who were acutely conscious of themselves as makers of verse, nevertheless did not self-identify as poets; even Aldhelm, who boasted of being the first Englishman to compose metrical Latin verse, called himself *poeta* only obliquely.

We are left, then, with two questions: what an Anglo-Saxon who composed verse would normally call him- or herself; and what *we* should call such people. The second question is the most easily addressed. In this study, I shall refer to any maker of verse (however incompetent) as a poet, and reserve the culturally specific terms *scop* or *poeta* for rare instances in which it seems warranted by context. No doubt this makes poets of many who never expected to be so – testers of pens, and scribblers in margins – but it is often hard to gauge intention by results. Since this study is concerned with all those who composed verse in Anglo-Saxon England, I think it best not to prejudge their efforts with my terminology: so I also mean no *more* by 'poet' than 'composer of verse'.

This definition naturally calls into question what constitutes 'verse' – a problem that would not necessarily have been simple in the Anglo-Saxon period, and is even more difficult today. For this study, I have used a conservative definition: language structured by socially accepted metrical patterns, with use across two or more unrelated texts as a proxy for social acceptance where no formal theory exists. I have deviated from this criterion in a few instances, where it seemed to me clear that the poet *thought* he was conforming to such metrical patterns. For unlike quantitative Latin verse, neither Old English nor rhythmic Latin metre had codified principles. Practitioners must have extrapolated rules from extant verse, and the rules they arrived at must therefore have been affected by the nature of the verse available. The process of understanding Old English and rhythmic Latin poetry relied, in Kant's terms, on reflective rather than determinant judgment, and necessarily had a subjective element. Such metres thus held a possibility of reinterpretation unavailable to users of handbooks on dactylic hexameter.[92] A full account of the historical dynamics of such 'reflective metres' is beyond the scope of this book, though Chapter 4 demonstrates how a poet could be mistaken about what he considered verse. Some of the poets in the following chapters, in other words, would certainly not have been called poets by their contemporaries.

As for what these poets called themselves, I consider it in general safest to say that they called themselves by their primary social role – priest, nun, warrior, king – and perhaps also by functions such as 'teacher'. In the next chapter, I shall present the surviving biographical information about those people who were known to have composed verse, and outline the social roles that they were most likely to fulfil. But when poets spoke of themselves and the craft of verse, the most common voice was active. 'Ic þysne sang siðgeomor fand' ('I, weary of journeys, made this song') is how Cynewulf opened *The Fates of the Apostles*, while Wulfstan Cantor introduced his poem on St Swithun with *prospera cuncta canam* ('I shall sing of all fortunate things').[93] In subsequent chapters, we shall see further how poets represented the practice of their art. But overall the evidence seems clear that being a poet in Anglo-Saxon England was a matter of what one did rather than what one was.

CHAPTER 2

Who became poets?

An Anglo-Saxon poet might aspire to an immortal reputation as a *scop* or *poeta*, but the actual composition of verse was generally a more mundane affair. Much surviving Anglo-Saxon poetry was transparently functional: it taught facts, recorded names, or filled a given space in the liturgy. The people called upon to create this verse often did so as an integral part of their roles in their communities. This is not to say that *every* poem sprang directly from a duty. Rather, those who could use the art of verse to do what was required of them were the most likely to acquire that knowledge – and would then be free to use their skill for less momentous occasions as well. No doubt some Anglo-Saxons learned to become poets for no reason beyond inclination; but the surviving evidence suggests that many Anglo-Saxon poets learned and practised their art for reasons we can still discern.

Such evidence as does survive is presented in Appendix I as a handlist of known poets who were born in, or spent a significant part of their careers in, Anglo-Saxon England. About fifty named individuals are securely known to have composed verse. Probably this number represents a minute percentage of the true population of pre-Conquest poets, but it is all that we can name with even relative certainty. The list is also biased towards Latin authors, though in a way that may well be representative of the manuscript culture of the period. In other words, while Latin works survive in numbers that are probably disproportionate within the total number of poems ever composed in Anglo-Saxon England, they may well mirror the proportions of Latin versus vernacular texts that were ever written down.[1]

Few long poems in Anglo-Latin have been transmitted anonymously. Even where no name is directly attached to a work, there is often corroborating information to identify, or at least localize, the author. The *Narratio metrica de S. Swithuno* is a good case in point: John Leland's attribution of this poem to Wulfstan, partly on the basis of a gloss to a line indicating the author was a cantor, was corroborated by the discovery of a stylistically similar poem prefaced by an acrostic yielding the name VVLFSTANUS.[2]

The *Miracula S. Nyniae* remains anonymous, but Alcuin's mention of it in a letter to the brothers of Whithorn indicates that it is a product of the late eighth century, probably from Whithorn itself.[3]

Old English represents almost a mirror-reversal of the Latin situation; only Cynewulf, who 'signed' his poems with runic acrostics, leaves a substantial poetic corpus. Though modern scholars have connected many names with *Beowulf*, and a few others (most notably Cædmon's) with the poems of Junius XI, no other poet has been securely ascribed more than nine lines of Old English verse.[4] Part of our difficulty is that Old English verse so often dealt with topics of broad appeal – the story of a universal saint like Andrew is far more difficult to localize than that of a local patron like Nynian or Judoc. Vernacular graphic conventions have contributed to our problems. The tendency not to separately lineate Old English verses, for instance, meant that one needed all of Cynewulf's technical ingenuity to make an acrostic salient. The result is that it was easy for a barely competent Latin poet to attach his name to a work (as with the Eadwald whose pseudo-metrical acrostic is preserved in CCCC 307), and much more difficult for an English poet to ensure he would be remembered after a copy or two.

The very small corpus of Anglo-Saxon letter-books and anthologies reminds us that we have only a glimpse into a widespread culture of poetry in early England. The dossiers of letters to and from St Boniface and Lull, his English-born successor at Mainz, preserve verses by many people – including women – whose competence as poets would otherwise have been unknown; the same is true of the collections of tenth- and eleventh-century archiepiscopal correspondence from Canterbury preserved in two Cotton manuscripts.[5] Likewise, though the *liber epigrammatum* collected by Milred of Worcester in the eighth century survives only in fragments, it illuminates a world of occasional and dedicatory verse in early Anglo-Saxon England whose scope is now difficult to gauge. The work of Patrick Sims-Williams and Michael Lapidge on this text makes it clear that Milred was not alone in his poetic interests.[6] We know that a variety of *tituli* for churches and ecclesiastical adornments were composed by Aldhelm in the seventh century, and Dunstan in the tenth; the sylloge of Milred of Worcester reveals that not only Bede, but many otherwise unknown people also composed poems under similar circumstances. It is hard for us now to discern how common poetry was in daily life; but many Anglo-Saxons, and not just monastics, may have lived with or regularly used things inscribed with verse.

Books, in the end, have proven among the most durable of the Anglo-Saxons' artistic creations. Though incalculable numbers of them were destroyed during the medieval period and at the Reformation, and even those in libraries have suffered from 'time and chance', well over a thousand volumes survive from the Anglo-Saxon period.[7] These, in the main, form the record from which the world of Anglo-Saxon poets must be deduced: and because medieval books were often more like ecosystems than static repositories of words, it is often possible to gather information from incidental markings, flyleaf scribbles, and significant juxtapositions when the words themselves are unrevealing. I have therefore also drawn upon anonymous poems in this discussion when there is context enough to infer the status of their authors and, thus, what sort of people were most likely to become poets.

With regard to the Latin tradition, I believe that the information in Appendix I does sketch out a generally accurate image of the sort of people most likely to become poets, and that the overall contours are plain enough to let us infer what once occupied some present gaps in the record. But in the vernacular, the picture is far less clear. We cannot even be certain how representative the surviving English poems are of the overall vernacular poetic tradition, and we must certainly consider the possibility that 'classical' Old English verse is the only survivor of a once larger cohort, preserved because of its popularity in the stratum of society most likely to become literate. We can no longer know if the servile classes, for instance, shared their masters' tastes, or if a tradition of slaves' songs is now lost to us. Such evidentiary biases cannot be altogether counterbalanced, and should be borne in mind throughout this discussion. I have incorporated vernacular evidence wherever possible, but in many cases this has involved analogy rather than exact correspondence, and I therefore emphasize that the taxonomy of poets in this chapter is a survey of tendencies, rather than an absolute law admitting no deviation.

That said, the surviving evidence points towards four social roles commonly played by people who became poets: from the best to least attested, these are teachers; scribes; musicians; and courtiers. Information about poets' occupations can be gleaned in various ways, from straightforward biography to subtle cues in manuscript context, and often differs in kind depending on the occupation itself. My discussion, therefore, will in each case focus on evidence for poets' activities within each of these social roles, and, more broadly, how poetry seems to have intersected with each particular occupation. A comprehensive account of any of these groups within Anglo-Saxon society would require a substantial monograph, so my intention here is simply to describe what can be known about how poets and poetry functioned within specific social contexts. But the study of poets as teachers, scribes, musicians, and courtiers can, I hope, tell us something about what it was to be these things in Anglo-Saxon England, as well as what it was to be a poet.

Teachers

Teaching is essentially communal: to be a teacher, one must have someone – and something – to teach. But beyond this basic logical requirement, there was no single experience or characteristic shared by all Anglo-Saxon teachers, just as there was no single, universal form of schooling. We have evidence for a broad range of educational methods, ranging from the groups of roughly coeval *pueri* under the guidance of a single master attested by Ælfric's *Colloquy*, to one special case in which a number of masters instruct a high-status adult.[8] We should therefore avoid making assumptions about what being a teacher meant during the Anglo-Saxon period – and, in particular, we should not assume that modern educational practices furnish a relevant paradigm. By expanding our notions of what constituted education, we can better comprehend why teachers might become poets.

Of the fifty named poets on the handlist, at least fifteen are known to have been teachers, while several more produced works that can be associated with formal schooling. Combined with the large amount of recent scholarship on Anglo-Saxon manuscripts associated with teaching, this provides us with a broad and diverse range of information on poets who were teachers, and on the teaching of poetry in early England. What emerges is a curiously mixed picture. The study of verse seems to have been integral to learning throughout the Anglo-Saxon period, often to a degree that sharply distinguishes English from Continental education. Yet much of this learning was passive: which is to say, while many people must have learned to read or recite verse, far fewer seem to have acquired the ability to compose it. Those who did learn how to compose frequently taught others, and often attained high station in the church. In this section, I will consider what this might indicate about expectations for advancement in the Anglo-Saxon ecclesiastical hierarchy, as well as the nature of literary education generally.

The laws of verse

The three surviving metrical treatises from early Anglo-Saxon England – Aldhelm's *Epistola ad Acircium*, Bede's *De arte metrica*, and Boniface's *Caesurae uersuum* – share certain assumptions, the first and most basic of which is that students will learn the art of verse by memorizing many authoritative examples. This fundamental tenet was also held by Late Antique metrists, for similar reasons: once the quantity of vowels had ceased to be salient even to native Latin speakers, the authority of grammarians and poets was the only reliable means of ascertaining the correct scansion of words.[9] The Anglo-Saxon textbooks were not really prolegomena to the study of verse, then, but a means of helping students systematize their knowledge of verse they had already learned by heart.

For Latin learners, this process of memorization would have begun almost at once, since prosody was considered a fundamental aspect of language. Syllabic quantity, as understood by Late Antique phonological and metrical theories, formed part of the most basic level of instruction, and thus *artes metricae* were used to supplement elementary parsing grammars like Donatus' *Ars minor*.[10] The textbooks on metre composed by early Anglo-Latin authors can be understood as part of their ongoing effort to adapt the tools available for teaching Latin to the immediate needs of people who had never heard that language's spoken descendants. These Anglo-Saxon *artes metricae* are the work of well-known teachers who were themselves poets, and the methods they thought best for conveying the principles of Latin versification reveal a great deal about what they thought verse was and what it ought to be. Their vision of poetry – partly derived from Late Antiquity and partly a response to contemporary circumstances – became a template for future generations' work within England and beyond it.

The emphasis on the dactylic hexameter in all three treatises, for instance, is both an inheritance from their Late Antique predecessors and a foreshadowing of the course of Anglo-Latin poetics. Of the three textbook authors, only Bede discusses quantitative lyric metres in any detail, and he is also the only one known to have written quantitative lyrics himself.[11] Quantitative lyric verse is in fact vanishingly rare in Anglo-Saxon England; only three people can be convincingly shown to have composed it.[12] But this widespread bias towards dactylic verse forms – particularly 'heroic' (hexametrical) verse, and secondarily elegiac couplets – does not simply stem from ignorance of, or inability to handle, more complex metres. The dactylic hexameter is presented as the paradigmatic form of Latin verse: 'more beautiful and nobler than all the rest', as Bede put it.[13] Aldhelm and Boniface likewise affirm the pre-eminence of heroic verse.[14] The metrical treatises show that the dominance of the dactylic hexameter in Anglo-Latin verse is not an accident of survival, but a reflection of actual aesthetic preferences.

Despite their shared assumptions about the best kind of verse and the best way to learn it, these three early handbooks reveal some important differences in their methods of presentation and – more critically – their ideas about what learning metre did for a reader of Latin poetry. That the treatises of Aldhelm and Bede were directed chiefly to *readers*, and only secondarily to aspiring authors, has been demonstrated by Carin Ruff: Boniface's *Caesurae uersuum* seems based on similar principles.[15] Yet that these three authors raised such different edifices upon such similar ground-work indicates that there was no universally agreed-upon structure to the 'curriculum' of an aspiring Latinist, and no absolute consensus on why one should learn the principles of Latin metre. This absence of consensus means that generalizations about the place of poetry in Anglo-Saxon scholarship must be treated with great care: but it also means that early scholars themselves were free to draw independent, sometimes radical conclusions about the utility of verse.

Of the three early treatises, Ruff observes that 'History seems to have voted for Bede's method.'[16] Nearly a hundred full texts or excerpts of the *De arte metrica* survive in manuscripts from across Europe, and the work was reprinted during the Renaissance as a practical handbook for students.[17] Basing his book on the structure of elementary grammars, Bede builds from simple to complex – through the letter, syllable, foot, and metrical line – and from left to right, showing how to determine the quantities of initial, medial, and final syllables in that order. This is an essentially readerly approach, as Bede himself emphasizes in his chapter 'De primis syllabis':

> Et ideo cum codicem exametri uel elegiaci carminis adsumis in manus, quacumque paginam aperiens inspexeris, quemcumque uersum arripiens leg-eris, absque ulla dubietate primam syllabam aut natura aut positione longam inuenies, quod nimirum siue spondei seu dactyli constat esse principium.[18]

> And so when you take up a book of hexameter or elegiac verse in your hands, whatever page you look at when you open it up, and whatever verse you happen to light on when you begin to read, you will find without any doubt whatsoever that the first syllable is long either by nature or position, because it invariably forms the beginning of either a spondee or a dactyl.

Ruff shows how the *De arte metrica*'s use of colometry, which was as much a rhetorical as a metrical system, also helps readers correlate metrical units with the sense of the verse.[19] The immediate practicality of Bede's textbook for readers – its obvious usefulness even to those with no desire to compose poems of their own – helped ensure its lasting popularity.

User-friendliness was not the only distinctive feature of the *De arte metrica*. Bede also presented it as a self-consciously modern work for Christian readers. The word 'modern' is his: he uses it to distinguish

Christian poets from pagans, as in his chapter 'Ut prisci poetae quaedam aliter quam moderni posuerunt' ('On why the ancient poets sometimes scan differently from the modern ones').[20] Bede replaced his Late Antique sources' quotations from Classical poets with examples from Christian Latin authors – the works of Prosper of Aquitaine, Paulinus of Nola, Sedulius, Arator, and others who would have been intimately known to the readers of his time. Bede's relation to *auctoritas* in the establishment of correct scansion is not essentially different from that of the Late Latin grammarians, but his presentation of Christian Latin poets as embodiments of that authority aligned his textbook with the experience of his readers. The *De arte metrica* was the first handbook designed for people educated as Christians, not Romans, and as such it brought quantitative metre within the sphere of knowledge proper to any Christian reader.

Bede also promoted a form of verse that many of his Late Antique sources considered vulgar: rhythmic poetry. Though we cannot be sure whether his reference to the 'carmina uulgarium poetarum' ('verses of common poets') as examples of rhythmic poetry is a holdover from his source or an allusion to Old English, he unequivocally praises the rhythmic hymn *Rex aeterne Domine* as 'praeclarus' ('extremely excellent').[21] Moreover, he indicates that rhythmic metre, like quantitative, is a skill that can be honed with study: the modulation of stress that structures the poems, he says, 'quem uulgares poetae necesse est rustice, docti faciant docte' ('which the common poets of course do coarsely, the instructed will do learnedly').[22] As with the quantitative poems of Christian Latin authors, Bede presents these rhythmic poems as worthy products of the modern world, rather than poor imitations of the lost glory of the ancients.

Following such logic, a reader of Bede's textbook would find no reason to believe that his or her own writings – so long as they followed the best practice of modern authority – would be inferior or unacceptable. It is difficult to know whether this attitude often inspired Anglo-Saxon students to become poets, or merely better readers. But if the Cuthbert to whom Bede addressed the *De arte metrica* is the same student who went on to become abbot of Wearmouth-Jarrow, we can answer that question for at least one individual. In his correspondence with Lull, Cuthbert ended his letter of thanks with a metrical valediction:

> Abbas Cutberctus tete bis terque salutat;
> Te Deus omnipotens saluum conseruet in evum.[23]

Abbot Cuthbert bids you farewell six times over; may almighty God keep you safe forever.

The casual competence of his verse shows that Cuthbert had learned his lessons well.

In contrast to Bede's widespread influence – his textbooks were brought to the Continent by various Anglo-Saxon travellers, including Alcuin as well as earlier missionaries – Aldhelm's *Epistola ad Acircium* was little disseminated as a complete tract.[24] The form of his treatise undoubtedly had much to do with this. Profuse, ornate, digressive, and technical, Aldhelm's work must have perplexed at least as many readers as it enlightened. As Ruff puts it, where 'Bede never lets the discussion of pattern stray far from the words that form the center of the text's meaning', Aldhelm conversely 'rejoices in the operation of meter as a system – finite and quantifiable, as well as quantitative'.[25] The system Aldhelm espouses is, in its way, logical; he divides the hexameter line into a grid, and enumerates the entire range of possibilities for filling the grid with syllables. The long lists of words in *De pedum regulis*, the final part of the tract, are grouped by part of speech, and give the curious impression that sense has little to do with the construction of verse. As a typical instance:

> Haec sunt nomina anapesto suffragrantia et concordi ratione respondentia utpote deitas, pietas, bonitas, novitas, brevitas, levitas, gravitas, probitas, feritas, species, sanies, macies, glacies, rabies, scabies, series, facies, acies et reliqua similia.[26]

> These are nouns conformable to the anapest and comparable in terms of concord: those like *deity, piety, integrity, novelty, brevity, levity, gravity, probity, savagery, appearance, gore, thinness, ice, madness, itchiness, sequence, countenance, keenness,* and others of the same sort.

The jazzy free-associative juxtapositions encourage students to think of words as shapes, rather than units of meaning. But this 'fill-in-the-blank' attitude towards versification, while doubtless confusing to those who simply wanted to know how to scan a line of verse, did offer a concrete compositional strategy for aspiring poets. As Lapidge observed of *De pedum regulis*'s lists,

> The utility of this section (as Aldhelm apparently saw it), would be that, when a student wished to fill a gap in his hexameter and needed a dactyl to do so, or when he was in doubt concerning the quantity of a particular word, he need only cast his mind back over the list of dactyls provided . . .[27]

This modular approach to verse was one Aldhelm practised himself, as Lapidge and Orchard have demonstrated, and the method was particularly embraced in early Southumbria and by the Wessex-trained missionaries to the Continent.[28]

But though the lists of syllabic permutations can give the *Epistola ad Acircium* the grimly practical character of a Scrabble guide, Aldhelm's goals for the book were much greater. The ostensibly irrelevant initial chapters on the mystic significance of the number seven reveal that he believed the entire cosmos was organized according to numerical patterns, and that metre provided one window into that rational organization. His hundred riddles on the theme of 'Creation' that illustrate the workings of the hexameter were thus an integral part of the theme of his treatise. Metre was a way of unlocking these riddles:

> Et ut evidentius harum rerum ratio claresceret, legitimos septies quaternos metrorum pedes, quibus universa non solum principalia octo genera progrediuntur verum etiam species, quae ex eadem stirpe pululantes centuplis metrorum frondibus contexuntur, subdidimus . . .[29]

> And so that the principle behind these [riddles] might shine forth the more clearly, I have set forth the four-times-seven licit metrical feet, from which spring not merely the eight principal kinds [of metre] but likewise all forms which, sprouting from the same stem, are interwoven into the hundredfold fronds of metres . . .

The distributive periphrasis Aldhelm gives for the 'twenty-eight legitimate metrical feet' is no stylistic trick: the sacred number seven appears here too, and provides a *ratio*, a 'deep structure', for the *enigmata*. Metre thus reveals the workings of Creation.

Before exploring further Aldhelm's riddles and the lessons they teach, I would like to conclude this survey of Anglo-Saxon metrical treatises with a look at Boniface's brief (and somewhat mistitled) tract, *Caesurae uersuum*. Culled from multiple sources – chiefly Isidore's *Etymologiae*, but also the grammars of Diomedes, Audax, and Pompeius, and Servius' *De centum metris* – Boniface's text offers an introductory glossary of prosodic and metrical terminology.[30] He includes notation marks for 'the twenty-eight feet' and a list of the 'eight principal metres' alluded to by Aldhelm in the passage quoted above. Boniface also includes a history of the dactylic hexameter which functions as a defence of its pre-eminence among other forms of metre. The entire tract, in fact, can be read as an *accessus ad Aldhelmum*, although the two texts are found together only in one manuscript, Vatican, Pal. lat. 1753.[31] Above all, Boniface was attempting in the *Caesurae uersuum* to open the study of metre to readers: by clarifying the arcane notations and Greek-derived vocabulary, he enabled students to use textbooks like Aldhelm's (or even Bede's) with confidence, and to understand grammatical commentaries on the poets. His goal was not to teach the structure of verse per se, but to teach students how to learn it. Boniface's work can be read, then, as the completion of the early Anglo-Saxon scholars' campaign to make the form of Latin poetry comprehensible to non-native readers of Latin – which, by the time of his writing, encompassed most of Europe.

For the most part, the metrical textbooks of the early Anglo-Saxon period were predicated on the notion that becoming a Latin poet was something that happened only after absorbing the works of a great many other poets. So far as we can judge from these scholars' own works and from the manuscript record, this was indeed the chief invariant of education in Latin literature throughout the Anglo-Saxon period. While it is usually unclear what methods teachers used, evidence suggests that Anglo-Latin poets came to exercise their art only after negotiating a long course of reading. We shall turn, then, to the works the Anglo-Saxon textbook writers helped their students read.

'The core curriculum'

Bede's textbook, as we have seen, was useful partly because it drew its examples from several well-known Christian poems. This set of 'core texts' seems to have been remarkably stable throughout the Anglo-Saxon period: an English student in the eleventh century would have read many of the same books as Aldhelm and Bede. I have listed the key poetic texts of this 'curriculum' in Table 2.1. The group is based on a flexible set of criteria – a combination of the number and type of surviving manuscripts, and quotations or echoes of particular works in Anglo-Latin texts.

Both of these criteria are problematic for different reasons. Interpreting the manuscript record requires addressing three crucial issues: identifying books used in education; discerning how and by whom such books were used; and understanding the significance of gaps in the surviving collections. Finding one or more specific elements in a medieval book may point towards its use in teaching: an apparatus of glosses, construe marks, and commentaries or *accessus ad auctores*;[32] formal grammars, especially elementary parsing grammars; and of course, curriculum texts. None of these, however, is a failsafe indication that a particular manuscript was used in the classroom. Lapidge especially has shown how textual apparatus developed through successive copying, and that Anglo-Latin glosses often depend on Carolingian exemplars.[33] Patrizia Lendinara has recently provided an invaluable guide to 'Anglo-Saxon Manuscripts (up to 1100) Containing

Table 2.1 *The Anglo-Saxon 'core curriculum': verse texts*

Period	Author	Work	Metrical form	Number of surviving MSS from ASE
Throughout	Sedulius	*Carmen paschale*	hexameter, elegiac couplets	7, 1f
		A solis ortus cardine	iambic dimeter	7 (?)
	Juvencus	*Libri IV euangeliorum*	hexameter	6
	Arator	*Historia apostolica*	hexameter, elegiac couplets	7, 1f
	Prosper of	*Epigrammata*	elegiac couplets	4, 1f
	Aquitaine	*Carmen coniugis ad uxorem*	anacreontics	4, 1f
	Prudentius	*Psychomachia*	hexameter, iambic senarius	11, 1f
		Cathemerinon	*multiple*	6
		Dittochaeon	hexameter	9, 1f
		Peristephanon	*multiple*	7, 1f
		Contra Symmachum	hexameter, asclepiad, glyconic	6, 2f
		Apotheosis	hexameter, iambic trimeter + dimeter	4
		Hamartigenia	hexameter, iambic senarius	4, 2f
	Symphosius	*Enigmata*	hexameter	4
	Virgil	*Aeneid*	hexameter	1, 4f
		Georgics	hexameter	1, 2f
Post-7th century	Aldhelm	*Carmen de uirginitate*	hexameter	5
		Enigmata	hexameter	5, 1f
	Bede	*De die iudicii*	hexameter	6, 1f
		Vita metrica S. Cuthberti	hexameter	10, 1f
Post-9th century	Boethius	*De consolatione philosophiae*	*multiple*	15, 4f
	'Cato'	*Disticha Catonis*	hexameter	5
	Martianus Capella	*De nuptiis Mercurii et Philologiae*	*multiple*	2, 7f

Addendum: other hypothesized school texts

Author	Work	Metrical form	Number of surviving MSS from ASE
Alcimus Avitus	*De spiritualis historiae gestis; De consolatoria castitatis laude*	hexameter	–
Cyprianus Gallus	*Pentateuchos*	hexameter	1
Lactantius	*De aue phoenice*	elegiacs	2
Paulinus of Nola	*Natalicia S. Felicis*	*multiple*	2f
Persius	*Satirae*	hexameter	5
Virgil	*Eclogues*	hexameter	1

Works with a Possible Instructional Use': the qualifier *possible* is a telling one.[34] Lendinara highlights our 'far from complete' understanding of Anglo-Saxon instructional methods, and also notes the ranges of possible interpretations for the purpose of glosses, construe marks, and other apparatus.[35]

A major source of the interpretative disagreement over the purpose of textual apparatus is the problem of audience. A gloss, for instance, presumably aids in the interpretation of a text, but this does not mean that the immediate user of the manuscript needed the gloss him- or herself; it might have helped in explaining the text to others.[36] This idea of the 'teacher's manual' is more or less accepted as the purpose of a striking set of miscellaneous manuscripts usually called 'classbooks', including 'St Dunstan's Classbook' (Bodleian, Auct. F.4.32),[37] and the 'Cambridge Classbook' (CUL Gg.5.35).[38] Almost all these books date from the mid-tenth or eleventh century, and their contents and form were clearly influenced by Carolingian scholarship and pedagogy.[39] A 'teacher's manual' is not as concrete a definition for these books as it might seem; disagreements remain as to whether they were actual classroom texts, resources for working or aspiring teachers kept in the monastic library, or perhaps owned by (or lent to) individuals for private reading and study.[40] These options are not mutually exclusive, and a single volume might have had several careers in the course of its lifespan.[41]

The question of the audience for 'classbooks' or volumes of curriculum authors is a crucial but difficult one for the present discussion. If we want to understand the importance of poetry and its composition in Anglo-Saxon

England, the difference is immense between a teacher who scans lines of verse with his students – perhaps also coaching them through their own first attempts at composition – and one who teaches the essentials of grammar and leaves his charges to discover the rest for themselves. But here, the manuscripts' testimony is ambiguous. CUL Gg.5.35, for instance, contains an elaborate metrical apparatus on the *metra* of Boethius, including names and brief descriptions of the metrical forms, and (usually) scansions of the first lines. This might indicate that students of Latin at St Augustine's in Canterbury routinely learned about difficult lyric forms; it might also indicate that they did *not*, and that this manuscript served as a reference for the rare and intrepid individuals who hoped to interpret the metre of Boethius' verse on their own. The same holds true for relatively bare manuscripts: they might indicate a low level of scholarship, or they might suggest the presence of well-trained masters in little need of *aides-memoires*. This dilemma may be insoluble in our present state of knowledge; the manuscripts themselves have not yet given up their secret.

The surviving books tell us what could be read, but not necessarily how or by whom. Conversely, verbal echoes in Anglo-Latin texts indicate that many well-known books have left little trace in the manuscript record. Virgil's *Æneid* is a prime example; it was apparently habitually read throughout the Anglo-Saxon period, but only one full codex and a few scraps remain.[42] The contrast with Prudentius (for instance) is striking. Patterns of use partly explain such discrepancies: manuscripts of the *Æneid* continued to be read (and worn out, and replaced) after the Conquest, while the Christian Latin epics fell out of favour; the Anglo-Saxon codices presumably survived as fit enough for purpose.[43] Enduringly popular texts are therefore likely to be under-represented in the manuscript record, as are utilitarian texts like grammars. Student 'workbooks' and manuals must have existed too, but none from Anglo-Saxon England has yet been found.[44] The content, number, and distribution of 'classbooks' and single-author codices are thus simultaneously enlightening and unreliable as guides to the 'Anglo-Saxon curriculum'.

Reading the works of Anglo-Latin poets can thus help counteract the ravages of time, while revealing some of the techniques by which their authors learned their craft. Orchard's study of Aldhelm's verse is the most thorough investigation of 'remembered reading' in the work of any Anglo-Saxon poet, and it shows that Aldhelm absorbed an astonishing array of Late Antique and Classical works, some – like the *Carmen ad Flavium Felicem* and collections of inscriptions – comparatively obscure, or even (as with Lucan's *Orpheus*) now lost.[45] Sometimes he directly quoted from the works he read, but earlier poets' words also resurfaced as elements of his normal diction. While undoubtedly exceptional in the range of his knowledge, Aldhelm was not unique in the degree to which his reading formed his style. Even a cursory examination of Anglo-Latin poets shows indebtedness to an evolving group of texts, and further research on Aldhelm's successors will help us better understand how the 'curriculum' evolved over time.[46]

Gauging authors' reading through their use of verbal parallels does, however, face some methodological obstacles. First, even the most striking borrowing does not imply knowledge of an entire work: verses and phrases circulated as isolated snippets in the works of the grammarians, Church Fathers, and poets, and were often reappropriated at second- or third-hand. Ogilvy's *Books Known to the English, 597 – 1066*, was particularly prone to false use of this kind of authorial metonymy, though Lapidge's recent *The Anglo-Saxon Library*, intended to replace Ogilvy's list, is far more cautious in this respect.[47] This problem particularly affects our understanding of poets' education when we encounter an Anglo-Saxon work that apparently shows knowledge of a text that was rare in England. In such a situation we must decide whether the author knew the rare work via the intermediary of a more common one; or if he studied his craft where the text was more widely known; or if he somehow acquired, and independently read, a book his teachers and contemporaries did not know. Our verdict in such a case must depend on many other judgments about the author and his work. But there is, of course, a fourth option; and that is simply that we do not yet know enough about Anglo-Saxon literary education. This last possibility must always be borne in mind.

Judging, however, from what we *do* know, many teachers of Latin in Anglo-Saxon England spent a good deal of time reading and expounding poetry, and if these teachers were themselves poets, the texts they taught were almost certain to affect their own compositions. A better picture of the kinds of text habitually read and taught can thus explain some notable qualities of the Anglo-Saxon verse corpus.

Epic's scope

The most important genre in the Anglo-Saxon 'curriculum' was undoubtedly the biblical epic. This specifically and self-consciously Christian mode arose from a mingled desire to bring educated readers of poetry to Christianity and make Latin verse serve the needs of Christians.[48] As a form of paraphrase, biblical epic was intimately linked to Roman literary and rhetorical education, and in turn the works of Juvencus, Alcimus Avitus,

Sedulius, and Arator were quickly integrated into Christian education – a tradition which, as Table 2.1 shows, the Anglo-Saxons enthusiastically perpetuated.[49] Over time, the New Testament epic metamorphosed from the connected, relatively linear narrative of Juvencus, who retells a synthesized version of all four Gospels, into Arator's and Sedulius' episodic, condensed meditations on the Acts of the Apostles and New Testament miracles.[50] Sedulius added the further innovation of a prose companion to his own poem, separating the biblical epic even more from straightforward paraphrase.

When the Anglo-Saxons adopted the genre they continued to develop it, at first along lines already sketched out by Gaulish predecessors. Hagiography had provided a new field for emulation of the biblical epics: Sulpicius Severus' paradigmatic *Vita S. Martini* had two verse paraphrases by the sixth century.[51] Early Anglo-Latin authors took up this new form with enthusiasm, and the *opus geminatum* – Sedulius' term for his 'twinned work' in verse and prose – became, for a time, a distinctively English mode of hagiography. Aldhelm's *Opus de uirginitate*, Bede's *Vita S. Cuthberti*, and Alcuin's *Vita S. Willibrordi* all participate in this mode; Alcuin's *Carmen de episcopis regibus sanctisque Euboracis* and Bede's prose *Vita S. Felicis*, were designed as 'twins' of Bede's *Historia ecclesiastica* and Paulinus of Nola's *Natalicia S. Felicis* respectively.[52]

It is no coincidence that Aldhelm, Bede, and Alcuin were teachers as well as hagiographers. Their choice of genre, and their understanding of the relation of verse to prose, were undoubtedly influenced by their extensive reading of Late Antique poets. The style of their verse, moreover, shows a close relation to that of Sedulius and Arator. The Anglo-Latin 'saints' epics' are likewise episodic, meditative, mainly non-narrative, especially when compared to their prose 'twins'. In his preface to the double *Vita S. Willibrordi*, Alcuin presents this difference as a reflection of audience and function:

> et duos digessi libellos, unum prosaico sermone gradientem, qui puplice fratribus in ecclesia, si dignum tuae videatur sapientiae, legi potuisset: alterum Piereo pede currentem, qui in secreto cubili inter scolasticos tuos tantummodo ruminari debuisset.[53]

> And I set forth two little books, one progressing in prosaic speech, which (should your wisdom deem it worthy) may be read publicly to the brothers in church, the other hurrying with Pierian foot, which should only be meditated over by your scholars in their private chambers.

For Alcuin, the difference between prose and verse is between exoteric and esoteric forms. Prose is straightforward and literal, to be taken in collectively by a heterogeneous group of listeners; poetry is difficult, reserved to *scholastici* for private contemplation, whose work involved decoding the words themselves and the pattern of 'Pierine feet' they formed. Alcuin's formulation inverts the ancient equation of verse with *dulcedo* seen in Late Antique Christian authors from Juvencus to Boethius.[54] Instead of the sweet syrup that made truth more palatable, Latin verse had become the more difficult form for the Anglo-Saxons, needing to be savoured rather than gulped. This view of the functional differences between verse and prose helps explain, I think, why Anglo-Saxon readers and authors so often preferred the complex, allusive style of Sedulius and Arator to the large-scale narratives of Juvencus or, indeed, Virgil.

Vernacular poetry somewhat alters this landscape. Biblical and hagiographical epic was a favourite form of Old English poets, too, and scholars have often drawn connections between these poems and particular Latin curriculum texts.[55] Some vernacular biblical epics do employ the allusive, nonlinear mode of the later Latin poets and their Anglo-Latin compatriots – *Exodus* is the most notable example, but *Christ and Satan* and, perhaps, *The Fates of the Apostles* might also qualify.[56] Other poets, like those of *Genesis A*, *Daniel*, *Andreas*, and *Judith*, preferred more straightforward narrative modes, akin to the amplifying but essentially linear form of Juvencus. As to the meaning or cause of this difference between the Latin and Old English corpora, many conclusions are possible – it might stem from differences of taste or education in authors or audiences, or differing theories about the purpose of vernacular poetry. Further research will undoubtedly reveal more about the connections between Latin and vernacular biblical epics.[57] What will be more difficult to discover is whether the close correlation we see in Anglo-Latin between knowledge of biblical epics, production of new verse paraphrases, and a profession as a teacher, should be read as holding true for Old English works. If *Exodus*, for instance, were the work of someone who demonstrably knew Alcimus Avitus and Sedulius,[58] is it therefore likely to have been composed by someone who taught the Latin epics? The correlation seems compelling but not ineluctable.

Riddles of Creation

Another popular and characteristic genre, the literary *enigma*, links teachers with poetry in both Latin and Old English.[59] Inspired by the Late Antique collection of 'Symphosius', Aldhelm composed his own century of

Table 2.2 *Two eleventh-century collections of Anglo-Latin riddles*

Gg.5.35		Royal 12.C.xxiii	
Eusebius	370^r–4^v	Aldhelm	79^v–103^v
Tætwine	374^v–7^v	Symphosius	104^v–13^v
Alcuin: *monitory poems to princes*	378^r–80^v	Eusebius	113^v–21^v
'Versus cuiusdam Scoti de alfabeto'	381^{r-v}	Tætwine	121^v–7^r
Boniface	382^r–8^r	Alcuin: *various monitory texts*	127^r–37^r
'Sancte sator' hymn	388^v	'Versus cuiusdam Scoti de alfabeto'	137^r–8^v
Alcuin's epitaph	388^v		
Symphosius	389^r–93^v		
Aldhelm	394^r–407^r		

hexametrical Latin riddles early in his career.[60] As we have seen, he incorporated it into his metrical treatise as a source of exemplary verse and an embodiment of his work's themes. Aldhelm's riddles were in turn reabstracted and re-incorporated into miscellaneous 'classbook' manuscripts intended – it is presumed – to provide literary education of a more general sort.[61] In two of these, CUL Gg.5.35 and BL, Royal 12.C.xxiii, Aldhelm's riddles are accompanied by those of Symphosius and of two Anglo-Latin authors, Tætwine and Eusebius; the Royal manuscript also prefaces Aldhelm's riddles with an excerpt from the *Epistola ad Acircium*, which describes the *enigma* as a genre and outlines the principles of scansion in the dactylic hexameter.[62] The order of the riddle collections in the two manuscripts is outlined in Table 2.2. In both, the *enigmata* are grouped together, preceded – and, in Gg.5.35, followed – by other kinds of text. Combined with the excerpt from Aldhelm's *Epistola ad Acircium* in Royal 12.C.xxiii, this consistent arrangement suggests, as Orchard has argued, that *enigmata* were understood as a distinct literary genre throughout the Anglo-Saxon period.[63]

The didactic associations of Anglo-Latin riddles extend beyond their manuscript context to the poems' content. Of the major collections, Aldhelm's are perhaps the least insistently focused on the physical and textual world of the classroom; as his subject, he took 'Creation', and sixty-nine of his hundred riddles describe animals or natural phenomena.[64] Yet he too turned his attention to the scholar's equipment. In addition to 'Alphabet' (xxx), 'Pen' (lix), and 'Book-chest' (lxxxix), Aldhelm ventriloquizes a set of writing-tablets:

xxxii. Pugillares

Melligeris apibus mea prima processit origo,
Sed pars exterior crescebat cetera silvis;
Calciamenta mihi tradebant tergora dura.
Nunc ferri stimulus faciem proscindit amoenam
Flexibus et sulcos obliquat adinstar aratri,
Sed semen segiti de caelo ducitur almum,
Quod largos generat millena fruge maniplos.
Heu! Tam sancta seges diris extinguitur armis.[65]

32. Writing-tablets. My first birth came forth from honey-bearing bees, but then my outer part grew from trees; shoes gave me a tough back. Now an iron goad scores my fair face, and with its turns flicks out furrows like a plough, but to the field it brings nourishing seed from heaven, which yields great harvests with thousandfold fruit. Alas, that such a holy crop must be removed with cruel weapons!

The structure of *Enigma* xxxii is typical of most of Aldhelm's riddles on man-made objects: it begins with the object's 'birth' from natural materials and proceeds to its present appearance and function. These tablets, however, are specifically *ecclesiastical* implements: they bear a passage from Scripture, the 'life-giving seed of heaven'. In a characteristically Aldhelmian gesture, we even learn that the tablets regret it when the words are smoothed out with the reverse of the stylus in preparation for new text. This is a clever manipulation of a stock metaphor: the New Testament image of Scripture as 'seed of life' was a favourite motif of Christian writers, but in Aldhelm's version, the smoothed-over wax tablet becomes the bare field after the 'fruits' have been cut by the reapers.[66] If Aldhelm's own poems were learned as lessons in this way, the image's immediacy was no doubt enhanced; but even when seen from a parchment page, the writing-tablets connect the created world of Aldhelm's *Enigmata* to the daily experience of a Latin-learner.

Even with 'natural' subjects, Aldhelm's riddles habitually foreground their textuality, and their interpretations have at least as much to do with the act of reading as of seeing or knowing. In his analysis of Isidore's *Etymologiae* as a source for the *Enigmata*, Nicholas Howe has shown how Aldhelm perceived words as keys to the nature of things.[67] A good example of this is the 'Crab' riddle:

xxxvii. Cancer

'Nepa' mihi nomen ueteres dixere Latini:
Humida spumiferi spatior per litora ponti;
Passibus oceanum retrograda transeo uersis:

Et tamen aethereus per me decoratur Olimpus,
Dum ruber in caelo bisseno sidera scando;
Ostrea quem metuit duris perterrita saxis.[68]

37. Crab. The ancient Latins said my name was *nepa*: I amble across the damp plains of the foamy sea. I cross the ocean in reverse, with backward strides – and yet heavenly Olympus is adorned by me when, red, I climb up twelve stars in the sky. The oyster fears me, terrified by hard stones.

This riddle is about neither the animal nor the constellation, but the Latin word *cancer*. The crab's enmity towards the oyster in the final line is derived from Isidore; the synonymy of *cancer* with the somewhat obscure word *nepa* is probably taken from a glossary or grammatical text.[69] While the crab's sideways skitter could have been learned by observation, it need not have been: this is typical of Aldhelm's *Enigmata*, where experience mainly reinforces the testimony of books. Creation manifests itself to readers through the filter of the Latin lexicon. This quality – in addition to keeping the *Enigmata* so popular with Latin learners – doubtless also helped promote the text's stated purpose, the elucidation of Latin metrics.[70] Scholars have often noted Aldhelm's focus on the inner workings of things, their *uiscera*.[71] Words, in his view, are a vital part of these workings: one understands a thing by knowing the right words for it. But as Aldhelm presents it in the *Epistola ad Acircium* – in the excerpt most frequently circulated with the riddles – metre is a way of understanding the inner workings of words themselves, and the secret rules of their arrangement.[72] This profoundly logocentric view of the world made the *Enigmata* philosophically, as well as practically, ideal for introducing readers to the interpretation of Latin texts.

Tætwine – archbishop of Canterbury from 731 to 734, and, according to Bede, a priest from the Mercian house of Breedon-on-the-Hill – seized on the strain of ecclesiastically oriented textuality in Aldhelm's *Enigmata* and developed it even further.[73] His group of forty riddles, linked by an intricate acrostic in the first and last letters of their first lines, owes a deep debt to Aldhelm's example.[74] Tætwine's subjects, however, are far more focused on the apparatus of the church and the scriptorium, and on grammar; more than half of his riddles describe abstract concepts or man-made objects. As a grammatical textbook survives under his name, perhaps his interest in the subject is unsurprising, but the choice of 'a preposition that takes two cases' for a riddle topic shows active delight in the formal aspects of Latinity:[75]

XVI. De prepositione utriusque casus
Emerita gemina sortis sub lege tenemur:
Nam tollenti nos stabiles seruire necesse est,

Causantis contra cursus comitamur eundo;
Sicque uicissim bis binae coniungamur ambis
Quippe sorores; decreta stat legibus urna.[76]

16. Prepositions that take either of two cases. We hold to a just twofold law of
fate: for when we are still, we must hold to the one who takes away; but in
motion, we accompany the course of the one on trial. Thus we four sisters
join ourselves to both in turn; our decreed fates stand by laws.

The prepositions *in*, *sub*, *subter*, and *super* appear as central figures in a
bizarre and scandalous marital case, in which the ablative case becomes an
abductor (*tollens*) and the accusative, the plaintiff in a trial (*causans*: for
Tætwine, a nonce formation). The latter hero is evidently connected to
Tætwine's definition of the case:

ACCUSATIVVS quod per ipsum accusamus aliquem aut aliquis nos accusat.[77]

Accusative, so called because through it we accuse something, or someone
accuses us.

The legalistic colour evidently caught his imagination, and what resulted
was the curious double bigamy trial – or is it a group marriage? – of *Enigma*
XVI. Tætwine's riddle is the work of someone who has spent a great deal of
time thinking about Latin grammar: its inflexible laws, and its occasional
absurdities. The *enigma* is less a student's mnemonic than a scholar's
fantasia; though as line 4 is helpfully glossed with the prepositions in
question in Gg.5.35, it seems that it could function as a teaching device
nevertheless.

The environment evoked by Tætwine's collections is predominantly
ecclesiastical.[78] So are the modes of thought demanded by his text. This is
perhaps clearest in *Enigma* III, on the fourfold interpretation of Scripture:

III. De historia et sensu et morali et allegoria
Bis binas statuit sua nos uigiles dominatrix
Thesauri cellaria conseruare sorori.
Diuersisque intus fulgent ornamenta metallis;
Omnigena et florum dulcedine serta uirescunt.
Gaudentes nostris hec mox reseramus amicis;
Ingratisque aditum sed iure negamus apertum.[79]

3. Historical, Spiritual, Moral, and Allegorical Interpretation. Our mistress
appointed us as her four vigilant guardians to keep our sister's storehouses of
treasure. Ornaments of varied metals glitter within, and all manner of things
flourish in fragrant wreaths of flowers. We are happy to unlock these things
quickly for our friends: but for the graceless, we justly block even the open
door.

The relatively transparent symbols in this poem – the four siblings with their sister and mistress; the treasure-chambers; the precious metals and flowers – invite the reader to interpret beyond the literal sense of the words, and thus enact the solution while guessing it. Martin Irvine has written of the *enigma*'s potential to transmit the form of literacy required by medieval modes of exegesis.[80] Tætwine's *Enigma* III elegantly exemplifies the kind of grammatically oriented texts Irvine analyses, which construct not only their own readers, but ideal readers of Scripture. Here we can see a close correlation between Tætwine's role as a teacher and his choice of genre: his *Enigmata* provide multilayered lessons on grammar, metre, and the processes of thought that transform naïve readers into literate interpreters of texts.

Tætwine's companion in the manuscripts is known only as 'Eusebius'. The sixty riddles of the *Enigmata Eusebii* precede Tætwine's collection in both the Royal and Cambridge manuscripts, and scholars have plausibly hypothesized that the pairing was designed to provide the 'canonical' total of a hundred found in both Aldhelm and Symphosius.[81] The author of the collection is customarily identified with Hwætberht, Ceolfrid's successor as abbot of Wearmouth-Jarrow, since Bede's preface to Book IV of his commentary on Samuel indicates that upon Hwætberht 'amor studiumque pietatis iam olim Eusebii cognomen indidit' ('love and zeal for devotion long ago bestowed the by-name "Eusebius"').[82] Abbot Hwætberht was certainly a Latinist and a teacher: in the *Historia abbatum*, Bede describes him thus:

> Eligitur itaque abbas Hwætberchtus qui a primis pueritiae temporibus eodem in monasterio non solum regularis obseruantia disciplinae institutus, sed et scribendi, cantandi, legendi ac docendi fuerat non parua exercitatus industria.[83]

> Chosen as abbot was Hwætberht, who from his earliest boyhood in this same monastery was not merely imbued with the observance of the Rule's discipline, but had been exerting himself with no small labour in writing, singing, reading, and teaching.

But the connection between Hwætberht-Eusebius and the Eusebius of the Cambridge-Royal riddles seems much less secure than that between the enigmatist Tætwine and the archbishop of the same name. We have little information on how many Anglo-Saxons took names in religion, or how persistently they used them, so it is difficult to know how distinctive the name 'Eusebius' was; Hwætberht of Wearmouth-Jarrow, judging by the *Historia abbatum*, seems to have used his English name more often than his cognomen. The riddles' internal evidence is mixed. Lapidge, drawing on unpublished metrical analyses of Neil Wright, argues that Eusebius' technique is closer to that of Aldhelm and Tætwine, and that he was probably 'an otherwise unknown Southumbrian poet'.[84] Orchard, however, has found that Eusebius' tendency towards dactylic rhythms in his hexameter lines groups his style with Bede and later Northumbrian poets.[85] Given how little we know of the literary connections between Mercia and Northumbria in the eighth century, the question will be difficult to resolve. Since Eusebius' riddles were apparently composed as a response to Tætwine's collection (and, thus, after his work), and since the only known site of either collection's transmission is Canterbury, I think it more likely that Eusebius was an otherwise unknown author working in Kent during or after Tætwine's archiepiscopate. This, however, is merely a conjecture.

Whoever Eusebius was, he too seems to have been fixated by the textuality of Latin and by the world of Christian learning. The cosmographical element of his work is particularly apparent in the first six riddles (on, respectively, God, Angel, Demon, Man, Heaven, Earth).[86] So is Eusebius' interest in binary opposites, which continues in other paired riddles like Sun and Moon (x and xi), Ox and Cow (xii and xiii), and a series of riddles whose single solutions are pairs of opposites: Wind and Fire (viii); Fire and Water (xv); Crime and Justice (xviii); Land and Sea (xxi); Life and Death (xxiv); Humility and Pride (xxvii); Day and Night (xlviii). Tætwine had created riddles with 'grouped solutions', but these invariably were ideas or items that went together – such as the 'Fourfold Interpretation' discussed above, or the more prosaic 'Sword and Sheath' (xxx). In the Anglo-Latin *enigma* tradition, Eusebius' use of paired opposites is paralleled only in Boniface's book of acrostic riddles on the virtues and vices.

Like his predecessors, Eusebius includes a series of riddles on medieval desk supplies: Inkhorn, Wax, Parchment, and Book-cover (xxx–xxxiii). Five of his *enigmata* concern the alphabet – Letters (vii), A (ix), X (xiv), V (xix), and I (xxxix) – and they are mainly interested in the polyvalence of the letters as symbols, rather as Aldhelm was concerned with the multiple resonances of his subjects as words. Perhaps more striking are Eusebius' two riddles on computistical subjects: *De die bissextile* ('Leap Day', xxvi) and Lunar Cycle and Leap (xxix). The second of these reads as a mnemonic:

> xxix. De aetate et saltu
> Rite uicenis cum quadragies octies una
> Quaeque sororum formatur de more mearum

Nempe momentis; tunc ego sola peracta uidebor.
Cicli nondecimus cum deficit extimus annus.[87]

> 29. Lunar Cycle and Leap. By rule, every one of my sisters is formed by twenty times forty-eight motions; then I alone appear to be completed when the nineteenth and final year of the cycle comes to an end.

The conceit of the 'sisters' is the only concession to the riddle genre; mainly, this is a versified definition. Eusebius' tendency towards straightforward verse paraphrase reaches its peak in the peculiar final set of riddles: beginning at about *Enigma* XL, most of the last twenty *enigmata* describe exotic creatures from Isidore's *Etymologiae* and, occasional ornamentation aside, essentially replicate Isidore's words. Eusebius' connection to Latin schooling seems plain – his subjects describe aspects of grammar and *computus*, along with natural history and basic theology. Yet the impression his collection of *enigmata* creates is less of a teacher reconsidering familiar topics, than of a student revisiting lessons while working through the rules of Latin verse. Aldhelm's claim to have written his riddles 'uelut in quodam gimnasio prima ingenioli rudimenta exercitari cupiens' ('seeking to exercise, as if in some gymnasium, the first rudiments of my small ingenuity') seems far truer of Eusebius.[88] But knowing as we do nothing of the circumstances of these riddles' composition, it is impossible to be sure.

Anglo-Saxons working on the Continent helped perpetuate the riddle tradition through the eighth century. Those enigmatists whose names we know, Boniface and Alcuin, were both teachers. Boniface's intricate set of *enigmata* on the virtues and vices seems least like the other Anglo-Latin collections, given its adherence to a consistent set of topics and use of acrostic solutions: the aim of *De uirtutibus et uitiis* was didactic, but in a way less transparently connected to the trivium; I will discuss this book further in Chapter 5. Alcuin's riddles, on the other hand, were straightforwardly educational, and encompassed mathematical as well as linguistic puzzles. These, however, were in prose: although fascinating as a window into early Carolingian educational practice, they fall outside the scope of this study.[89] For the present, we should turn to the most famous set of Anglo-Saxon *enigmata* – the Old English riddles of the Exeter Book.

The question of who wrote the Exeter riddles, and why they were included in the manuscript, has exercised scholars as much as the most insoluble of the riddles themselves. Once enthusiasm for attributing the entire Exeter Book to Cynewulf had abated, a consensus – still held – grew that, as Moritz Trautmann put it: 'When ... the difference between individual riddles in style, tone, learning, and language is weighed, one quickly comes to the conclusion that, not only are the Exeter *Riddles* not a coherent and uniform collection, but that they must stem from different poets.'[90] Linguistic features of many of the riddles seem to indicate a relatively early date for some groups of poems.[91] The single riddle with a text paralleled outside the Exeter Book – *Riddle* 35, a translation of Aldhelm's *Enigma* XXXIII: *Lorica* – shares a common source with the *Leiden Riddle*, which is composed in a distinctively eighth-century Northumbrian dialect.[92] However, Katherine O'Brien O'Keeffe has demonstrated that *Riddle* 40, at least, must postdate the beginning of the tenth century.[93] But while the Old English riddles cannot be read as a single planned text like the Anglo-Latin collections, it is not impossible that the Exeter Book's compiler envisioned the manuscript as a parallel to the sorts of teaching-oriented books that preserved the Anglo-Latin riddles. Irvine and Lerer compare its structure to that of CUL Gg.5.35.[94] Individual riddle-authors, too, could be plausibly read as teachers. The translator of *Riddle* 40, who handles the Classical references in Aldhelm's *Enigma* C: *Creatura* with confidence, must certainly have studied Latin poetry.[95] More broadly, Dieter Bitterli has traced the etymological and logogriphic games beloved by Latin enigmatists in many of the Exeter riddles.[96] But though it is possible to fit them within an Anglo-Saxon educational context, the Old English riddles' anonymity, combined with the absence of specifically grammatical topics, means that it is impossible to attribute any of them definitively to a teacher or a classroom setting. For at least some, the scriptorium seems a more likely birthplace, as we shall see below.

Learning and verse

Other Old English poems of the Exeter Book could plausibly be attributed to teachers: *Precepts*, for instance, has the monitory tone and concatenate structure of the *Disticha Catonis*. But wisdom verse need not be the work of a professional teacher, since as a vernacular genre it seems to have been widely enjoyed and may have been widely produced.[97] However, though it is possible that some texts of this sort have yet to be identified as English, we have few examples of purely factual Anglo-Saxon didactic verse. While on the Continent, Alcuin wrote a poem to help readers distinguish long and short syllables; but if he sent it to York, his correspondents evidently did not imitate it.[98] Continental authors were much fonder of writing didactic verse, and their efforts were sometimes preserved in Anglo-Saxon manuscripts. Israel the Grammarian's poem *De arte metrica* was seemingly well known in tenth-century England, for instance; Israel, who was probably a Breton, may also have brought two mnemonic poems on medical terminology to England.[99] Perhaps the most interesting Anglo-Latin didactic poem is Oswald of Ramsey's exemplary text on retrograde hexameters, which begins:

> Centum concito sic qui nouit condere uersus
> nullo crimine commaculatos, ordine gratos,
> sensu denique confertos et cursibus aptos –
> laudis munera dat dictanti scansio lucens:
> Virgilianus hic dicetur maxime uates . . .
> istos texuit Osuuoldus, qui est nescius artis . . .[100]

He who knows how to swiftly forge a hundred verses like this – blotted by no fault, pleasing in arrangement, packed (naturally) with meaning, and in orderly sequence – such resplendent scansion grants the speaker gifts of praise: he is rightly called a Virgilian poet . . . Oswald, who is ignorant of the art, composed these verses . . .

Oswald stops seventy-nine lines short of being a *Virgilianus . . . uates*, but his assessment of the skill needed to compose a hundred lines in this manner (that is, scanning identically forward and backward) seems apt. If any at Ramsey took up his challenge, though, their efforts have been lost.[101] The poem circulated in Canterbury, which we know through the indefatigable generosity of the compilers of CUL Gg.5.35. But as a representative of the tradition of didactic verse – and especially of didactic verse about verse – Oswald's poem remains isolated. It seems that Anglo-Saxon teachers created versified lessons far less often than their contemporaries on the Continent.[102]

We know much less about the place of poetry in the education of monoglot English speakers than we do about Latin. After the first Viking invasions, it seems clear that some people learned to read English but not Latin; but no English primers – at least, that we recognize – have survived. But Asser's description of the education of Alfred of Wessex and his children suggests that poetry did hold an important place in the upbringing of aristocrats. The famous incident of the 'book of poetry' deserves repeating:

> proh dolor! indigna suorum parentum et nutritorum incuria usque ad duodecimum aetatis annum, aut eo amplius, illiteratus permansit. Sed Saxonica poemata die noctuque solers auditor, relatu aliorum saepissime audiens, docilibilis memoriter retinebat . . .
> Cum ergo quodam die mater sua sibi et fratribus suis quendam Saxonicum poematicae artis librum, quem in manu habebat, ostenderet, ait: 'Quisquis uestrum discere citius istum codicem possit, dabo illi illum.' Qua uoce, immo

diuina inspiratione, instinctus <Ælfredus>, et pulchritudine principalis litterae illius libri illectus, ita matri respondens, et fratres suos aetate, quamuis non gratia, seniores anticipans, inquit: 'Verene dabis istum librum uni ex nobis, scilicet illi, qui citissime intellegere et recitare eum ante te possit?' Ad haec illa, arridens et gaudens atque affirmans: 'Dabo,' infit, 'illi.' Tunc ille statim tollens librum de manu sua, magistrum adiit et legit. Quo lecto, matri retulit et recitauit.[103]

Alas! by the neglect of his parents and tutors, he remained illiterate up to twelve years old, or even longer. But, as he was a discerning auditor of Saxon poetry by day and night, listening very frequently to the recitations of others, he (being very apt for learning) retained them in his memory . . .

One day, then, when his mother was showing him and his brothers a certain Saxon book of the poetical art, she said: 'I will give this book to whichever of you can learn it the quickest.' Inspired by that speech (or, rather, by divine urging), and attracted by the beauty of the initial letter of the book, he got ahead of his brothers (his seniors in years, though not in grace) and replied to his mother, 'Will you really give that book to whichever of us can most quickly learn it and recite it before you?' To which she – smiling, pleased, and encouraging – said, 'To him I will give it.' Then, immediately taking the book from her hand, he went to his master and read it. And, having read it, he brought it back to his mother and recited it.

A considerable literature surrounds this passage, which raises a host of interesting questions about issues such as women's literacy and book own-ership, the luxury book trade, even the meaning of 'reading' in the society Asser describes.[104] For us, two elements are particularly important. One is the stress Asser puts on the memorization of large quantities of verse; this strongly resembles the experience of Anglo-Saxon students of Latin. The other is the role of the *magister* glimpsed helping Alfred learn his book: did he read passages aloud, coaching his young pupil through the correct repetition of them? If so, did teachers of Latin do the same? It would be valuable to know the status and training of Alfred's early teacher, but Asser says no more about him.

Equally important for this study is the essential passivity of Alfred's experience, which is not unlike that of the readers of *artes metricae*. He is not being encouraged to make up a new poem as good as those in the book; his mother expects him to repeat back the words as written. The *Saxonica poemata* of which young Alfred was such a dedicated listener were also the works (and indeed the performances) of others. This has interesting con-sequences for interpretations of the role of courtiers in the production of verse, as we shall see later on. Those of Alfred's children who were brought up for secular, aristocratic life seem to have been raised along lines similar to their father:

> Eadwerd et Ælfthryth semper in curto regio nutriti cum magna nutrito-rum et nutricum diligentia, immo cum magno omnium amore, et ad omnes indigenas et alienigenas humilitate, affabilitate et etiam lenitate, et cum magna patris subiectione huc usque perseverant. Nec etiam illi sine liberali disciplina inter cetera praesentis vitae studia, quae nobilibus con-veniunt, otiose et incuriose <vivere> permittuntur, nam et psalmos et Saxonicos libros et maxime Saxonica carmina studiose didicere, et fre-quentissime libris utuntur.[105]

> Eadweard and Ælfthryth, having been entirely brought up in the court under the great care of their tutors and nurses, live to this day with the great esteem of all, and with modesty, affability, and kindness towards both native-born and foreign people, and with great respect for their father. Nor were they allowed to live idly and ignorantly, without the liberal disciplines among those other worldly pursuits befitting the nobility; for they studiously learned both the Psalter and Saxon books, and most especially Saxon poems, and very often made use of books.

Alfred and his court evidently regarded Old English poetry as worthy in its own right, not merely an illiterate's substitute for true learning; Asser's final sentence makes it clear he thought learning vernacular poems was a more intellectual pursuit than hawking and hunting. Knowing many poems by heart, moreover, seems to have been a major step towards becoming cultured in this society. What is less clear, though, is the role of teachers. The *nutritores* and *nutrices* were obviously important, but we cannot tell if they were educators as well as caretakers. As for their 'liberal studies', the young prince and princess might have been coached by teachers through a set of texts chosen for them; or they might have simply been allowed to listen to whatever was being recited before the court, and expected to absorb it. Old English poems could have been widely learned in this way without being commonly taught.

While Asser's *Gesta Ælfredi* answers few of our questions about the role of teachers in the transmission of Old English verse, it at least assures us that one significant similarity did exist between Latin and vernacular literary educa-tion. The absorption of large quantities of verse was obviously a prerequisite, in either language, for status as a cultured person. Even if the tutors at Alfred's court did not spend much time explaining morphology or rhetorical tropes in the way a *grammaticus* teaching Sedulius would have, it seems they would have often heard, and perhaps read and recited, Old English verse.

Some prosopographical conclusions

Judging from the Latin evidence, the teacher–pupil relation was significant for both parties. In many cases, we know of poets' fame as teachers because their students wrote to them years later, asking for favours including the correction of their own poems; Æthilwald's *Carmina rhythmica* attest this.[106] The strength of this bond undoubtedly helped disseminate the works of many Anglo-Saxon poets within England, and abroad through English travellers and missionaries. Moreover, the link between the teaching and composition of verse seems solid enough to hypothesize that two named teachers at least – Æthelwold of Winchester and Eadburg of Minster-in-Thanet – must have composed verse, even if it has been lost. Æthelwold's disciples praised his teaching, and one of them, Wulfstan Cantor – probably the most accomplished Latin metrist in Anglo-Saxon England – emphasized that Æthelwold gave instruction in the art of metre.[107] Several Latin poems are apparently the work of a student in his school, and the scribe Godemann was also his pupil.[108] We know that Æthelwold's older contemporary (and teacher) Dunstan wrote poems, including *tituli* for new ecclesiastical furnishings.[109] Though no poems have been attached to Æthelwold's name, it seems most probable that he composed verse.

The same can be said of Eadburg, Boniface's friend and correspondent, and abbess of Minster-in-Thanet. Her student Leofgyth – who eventually joined Boniface's mission as a teacher and abbess herself – attributes her own metrical knowledge to Eadburg's teaching.[110] Leofgyth's hexameters make clear that her literary education entailed a stiff dose of Aldhelm, of which Eadburg must necessarily have also partaken. And if the student practised her skill by composing verse, it seems likely that her teacher did too.[111] Leofgyth's letter to Boniface also demonstrates that women, at least in the earlier period, could and did become Latin poets. It is possible that many of the great abbesses of the seventh and eighth centuries taught and composed verse, though few records of this survive.[112] We know relatively little about the sort of education given to girls and women in convents during the tenth century and later: if such students learned large quantities of verse (as we see in monasteries, and in the education of Alfred's daughter Ælfthryth), it may well be that convent teachers were also likely to be poets.

One other noteworthy aspect of the careers of teacher-poets is their tendency to reach high ecclesiastical office. Bede and Byrhtferth of Ramsey are unusual in gaining a significant reputation as teachers without achieving a rank higher than priest and monk. In this respect, the frequency with which abbots and bishops are praised for their teaching is worth further consideration: in some cases, such words were perhaps merely an encomiastic tradition, but it may also have been commonly true that an Anglo-Saxon abbot was expected to provide advanced teaching to his monks. Facility in Latin must have been an important consideration in such cases: in which case, for Anglo-Saxon teachers, becoming a poet would have been a good way of getting promoted.

Scribes

Teachers have occupied so much of this chapter partly because the evidence for poet-teachers is so strong, but also because their work sheds light on the entire process of becoming a poet. It was possible for an Anglo-Saxon to learn the art of poetry with little or no formal teaching, as we shall see in Chapter 4; but this was probably not the most common experience. All poets learned somehow or other to compose verse, and many of them probably learned from other poets. The work of scribes is of similarly universal relevance, since all the surviving Anglo-Saxon poems were written down by someone: so much is self-evident. Each poem was also composed by someone. How often these categories of *someone* overlapped is the central problem of this section.

Several known poets worked as scribes. Two or three of those listed in Appendix I seem to have been scribes primarily; others may have considered the physical writing of books as a part of their other duties. Bede and Dunstan are examples of this latter category; both are reported to have written books, but the work they did in their respective monasteries was clearly not confined to copying others' words. This raises the question of what constitutes a scribe. Learning to read in the Middle Ages did not necessarily entail learning to write, and it is very difficult to ascertain what percentage of readers could copy down others' words or their own thoughts. But someone who can form letters is not necessarily a scribe: we normally assume that after learning the rudiments of writing, a person must have undergone a period of training before being entrusted with the replication of texts – not to speak of the investment of parchment, pens, and ink. It is not, however, clear that all working scribes did have such training, or how apprentice or amateur work is to be differentiated from the professional but incompetent. As a basic definition, then, I will consider as a scribe anyone who has written or contributed to the writing of a complete text. This excludes only a few categories of activity – mostly isolated glosses and doodles – and would perhaps be considered overly capacious by the standards of a well-run scriptorium. But establishing standards for professionalism in Anglo-Saxon scribal activity is far beyond the remit of this study.

Conversely, in other cases it is indisputable that an individual was a scribe, but whether he was a poet is more open to doubt. This particular problem takes two forms. First, much of the evidence we have for independent composition by scribes consists of colophons, and these were often re-transcribed along with the rest of a manuscript.[113] The author of a particular colophon might have been *a* scribe, in other words, but not the scribe of the manuscript we have. Alternatively, it may be unclear that an inscription is intended as verse. The famous colophon to the Eadwig Gospels is an excellent example of this. Its author, a monk of Christ Church Canterbury in the early eleventh century, was much in demand for high-status book production, and his elegant Anglo-Caroline script became extremely influential.[114] As Eadwig wrote it, the colophon reads:

> Pro scriptore precem ne tempnas fundere pater.
> Librum istum monachus scripsit EADUUIUS. cogno
> mento BASAN. Sit illi longa salus. Vale seruus
> dei. N. et memor esto mei.[115]

For the scribe, Father, do not scorn to pour forth a prayer. The monk Eadwig, called Basan, wrote this book: may he have long-lasting health. Farewell N., servant of God, and remember me.

Is this meant as heightened prose (emphasized by the alternate coloured inks),[116] or as a peculiarly freeform poem? David Dumville's cautious conclusion is that an earlier version of the inscription *had* been metrical, and that

> an 'Eaduuius Basan' had intruded his own name when copying a text which contained a different one or none . . . The intrusion of names in lines 2 and 4 and (if we wish to explain faults of quantity thus) the possible rewriting of line 1, both in defiance of metre, would satisfactorily explain the colophon's present shape.[117]

While Eadwig's inscription is indeed hopelessly incorrect by quantitative standards, the first line forms a perfectly ordinary rhythmic hexameter:[118]

> Pro scriptore précĕm | ne tempnas fúndĕrĕ pátĕr.

The final part of the inscription is also rhythmic, with a form 6p+7p if *N.* – the reader/recipient's name – is inserted extrametrically. This still leaves the midsection of the inscription unscannable; but this, I think, was probably the intention. In other words, the form of the colophon is most likely a prose sentence framed by two lines of rhythmic verse.[119] Such a reading does not at all preclude Dumville's hypothesis that Eadwig simply copied, rather than created, his verse. Until an original is discovered, though, the most economical explanation is that Eadwig composed this prosimetrical inscription himself.

Other colophons are similarly mixed in form, perhaps suggesting a certain spontaneity in composition. Owun, one of the glossators of the MacRegol Gospels, added an inscription which may be laid out thus:

> Ðe min bruche gibidde fore owun þe þas boc gloesde. Faermen ðaem preoste aet harawuda.

> Haefe nu boc awritne   bruca mið willa
> symle mið soðum gileofa   sibb is eghwaem leofost.[120]

> Pray, whosoever uses me, for Owun who glossed this book, [and] for Færman the priest at Harewood. Take now the fully written book, and enjoy it gladly, always with true faith: amity is dearest to everyone.

Much like Eadwig's, Owun's colophon is both formulaic and structurally miscellaneous, with a prose sentence, a standard Old English long line, and a hypermetric long line. As Gameson's survey demonstrates, the colophon was not a standard or well-defined form in Anglo-Saxon England, and scribes approached it rather casually. Poetry was not mandatory, but an adornment for an inscription that by its nature was already somewhat idiosyncratic.

Naming oneself was also not a necessity, as the metrical epilogue to the *Old English Bede* in CCCC 41 demonstrates:

> Bidde ic eac   æghwylcne mann,
> brego, rices weard,   þe þas boc ræde
> and þa bredu befo,   fira aldor,
> þæt gefyrðrige þone writre   wynsum cræfte
> þe ðas boc awrat   bam handum twam,
> þæt he mote manega gyt   mundum synum
> geendigan,   his aldre to willan,
> and him þæs geunne   se ðe ah ealles geweald,
> rodera waldend,   þæt he on riht mote
> oð his daga ende   drihten herigan. Amen. Geweorþe þæt.[121]

I likewise beg every man, the kingdom-guarding warrior who reads this book, the lord of men who holds the covers, that he should assist the writer with pleasant skill who wrote this book with his own two hands, so that he might complete many more with his hands, as his life's joy; and that the

Ruler of the heavens, who has all power, might allow him to properly praise the Lord until the end of his days. Amen, so be it.

Robinson's re-edition of this poem in its context shows that *ic* in line 1 is Bede.[122] This is the third text following the Old English version of Bede's own colophon to the *Historia ecclesiastica*; the two that precede it are first person prose prayers, also translations of Bede's Latin. The metrical colophon is distinguished from the prose texts by its use of alternating coloured lines (and the space left for a capital, perhaps to be coloured) but is not separated from them.[123] The continuation of the first person joins the poem organically to the *Old English Bede*'s sequence of pendant texts, and such a colophon could be recopied successively, allowing each new scribe to attribute the poem to himself – adopting it without recomposing it. So far as we can ascertain, though, the metrical epilogue was not recopied. The text of the *Old English Bede* in CCCC 41 is uniquely divergent; Robinson suggests that the redactor of the Bede text and the author (or redactor?) of this poem are the same, and that he may be the scribe of the main text.[124] If so, a pseudo-Bedan prayer for an anonymous 'writre' is a fitting tribute to the invisible individuality of his work.

Other anonymous Old English inscriptions may well be the work of scribes. *Aldhelm* – the exuberant trilingual verse bridge between the contents list and main text of Aldhelm's *Prosa de uirginitate* in CCCC 326 – was discussed in Chapter 1; its uniqueness and indissociability from its place in that particular book point towards scribal authorship.[125] Another candidate is *Thureth*, a dedication inscription for the pontifical now bound in Cotton Claudius A.iii:

> Ic eom halgungboc;   healde hine dryhten
> þe me fægere þus   frætewum belegde.
> Þureð to þance   þus het me wyrcean,
> to loue and to wurðe,   þam þe leoht gesceop.
> Gemyndi is he   mihta gehwylcre
> þæs þe he on foldan   gefremian mæg,
> and him geþancie   þeode waldend
> þæs þe he on gemynde   madma manega
> wyle gemearcian   metode to lace;
> and he sceal æce lean   ealle findan
> þæs þe he on foldan   fremaþ to ryhte.[126]

I am a consecrating-book; may the Lord protect him who thus beautifully arrayed me with adornments. Thureth had me so constructed, in gratitude, love, and worship of Him who made the light. He is mindful of every power whereby he can do good on earth, and may the Ruler of hosts thank him for his intention to consecrate many treasures as an offering to the Creator; and he shall receive eternal reward for all good deeds he does on earth.

The book itself speaks to commend two people – Thureth the donor, who receives a eulogistic blessing, and the man who 'me fægere ... frætewum belegde'. The latter might possibly have been the binder, but the appearance of the text makes the scribe the likelier candidate. 'Ic' begins with a decorated initial terminating in a vegetal flourish, and the final long line of the poem is figured into a six-line diminuendo enclosed in a large ink V. The overall effect is odd, but nevertheless decorative: the scribe *is* adorning the book.[127] *Thureth* is unique to Cotton Claudius A.iii, it depends for its meaning on the particular purpose of that manuscript, and it draws attention to the scribe's effort both textually and graphically: this combination of factors, I think, implies the scribe created it himself.

The forms of scribal composition examined so far have been consciously paratextual. They are presented as accessories to the main text through their position at their books' boundaries: when the reader has just opened, or is about to close, the covers of a book or the last page of a text, a discreet signal from the maker of that text's physical form was no interruption. The scribal riddles, however, *are* the text: this subgenre of *enigma* actively encourages contemplation of the physicality of words and the life-processes of the apparatus of writing. Encompassing a number of Anglo-Latin *enigmata* as well as at least seven of the Old English Exeter poems, the scribal riddles have been the subject of several studies – most lately by Dieter Bitterli, who considers both linguistic traditions.[128] But as we saw above, the riddles of Aldhelm and Tætwine, and perhaps Eusebius, are more likely the work of people whose primary work was grammatical teaching, rather than the copying of books, familiar though they obviously were with the scribe's tools. Shook argues that the Old English riddles were essentially different in purpose:

> the riddles of Aldhelm and Tatwine (and possibly of others too) were composed to teach Latin hexameters, much as Latin colloquies were written to teach Latin vocabulary and sentence structure. It is doubtful that the vernacular riddles of the Exeter Book were written to teach anything. They are probably to a great extent scribal diversion.[129]

The Old English riddles were not the diversion of the scribe of the Exeter Book itself: they were copied into the ruled main page with the same dignified Square Minuscule as the rest of the text, and a series of small but significant errors in word division and orthography (such as *speop* for *speow*, or *hwilū mon* for *hwilum on*) reveals he was working from a written exemplar.[130] But of course this does not mean that the Exeter riddles could not have been composed by earlier scribes: the difficulty is in establishing any degree of certainty.

Certainty, however, is what riddles are calculated to elude. Consider, for instance, *Riddle* 51:

> Ic seah wrætlice   wuhte feower
> samed siþian;   swearte wæran lastas,
> swaþu swiþe blacu.   Swift wæs on fore,
> fuglum framra;   fleag on lyfte,
> deaf under yþe.   Dreag unstille
> winnende wiga   se him wegas tæcneþ
> ofer fæted gold   feower eallum.

I saw four creatures going on a journey together in a marvellous fashion; their footprints were dark, their track very glistening. The journey was quick, more vigorous than birds: it soared into air, and dove beneath the wave. He was ceaselessly busy, the striving warrior who marks out the paths for the four creatures over sheets of gold.

The *ic*, the detached, bemused observer who finds all things *wrætlic*, is a common persona in the Old English riddles; four of the next eight riddles also begin with *ic seah*.[131] The four journeying creatures – the three fingers and their pen – are common in medieval descriptions of scribes and stem from actual practice, as Bitterli shows.[132] So are complaints about the physical work involved, as reflected in this hexametrical colophon from an Aldhelm manuscript:

> Tres digiti scribunt totum corpusque laborat
> Scribere qui nescit nullum putat esse laborem.[133]

Three fingers write, and the whole body labours: he who doesn't know how to write thinks it no labour at all.

Gameson points out that this couplet could not have been the scribe's own composition, but was probably nonetheless deeply felt.[134] *Riddle* 51's focus on the *winnende wiga* who *dreag unstille* echoes such reminders to complacent readers of the labour required to apply words to a page. This consciousness of the difficulty and invisibility of scribes' effort also accounts for the violent imagery of the 'inkhorn' riddles (Riddles 88 and 93) more plausibly than DiNapoli's hypothesis of a subconscious yearning for a purely oral culture.[135] Such a profound (and rather defensive) sympathy with scribes' work is surely consonant with scribal authorship of this group of riddles.

Yet there are difficulties with this connection. The sympathy shown for the experience of 'seo friþe mæg' ('the protecting kinswoman') who fed the speaker of *Riddle* 9 and 'hæfde swæsra þy læs / suna ond dohtra þy heo swa dyde' ('had the fewer dear sons and daughters for doing so') does not mean the author was a songbird victimized by a cuckoo. This may seem a trivial point – after all, scribes *could* compose poems and certainly did write them down, while birds do neither – but we should be wary of assuming authors lacked the imaginative sympathy to portray experiences not their own. The Old English riddles also tend to be slipperier in their referents than appears at first glance. The scribe in *Riddle* 51, for instance, is not writing just any book; he is guiding his pen *ofer fæted gold* 'over gold beaten out', i.e., gold leaf. Gilding in itself indicates a high-status, and usually a sacred manuscript: the riddle thus cannot be describing its own creation.[136] Other Old English book riddles display a similar bias towards depicting sacred texts: *Riddle* 26 describes the making of a gospel book, while Bitterli's study of *Riddle* 28 indicates that it might be best interpreted as parchment made into a martyrology.[137] The images of scribes glimpsed in the Exeter *Riddles* are idealizations. They might be self-portraits, too – but if so, they are fittingly enigmatic.

Identifying any particular poem as a scribe's original work will nearly always involve some degree of uncertainty. Yet where scholars have been able to compare scribal behaviour in recording Old English verse – that is, within the small corpus of poems existing in more than one copy – the picture that emerges is of individuals who were not simply copying, but reprocessing what they wrote through the engine of their own knowledge. Katherine O'Brien O'Keeffe demonstrates how scribes 're-performed' the texts they wrote, sometimes substituting phrases with formulaic equivalents, and punctuating for oral delivery.[138] Her analysis shows that the status of a manuscript text of Old English poetry was essentially different from that of, say, a Latin commentary by Augustine; scribes of the vernacular behaved as if they felt their own knowledge to be an authority nearly equal to that of their copy texts. I will explore further in Chapters 3 and 4 the way poets perceived their own status in respect to that of books. Here, I should like to suggest that experience as a scribe reinforced the sense of expertise that many of those who copied Old English poetry seem to have felt. Whether they gained their prior understanding from reading verse, or from hearing it read or recited, is in this respect irrelevant: the act of copying enforced close engagement with the text before them, and provided at least some basis of knowledge. Some of this sense of expertise may well have been false – scribes did sometimes misunderstand or reinterpret their copy texts, as we shall see in Chapter 4. But on the whole, a scribe who copied vernacular poetry must, through his work, have acquired some knowledge of Old English verse, even if his understanding was limited mainly to formulaic phrases. For Latin literate scribes, the same effect probably held true: this would explain the eccentric metre of Eadwig's colophon, for instance. It seems to be the work of someone who knew what a metrical colophon ought to sound like, but was unacquainted with (or uninterested in) the principles of quantitative verse.

If we hypothesize, then, that the nature of scribes' work gave them considerable opportunities to become poets, we can begin to investigate the types of poem most likely to have been scribal compositions. We have already looked at colophons and donation inscriptions as classes of verse often written by scribes (even if not always by the scribes of the manuscripts in which they are now preserved). On the other end of the spectrum, poems that are not indigenous to particular books are almost impossible to attribute to scribes. The Old English *Genesis B*, for instance, is conceivably the work of a poet-copyist at a stage prior to the Junius XI manuscript, but it would require extraordinary (and extraordinarily improbable) discoveries to prove such a theory.

But a class of poems specific to particular texts (rather than particular manuscripts) may be worth investigating in respect to scribal composition. Prefaces and encomia on authors, some metrical, are familiar features in manuscripts of both Latin and Old English. Some are authorial, like the concluding prayer that circulated with Bede's *Historia ecclesiastica*, or invested with a kind of historical authority, as with the various *vitae* of Boethius frequently attached to his *De consolatione philosophiae*.[139] But many verse paratexts inhabit a more ambiguous realm, such as the poems in praise of Sedulius copied in five Anglo-Saxon manuscripts of the *Carmen paschale*. Such verses may have provided a model for the metrical prefaces attached to several Alfredian prose texts – the *Pastoral Care*, the *Old English Boethius*, and Gregory's *Dialogues*. The *Pastoral Care* is also equipped with a metrical epilogue in two of its witnesses, including Bodleian, Hatton 20.[140]

None of these paratexts claim an authorial voice, although the metrical preface to the *Pastoral Care* occurs or did occur in all the known manuscripts and is therefore, at minimum, authorized. This poem is particularly interesting because its final third addresses the copying of the text:

> Siððan min on englisc   Ælfred kyning
> awende worda gehwelc,   and me his writerum
> sende suð and norð,   heht him swelcra ma

brengan bi ðære bisene, ðæt he his biscepum
sendan meahte, forðæm hi his sume ðorfton,
ða ðe lædenspræce læste cuðon.[141]

> Afterward King Alfred turned each of my words into English, and sent me
> south and north to his scribes, commanding them to bring forth more like it
> according to the exemplar, so that he could send them to his bishops: for
> some of them had need of it, those who least understood Latin.

That part of the function of this metrical preface includes justifying to
copyists the necessity of their work implies that scribes are most conscious
of their own role in the texts surrounding 'The Text'. The metrical preface
to the *Pastoral Care* is perhaps not the work of a scribe, but it was composed
by someone who knew how scribes thought: and, as O'Brien O'Keeffe has
shown, it provides an interesting insight into how scribes did think.

The official disseminators of the *Pastoral Care* thus seem to have anticipated the tendency for books to accrete unauthorized proems, and controlled for it with verses that addressed scribes directly. The metrical proem
to the *Old English Boethius* does not mention the text's transmission, but its
ascription of authorship to Alfred may stem from a similar impulse to
control the growth of scribe-generated paratexts.[142] Non-Alfredian works,
though, did acquire new apparatus in transmission. We have already seen
that the metrical epilogue to the *Old English Bede* in CCCC 41 is likely to
have been scribal. So too, I think, is the metrical preface to Wærferth's
translation of Gregory's *Dialogues* found uniquely in BL, Cotton Otho C.i.
This text, evidently written at the request of Wulfsige, bishop of Sherborne,
is in the first person voice of the book, and includes third person prayers for
Wulfsige 'and eac swa his beahgifan, þe him ðas bysene forgeaf . . . Ælfryd
mid Englum' ('and likewise his ring-giver, who gave him this exemplar,
Alfred of the English': ll. 23, 25a). It seems to be the work of someone with a
far better knowledge of prose than of verse; the mention of the exemplar,
together with the poem's specificity to that particular book, make it likely
that that author was the scribe.

This survey of scribes as poets has considered a fairly diverse range of
verse in Latin and Old English. Understanding the full range of scribes'
poetic work, however, may require us to venture beyond the virtual cer-
tainties of colophons and dedication inscriptions. One area in which I
believe scribal composition can be located is within the zone of paratexts
at the beginning and end of longer and more canonical texts. Many of these,
especially in Latin, are unpublished; they are also frequently anonymous,
and may have extremely complex transmission histories, which will make

ascertaining the occupation (and nationality) of their authors the more difficult. Yet if we wish to understand the work of scribe-poets, I believe that it will be most readily found in these spaces at the thresholds of texts. There, too, I think we may find some hints as to why scribes became poets. As we have seen in the texts considered in this section, scribes did not confine their commentary to complaints about the weary length of their labour: many (such as the authors of *Aldhelm*, *Thureth*, and the Alfredian paratexts) reflected on the value of the works they copied. Perhaps not all scribes read their exemplars, but many did, and approached their work as an act of interpretation, as O'Brien O'Keeffe showed in *Visible Song*. Copying texts was one route to acquiring the mental store of verse that the Anglo-Saxons seem to have considered a prerequisite to composition. Scribes, then, had the means and the tools to become poets. Their praise in proems and epilogues – and, perhaps, in riddles – of the wisdom to be found in books, indicates that many also had the inclination.

Musicians

As with scribes, speaking of Anglo-Saxons as musicians raises questions of definition. In monasteries, *everyone* was a trained performer: chant was the first skill taught to novices and oblates, who began to sing the psalms before they could necessarily understand them.[143] Any monk who became a poet was therefore also in some degree a musician. But the music theory of the early Middle Ages drew a sharp distinction between true *musici*, who understood the principles of harmonics, and performers who brought forth music without comprehending it. By the more rigid medieval definition of 'musician' as someone with mastery of music theory, we can identify only three named musicians in Anglo-Saxon England: Abbo of Fleury, who trained in Orléans; Wulfstan Cantor; and (just after the Conquest) Osbern of Canterbury, who trained in Bec. All worked in or after the tenth century; all were likely or certainly poets,[144] and all were quite exceptional individuals.

Such strict criteria for musicianship unquestionably exclude many for whom music was of daily importance. Monks and nuns are the best-attested group, but secular Anglo-Saxons valued music as well. So the catalogue poem *Fates of Men* describes a performer:

> Sum sceal mid hearpan æt his hlafordes
> fotum sittan, feoh þicgan,
> ond a snellice snere wræstan,

lætan scralletan   sceacol, se þe hleapeð,
nægl neomegende;   biþ him neod micel.[145]

One shall sit with his harp at his lord's feet, receive money, and always quickly pluck the strings, his leaping pick causing them to resound sweetly; there is great need for him.

That the harper will *feoh þicgan* ('receive money') makes him by definition a professional, but there are many things we cannot know about his situation. First, no surviving texts make clear how widespread his skill was – did he have special training unavailable to most people, or did he simply possess in superlative degree an ability that many possessed? It would be useful to know how many amateur musicians Anglo-Saxon England had, for if such training were common, it might well be that most poets had some musical skill. But there is not enough evidence to assure ourselves that knowledge of the harp (or any other instrument) was a habitual accomplishment of any class in the way that hunting was among aristocratic men. Moreover, Opland has argued forcefully that professional musicians were a class apart from poets in Anglo-Saxon society; not all of his conclusions are tenable, as we saw in Chapter 1, but the distinctions in Old English terminology he outlines seem to be real.[146] The harper was not *ipso facto* a poet, and we do not know what part – if any – words played in his performance. We also do not know how closely his playing resembled that of Cædmon's friends at the farm workers' gathering described in the *Historia ecclesiastica* IV.24: if the Anglo-Saxons distinguished between high and low musical cultures, we can no longer perceive how and why. After the Conquest, writers like William of Malmesbury speak of narrative *cantilenae* sung among the common people; given their subjects (King Edward's liaison with a shepherdess, for instance), one would guess these alleged folk songs predated the Normans.[147] But the twelfth-century historians give us little idea of what these songs were like, or who sang them. For our purposes, the secular songs of Anglo-Saxon England have vanished without more than a few blurred traces.

This loss of evidence means that using the more stringent medieval criteria for identifying a musician has seemed to me wisest. We know that in the church, an acquaintance with some practical musicianship, mainly in the form of chant, was nearly universal. Something similar might have been true in secular society – there is no evidence for this, yet also no compelling reason to assume otherwise. Distinguishing between the many people with some knowledge of music, and the few who understood its principles and for whom its creation and perpetuation was a primary responsibility, therefore seems important for our present purposes. There would be no value in designating every poet a musician; but at the same time, someone who was not primarily a musician may have known quite a lot about music.

The use of chant in teaching Latin poetry illustrates how music permeated quite unexpected aspects of medieval life. Jan Ziolkowski's *Nota Bene* outlines a variety of uses teachers and readers of Classical Latin verse had for neumes, such as elucidating metrical and rhythmic form, *aides-memoires*, and heightening the effect of stirring passages.[148] Anglo-Saxon manuscripts reflect this practice much less often than the German and Frankish books that form the majority of Ziolkowski's examples. As his focus was on Classical verse, however, and not the Christian Latin epics that constituted the backbone of the Anglo-Saxon curriculum, it may be that a similar study of (say) Sedulius and Arator would uncover analogous results. Conversely, Anglo-Saxon schools may have resisted this Continental innovation in fusing song with the trivium. The great majority of surviving manuscripts containing pre-Conquest musical notation are (as one would expect) liturgical; among the exceptions are manuscripts of Boethius' *De consolatione philosophiae*; Prudentius' lyrics; and the famous 'Cambridge Songs' collection, which includes excerpts from Statius, Virgil, and Horace.[149] It is not clear if the melodies in these texts were actually used, or simply recopied from exemplars. Whatever the actual prevalence in England of music in the teaching of Classical verse, we must recognize that this practice was never intended as a direct route to becoming a poet: Ziolkowski concludes that neumes were not used as guides to the principles of Latin quantitative metre.[150]

Evidence for the advanced study of musical theory is fairly rare in Anglo-Saxon England. Only three surviving manuscripts contain significant theoretical discussions. Two of these – CCCC 260[151] and CUL Gg.5.35[152] – are from Canterbury. The third, Avranches, Bibliothèque municipale 236, was probably written in southern England.[153] Wulfstan Cantor, the only Anglo-Saxon known to have written a treatise on music, composed a *Breuiloquium super musicam* which is now mostly lost, but was known to William of Malmesbury and to an anonymous English commentator on Boethius' *De institutione musica*.[154] From the scraps that remain, we can tell that Wulfstan's treatise dealt with the definition and purpose of music, the harmony of the spheres, and technical definitions – all standard fare in medieval music theory. But for his sources and intellectual affinities to be identified, the *Breuiloquium* would have to be rediscovered.

Most elements of practical musicianship, however, were passed on orally. When Benedict Biscop wanted to improve the musical skill of his house at

Wearmouth in the late seventh century, he brought back not books, but a man, John the Archcantor.[155] It is usually assumed that almost all practical musical knowledge, including most of the music itself, was conveyed without writing during the Anglo-Saxon period.[156] Some of this tradition may have included what the authors of musical treatises would have considered the basis of 'true' musicianship: a theoretical understanding of harmonics based on proportions.

In Boethius' influential definition, a *musicus* differs from a performer in the same way an architect differs from a stonemason or a general from a foot soldier:

> Is vero est musicus, qui ratione perpensa canendi scientiam non servitio operis sed imperio speculationis adsumpsit. Quod scilicet in aedificiorum bellorumque opere videmus, in contraria scilicet nuncupatione vocabuli. Eorum namque nominibus vel aedificia inscribuntur vel ducuntur triumphi, quorum imperio ac ratione institute sunt, non quorum opere servitioque perfecta ... isque est musicus, cui adest facultas secundum speculationem rationemve propositam ac musicae convenientem de modis ac rythmis deque generibus cantilenarum ac de permixtionibus ac de omnibus, de quibus posterius explicandum est, ac de poetarum carminibus iudicandi.[157]

> He, therefore, is a musician who gains knowledge of singing through rational contemplation: not by the servitude of labour, but rather by the ruling power of theoretical thought. We see this same phenomenon of naming by opposition in architecture and warfare: for the names inscribed on a building or raised up in a triumphal procession are those of them by whose command and design the things were planned, not of those by whose labour and servitude they were achieved ... And he is a musician who, through theoretical thought or logical reasoning, attains expertise pertaining to music with regard to mode or rhythm; to the genres of songs; and to their combinations; and to all those things which shall be explained below; and to judgment on the works of poets.

The *De institutione musica* was at the heart of the early medieval canon of music theory from the ninth century onwards, and so too was this divide between theoretical and practical expertise. As Susan Boynton has shown, the implications of the distinction troubled medieval commentators.[158] Yet the medieval curriculum seems to have combined with the monastic power structure to reinforce the *imperium* of the few. As an advanced element of the study of the liberal arts, the *ars musica* would have been the concern of the most proficient Latinists in a community.[159] Likewise, the musical repertoire of a religious community was controlled by a very few individuals: in post-Benedictine-reform monasteries, the precentor (cantor) had

final authority over everything that was sung.[160] The educational attainments of the cantor are not stipulated in surviving Rules, and in many cases
he may not have been a *musicus*. Yet the larger and more influential a
community was, the more likely it is that its senior musical official was also
one of its most advanced scholars. Osbern, for instance, spent several years
studying with Anselm at Bec before becoming precentor of Christ Church
Canterbury. While this sojourn abroad was at least partly a disciplinary
measure, it also provided then-archbishop Lanfranc with a Continentally
trained supervisor of Canterbury's books and music.[161] Sending a talented
monk for a period of training elsewhere may have been a convenient way for
monasteries to gain a better-educated precentor than they could have
otherwise obtained.

Music and the saints

The distinction between a proficient practical musician and a *musicus*, who
must also have been a highly educated Latinist, helps explain a notable
pattern in the careers of the few identifiable musician-poets in Anglo-Saxon
England. All left Latin prose writings in various genres, but the one form
they all practised was hagiography, and in at least two instances composed
hymns for the saints they chronicled. Of the three known *musici* in Anglo-
Saxon England, Abbo of Fleury – who according to the *vita* of him by Aimo
'paid a considerable sum of money' to learn music theory in Orléans – left
few traces of his musicianship during his stay in Ramsey from 985–7.[162]
However, at least one hymn to an Anglo-Saxon saint can be attributed to his
hand with a fair degree of certainty: evidence of metre and internal content
combine to suggest that the poem *Laurea regni* was almost certainly written
by Abbo as an accompaniment to his *vita* of St Edmund.

Commissioned, as its prologue asserts, by Archbishop Dunstan of
Canterbury, Abbo's *Vita S. Eadmundi* embellishes its central narrative
with Classical as well as biblical echoes. In his edition, Winterbottom
notes parallels with Virgil, Persius, and – especially important for our
purposes – Horace.[163] The Horatian echoes in the *Vita S. Eadmundi* all
derive from the *Carmina*, although Abbo apparently had a relatively
broad knowledge of Horace's works.[164] All the surviving manuscripts of
Horace from early England, however, stem from the mid-eleventh century or later; most postdate the Conquest.[165] It is likewise clear from
the evidence Lapidge adduces in *The Anglo-Saxon Library* that knowledge
of Horace was never widespread in Anglo-Saxon England, and that
Bede (for instance) may only have known his works via second-hand

quotations.[166] Abbo's direct acquaintance with Horace's poems, then, was another element of his Continental education that set him apart from his Anglo-Saxon colleagues.

Strikingly, the poem *Laurea regni* contains an allusion to *Carmen* 1.22 that suggests actual knowledge of Horace's poem. This hymn to St Edmund, composed in quantitative Sapphic stanzas, is found only in two manuscripts: BL, Cotton Vespasian D.xii, and London, Lambeth Palace, 362. The former is an eleventh-century glossed hymnal from Canterbury; the main contents of the latter are the *Vita S. Eadmundi* of Abbo, together with other materials for Edmund's cult.[167] A second hymn to St Edmund, *Laus et corona militum*, accompanies *Laurea regni* in both manuscripts, and the Vespasian hymnal uniquely contains one further hymn to Edmund. All three are edited by Milfull in *Hymns of the Anglo-Saxon Church*; her textual notes make it clear that the Lambeth manuscript preserves a better text than Vespasian, although neither is without errors of transmission.[168] In the Lambeth manuscript, the fourth stanza of *Laurea regni* reads:

> Unde, rex martyr, tibi, magnus heres,
> integer membris maculeque purus,
> fungeris digno meritis honore
> talibus hymnis.[169]

Therefore, O king and martyr, great inheritor, intact in limbs and spotless, you are honoured as befits your merits in such hymns [as this].

The second line of this stanza 'preserves the Horatian tag' from *Carmen* 1.22, as Milfull notes:[170]

> Integer vitae scelerisque purus
> non eget Mauris iaculis neque arcu,
> nec venenatis gravida sagittis,
> Fusce, pharetra . . .[171]

The man pure of life and unstained with sin needs not Moorish javelins nor the bow, nor a quiver laden with envenomed arrows, O Fuscus. . .

As mentioned above, this poem is alluded to in Abbo's *Vita* of St Edmund. The passage reads:

> Ille quidem *purus sceleris* in columna ad quam uinctus fuit sanguinem non pro se sed pro nobis flagellorum suorum signa reliquit; iste pro adipiscenda gloria immarcescibili cruentato stipite similes poenas dedit. Ille *integer uitae* ob detergendam rubiginem nostrorum facinorum sustinuit benignissimus immanium clauorum acerbitatem in palmis et pedibus; iste propter amorem

nominis Domini toto corpore *grauibus sagittis* horridus et medullitus asper-
itate tormentorum dilaniatus in confessione patienter perstitit . . .[172]

> He [Christ] indeed, unstained with sin, left his blood upon the pillar to
> which he had been tied as signs of his flagellation not for himself, but for us;
> the other [Edmund], in order to gain unfading glory, underwent like suffer-
> ings upon a bloodstained post. The first, pure of life, in order to expunge the
> stain of our crimes most graciously endured the unspeakable agony of nails in
> his hands and feet; the other, for love of the Lord's name, while bristling with
> painful arrows all over his body, and willingly torn with the cruelty of
> tortures, patiently endured in confession . . .

Comparison of these passages makes two things immediately apparent.
First, the allusion to Horace in the hymn could not have been reassembled
from Abbo's prose: *Laurea regni* retains the order and metrical position of
integer . . . purus, as the *Vita* does not. Moreover, someone who had not read
Carmen 1.22 would not have understood why the reference was appropriate
to a poem in honour of a saint tortured with arrows. As in the *Vita
S. Eadmundi*, the echo of Horace in *Laurea regni* is not a mere tag or filler,
but a precisely chosen allusion.

The choice of metre for *Laurea regni* also implies knowledge of Horace;
like *Carmen* 1.22, it is in quantitative Sapphic strophes. This form was not
unknown in Anglo-Saxon England: Bede defines it in his *De arte metrica*,
chapter XVIII, giving an example from Paulinus of Nola, and various hymns
in this metre were in fairly widespread use.[173] However, it seems to have
been very rarely practised in England. Besides *Laurea regni*, only a single
poem in quantitative Sapphic stanzas can be attributed to an Anglo-Saxon
author: *Inclitus pastor*, a hymn for St Æthelwold almost certainly composed
by Wulfstan Cantor.[174] Few poets, it seems, had the ability and inclination
to compose quantitative verse in complex lyric metres. It seems most likely,
therefore, that Abbo of Fleury composed this unusual hymn to accompany
his prose *vita* of St Edmund.

There are several implications of such an attribution. First, it may be that
the other liturgical material in the St Edmund *libellus* in Lambeth 362 – the
hymn in iambic dimeter, and the mass – should also be attributed to Abbo.
More broadly, however, we can be certain that trained *musici* in Anglo-
Saxon England were commissioned to create saints' cult materials, which
included narrative prose, liturgical prose, and verse. This prosopographical
fact may help us understand the careers of less-known individuals, and may
also clarify the relations between various anonymous texts. While it would
be rash to (for instance) reflexively attribute all a cathedral's liturgical
material to its precentor, the relations between hagiography and hymnody

are worth exploring further – as is the office of the precentor itself during the Anglo-Saxon period. If a good cantor were expected to create as well as perpetuate liturgical verse, men with musical talent and ambitions towards such an influential office might well have found that becoming a poet furthered their plans.

Practical hymnody

But, as Abbo's example shows, *musici* were not necessarily precentors. Before his ill-fated abbacy, Abbo himself was a teacher of the liberal arts, including the more advanced branches of rhetoric and *computus*, and perhaps it is among teachers that we should seek other Anglo-Saxon *musici*.[175] The *ars musica*'s status as a scholarly discipline explains why musical treatises were preserved in manuscripts like CUL Gg.5.35, and glossed hymns were certainly used for a variety of teaching purposes.[176] But the composition of hymns may nevertheless have been taught. Worcester, Cathedral Library, Q.5, a late tenth-century grammatical manuscript attributed to Canterbury, contains a peculiar scansion table.[177] As well as giving names for complex metrical feet, the table lists the patterns of long and short syllables created by combining metrical feet, arranged in ascending order of length.[178] As a 'field guide' for students of lyric metres, the table could conceivably have helped would-be composers perceive the regularities underlying complex forms. While the passive, readerly orientation of most medieval metrical treatises has rightly been emphasized,[179] texts like this one may nevertheless have served as aids for would-be *musici* called upon to produce new songs. Though much of the musical learning of the Anglo-Saxons necessarily disappeared with the passing of the oral tradition that perpetuated it, books intended for advanced training in the liberal arts may yet preserve unexpected clues to the work of hymnodists.

Hymns, certainly, must have embodied many Anglo-Saxons' most frequent and intense experiences of poetry. They were sung by many with little training in Latin, and perhaps no understanding of Classical prosody. They were also created by people who did not know, or who rejected, the systems of quantitative metre which had long been divorced from pronunciation: hymns, indeed, began as a semi-popular form.[180] Rhythmic hymns were common from the very beginning of the Anglo-Saxon period, and as mentioned earlier, Bede included a chapter on rhythmic metre in his textbook *De arte metrica*.[181] Because a thorough understanding of Latin quantity and metre was *not* required to compose a functional hymn, the practical art of hymnody is unlikely to have been restricted to *musici*, even as some *musici* might choose to compose rhythmic verse as well. What a hymnodist would need was a practical grasp of music and of Latin pronunciation, which a life of liturgical training would undoubtedly provide.

In late tenth- and eleventh-century Canterbury, the growing importance of the cult of St Dunstan required the composition of new hymns, and in a set of texts which survive in several manuscripts we can see the poetry of at least one individual who may have been a musician without being a *musicus*. Helmut Gneuss, who first edited and studied these texts, believes that the three surviving hymns are the work of at least two authors, and that those for the nocturns and lauds may date from Lanfranc's archiepiscopacy.[182] The first hymn, *Ave Dunstane presulum*, however, unquestionably dates to the era of the Danish wars, as the third and fourth stanzas make clear:

> Tibi pater nos credimus
> Quibus te nil iocundius
> Ad te manus expandimus
> Tibi preces effundimus.
>
> Oves tuas pastor pie
> Passim premunt angustię
> Mucrone gentis barbare
> Necamur en cristicole.[183]

> In you we trust, father: to no one more gladly than you. To you we stretch out our hands: to you we pour forth our prayers. Holy shepherd, afflictions oppress your flock everywhere: we the servants of Christ are dying by the sword of a barbarous race.

Though the fourth stanza was omitted from later copies of the text, it illuminates the impetus for the creation of the hymn: the appeal to St Dunstan arises not from an abstract desire for a patron's aggrandizement, but from immediate and visceral need. Gneuss even suggests that it may date from the 1011 siege and capture of Canterbury, which led to the murder of St Ælfheah.[184] About the author we know nothing, but the metre of the hymn suggests that he was not striving for a quantitative form (e.g., *Tĭbĭ păter*, 9; *Quibus tē*, 10), but rather the standard rhythmic 'Ambrosian' hymn metre, 8pp+8pp.[185] Interestingly, though, the actual word-stress often conflicts with the basic iambic template: this is particularly apparent in line 13, *Óves túas pástor píe*, a perfectly trochaic line ending in an alliterating word-pair. The aesthetic here, as the hymn rises to its desperate plea, is essentially Old English. It is impossible to be sure how acquainted *Ave Dunstane presulum*'s author was with the *ars musica*, but the poem is the work of someone sensitive to the rhythm of Latin as it must have been spoken – and sung – in England. He may not have been a great scholar, but judging by all we know of ecclesiastical life in the period, he must have been a practical musician.

Further than this it is difficult to go, at least while attached to any kind of prosopographical anchor. Yet many intriguing possibilities for the connections between music and poetry remain unexplored, particularly in the vernacular tradition. The Old English metrical versions of the Psalms, for instance, could conceivably have been intended to be sung, as could the Old English poetic version of the daily office found in Junius 121.[186] The 'Kentish Hymn' is found in Cotton Vespasian D.vi, a Canterbury manuscript containing grammatical material (such as the *Distichs of Cato* in Latin, and a glossary on the Book of Proverbs); hagiography, including an excerpt from the *Vitae patrum*; and liturgical material, including a verse antiphon for St Augustine of Canterbury.[187] These juxtapositions suggest the kind of complex nexus of relationships between literary study, hagiography, and music that we have seen in the careers of *musici* such as Abbo, Wulfstan Cantor, and Osbern – but with the tantalizing addition of vernacular poetry.

While we know painfully little about the work of musician-poets in Anglo-Saxon England, the seeming interconnectedness of these arts offers hope for future discoveries. We know that much Latin poetry was experienced as song, as neumed manuscripts indicate. The full range of effects this had on composers of verse in Latin – and Old English – is still not fully understood. Moreover, the early medieval divorce between music theory and practice may paradoxically open doors to the better understanding of musicians' work, through the medium of seemingly unrelated grammatical manuscripts. Though the *musici* examined in this section are but three isolated points, the implications of their work may help us to draw unexpected lines of connection between broader fields of Anglo-Saxon culture.

Courtiers

The courtier is simultaneously the most familiar and elusive of possible roles for Anglo-Saxon poets. For centuries, scholars have imagined *scopas* singing in the halls of Northern kings; and yet surprisingly little can securely be attributed to such a milieu. Because so many cultures in close contact with the Anglo-Saxons certainly did encourage court poetry, the presence of poets in various kinds of Anglo-Saxon court, and their lords' patronage of poetry, has often been taken for granted. Court poets were retained by rulers in medieval Wales, Ireland, and Scandinavia, and all of these countries possess a substantial corpus of verse attributed (with varying degrees of reliability) to named historical figures. In most of these places, the making of poetry was also regulated by law, and the wealth of evidence about poetry's social role in these areas has sometimes tempted scholars to supplement the far scantier evidence from early England.[188] Cross-cultural anthropology, too, has proved a popular source of comparands from societies whose distance in time or space means that direct contact with Anglo-Saxon societies was impossible, but whose ways of life somewhat resembled those of the early English. Jeff Opland's work on South African Xhosa traditions, for instance, informed his reading of Anglo-Saxon verse as essentially courtly and panegyric.[189]

Moreover, the 'mythic poet' of *Beowulf*, *Widsith*, and *Deor* was a denizen of royal or aristocratic courts, as can be seen from the passages examined in Chapter 1.[190] No doubt partly for this reason, the royal court has been a favourite critical site of origin for Old English literature, especially *Beowulf*, since at least the early nineteenth century. I have already noted Sharon Turner's belief in the genesis of Old English poetry as 'the rude exclamations of a rude people . . . greeting their chieftains', and its perpetuation by 'the bards of the chiefs'.[191] Somewhat more charitably, John Earle – Professor of Anglo-Saxon at Oxford from 1876 until his death in 1903 – interpreted *Beowulf* as a 'mirror for princes' intended for the court of Offa of Mercia. The poem, he argued, 'is the work of an eminent person, of one who could speak with authority to the highest in the land' and he suggested this person was Offa's advisor Hygeberht, archbishop of Lichfield.[192] In the twentieth century, A. S. Cook attributed *Beowulf* to a courtier of King Aldfrith of Northumbria,[193] while Dorothy Whitelock – though more circumspect in particularizing the historical setting – firmly situated the poem within a royal court.[194] More recently criticism has connected the poem with Alfred and his immediate descendants, or with courts ranging from those of the East Angles in the seventh century to those of various Mercian rulers through the tenth century.[195] While this thread of interpretation is rarely prominent enough to give it the status of orthodoxy (and has perhaps been less often brought to the fore in the last twenty years), the idea of a courtly origin for *Beowulf* is an important tradition in Old English scholarship.

In this section, therefore, I shall be considering the possible role of courtiers in the creation of Anglo-Saxon poetry in a somewhat expanded framework. Our prosopographical information is extremely limited – with the notable exception of Scandinavian-language poets, to whom I shall return below. Of named poets of Anglo-Saxon origin or working in Anglo-Saxon England, we can place perhaps four within courts. Of these, Alcuin of York is the best-known by several orders of magnitude; he is also the only court poet certainly born and educated in England. The others – John the Old Saxon, Israel the Grammarian, and one Peter – all seem to have been foreigners sojourning at the West Saxon court in the late ninth or early tenth centuries. All four composed in Latin.

Alcuin is among the most-studied figures of the early Carolingian period, and while some aspects of his career remain in dispute, the overall contours of his life are well known.[196] He was born in Northumbria, most likely during the 730s or 740s, and studied at York with Ælberht, who eventually became archbishop and whose teaching and character Alcuin revered for the rest of his life. With Ælberht, Alcuin first visited Rome, and he succeeded to his position at the cathedral school.[197] Alcuin also inherited Ælberht's books after his master's death in 780.[198]

At York Alcuin acquired much of the learning that would make him one of the most famous teachers in Europe, but his association with Charlemagne made him a court poet. In 781, while in Italy to acquire the pallium for Ælberht's successor Eanbald, Alcuin met the Frankish king at Parma. They had met before; this time, he was invited to join the royal entourage. It is usually thought that Alcuin took up this invitation quickly, and returned to the Continent within a year of fulfilling his mission to Eanbald; Bullough, however, has argued that he did not join the itinerant court until 786.[199] This difference is significant for our understanding of Alcuin's role in Charlemagne's court school, as well as for his own relations to the king. Alcuin was certainly in England during part of 786, and between 790 and 793; from 796 onwards, he resided at Tours as abbot of St Martin's. If Bullough is correct, Alcuin would only have spent about six years altogether in Charlemagne's court, and could not have been the formative influence on the king's opinions and policies which he is often held to be.[200]

Important as it is, the question of Alcuin's arrival at court is one I cannot settle here. But it is crucial to point out that Alcuin's formation as a poet had largely taken place before 781, as demonstrated in a circular poem sent to his friends on the Continent sometime from 778–80.[201] The poem, *Cartula, perge cito*, is addressed to the letter itself (and perhaps also its carrier) in a series of requests to remind others of its author. Most important of these acquaintances is Charlemagne himself:

Si te forte velit regis deducere ad aulam,
Hic proceres patres fratres percurre, saluta.
Ante pedes regis totas expande camenas,
Dicito multoties: 'Salve, rex optime, salve.
Tu mihi protector, tutor, defensor adesto,
Invida ne valeat me carpere lingua nocendo
Paulini, Petri, Albrici, Samuelis, Ione,
Vel quicumque velit mea rodere viscera mursu;
Te terrente procul fugiat, discedat inanis'.[202]

If [Neptune] should perchance see fit to deliver you to the king's hall, hasten to greet the dignitaries, priests, and monks. Before the king's feet unfold all your verses, and say over and over, 'Hail, greatest king, hail! Be to me a protector, a shield and defender, so that the jealous and hostile tongues of Paulinus, Peter, Alberic, Samuel, Jonas – or whoever might wish to gnaw at my vitals with biting attack – won't be able to pull me apart for my faults; they'll flee far away in terror, and be dispersed into empty breezes.'

This entreaty – at the exact centre of the eighty-one-line poem – flatters both the king and the scholars named in line 42; in the lines following, the letter is instructed to give further messages to the first two, Paulinus of Aquileia and Peter of Pisa. Charlemagne himself, however, is figured as one beyond pedantry: a conqueror whom scholars fear, and at whose feet verses are strewn. Godman argues that the poem's tone indicates not just Alcuin's confidence in the king's interest, but significant experience at the court during his early travels, though Sinisi has more recently suggested that it was intended primarily as a *vade mecum* for a friend who would carry the letter and transmit Alcuin's greetings.[203] At very least, *Cartula, perge cito* shows that Alcuin understood the value of poetry in maintaining his status *in absentia*, and that he had developed this sensibility before his long-term association with Charlemagne's court.

Absence is at the heart of Alcuin's poetic persona, and is perhaps the key to its formation. Many of his surviving poems are epistles, or seem to have been composed on the occasion of arrivals or departures; they are often elegiac in tone and in form.[204] *O mea cella*, perhaps his best poem and certainly the only one still widely read, begins like a love elegy:

O mea cella, mihi habitatio dulcis, amata,
Semper in aeternum, o mea cella, vale.
Undique te cingit ramis resonantibus arbos,
Silvula florigeris semper onusta comis.
Prata salutiferis florebunt omnia et herbis,
Quas medici quaerit dextra salutis ope.[205]

O my cell, sweet dwelling and beloved: forever and always, my cell, farewell. A tree girds you round about with rustling branches, foliage bearing always its flowery hair. All the meadows flower likewise with healthful herbs, which the doctor's hand seeks for his labour of health.

The sweetness of the beloved, praise of her physical attributes, even the beloved as medicine – these are elegiac commonplaces which Alcuin has transmuted here into a remarkable and strange lament for a lost home, with possible debts to Ovid and Tibullus as well as Bede.[206] It is surely right to see genuine sentiment here, as many critics have.[207] But Alcuin's poetry to his court patrons is often similar in tone. This poem, for instance, includes an address to Charlemagne on the king's departure:

> Semper ubique vale, dic dic, dulcissime David,
>   David amor Flacci, semper ubique vale.
> O mihi dulcis amor David, per saecla valeto,
>   Quam te praesentem semper habere velim,
> Pieri ut tecum liceat mihi ludere versu,
>   Scandere vel summi sidera celsa poli . . .[208]

Say, say O ever farewell, sweetest David; David, Flaccus' beloved, ever farewell. O my sweet love David, flourish forever, you whom I would always wish here, that with you I might trifle in metred verse, or climb the lofty stars of the high heaven . . .

He goes on to enumerate other studies besides poetry and astronomy that he wishes he could always share with the king. Though presenting the catalogue of scholarly disciplines in the form of a personal lament for the lost pleasures of Charlemagne's company, Alcuin's poem also serves as a versified CV – a portable reminder of his own indispensable skills. In his courtly verse, Alcuin adapted the absent presence of the Classical elegy into an effective machine for maintaining his own valued relationships, whether at the royal court (as seen here) or in the hearts of his distant friends.

The prevalence of this elegiac tone in Alcuin's courtly verse is perhaps an accident of survival. Poems intended for delivery as letters must be written down, while lighter occasional verses could be composed and kept in mind for oral delivery, and as quickly forgotten once the occasion has passed. Garrison has pointed out that Charlemagne's court poets did not make a point of preserving or anthologizing their own work, and many instances of Alcuin's efforts to 'Pieri . . . ludere versu' ('trifle in metred verse') have probably been lost.[209] However, I think it likely that the 'absent presence' was a core feature of Alcuin's court-poet persona from the beginning. Whatever might have been the vernacular cultural experiences of Charlemagne's clerical entourage,

Latin court poetry was a new creature for them, and one crossbred from disparate elements. Godman has argued persuasively for the influence of Venantius Fortunatus, one of the last court poets of Late Antiquity.[210] But other models are also at work. I have already noted the role of rediscovered Classical elegy, which a number of scholars have explored.[211] Orchard, however, has drawn attention to the importance of another genre with which Alcuin was clearly familiar: epistolary verse. In a letter to Lull, archbishop of Mainz, a master at York called Koaena (who may be identical with Alcuin's teacher Ælberht) concluded with a few hexameters:

> Vive Deo felix, Christi laurate triumphis,
> Vita tuis saeclo specimen, carissime caelo,
> Iustitiae cultor, verus pietatis amator,
> Defendens vigili sanctos tutamine mandros,
> Pascua florigeris pandens prędulcia campis,
> Iudice centenos portans veniente maniplos.[212]

> Live blessed in God, O man crowned with the victories of Christ: your life is a model to your people in this world, and you yourself are most dear to heaven. You are a supporter of justice and a true lover of piety, defending the holy flocks with your tireless guardianship, revealing the sweet pastures in the flowery fields, and bringing hundredfold sheaves before the approaching Judge.

In his examination of these verses, Orchard demonstrated that whether Ælberht's or not, Alcuin knew them well and recycled their diction in his own work. He notes too that

> the phrase *vive deo felix*, employed by Alcuin on at least two occasions, appears to have become something of a favourite: later poets (such as Hrabanus Maurus, Theodulf of Orléans, Walahfrid Strabo and Sedulius Scotus) who use the phrase can be linked with Alcuin, from whom they may have learnt it directly.[213]

Much of the tone and function of Alcuin's court poetry is present here alongside the phraseology: Koaena's epistolary verses are a brief panegyric intended to maintain friendship between York and the missionary archbishopric founded by St Boniface. Epistolary poetry was already a long-standing genre in Anglo-Saxon England.[214] Alcuin, it seems, perceived that its forms could be adapted to a new need: pleasing secular patrons, as well as fellow servants in the church.

In becoming a court poet, then, Alcuin made novel use of material already at hand, and the nature of that material has left its imprint on his surviving verse and the verse of his contemporaries. The astuteness and versatility with which he conformed to his new role indicate some of the personal qualities for which Charlemagne valued him. As a poet at the Frankish court, Alcuin had occasion to compose a variety of poems, including amusing *ludi* (like riddles) and 'official' verse, including an epitaph for Pope Hadrian.[215] But his most characteristic works were instrumental to himself, in maintaining his own relationships rather than his patrons': he seems to have written relatively few poems in the king's name, and his large-scale historical verse narrative (the poem on York) apparently had nothing to do with the Frankish court.[216] Alcuin's skills as a poet made him useful as a courtier, as he took care regularly to remind King Charles; but his poems were created much more often in his own service than the king's.

Whether the same was true of the three named Latin poets working at English courts is difficult to say, since the record of their life and activities is minimal. Such knowledge as we have is based mostly on Michael Lapidge's research: as court poets, the reputations of both John the Old Saxon and one 'Peter' are inferred from verses gathered in a single study, 'Some Latin Poems as Evidence from the Reign of Athelstan'.[217] From Bodleian, Rawlinson C.697 Lapidge printed a double acrostic which spelled ADALSTAN down the left margin, and IOHANNES on the right. The former is unquestionably the addressee, since the poem plays repeatedly on the etymology of his Old English name, and figures the speaker as Samuel prophesying the greatness of a future king.[218] As an acrostic, though, the poem is inept (it relies on several instances of tmesis and a reversed word to make the names come out right). Partly on this basis, Lapidge attributes two other poems, which try and fail to spell AELFRED/ELFRED in acrostic and telestich, to the same unskilful hand.[219] This hapless poet he identifies as John the Old Saxon, known from Asser's life of Alfred and a few other contemporary sources. In the same article, Lapidge reconstructs a letter-poem, *Carta dirige gressus*, in which Peter, possibly a cleric at Winchester of Continental origin, announces King Athelstan's victories in the north to the royal household.[220]

Judging by this set of poems, the royal court of Wessex was provided with at least a few clerics willing and (more or less) able to produce some of the modes of verse fashionable on the Continent. We have already noted the prevalence of letter-poems among Alcuin's work; his successors, too, practised the form. Acrostic and figured verse – the more complex of which was based on the models of Optantianus Porphyrius – had been practised by early Anglo-Saxon authors including Boniface. Alcuin helped to popularize the form again for secular literature, and his student Hrabanus Maurus produced an elaborate series of figured devotional poems.[221] Both John and Peter, then, were drawing on established traditions when creating verse in service of royal patrons.

The creation of verse was certainly not the primary responsibility of John the Old Saxon, whom we know as a priest and (later) abbot who acted as tutor and advisor to King Alfred.[222] Of Peter we can say much less, but a cleric at Winchester would have had multiple duties, cathedral services probably most important among them. Yet the ability to create occasional verse in the king's service must have added to the value of these foreign scholars in their patrons' eyes. The same is possibly true of Israel the Grammarian, a (probably Breton) scholar of distinction who spent some time at the court of King Athelstan. Israel's own verse included didactic poems like the *De arte metrica*, and manuscript evidence suggests that he introduced some Greek texts to Anglo-Saxon readers.[223] Though these three foreign scholars were unlikely to have been retained as court poets by English kings, nevertheless their poetic abilities may have added lustre to their positions at court. We know that both Alfred and Athelstan imported Continental books and learning to England, and the poetic works of John, Peter, and Israel form a modest but coherent part of that endeavour.

King Charles and his successors were not the only royal patrons of poets in the northern world, however. The Viking age brought the English-speaking peoples into permanent contact with Scandinavian-language cultures. During the ninth century, a new and ornate form of Old Norse court poetry had developed and was rapidly disseminated by the highly mobile warrior class which practised it.[224] To the Anglo-Saxonist, one of the most striking aspects of skaldic verse is its attachment to named individuals: the thirteenth-century *Skáldatal*, for instance, lists the names of poets who served particular kings, and an entire genre of saga narrative grew up around the biographies of notable poets.[225] Icelanders were particularly renowned for their skill in *dróttkvætt* and the other skaldic metres, but mainland Scandinavians also practised these forms, and we know of many poets who served Cnut, king of Denmark and England.[226] Cnut's Anglo-Danish court, however, was not the first to host skalds; Appendix II provides a full list of Old Norse court poets known to have worked in England. Verse from the Norse-speaking kingdom of York aside, a poem in praise of Æthelred survives, while Athelstan is remembered as patron of the great Egill Skallagrímsson. Scholarly opinion as to the effect of skaldic verse on Anglo-Saxon culture has varied; Roberta Frank has argued for the significance of the genre's influence on a wide range of Old English literature (including *Beowulf*), but on the whole the impact of this line of research has remained limited.[227] Recently, however, Matthew Townend has made a strong case for regarding the earlier verse in the *Anglo-Saxon Chronicle* as inspired by the example of skaldic court poetry. He argues that *The Battle of Brunanburh* and the *Capture of the Five Boroughs* in particular may have been created for the royal court of the newly united England (probably that of Athelstan's half-brother and successor Edmund) and circulated separately before their inclusion in the *Chronicle*.[228]

Skalds provide such an attractive model for understanding the Anglo-Saxon court poet because they seem to be everything that the elusive 'courtly scop' is not: named, datable, the creators of poems associated with historical kings and historical events. But they also present a critical problem: are Anglo-Saxon parallels with skaldic verse analogous, or derivative? Does the example of Anglo-Scandinavian verse simply allow us to see more clearly an already extant element of English culture, or did it actually prompt a change in the native literature?

The difficulty of answering this question is particular to the texture of Anglo-Saxon literary history. Simply put, virtually no vernacular literature is securely datable to the era prior to the Viking age, and it is therefore difficult to argue for points of change, whether based on foreign contact or otherwise. Constructing a narrative for the history of Anglo-Saxon court poetry would require the identification of a larger and more secure set of texts: which brings us in turn to some central problems of definition.

Panegyric is the form most classically associated with courts. This connection is indeed so ingrained that panegyric-like moments in quite different kinds of literature are used to anchor works to specific courts. (The Offa episode in *Beowulf* is perhaps the *locus classicus* for this tendency in Old English.[229]) In medieval literature, secular or semi-secular historical writing is often viewed as oblique panegyric for the dominant rulers. By recounting the origins of a royal or noble lineage, its legitimacy is reinforced, and the power of its current representatives thus enhanced. Such rhetorical uses of history are very ancient; but in poetry, the particular example of the *Æneid* would undoubtedly have been available in Anglo-Saxon England. Servius' commentary, for instance, made Augustus' patronage of Virgil the key to the poem.[230] While I would not here contend that the *Æneid* actually *was* a model for Anglo-Saxon historiography, its example does at least demonstrate that poetry could be (and was) read as participating in a discourse of official power through the medium of patronage.

Critics seeking to locate specific instances of courtly influence in Anglo-Saxon literature have therefore turned most often to the *Anglo-Saxon*

Chronicle, since it seems to offer both panegyric per se (in the form of *The Battle of Brunanburh* and *Capture of the Five Boroughs* especially), and historical narrative calculated to aggrandize the West Saxon royal dynasty. In recent years, for instance, Anton Scharer has argued forcefully for the production of the early phases of the *Chronicle* at Alfred's court, and Bredehoft has furthered this line of inquiry with regard to later material, including the tenth-century verse.[231] Of surviving Old English poems, *Brunanburh* and *Five Boroughs* are the two perhaps most likely to be accepted as the work of courtiers.[232]

For the purposes of this study and of further research, however, it is worth disentangling some closely entwined categories. The distinction between a courtier and a client is perhaps the most critical. As I would define them, a *courtier* is one whose physical presence at a court forms an important part of his or her social role, while a *client* is one dependent for some benefit (most commonly money, tangible goods, or status) on a patron. Most courtiers would thus be clients, but a client need not be a courtier. For Anglo-Saxon England – most of whose surviving literature was preserved by ecclesiastics, some of whom were cloistered – this distinction is of real significance. A monk, for instance, might well produce verse panegyrics for a royal patron whom he has never seen. To read such a poet as a courtier would be to erase, to my mind, critical aspects of a court: a physical space, and proximity to the ruler.[233]

Too reflexive an identification between a generic form and a cultural site of origin may therefore distort our understanding of the literature, and may perhaps also prematurely close certain avenues towards a better knowledge of patron–client relations. Yet at the same time, we should also be open to the potential of broader definitions of the court. We know, for instance, that Anglo-Saxon bishops retained a *familia* much like secular aristocrats did. Partly itinerant, but centred around the cathedral, the episcopal court could certainly be read as organizing power in much the same way as that of the king. This would mean that the works of St Dunstan's follower 'B', for instance, might be read as courtly literature; but pursuing such a line even further, certain works of hagiography could be considered panegyric history. The various texts associated with St Swithun could thus be read as bearing roughly the same relation to Æthelwold of Winchester as the history of King Ecgberht of Wessex did to King Alfred. Redefining the Anglo-Saxon court so radically might be of limited use to historians seeking to understand the function of secular central governments, but it might help to explain why certain clerics – or even secular retainers – became poets.

Limiting ourselves, however, for the present to the commonly received definition of an Anglo-Saxon court,[234] we might still consider the possibility that courtiers' poetry extended beyond the panegyric or historical-panegyric. To give but one potential example: we know that religion was a major feature of court life in Anglo-Saxon England, that bishops and house clerics formed an important part of kings' retinues, and that rulers were interested in owning personal prayerbooks. Scharer, for instance, suggests that the 'Book of Nunnaminster' may have been kept at Alfred's court, and that Alfred's own lost 'liber manualis' may have been a private prayerbook.[235] Most of the prayers in the 'Book of Nunnaminster' are in prose: but prayers in verse may also have been commissioned from court clerics for private use. Royal women might be as likely to have been patrons of such poems as men.[236]

Future work, therefore, may uncover new dimensions to the work of courtiers as poets in Anglo-Saxon England. In our present state of knowledge, it is worth returning to a few points. First, the works of Alcuin – our earliest known Anglo-Saxon court poet – show evidence of a canny, versatile courtier forging a new mode of Latin poetry from many elements of his wide reading. Though formulaic in phrasing, in genre Alcuin's courtly works seem to derive from several disparate literary traditions, particularly epistolary verse and elegy, rather than inheriting well-established courtly forms. It is thus, I suspect, quite significant that all of the texts surveyed in this section which are associated with *English* courts date from Alfred's reign or later. Extensive Continental influence is visible in the Latin poems, which were indeed probably composed by Continental scholars. We know from a variety of sources that Alfred invited scholars from many countries to Wessex, as a means of reinvigorating national culture.[237] His grandson Athelstan was equally receptive to foreigners, though we know far less about his programmatic intentions.[238] Given this openness to foreign influence, it seems to me not unlikely that courtly poetry as we commonly define it was introduced to English courts under the ægis of Alfred and his descendants, and that the panegyric verse of the *Anglo-Saxon Chronicle* was a hybrid product of cultural change in tenth-century England, rather than the heir of a longstanding tradition.[239] Thus, to answer the question posed a few pages back: at least in our present state of literary-historical understanding, I think that contact with skalds – and with the work of Carolingian Latin court poets – did change the character of Anglo-Saxon literature.

Perhaps paradoxically, though, I would be less willing to assert that the *Chronicle* verse was therefore necessarily the work of courtiers. I believe that more work on client–patron relationships in Anglo-Saxon England is imperative before we can adequately describe how and why royal influence affected the production of the surviving vernacular poetry. Only by better understanding what a courtier was – and was not – can we come to a real understanding of why such a role might have led an Anglo-Saxon to become a poet.

Conclusions

In the course of this chapter, we have surveyed the social roles most common among identifiable Anglo-Saxon poets. It has become apparent in the process that much of the poetry they created was instrumental to these roles, and that certain genres or modes are characteristic of certain activities. Some of these correspondences are transparent – teachers' didactic riddles; scribes' colophons; musicians' hymns; and courtiers' panegyrics. Other connections, such as those between musicians and hagiography, and courtiers and prayer, are more speculative and require further research to clarify. More work may also find new generic correspondences, and uncover other social positions occupied by poets. In several cases, we can see that some people who began in humbler roles went on to positions of considerable authority in their communities – teachers who became abbots or bishops, for instance, or musicians who became precentors of their cathedrals. Here, it seems likely that skill as a poet assisted them in their rise: that becoming a poet, in other words, helped them to play their parts in the community more effectively. Certainly social ambition could not have motivated every would-be poet, but it may explain the attainments of some. In Anglo-Saxon England, poetry and labour are mutually illuminating, and further study of either is likely to bring surprising new connections to light. Since Anglo-Saxon poetry, as this chapter has shown, was thoroughly integrated into the workings of society, in the next chapter I shall investigate the effect that social communities had on the experience of poets and on the poetry itself.

CHAPTER 3

The poet in the community

If, after days and nights of incredible labour and fatigue, we were to discover the principle by which an Anglo-Saxon poet might be generated, we would find that the elements required for our experiment were these: the individual to be made a poet; a quantity of poetry as distinguished from other kinds of language; and a community to tell good poetry from bad. The last chapter has been spent in examining the qualities of the first ingredient and some aspects of the second. In this chapter and the two following, we shall consider the nature of the third, and the effect on the result when the kind and quantity of the community is varied.

As a unit of analysis, 'community' itself requires definition. For my purposes, I shall consider a community to be any group that a member would – however reluctantly – call 'us'. It can therefore depend on bonds of self-identification as well as proximity, and so includes 'communities' joined by a common profession, religion, tribe, or caste. Some members of the groups I shall discuss here could never have met: but as Benedict Anderson points out, all communities are to some degree creatures of their members' imaginations; a sense of belonging to others through some shared bond makes a group a community.[1] Under this definition, most people of any era must have belonged to several communities simultaneously, and poets can have been no exception. One challenge of this study, therefore, is to identify overlapping social groups, and to understand the different forces that each exerted.

Since distinguishing multiple interacting variables is a problem faced by many kindred disciplines, investigators have devised a wide and versatile array of tools for attacking such questions. During the course of the last half-century, linguists, sociologists, and historians have grown increasingly interested in tracking the reciprocal effects of individuals on (and in) groups across time. Judicious adaptation of analytical methods from these neighbouring disciplines can prove extraordinarily useful to literary scholars seeking to understand the mechanisms by which social groups affected authors.

Before I turn to particular case studies, then, I shall describe the tools in my particular kit, and explain the principles that make them useful for dissecting the relations between Anglo-Saxon poets and their communities.

Many of the tools are familiar ones. Both rhetorical analysis and close reading are time-tested methods for demonstrating how texts are oriented towards an audience. Though the texts that most fully articulated the Greek and Roman rhetorical tradition – tracts by Aristotle or Quintilian, for instance, or the *Rhetorica ad Herennium* – did not reach Anglo-Saxon England, rhetoric in its broader sense is universal in human discourse: the Classical rhetors, after all, named and systematized the figures, but did not create them.[2] Close reading as a method is inseparable from rhetoric, though focused on product rather than process. Not only is close reading heavily invested in identifying and accounting for rhetoric's figures of speech – the 'schemes and tropes' that Anglo-Saxons recognized – but 'tone' and 'intention', which form half I. A. Richards's list of the components of meaning, largely describe the dynamics of speaker and audience.[3]

Close reading and rhetorical analysis are so fundamental to modern literary scholarship that it may seem superfluous to discuss them. But Anglo-Saxon poems differ in some crucial ways from modern texts, and it cannot be casually assumed that they can be read like modern works. Most importantly, both vernacular and Latin verse in the Anglo-Saxon period were formulaic, and even unquestionably literate works show the characteristic thought-patterns of oral composition.[4] Oral-formulaic composition poses two serious problems for close readers. First, individual words may not signify individually: if blocks of words are interchangeable, or their choice prompted by factors other than meaning, intense scrutiny may lead to meaningless results. Moreover, if Anglo-Saxon poems truly sprang from an oral tradition, then they were not art-objects as we understand the term; as unpremeditated responses to a performance context, they would evade or collapse under attempts to freight particular word-choices with fixed meaning. It may be that an Anglo-Saxon poem can be experienced, but *es ließ sich nicht lesen*.

In practice, however, these problems are not insuperable. Scholars working through the implications of oral-formulaic theory for Old English have reached several conclusions that are important for close readers. First, Old English formulas are extraordinarily malleable. Poets working within a formulaic system could innovate (generating, for instance, entirely novel compound words), and many poets demonstrably preferred more difficult diction.[5] Moreover, formulas can themselves be close-read as supra-lexical units with their own range of meaning.[6] Although Anglo-Saxon poetry may be differently structured from modern verse, its diction or arrangement need not be considered less intentional. Such a conclusion obviates fears that Anglo-Saxon (and particularly Old English) verse is radically resistant to reading. Even were it to be proven that particular texts had been composed orally, their poets' demonstrable freedom to choose their words means that such texts are art-objects and, as such, fit subjects for analysis.

We have, then, very suitable methods for examining texts in the finest grain of detail, and for understanding the means by which those texts might seek to affect audiences' reactions. We also require a technique for identifying communities' effects on poets, and a mechanism that would explain how such effects come about. Both these needs can be supplied by adapting some methods and insights from sociolinguistics. By examining and quantifying the ways that individuals in modern speech communities affect each other, sociolinguists have generated models that let us perceive the particular stamp that communities leave on discourse. These models can be extended or reverse-engineered to help us understand literature of the Anglo-Saxon period: though we cannot, of course, conduct field studies, we can examine the surviving poems to ascertain how communities are most likely to have affected them.

For the work of this chapter, I have found two sociolinguistic tools particularly useful: a taxonomy of oral narrative presented in the work of William Labov, and the theory of social networks devised by Leslie and James Milroy. Labov's classifications, developed in conjunction with Joshua Waletsky for various American dialect groups, identify recognizable strategies that oral narrators use to shape their audiences' reactions.[7] By examining these strategies in *The Battle of Maldon*, we can see how its poet pre-emptively redirects a community's response from judgment of the poem to judgment of the historical characters within the poem. Social network theory, meanwhile, provides a larger-scale method for understanding the structure of communities and poets' places within them. The Milroys' studies of speech patterns in working-class Belfast communities in the 1970s provided substantial evidence for their contention that the community is a mechanism of linguistic stability: it is possible to predict how typical a speaker's language is of his or her community by knowing how many and what kind of ties he or she has to others in the group. Those with more and stronger ties hew closely to a standard, while outliers tend to have irregular usage.[8] This insight – which corresponds closely to Labov's observations of Black English Vernacular speakers – is essential to my argument in the following chapter as well as this one. For many Anglo-Saxon poets, social groups were a constant and influential presence. Others, however, seem to have practised their art in isolation. This key difference resulted in certain peculiarities in the work of isolated poets, which I shall investigate in Chapter 4.

To understand how Aldhelm's Latin style spread so quickly across seventh-century England, I have used surviving evidence to reconstruct his various intersecting social networks. This method has proved productive before for the Anglo-Saxon period: thus Ursula Lenker used the relative wealth of material from reformed Benedictine monasteries of the mid-to-late tenth century to explain the spread of 'Winchester vocabulary' via networks, rather than from the decrees of a central authority.[9] Reformed monastic communities were an ideal subject for such work, since the Rule of Benedict provided a blueprint for all social interactions; by identifying particular individuals within such communities, Lenker could deduce something about those individuals' probable social interactions without actually observing them.[10] Though fewer rule-governed communities are known from the earlier period, social networks can still be extrapolated from association with entities like schools, royal courts, and foreign missions. Letters provide another kind of evidence for early medieval social connection, and although these must be used with care, such documents are nevertheless invaluable for identifying social ties sustained across spatial or temporal distance.[11] Letters, accordingly, form an important part of my analyses of the networks of Aldhelm and (in Chapter 5) of Boniface and his companions.

Even in the many cases where a poet's historical social ties can no longer be discerned, we can often see traces of the means by which his community affected him: the judgment of others in the group. Such judgment was (and is) a complex phenomenon, based on standards that are not always transparent to those who judge. Cicero gives an excellent example of this:

> quotus enim quisque est qui teneat artem numerorum ac modorum? at in iis si paulum modo offensum est, ut aut contractione brevius fieret aut productione longius, theatra tota reclamant.[12]

> Hardly anyone, really, can master the art of metre and rhythm; and yet at the slightest mistake in either of these – so that a syllable is clipped too short or drawn out too long – the whole theatre roars out.

In this section of De oratore Cicero marvels at the unerring ability of the untaught to recognize and judge aural patterning, and concludes that it must stem from some natural law. The keen metrical sense of Roman theatregoers must have stemmed partly from their native intuition as speakers of a quantitative language; it must also have had an aesthetic component, extrapolated from other plays they had heard. For the theatra tota to react, this linguistic/aesthetic judgment must have been widely shared, not idiosyncratic. It is perhaps helpful here to recall that Kant regarded judgment as by its nature referring to a *sensus communis*, which was not 'common sense' but 'a public sense, i.e. a critical faculty which in its reflective act takes account (*a priori*) of the mode of representation of every one else, in order, as it were, to weigh its judgment with the collective reason of mankind'.[13] Intuitive reference to 'what everyone else would think' is essential to the nature of judgment, and is one reason that it cannot be reduced to a single dimension of critique. Even when confined to linguistic and aesthetic phenomena like poetry, judgment readily takes on an ethical tinge: it is easy, in other words, to slide from 'Why did you say that?' to 'What is wrong with you?' Anglo-Saxon poets were well aware of this, as we shall see.

We are dealing, therefore, with but one aspect of a powerful social force. That judgment is an operative mechanism of the social group is indicated by a wide range of research; 'policing' and 'norm maintenance' are commonly used terms to describe the action and results. Overt negative judgment (like mockery) is one method of correcting those who stray from the group's norm.[14] Other means are more subtle: for instance, when individuals note their own differences from the norm, they often attempt to self-correct.[15] At the same time, many key sociolinguistic studies have highlighted the positive – rather than corrective – influence of example, as individuals seek to affiliate themselves with peers or emulate those whom they wish to be their peers.[16] These latter impulses might be described as 'self-policing', as individuals seek to conform to their group's expected judgment. But while people isolated from a social network might engage in self-policing, they would lack the means of correcting their self-judgments – of calibrating their *sensus communis*. The self-policing of those embedded in a network, in other words, is more likely to bring them closer to the norm because they have others at hand to verify their self-assessments; whereas those at the edge of a group, or outside it, would be left to their own inferences. In practice, this leads to the distinctive peculiarities found in isolated individuals which we shall examine in Chapter 4.

To exist within a community, then, is to expect the judgment of others. What has not, I think, previously been recognized is that this equation can be meaningfully reversed: so that the pervasive expectation of judgment which we find in Anglo-Saxon poetry can and should be read as indicating that many, perhaps *most*, poets practised their art within communities of others capable of judging their work. These others need not have been poets themselves; perhaps the majority were not. But, like the theatrical audiences of Cicero's time, they must have possessed enough knowledge and discernment about the poets' art to have been able to evaluate works in a way that transcended simple liking or disliking. The judgment of these readers and listeners is perceptible to us in the imprint they have left upon the poems themselves, as poets anticipate and attempt to manage their audience's reactions.

The engagement of poets within networks joining other poets with discerning readers and critics is hardly unique to Anglo-Saxon England: we can see traces of the expectation of judgment in the literature of many other cultures.[17] What is particularly interesting in Anglo-Saxon literature is the range of apparently long-established techniques for explicitly engaging others' judgment within the poems themselves. These methods vary from direct addresses to respected authorities to complicated dynamics of voice alternating between the first person singular, second person, and first person plural within a relatively brief space. But perhaps the most perennially successful of the Anglo-Saxons' techniques for managing the judgment of others can be found in the literary riddles. Here, the poet's encounter with the judgment of others becomes the purpose of the poem, which thereby ceases to be the passive object of judgment and instead is transformed simultaneously into a weapon and a battlefield in a playful clash of wits. The variety and sophistication of these modes of engagement suggest that the judgment of others was expected and sometimes welcomed by poets, and that this reciprocal bond was a pervasive aspect of most Anglo-Saxon poets' experience.

A few poems seem to offer glimpses of the context for social judgments. The Exeter Book *Maxims* begin with a direct challenge and demand for reciprocity:

> Frige mec frodum wordum.   Ne læt þinne ferð onhælne,
> degol þæt þu deopost cunne.   Nelle ic þe min dyrne gesecgan,
> gif þu me þinne hygecræft hylest   ond þine heortan geþohtas.
> Gleawe men sceolon gieddum wrixlan.[18]

> Question me with wise words. Do not keep your mind concealed, leaving hidden that which you know most deeply. I will not tell you my secrets if you hide from me your mind's power and the intentions of your heart. Wise men ought to exchange sayings.

This exchange is figured as between two equals; the poem's speaker requires both question and response of its addressee, who is an individual (*þu*), not an undifferentiated mass. It is not clear whether this passage represents a monologue or dialogue. If the latter, the voices are not distinguished from each other, perhaps suggesting that all *gleawe men* hold a common stock of knowledge and opinion. But if the *ic*, the speaker, remains stable and singular, then the condition expressed – that if his interlocutor remains silent, he will reveal nothing – reaches beyond the boundaries of the poem to demand an equivalent *gied* as a fitting exchange for *Maxims I* itself, or at least this first grouping. It is possible that the Exeter Book scribe answered this challenge with the two collections of maxims that follow.[19]

The beginning of *Maxims I*, then, establishes a friendly competition between wise speakers that invites judgment upon each speech – not in the form of a critique of what has been spoken, but of a new utterance of equal or greater value. The unit of measurement is not skill, but content: what must be spoken is something wise or formerly hidden. This context places the Exeter *Maxims* in the ancient genre of the wisdom contest, but this generic specificity may limit its relevance as a model for judgment in other kinds of poem.[20] Other Exeter Book poems depict less rule-governed verbal exchanges; *Vainglory*, for instance, contains a scene in which warriors

> sittaþ æt symble,   soðgied wrecað,
> wordum wrixlað,   witan fundiaþ
> hwylc æscstede   inne in ræcede
> mid werum wunige . . .[21]

sit at feast, pronouncing true sayings, exchanging words, seeking to find out which battlefield might still dwell among men within the hall . . .

The verb *wrixlan* 'to interchange' and the creation of *gied* – here *soðgied*, doubly true sayings – links this passage with the challenge of *Maxims I*. But instead of a dialogue, *Vainglory* depicts a many-sided conversation focused on shared memories; the generic scope of *gied* allows for the possibility that some of these speeches took the form of poems. There is perhaps a competitive edge – later in the poem, arrogant words lead to bloodshed – but here the exchange of words is chiefly a medium of social solidarity. These passages imply a society where friendly conversation is taken seriously, whether via the ritualized exchange of wisdom in the Exeter *Maxims* or the emphasis on *soð* ('truth') in the warriors' debate in *Vainglory*. But they tell us little about the specific expectations a poet might have had of those around him. To understand these, it is helpful to examine some of the techniques poets used for managing others' judgments: by analysing these, we can perceive more clearly what poets believed they might encounter in their readers and hearers, and how they hoped to elicit sympathetic judgments of their work.

Some, as mentioned above, preferred the direct approach: the prefaces of Anglo-Latin poems are particularly revealing in this regard, but some poems also feature asides or codae to influential readers. Such direct addresses were often of substantial scope: it is clear that they were not separable and particular – not, for instance, a sort of personal note in a dedication copy – but rather were integral to the entire work. One particularly spectacular example is the *Epistola specialis ad Ælfegum Episcopum* prefacing Wulfstan Cantor's *Narratio metrica de S. Swithuno*. This 334-line poem in elegiac couplets is couched as a direct address to Ælfheah, bishop of Winchester (*r.* 984–1006); it describes the fabric of Winchester Old Minster and the dedication ceremonies that accompanied the ambitious building pro- grammes of Ælfheah himself and of his predecessor, Æthelwold. The bishop, Wulfstan says, is a particularly fitting patron:

> Haec igitur commendo tibi munuscula patri
>   quae uoui Domino reddere corde pio,
> ut tua dignetur haec corroborare potestas
>   haec et ab infestis protegere insidiis.
> Dignus apostolica resides qui presul in aula,
>   instruis et populum dogmate catholicum
> hocque monasterium uariis ornatibus ornas,
>   intus et exterius illud ubique leuans.[22]

> Therefore, father, I entrust to you these little gifts, which, with devout heart, I vowed to render up to the Lord: so that your power might see fit to strengthen these things, and protect them from underhand attacks. You preside worthily as bishop in the apostolic hall, and you instruct the Catholic people in orthodoxy, and you adorn this monastery with various ornaments, elevating it on all sides, inwardly and outwardly.

Wulfstan requests support against *infestis . . . insidiis*; in the following lines, his praise can be read as an explanation of the special qualifications Ælfheah possesses as a defender of Wulfstan's verse: he has the authority of a bishop; he is concerned to instruct others in Christian truth; and he delights in adding to the beauties of the monastery. Wulfstan's poem, designed as an elegant metrical counterpart to Lantfred's prose account of the translation and recent miracles of St Swithun, was in itself a kind of adornment for the shrine of Winchester's most important saint. Ælfheah, therefore, was its natural promoter, and the bishop's concern for instructing others in Christian teaching would lead him to counter any 'underhand attacks' on the poem's narrative. While Wulfstan's plea for the bishop's patronage employs a humi- lity topos,[23] it simultaneously suggests that an attack on the *Narratio metrica* is an attack on the judgment of the bishop of Winchester.

Invocation of a formidable patron is a fairly common technique in Latin literature: what is striking about Wulfstan's *Epistola specialis* is not just its scale, but that it is balanced with a shorter, hexametrical *Epistola generalis* to the brothers of his own monastery. In it he requests their aid in correcting his own judgment:

> Vos quoque, uos seruo precibus succurite uestro,
> ne flatus per falsa queat me fallere fallax:
> inretitus enim curis et deditus imis
> haud animus quicquam poterit dinoscere ueri,
> ni prius errorem tetrae caliginis omnem
> expulerit sanctus donorum spiritus auctor.[24]

You too, all of you help your servant with your prayers, so that deceitful pride will not seek to lead me astray with its lies: for the mind, ensnared and given over to base preoccupations, will be quite unable to discern the truth, unless the Holy Spirit, source of all gifts, will first dispel every error of blind darkness.

In this remarkable passage, Wulfstan asks his brothers to help him avoid the errors of pride and self-deceit. He acknowledges the spiritual dangers in the singularity of his position as poet of St Swithun's cult, but frames their correct response to this as intercessory prayer, rather than direct correction of the poem or of Wulfstan himself – *that* he prefers to leave to the Holy Spirit. Wulfstan Cantor thus handles the possibility of harsh judgment by deflecting it into indirect channels, while still asserting deference towards and solidarity with his immediate audience, the monks of Old Minster Winchester.

Part of the oddity of Wulfstan's position stemmed from the fact that he was almost certainly a better poet than those around him.[25] In contrast, poets who portray themselves as students often ask for criticism directly, or acknowledge its likelihood by praising the mercy, justice, and wisdom of their teachers. The author of the *Carmen de libero arbitrio* provides a good example of this.[26] In the passage discussed briefly in Chapter 1, the poet goes on to address his bishop:[27]

> dogmate quodque mones claris prius actibus imples,
> solamen, uirtus, pastor et exulibus.
> claret hoc a domino quod celsa talenta benigno
> sint tibi, summe pater: te decus omne decet.
> mente meos sensus stolidos tu conspice, rector,
> quod male dico loquens, corrige, posco cliens.[28]

Whatever you advise in your teaching, you first fulfil in your shining deeds: you are a comfort, strength, and guide for exiles. Through the kindly Lord it is clear that the highest rewards shall be yours, best of fathers: you are worthy of all worthy things. With your mind, master, supervise my obtuse expressions, and correct, your servant begs you, what I express badly.

The bishop's integrity and merit, and his kindness to foreigners, are implicitly linked to the request for correction: such an illustrious man is not only *qualified* to judge this poem, but will surely do so in the best and fairest way. The pairing of *rector* and *cliens* in the last couplet quoted emphasizes the relative positions of the bishop and poet: judgment becomes an act of kindness, and the seeking of it a gesture of humility.

The dynamics of poetic voice in these passages are more complex than might first appear, since the second person voice also constructs a hierarchy among the audience. Those beyond the named addressees are temporarily reduced to uncomfortable spectators, their own reactions to the work shaped by the connection between the poet and those to whom he claims to speak. Often, this stratified second person is troubled still further by complications the poet introduces into the *first* person voice. For instance, in this epilogue to *De abbatibus*, Æthilwulf's ostensible addressee is Ecgberht, bishop of Lindisfarne (*r.* 803–21):

> hic locus ut Christo semper memorabilis almo
>   existat meritis, accumulent monachi,
> omnipotens meritis semper quos augeat istic,
>   et puram capiant corpore, mente fidem.
> sit deus omnipotens per secula cuncta beatis
>   seruator mitis dum meliora uelint;
> cum quibus hec cantans, cupiens sua miscere uota,
>   non cessat famulans, quandoque non uitiis.
> tu, pater, hec recitans nostros non sperne labores,
>   quin magis hec cernens gaudia digna tene;
> quod tua tam clari meruerunt sanguine patres
>   esse, deo grates reddere te moneo.[29]

> So that this place may always stand in its merits before the blessed Christ, may monks gather, and may the Omnipotent One ever increase them in their merits there – may they obtain a pure faith in body and mind. While these blessed ones desire the better path, may the Omnipotent God be a gracious Saviour to them through all ages; along with them, may the one singing these things – seeking to add in his devotions – not cease to serve, so long as it is not in vice. And you, father, as you read over these things, do not scorn our labours, but rather, perceiving these things, engage in fitting joy; I advise you to give thanks to God that from your blood such distinguished fathers have deserved to arise.

Normally the first person plural is merely a rhetorical convention, but here, in line 808, the *nos* of *nostros labores* seems to fulfil the wish expressed in the preceding couplet: that Æthilwulf should be joined to his fellow monks in their observances. A subset of his audience is thus subsumed, not into the *tu* that judges, but the *nos* who are being judged, and the *labores* are extended to include not merely *haec* – 'these things', the poem before the reader – but all the works and observances carried out by the brothers of this cell. By this means, key portions of Æthilwulf's likely audience – those around him – are effectively made into honorary authors. Judgments they might pass upon the poem are in some sense upon themselves.

This reaching outward into the first person plural, joining the audience with the author, is very characteristic of Anglo-Saxon verse; it is especially common in Old English. Many scholars have seen homiletic or liturgical influence here, and often the direct influence of the 'hortative we' – the voice in which most sermons and homilies conclude – seems clear.[30] But the extension of the first person is not a simple mirror of homiletic style: in most cases it is part of a multilayered interaction between the poetic voice and implied audience, interaction that seems to presume knowledge of multiple conventions for representing the poetic self in relation to the audience. These techniques work by presuming commonality with the audience: shared knowledge; shared identity; shared experience past or future. Presumptions of shared knowledge and identity I shall discuss below;[31] here I would like to point out how the notion of shared future experience joins the narrator and audience of *The Dream of the Rood*, and helps shape reactions to the poem.

The layered construction of voice in *The Dream of the Rood* is one of the poem's most striking qualities. The narrator's vision of the True Cross gives way to the Rood's own first person monologue – a speech that begins in the particularity of the Rood's own history and ends in the Last Judgment – before returning to the Dreamer's own meditations, which seem to include the Harrowing of Hell.[32] The presence of the first person singular is insistent: there are forty instances of *ic* or *me* in the poem's 156 lines, a little more than once every 4 lines (as compared to, say, *Elene*, where these pronouns occur only once every 27 or 28 lines). Despite the apparent particularity of the Dreamer's experience, his prayer at the end of the poem suddenly transforms into a general one:

> Si me dryhten freond,
> se ðe her on eorðan   ær þrowode
> on þam gealgtreowe   for guman synnum;
> he us onlysde,   and us lif forgeaf,
> heofonlicne ham.[33]

May the Lord be a friend to me, he who here on earth once suffered on the gallows-tree for the sins of man; he redeemed us and gave us life, a heavenly home.

Before this moment, the poem has been peculiarly intimate; the solitary Dreamer is addressed individually, as *ðu* or *hæleð min se leofa* ('my beloved warrior': 78b, 95b), by the solitary Rood.[34] But with the extension of the first person from the singular to the plural in line 147, the poet acknowledges the general import of the vision, and draws the audience into the circle of its witnesses. The use of *us* instead of *eow* ('you' pl.) does not diminish the intimacy of the preceding narrative, but perpetuates it. In the process, the audience is led to identify more strongly with the Dreamer's reactions, since it has been made a sort of co-recipient of his vision: the first person plural places the audience in the position of witnesses, not judges. This is emphasized all the more by the image of Christ as judge of all mankind introduced at the end of the Cross's speech (lines 103–21); the poem's readers and hearers are joined by implication with the Dreamer himself in the multitude standing before the Lord on the last day. The Rood's promised aid is thus extended to the audience as it has been to the Dreamer.

The central conceit of *The Dream of the Rood* – the speech of the personified Cross – has led many scholars to connect this poem with the Anglo-Saxon *enigmata*, since the personification of unlikely creatures and objects is an essential component of riddles in both Latin and Old English.[35] But the Rood's speech is confined within the poem: it addresses a human figure whose reaction constructs an interpretative framework for the strangeness of the vision. In the riddles, no barrier stands between the audience and the impossibilities posed by the narrator. This is, indeed, the purpose of the genre: to challenge the audience directly, allowing readers or hearers to test their interpretative skill against the poet's ingenuity.

Many of the riddles express this challenge openly, almost belligerently. Aldhelm ended his *Enigma* C ('De creatura') with this quatrain:

> Auscultate mei credentes famina uerbi,
> Pandere quae poterit gnarus uix ore magister
> Et tamen infitians non retur friuola lector!
> Sciscitor inflatos, fungar quo nomine, sophos.[36]

> Listen, believing, to the discourse of my words, which the skilled teacher will scarcely be able to explain aloud, though all the same the hesitating reader will not consider them trifling. I ask puffed-up wise men what name I go by.

The distinction between the singular *lector* and plural *inflati sophi* allows the reader (just) to exempt himself from being 'puffed-up', but the speaker – here still the riddle-persona – portrays the discovery of its[37] identity as a dose of humility for those impressed with their own wisdom. This is appropriate to the riddle's theme, since the series of paradoxes with which Aldhelm describes 'Creation' hinges on its embrace of unthinkable extremes; but as these are the final lines of the entire collection of riddles, it is hard not to read them simultaneously as a hyperbolically aggressive challenge to Aldhelm's own readers. Those who struggle with the solutions, in other words, are possibly not as clever as they think themselves.

Many of Aldhelm's successors echoed this closing line. The last verse of the final riddle in Tætwine's collection, for instance, is very similar if rather milder-mannered:

> Corporis absens plausu quid sum pandite sophi![38]

In the absence of a form, reveal what I am, wise men, with applause.

Again the riddle-creature (in this case, a sunbeam) demands to be named by *sophi*, but here with the curious addition of *plausu*, whose grammatical connection is ambiguous. The alliteration seems to link this word with *pandite*, as if the act of revelation were to be performed with applause as its instrument – or goal. The ambiguity makes it possible to see the praise extending to both the poet and the successful solver of his riddles: in Tætwine's formulation, the act of interpretation is an act of positive judgment that is both transitive and reflexive. The Old English 'storm' riddle, however, maintains something of the aggression of Aldhelm's formulation:

> Hwylc is hæleþa þæs horsc   ond þæs hygecræftig
> þæt þæt mæge asecgan,   hwa mec on sið wræce,
> þonne ic astige strong . . .[39]

Who among men is clever and wise enough in mind that he can tell this: who drove me on my path when I rise up in strength. . .

> Saga, þoncol mon,
> hwa mec bregde   of brimes fæþmum,
> þonne streamas eft   stille weorþað,
> yþa geþwære,   þe mec ær wrugon.[40]

Tell, O wise man, who draws me from the sea's embrace when the currents again grow calm, and the waves which had covered me grow peaceful.

The success or failure of the audience's claim to perceptiveness lies in its members' ability to decode the statements of the poem's speaker. The persona of the riddle-creature prevents this dynamic from becoming an outright contest between *poet* and audience; but still, as with Aldhelm's riddles and Tætwine's, the title to wisdom has been put at stake. In this sense, the normal process has been ingeniously reversed: the poems pass judgment upon their audience.

It is this conscious reciprocity of judgment that makes the riddles part
of a game. But the game is rigged in favour of the poet: the audience loses if
it cannot guess the solution, but if it does guess, then, as Tætwine's *Enigma*
XL suggested, *both* players win. Consider, for instance, the framework of the
famous *Riddle* 42:

> ...Ic on flette mæg
> þurh runstafas rincum secgan,
> þam þe bec witan, bega ætsomne
> naman þara wihta. Þær sceal Nyd wesan
> twega oþer ond se torhta Æsc
> an an linan, Acas twegen,
> Hægelas swa some. Hwylc þæs hordgates
> cægan cræfte þa clamme onleac
> þe þa rædellan wið rynemenn
> hygefæste heold heortan bewrigene
> orþoncbendum? Nu is undyrne
> werum æt wine hu þa wihte mid us,
> heanmode twa, hatne sindon.[41]

Upon the floor I can tell through rune-staves to men – those who understand
books – the names of both those creatures. There must be two Needs, and
the bright Ash all alone, two Oaks, and likewise some Hail. Who has
unlocked with the device of the key the bars of the vault door that secured
the riddle, its heart encircled with cunning bands, against thoughtful men
who know secrets? Now it is no mystery to men at their wine how these two
vulgar-minded creatures are named among us.

Seth Lerer and Dieter Bitterli have discussed the interpretative difficulties
of this riddle, especially its peculiar intermingling of the learned with the
popular.[42] What I would like to point out is the clever way it manipulates
the audience's solidarity. The clear distinction initially set up between the
speaker and his audience (*Ic*, 5b, versus *rincum*, 6b) is effaced by the process
of solving the riddle: the name is revealed *mid us* ('among ourselves', 16b),
who all seem to be equally *weras æt wine*. The riddle's difficulties are not
insuperable, since it is repeatedly asserted that the audience has overcome
them: *onleac* is in the past tense, implying that someone has already solved
the riddle, and the final sentence begins with the assurance that *nu is undyrne*
('now it is clear'). The problems posed by the *clamme* and *orþoncbende* are
thereby transformed into praise of the cleverness of the solvers and, in the
process, of the poet himself.

Part of the fascination of *Riddle* 42 is how it makes explicit the dynamic
relations between poet, persona, and audience underlying the entire

riddle-game.[43] Most riddles, in both Latin and Old English, leave unspoken the complicated way in which the audience is first antagonized and then, by the process of solution, brought into solidarity with the poet's aim. What remains stable is the sense that relations between poet and audience are inherently *un*stable – that the potential for conflict is ever-present, while the interests of each can be harmonized only by the poet's active management and the audience's goodwill. The riddle-game thus formalizes an essential aspect of almost all Anglo-Saxon poetry: the poet's expectation of the audience's judgment.

This pervasive expectation of judgment is the concrete trace of an otherwise vanished entity: the network of poets, listeners, and readers who made up the community in which poems were conceived and delivered. As with the imprints left in stone that witness the texture of a dinosaur's skin once the soft tissue itself has long vanished, the imprint of judgment is partial, but crucial, evidence for the existence of networks which cannot be directly examined. When we can perceive that a poet must have worked within a community, we are better placed to delve further into the poet's individual experience, and into the implications this has for our understanding of what poems were and what they were for. In the remainder of this chapter, I examine the traces of three poetic communities: those surrounding the author of *The Battle of Maldon*; the author of the poems signed 'Cynewulf' in runes; and Aldhelm of Malmesbury. My goal is to show the power and role of poetic communities in shaping the literature of Anglo-Saxon England from the beginning of the historical period to its end.

Evaluation and Judgment in *The Battle of Maldon*

As an artifact of Anglo-Saxon literary culture, *The Battle of Maldon* poses some curious ontological problems. The earliest surviving copy of it is an eighteenth-century transcript by David Casley, under-keeper of the Cotton library.[44] Even before its destruction in the 1731 fire, however, the manuscript was incomplete. The text as we now have it begins and ends in mid-sentence, but the notes of early modern scholars who saw the manuscript indicate that in the late seventeenth century, the first lines were as they now stand.[45] As the text encompassed six manuscript folios, it seems likely that a single outer sheet had been lost from an original quire of eight, and that fifty to sixty lines of verse have thus been lost from the poem's beginning and conclusion.[46]

Besides the uncertain nature of its manuscript record, the poem's subject is also problematic. It describes the death of the *eorl* Byrhtnoth in a battle with the Vikings on the tidal shores of the *Pante*, a river in Essex now known as the Blackwater. This event evidently corresponds to one recorded in the CDE versions of the *Anglo-Saxon Chronicle* under 991:

> Her wæs Gypeswic gehergod, and æfter þon swiðe raðe wæs Brihtnoð ealdorman ofslegen æt Mældune.[47]

> Here Ipswich was ravaged, and very soon after that *ealdorman* Byrhtnoth was killed at Maldon.

Maldon itself is never named in the surviving text of the poem, and the modern title is derived from historical sources. *The Battle of Maldon*'s exact relation to history, however, has been much disputed. Some scholars have argued that it is effectively historical fiction assembled from later sources, and dates from as much as a generation after the battle itself.[48] Most recent scholarship has tended to view the poem as composed fairly soon after 991, but also emphasizes the heavy stylization of character, plot, and action.[49]

As a text, then, *The Battle of Maldon* has an ambiguous relationship to reality. The poem we know is based on the simulacrum of a damaged text presenting a simulacrum of a historical event.[50] Yet despite its twilight existence, the poem presents excellent credentials as a case study. First, it indisputably stems from the later Anglo-Saxon period, and thus offers a glimpse into the development of the vernacular poetic tradition at the turn of the millennium. *Maldon* is also explicitly concerned with a textured view of history. It is a poem about the remembrance of individuals and of localized events, but it also engages the national implications of these events.[51] For us, therefore, *The Battle of Maldon* provides an opportunity to explore how a poem interacts with a relatively identifiable community. Using sociolinguistic categories for understanding oral narrative, I shall first consider the ways in which the *Maldon*-poet uses evaluative statements to direct the audience's interpretation of his work, and then turn to the crucial role that judgment plays at multiple levels of the poem. By understanding this poem's embedded expectations of its audience – and the means by which it seeks to anticipate and direct that audience's judgment – we can, I believe, perceive some features of a late Anglo-Saxon vernacular poetic community.

Tō fela: *evaluation in* Maldon

For an oral narrator – indeed, for any narrator – the attention of the audience is a perpetual challenge. Getting and keeping it is a test in its own right; but once a narrator has persuaded those around him or her to focus on the performance, he or she must continue to direct that focus. Otherwise, from the performer's point of view, there is a constant danger of misapprehension: idle details may be seized on and important points neglected, while the significance of the story as a whole may be mistaken – or missed altogether. Sociolinguists who have studied oral narratives have identified a class of techniques a speaker can use to frame the interpretation of a discourse, so that, as Labov puts it, 'when his narrative is over, it should be unthinkable for a bystander to say, "So what?"'.[52]

In narrative, then, evaluations are distinct from moral or ethical judgments, though they may sometimes take that form. Evaluations may also bear various relations to the narrative itself. They may occasionally be expressed extradiegetically, in the voice of the narrator: for instance, the *Beowulf*-poet evaluates Scyld Scefing's funeral with the statement

> ne hyrde ic cymlicor   ceol gegyrwan
> hildewæpnum   ond heaðowædum ...[53]

Never have I heard of a ship more splendidly adorned with battle-weapons and war-garments ...

But evaluation may also be embedded within the narrative. Often, the thoughts, words, and actions of characters point out incidents' significance. To take another example from *Beowulf*: Grendel himself is never described clearly, but the magnitude and horror of his appearance – and thus the significance of Beowulf's victory – are suggested through onlookers' reactions:

> Ða wæs swigra secg,   sunu Eclafes,
> on gylpspræce   guðgeweorca,
> siþðan æþelingas   eorles cræfte
> ofer heanne hrof   hand sceawedon,
> feondes fingras ...[54]

Then [Unferth] the son of Ecgtheow was a man more silent in boasting of deeds in battle, once the noblemen, through the lord's might, saw the hand above the high roof, the enemy's fingers ...

To strike Unferth with the sense that all his own deeds are not worth mentioning, the severed hand must be far beyond ordinary experience – as must the *eorles cræft*. But many more subtle evaluative techniques are often used by skilful narrators, including the embedding of comparatives, superlatives, and other means of indicating the notable qualities of the narrative action. Particular oral traditions may also develop their own conventions: for instance, Suzanne Fleischmann has shown that in medieval French, narrators switch to the present tense to foreground the action, signalling its importance by bringing it more immediately before the audience.[55]

In *The Battle of Maldon*, the poet uses a wide range of techniques for evaluating the action. Some are overt; others are so subtle that they are rarely consciously recognized, though they guide interpretations of the poem just as effectively. The *Maldon*-poet has a particularly strong preference for intra-diegetic evaluation, and his often-praised work of characterization contributes to this. The famous instance of the hawk helps illustrate some of his methods:

> Þa þæt Offan mæg   ærest onfunde,
> þæt se eorl nolde   yrhðo geþolian,
> he let him þa of handon   leofne fleogan,
> hafoc wið þæs holtes,   and to þære hilde stop.
> Be þam man mihte oncnawan   þæt se cniht nolde
> wacian æt þam wige   þa he to wæpnum feng.[56]

> When Offa's kinsman first perceived that the lord would not endure coward-ice, from his hands he caused his beloved hawk to fly off to the woods, and advanced to the battle-line. By that it could be perceived that the young man had no intention of weakening in the fight, when he took up weapons.

This brief passage intertwines several evaluative techniques. Most obvious are lines 9–10, in which the poem's narrator interprets the young man's behaviour. But the actions interpreted are themselves evaluative: Offa's kinsman sets free his hawk (7–8) in response to his own understanding of Byrhtnoth's intentions (5–6), since in the lines before, Byrhtnoth has ordered the horses to be driven from the battlefield. The *cniht*'s actions confirm and extend the implications of Byrhtnoth's. Seen through the lens of the abandonment of the hawk, the abandonment of the horses cannot be read simply as preparation for battle with infantry: it too must be inter-preted as a gesture of total commitment, a pre-emptive forfeiture of worldly goods. The preparations for battle are thus invested with fatal significance.

It is probably no coincidence that Offa's kinsman was the owner of the portentous hawk, since Offa himself is the most important avatar of diegetic evaluation. To Offa is attributed the prophecy of cowardice in the ranks in lines 198–201, and once his prediction is justified, he interprets the con-sequences of the Oddassons' flight:

> wende þæs formoni man,   þa he on meare rad,
> on wlancan þam wicge,   þæt wære hit ure hlaford;
> forþan wearð her on felda   folc totwæmed,
> scyldburh tobrocen.   Abreoðe his angin,
> þæt he her swa manigne   man aflymde.[57]

> when he rode off on that fine horse, all too many men believed that it was our lord: and so the people were divided here on the battlefield, and the

shieldwall broken. A curse upon his birth, that he should have put so many men to flight here.

Reading Offa's speech as evaluation, we can understand the full meaning of what he is telling his comrades. In purely narrative terms, his explanation of the motivations of the army – their false interpretation of Godric's escape on Byrhtnoth's horse – justifies the poem's description of that escape in lines 185–97. But Offa's language goes further: the words he uses – *formoni* (239a) and *swa manigne* (243a) – do not simply mean 'a lot'. As specifically evaluative terms, they describe not just the scale, but the significance of the army's flight. What Offa is saying is that the English are now fatally outnumbered.[58]

Offa's speech thus accomplishes several goals. In its narrative context, it confers tragic significance upon the remaining fight by dramatizing the remaining men's full awareness of their choice. For the audience, however, it does even more: it pre-empts rumours of Byrhtnoth's flight (which could plausibly have been spread by deluded survivors), and makes the battle's loss more palatable by opening space for a counternarrative. Had Godric not fled – had those *formoni* men remained – then perhaps the Vikings might have been defeated. As a vehicle for embedded evaluation, Offa helps the audience understand the kind of story they are witnessing: an account not of weakness, but of treachery. His final curse on Godric has the narrative's full weight behind it.

The comparatives, intensifiers, and adjectives of quantity investing Offa's speech with its particular force are characteristic of the evaluative language embedded within the narrative. So, for instance, when the tide ebbs over the causeway, we are told that

> Þa flotan stodon gearowe,
> wicinga fela,   wiges georne.[59]

The sailors stood ready, many Vikings eager for battle.

This seems a simple description; but in context the number *fela*, and to a lesser extent the descriptors *gearowe* and *georne*, do not merely tell the audience what the enemy host was like. These words are evaluative devices indicating the *meaning* of these qualities: 'many Vikings eager for battle' thus implies a larger, better-prepared army.[60] We see similar devices in the sequence of encounters leading to Byrhtnoth's death. Compare, for instance, the accounts of the first two wounds he receives:

> Sende ða se særinc   suþerne gar,
> þæt gewundod wearð   wigena hlaford;

> he sceaf þa mid ðam scylde,   þæt se sceaft tobærst,
> and þæt spere sprengde,   þæt hit sprang ongean.⁶¹

Then the sailor cast a southern-made spear, so that the warriors' lord was wounded; then he struck out with his shield so that the shaft broke and the spear quivered, so that it sprang back out.

> Forlet þa drenga sum   daroð of handa,
> fleogan of folman,   þæt se to forð gewat
> þurh þone æþelan   Æþelredes þegen.⁶²

Then a certain one of the Scandinavian warriors cast a flying spear from his hands, so that it pierced the noble thegn of Æthelred too deeply.

Though the narrative of the first encounter is longer and more detailed, it gives no indication of the seriousness of Byrhtnoth's wound. Instead, through his actions, we are led to think that it was insignificant. In the second passage, however, the evaluative statement *to forð* points to the seriousness of this injury. The spear has gone in too deeply: though it is pulled out and the wound avenged by one of Byrhtnoth's retainers, it is already too late. At least one more encounter is required to finish him off (he is maimed in his sword-arm when 'To raþe hine gelette lidmanna sum', 'a certain one of the sailors hindered him *too swiftly*', 164), but Byrhtnoth's death, we know, is inevitable.

Given that the audience must have known the conclusion, it is unsurprising that the poem's evaluative language points so emphatically towards the English army's doom. The poem's most famous evaluation makes the outcome explicit by line 90:

> Ða se eorl ongan   for his ofermode
> alyfan landes to fela   laþere ðeode.⁶³

Then in his pride the lord began to allow too much land to the hateful tribe.

Historians have repeatedly defended Byrhtnoth's tactics against the criticism that he conceded *landes to fela*. Given the terrain, his imperative to engage the invaders, and his lack of naval forces, he may have had little choice but to fall back.⁶⁴ This is not, however, relevant to the poet's phrase as evaluation, rather than tactical judgment. In its narrative context, *to fela* indicates the manoeuvre's significance: as it turned out, too much land – indeed, the whole battlefield – *was* conceded to the Vikings. The evaluative device does not tell us how effectively Byrhtnoth used the terrain; it signals the battle's outcome.

These lines, however, contain a second evaluation which is also a moral judgment. Gneuss has conclusively demonstrated that *ofermod* must mean 'pride', with all the theological baggage the word brings.⁶⁵ Byrhtnoth's *ofermod*, then, seems to have a double function. As a judgment – a word with undeniable moral freight – it assigns blame for this predicted outcome. That blame for failure rests upon a flaw in the leader is in keeping with what we understand of contemporary Anglo-Saxon ideas about the conduct of war. Byrhtnoth was clearly no coward, but he lost – so his fault must have lain in the opposite direction.[66] The fact, though, that the poet finds him blame-worthy is itself an evaluation. In learning of Byrhtnoth's pride in conjunction with his concession of *landes to fela*, the audience is led to understand the narrative significance of this moment. He will not retreat further – perhaps he even believes he might win – but the English army's fate is sealed.

Narrative and judgment

The external judgment passed on Byrhtnoth is echoed within the world of *The Battle of Maldon*, where the community's verdict preoccupies most of the characters. So Ælfwine, grandson of the ealdorman of the Mercians, declares:

> Ne sceolon me on þære þeode   þegenas ætwitan
> þæt ic of ðisse fyrde   feran wille,
> eard gesecan,   nu min ealdor ligeð
> forheawen æt hilde.[67]

The noblemen among that people shall not reproach me for wishing to retreat from this army and seek that land, now that my lord lies cut down in the battle.

Leofsunu, evidently of less illustrious lineage, nevertheless expresses identical motivations:

> Ne þurfon me embe Sturmere   stedefæste hælæð
> wordum ætwitan,   nu min wine gecranc,
> þæt ic hlafordleas   ham siðie,
> wende from wige . . .[68]

The faithful warriors around Sturmer will have no cause to reproach me in speech, now that my friend is dead, for going home lordless and retreating from the battle . . .

In these characters' view, death is preferable to their home communities' contempt. Many scholars have considered the cultural implications of such sentiments, particularly in relation to ancient ideals like those described in Tacitus' *Germania*.[69] What I would emphasize here is that narrative is a critical element in the formation of these all-important judgments. Both Ælfwine and Leofsunu present their concerns about judgment via miniature embedded narratives whose main verbs are contrary-to-fact subjunctives (221, 251): *were* they to return home after Byrhtnoth's death, then the people would blame them. Were such things even to be said of them, they would have died in vain.

The speeches each man is given in the poem act as correctives to any such false tales, but the possibility of counternarrative remains a danger in *Maldon*, with the army's false belief in Byrhtnoth's flight acting as model for such misjudgments. The poem itself is constructed so as to present itself to the audience as a bulwark against these false beliefs. By providing the 'true' version of events, it seems to offer a transparent window for the audience to witness the action – and thus to pass its own judgment on the battle's actors. This focus on ethical judgment is accomplished partly through skilful use of evaluative devices in the narrative, and has significant consequences for the aesthetic reception of the poem.

The audience's judgment is flattered throughout the text. Byrhtnoth's dying prayer for mercy is an excellent example of this. The importance of the prayer itself is signalled internally ('Nu ic ah, milde Metod, *mæste þearfe*', 'Now, gracious Ordainer, I have the greatest need', 175), and in a different kind of work – Cynewulf's, for instance – this would have provided an opportunity to assert the final authority of *God*'s judgment, not man's. Here, however, the lack of closure – of assurance as to Byrhtnoth's ultimate fate – returns the power of judgment back upon the audience. While it is difficult to say how contemporary audiences responded, modern critics have been delighted to take up the question.[70]

The poem thus invests the audience with a sense of immense power. As Offa explained, the outcome of the battle was determined by the treachery or delusion of those who fled – whose accounts are therefore unreliable and must be countered with the actual events. The reputations of Ælfwine and Leofsunu meant more to them than their lives, but those reputations depend on the true story of their courage reaching Sturmer or the Midlands. Even the salvation of Byrhtnoth's soul seems to depend on the judgment of the poem's audience. This powerful sense of the real-world consequences of hearing and absorbing the poem is the *Maldon*-poet's greatest artistic triumph, and also the greatest barrier to the judgment of his art.

Judging Maldon

By relentlessly directing the audience's attention to its own power of judging the events of the narrative, the *Maldon*-poet creates the illusion that real men, not lines of verse, are the objects of judgment. This is by no means the only method by which Old English poets could consider ethical questions of this sort. In *Beowulf*, for instance, Hæðcyn's killing of his brother Herebeald, and Beowulf's retainers' desertion of him in the dragon-fight, raise significant moral dilemmas for the society within the poem. The poet deals with both in the same way: by having characters evaluate the action through elaborate fictional scenarios. Wiglaf's prediction of disgrace for the cowardly retainers (2864–91) resembles a prophecy much more closely than does Beowulf's epic simile of an old man's debilitating grief for a hanged son (2444–62a), but neither incident actually occurs within the poem's time-frame. While such incidents in *Beowulf* function as evaluation within the poem's narrative, they simultaneously focus attention on the act of narrative. Characters react to the story's events by telling more stories, and the result is an inescapable awareness of the artificiality – and the artfulness – of *Beowulf* itself. In *Maldon*, however, the poet redirects judgment from the poem to the poem's subjects, and the net effect is an illusion of transparency. It has been remarkably successful, as the many readings of the poem as naïve historiography testify.[71] But *ars est celare artem*: and I should like finally to consider this poet's particular form of art as a response to a particular type of community.

First, the fixation with reputation, and the assignment of praise and blame, must have reflected a real priority among the audience. This corresponds with much of what is already known about historiographical thought in the period.[72] What is less clear is what we should deduce from the poem's interest in the reputations of men who seem – at least from our vantage point – to have been known only locally. The work of Margaret Locherbie-Cameron strongly suggests that few, if any, of the named characters in *Maldon* were invented, but that people such as the *geneat* Byrhtwold, or even the Ælfnoth who apparently was a small landholder in Bedfordshire or Cambridgeshire, cannot have had much influence outside their home regions.[73] It does not necessarily follow from this that *Maldon* is and has always been a local poem for local people. Many have pointed out the appearance of characters from at least three of the old kingdoms and numerous social ranks, and some have argued that this points to a desire for a national audience, or at least national significance.[74] The loss of the manuscript is particularly unfortunate in this regard, since it is impossible now to know whether the poem's text was attested outside of the southeast. However, *Maldon*'s insistence on the power of the audience in determining its characters' reputations suggests that its immediate context was among those who would have felt an interest in these particular reputations. Such a view does not invalidate arguments for the poem's national concerns. It implies, rather, that the community was envisioned as a series of concentric circles, spreading outwards from those who knew the fallen to encompass the whole of England. To draw upon living memories of men like Byrhtwold and Ælfnoth, the inmost circle – the poem's site of origin – must have been located in the southeast, most likely in Essex or Cambridgeshire, and probably within a few years of the battle itself. Such an origin would have fed upon active interest in, and knowledge of, the reputations of the dead – and the living.

The poet of *The Battle of Maldon* therefore most likely lived in the southeast counties during the late tenth century.[75] We can say a little more than this, however, about his circumstances.[76] His extremely skilful use of evaluative language, and particularly embedded evaluation, suggests a talented and experienced oral narrator. While it is uncertain how transferable studies of modern speakers are to premodern milieux, Labov's observation that the use of evaluative devices develops into adulthood, and that dramatic embedded evaluations are used 'only by older, highly skilled narrators from traditional working-class backgrounds', suggests that cognitive development may be as important as acculturation in creating complex narrative.[77] Probably, then, the poet was born by 960 or before. There is much less evidence to identify his social role or status. Stafford has suggested that 'the lesser nobles who feature so prominently in [the poem] seem its likely hearers', and if so, the poet himself may have been one of the minor gentry.[78] Such an origin would not preclude a career as a secular cleric or even a monk; but there is no reason to identify the author of *Maldon* with any of the roles identified in Chapter 2.

The language of *Maldon* is relatively progressive. The poet uses a number of Scandinavian words, sometimes for dramatic effect, which perhaps implies in turn a degree of linguistic self-consciousness among the audience.[79] Metrically, the poem is often regarded as rather inept, and the regulation of unstressed syllables especially differs from the practice of the *Beowulf*-poet.[80] Most of *Maldon*'s metrical anomalies, however, are characteristic of late Old English verse, and many stem directly from linguistic changes. The decline of compounding, in particular, set off a cascade of stylistic and metrical shifts that include the rise of end-stopped verses; a restricted range of rhythmic patterns (since the patterns represented by Sievers's C, D, and E types relied heavily on poetic compounds); and the increased prominence of rhyme.[81] Despite the flavour of archaism many have detected in the poem, then, its style was largely contemporary.[82]

Yet not all *Maldon*'s aesthetic peculiarities can be explained as inevitable features of late metre. Scragg has pointed out that the poem contains much close verbal repetition, and that justifying *all* of it as purposeful incurs 'a danger of the critic working harder than the poet'.[83] There is also limited variety in the way the poet maps sentence structure onto the verse line. For example, more than half (51 per cent) of the B-verses end in finite verbs, and two thirds of B-verses have a verb form in the final position.[84] By contrast, less than a third of B-verses in the *Battle of Brunanburh* end in finite verbs (with about 40 per cent of the 73 lines ending in some form of verb), while in the late, stanzaic *Seasons for Fasting*, about one third of lines end in a finite verb, and a little under half end in some form of verb.[85] The texture of *Maldon*'s verse is significantly less varied than that of many other mid-to-late tenth-century poems.

The poet of *Maldon*, then, was a very skilled narrator but not an especially accomplished stylist. It is impossible to know whether he was incapable of more polished verse, or simply not interested in it. However, the focus of his artfulness on narration helps explain how the poet handles the audience's expected judgment. By transferring attention from the poem-as-artifact to the reputations of the men it describes, the *Maldon*-poet sidesteps judgment of the verse itself. We have now no way of knowing whether such poetic jujitsu was common in oral narrative poems or an ingenious contrivance of this poet, but it does suggest how a canny artist might harness the easy slide from aesthetics to ethics which is inherent to judgment as a social phenomenon. By channelling the community's interest in reputation, *Maldon* focuses judgment *through* rather than upon poetry, affirming the force and necessity of social judgment without being harmed by it. This may paradoxically have given its style *more* rather than less influence, by normalizing some of its peculiarities and innovations. While the audience considers whether Byrhtnoth was wrong or right, its attention drifts from the question of whether any particular verse is wrong or right by contemporary standards. In so doing, 'wrong' verses could be absorbed into the repertoire of acceptable forms.

There is profound irony, then, in the circumstances of *The Battle of Maldon*'s survival. The style of its narrative, and particularly its skilful use of sophisticated evaluative techniques, points to an oral origin and an investment in the reactions of a particular local community. The course of its life has separated it from virtually all its original context, until it comes to us *sans* companions, *sans* manuscript, *sans* beginning and end, *sans* everything but the somewhat unreliable text itself. And yet the poet's narrative strategies remain so effective that *Maldon* continues to persuade readers of the reality of its world, enticing modern readers into passing judgment on the actions of those long dead. Thus, a thousand years later, it perpetuates the values of its original community, and gives even those who never fought at Maldon a kind of immortality. The judgment of the community is the essence of the poem's power and the reason for its creation.

Prayers for Cynewulf

The Battle of Maldon is atypical among Old English works in its unusually overt connection to a specific place and set of people. Cynewulf is atypical in a different way: the survival of his name. He might seem a quixotic focus for a study of the Anglo-Saxon poet, given that in the century and three quarters since the discovery of his runic acrostics, Cynewulf has become metonymous for the shoals on which all 'biographical' criticism of Old English verse must break.[86] The only salvaged facts about the poet himself are these:

1. Runic acrostics spelling out *CYNWULF* or *CYNEWULF* are attached to four poems, *Juliana* and *Christ II* in the Exeter Book, and *The Fates of the Apostles* and *Elene* in the Vercelli Book.[87]

2. Given the spelling of his name with a medial *E* (rather than *I*) and various features of the four poems, he is likely to have flourished after the eighth century in one of the Anglian dialectal regions. But there is no compelling reason to believe that the Cynewulf of the signatures is identical with any of the Cynewulves known to history.[88]

3. All the signed poems draw extensively upon Latin texts, mostly hagio-graphical but also homiletic or devotional.[89] Given what we know about literacy in Anglo-Saxon England, it is overwhelmingly likely that Cynewulf was educated within the church and maintained some official affiliation to it.

All else remains in flux, from the number and identity of the poems actually composed by 'Cynewulf', to their date, mode of composition, and literary merit.[90] The present study is not intended to settle any of these issues, though it will have most to say about the two last; instead, my concern is to explore how a unified group of poems is situated within a perceived community of readers and (perhaps) hearers. Our lack of a secure historical anchor for Cynewulf himself means that the nature of his community cannot be externally determined; we do not know whether his immediate audience was male or female, monastic, clerical, or lay. We can make no assumptions about the people who surrounded Cynewulf or the customs governing them. Nevertheless, the poems themselves reveal an abundance of techniques for reaching outwards, enlisting and anticipating the judg-ment of their audience, and these suggest a great deal about their author's experience, even if they reveal no concrete evidence of his identity. The poems also illuminate one of the most significant, yet problematic aspects of Anglo-Saxon literary culture: how written texts were incorporated into an originally oral mode of art. Cynewulf's works show us one poet's method for addressing a double audience: one seen, one unseen. For us, as modern readers, the circle of hearers who made up the first category are now merely an abstraction; but as part of the second group – the imagined readers of the written text – we can still belatedly enter the community Cynewulf envisioned. In doing so, we can catch glimpses of what these poems were and did for the Anglo-Saxons.

My primary focus will be the four signed poems: the device of the runic signature itself unifies them, and – as will become clear below – I believe they share striking similarities in tone, style, and motifs. All, in particular, show a preoccupation with judgment, both human and divine, and all reveal a sophisticated understanding of the dynamics of voice and techniques for audience engagement explored in the previous sections. In Cynewulf's verse, we see the art of a poet well practised in speaking to his community.

Judges and judged in the signed poems

Death is the end of a performance, as Hamlet knew; given how often Old English poems conjoined the end of a poem with the end of life, they must have felt that the converse was also true – that the end of a performance was a kind of death. Beowulf's funeral is only one example of this mode of conclusion: *Exodus* ends with the stripping of the Egyptians' corpses, *Judith* with its heroine's peaceful passing; *Maxims II* concludes with the unfathomable mystery of the departure from this life, while *The Seafarer* reminds its audience of the life to come. The silence after the final word must have seemed like that of the grave.

Cynewulf's insistent return to postmortem judgment in each of his epilogues is therefore in keeping with a strong current in Old English literature. But what gives his version of this motif its peculiar power is the way he fuses the universal nature of mortality with the specific and personal. The runic acrostics speak at one level of a generic Anyman preparing for judgment, but with thought and interpretation they reveal a particular individual who has composed a particular poem. In the process of discovering Cynewulf's name, the audience is prompted to enter into a reciprocal relationship with the poem and its creator, and to assist him in his task.

This dynamic is perhaps clearest in the shortest of the poems, *The Fates of the Apostles*. Damaged as the conclusion is,[91] it is readable enough to demonstrate how Cynewulf links judgment of the poem with divine judgment:

> Nu ic þonne bidde   beorn se ðe lufige
> þysses giddes begang   þæt he geomrum me
> þone halgan heap   helpe bidde,

friðes ond fultomes.   Hu, ic freonda beþearf
liðra on lade,   þonne ic sceal langne ham,
eardwic uncuð,   ana gesecan,
lætan me on laste   lic, eorðan dæl,
wælreaf wunigean   weormum to hroðre.[92]

> Now therefore I beseech the man who loves the course of this song, that he
> beseech for me in my sorrow the help of that holy troop, their protection and
> comfort. Indeed, I have need of kind friends upon the deep, when I must
> venture alone to my long home, the unknown country, leaving behind me in
> my track my body, earth's share, plunder remaining as a consolation for the
> worms.

In this first section, the first person speaker is figured as a solitary, sorrowful
wanderer, in contrast to the apostles (*þone halgan heap*) and their implicit
ally the sympathetic audience member – the *beorn se ðe lufige / þysses giddes
begang*. The poet speaks to the *beorn* with the same verb with which the
saints are to be beseeched in turn (*bidde*, 88a, 90b), constructing a chain of
clientage with the audience in the centre.[93] The statement that *ic freonda
beþearf / liðra on lade* thus encompasses both requests; the 'kind friends'
the poet needs include the audience, as well as the apostles. The image of
death, on the other hand, is emphatically solitary, with stress on *ana*, and a
reflexive pronoun in 94a. But the emphasis is shifted from body back to
poem as the anagram itself (FWULCYN) is embedded in an elegiac passage
continuing the theme of the speaker's impending death; by dissolving his
name into individual letters, the poet associates himself even more strongly
with human mortality (96–106). The runic sequence is bracketed by two
promises to reveal the poet's name. The first is stated impersonally, to an
appreciator of poetry who is *forepances gleaw* – a flattering description for
any critic. After the last rune, the audience is again addressed, as *ðu* (105b).
The second person singular constructs an intimacy between speaker and
audience of the sort we saw in *The Dream of the Rood*; it also, I think, implies
a *reading* audience, a solitary interpreter alone with the text.[94] And, having
established this intimacy, 'Cynwulf' goes on to a personal request:

Sie þæs gemyndig,   mann se ðe lufige
þisses galdres begang,   þæt he geoce me
ond frofre fricle.   Ic sceall feor heonan,
an elles forð,   eardes neosan,
sið asettan,   nat ic sylfa hwær,
of þisse worulde.   Wic sindon uncuð,
eard ond eðel,   swa bið ælcum menn
nemþe he godcundes   gastes bruce.[95]

May the man who loves the course of this chant remember this, so that he may help me and provide comfort. I must go far from here, alone into foreign lands, seeking out a country and setting a course to a place I myself do not know: outside this world. The dwelling-places are unknown, the country and homeland, and it must be so for every man, unless he partake of a divine spirit.

In his plea for prayers under his own name, 'Cynwulf' constructs the reader as his spiritual patron, one capable of providing the postmortem 'help' and 'comfort' expected of a kinsman or a kindly disposed saint. Intercessory prayer thus becomes a direct result of literary interpretation, since the reader must have both deciphered the runic anagram and 'loved the song's course'. The reflections on the journey of death to which the speaker proceeds (in terms very similar to lines 88–95) magnify the value of the reader's prayers by re-emphasizing Cynewulf's solitude (110a) and the blank totality of his ignorance of the world to come. But by moving outwards to a general statement connecting his lack of knowledge to the condition of mankind (112b–14), the speaker prepares the way for a turn to an inclusive plural at the poem's end (115–22). By joining the reader with himself in the first person plural, Cynewulf reminds the reader that both of them are subject to God's judgment and in need of prayer as a means of reaching heaven. As a fellow object of judgment, the reader is thus made even more integral to the poet's enterprise; he becomes part of a cycle of prayer which must extend beyond the death of both. But the final lines of *Fates* obliquely reaffirm the independent power of the poem. *Nu a* (120b, 'now forever') connects the immediate time of the poem's end with eternity, and each reading of the poem brings a new moment into the sphere of God's timelessness. God's praise and glory may exist independently of the poem, but they also exist *through* the poem, and the use of *nu* brings to the forefront the participation of *The Fates of the Apostles* in the eternal praise of the Creator. The poem thus makes itself immortal; and the reader in turn has been transformed from the poet's judge into a witness to the work's transfiguration.

Cynewulf's other signatures also feature this fusion of submission to individual judgment with faith in the immortality of poetry, but where each differs is in the role of the readership in the approach to judgment. *Elene*, perhaps the most famous of the four, is unique in that readers' prayers seem to have no direct effect. The poem culminates in an extended Last Judgment scene describing the threefold division of humanity within the purgatorial flame of judgment.[96] Those not irrevocably damned will be

asundrod fram synnum,   swa smæte gold
þæt in wylme bið   womma gehwylces
þurh ofnes fyr   eall geclænsod,
amered ond gemylted.   Swa bið þara manna ælc
ascyred ond asceaden   scylda gehwylcre,
deopra firena,   þurh þæs domes fyr.[97]

parted from sins, like the smelted gold that through the oven's fire is entirely
cleansed in flame of all impurities, refined and melted. In the same way, each
of those men will be scoured and cleansed of every sin, of deep-rooted crimes,
through the fire of judgment.

Yet salvation is promised for those who prayed to their Saviour:

Him bið engla weard
milde ond bliðe,   þæs ðe hie mana gehwylc
forsawon, synna weorc,   ond to suna metudes
wordum cleopodon.   Forðan hie nu on wlite scinaþ
englum gelice,   yrfes brucað
wuldorcyninges   to widan feore. Amen.[98]

The guardian of angels will be kindly and gracious to them, for they despised
all crimes, the deeds of sin, and cried out with words to the son of the
Creator. Therefore they now shine in glory like the angels, and partake of the
inheritance of the King of glory forever. Amen.

In the epilogue to *Elene*, judgment is a process of purification whereby all
faults are purged, leaving perfection. It is impersonal in the sense that the
divine is indifferent to worldly status; not coincidentally, the sole acknowledgement of the audience in *Elene* is the first person plural *ure*, a homonym
for the name of the runic letter U.[99] There is no hint of intercession here, as
there was in *Fates*, but the saved are those who 'to suna metudes / wordum
cleopodon'. The efficacy of words recalls the epilogue's beginning:

Þus ic frod ond fus   þurh þæt fæcne hus
wordcræftum wæf   ond wundrum læs . . .[100]

Thus I, old and eager to depart because of that treacherous house [the body],
wove with word-craft and gathered miracles . . .

The poem's last words, then, offer a reminder that poetry like *Elene* is an act
of prayer, and that prayer saves despite the inevitability of judgment. But
the poet seems alone, and his state of darkness alleviated only by his reading
about the Cross.

The companionship – and judgment – given by books is a theme I will
return to below. First I would point out the contrast the stark and

uncompromising judgment in *Elene* presents to the social, supportive judgments in *Fates* and also in *Juliana*. As we saw above, in *The Fates of the Apostles* 'Cynwulf' invests his readers' literary opinion of his poem with salvific power, even as he reminds them subtly that they too must undergo judgment. At the end of *Juliana* – a poem about judgment, just and unjust – the speaker takes an even more emphatically submissive position towards his readers:

> Bidde ic monna gehwone
> gumena cynnes,   þe þis gied wræce,
> þæt he mec neodful   bi noman minum
> gemyne modig,   ond meotud bidde
> þæt me heofona helm   helpe gefremme,
> meahta waldend,   on þam miclan dæge,
> fæder, frofre gæst,   in þa frecnan tid,
> dæda demend,   ond se deora sunu,
> þonne seo þrynis   þrymsittende
> in annesse   ælda cynne
> þurh þa sciran gesceaft   scrifeð bi gewyrhtum
> meorde monna gehwam.[101]

I beseech every man of the kin of humankind, whosoever might recount this poem, that he, magnanimous, might remember me in my need by my name, and might beseech the Creator that the guardian of heaven, the ruler of powers, might provide me aid on the great day in the time of peril: Father and Holy Ghost, and the beloved Son, the Judge of deeds, when the undivided Trinity, enthroned in might, through the glorious decree allots rewards to the kin of humans, to every man, according to their works.

The power of judgment is still reserved to God, but the poet petitions his *modig* reader in the same terms that this reader is asked to petition the Creator for help on the Day of Judgment. The reader, in fact, is made a kind of co-creator. Normally in Old English verse, the subject of the phrase *gied wrecan* is the author of the poem.[102] Here, however, the subjunctive form of *wrecan* makes *monna gehwone* the more logical, as well as the closest referent, though the indeclinable *þe* leaves open the possibility that *ic* – as manifested in the mysterious rune clusters – is also a subject. In other words, the first line and a half mean both 'I (who would have made this poem) beseech every man of the kin of humankind' and 'I beseech every man of the kin of humankind who might recount this poem.' Creation and perpetuation are collapsed into a single act, both of which are acknowledged through intercessory prayer. In the poem's final lines, Cynewulf preemptively reciprocates those prayers:

> Forgif us, mægna god,
> þæt we þine onsyne, æþelinga wyn,
> milde gemeten on þa mæran tid. Amen.[103]

Grant us, God of powers, joy of princes, that we might encounter your gracious countenance at that great time. Amen.

The end of *Juliana*, then, constructs the reader both as an intercessor almost on a par with St Juliana – whose help is besought just before – and as a stand-in for Cynewulf himself.[104] The result is a curious reflexivity. The reader *þe þis gied wræce* has assumed a kind of responsibility for the poem, as well as for Cynewulf's spiritual welfare, and in the final *we* he is joined with the poet *on þa mæran tid*. The reader has thus become the object, rather than the subject, of judgment.

By this point in the poem, judgment has already been invested with crucial power. In the second line, *deman* is used as a synonym for 'recount', conflating the act of judgment with that of narration. The central conflict between Juliana and her oppressors – her father Affricanus, and the prefect Heliseus, her suitor – is figured initially as a problem of flawed individual judgment. Once Juliana refuses to marry the pagan Heliseus, her father reproaches her as foolish, self-willed, and rash:

> Þu on geaþe hafast,
> þurh þin orlegu, unbiþyrfe
> ofer witena dom wisan gefongen;
> wiðsæcest þu to swiðe sylfre rædes
> þinum brydguman . . .[105]

Through your hostility you have foolishly and unprofitably chosen a path contrary to the judgment of wise people; on your own counsel, you too hastily alienate your bridegroom . . .

Affricanus supports his position with assertions of expediency and threats of force. Juliana, however, is adamant:

> Ic þe to soðe secgan wille,
> bi me lifgendre nelle ic lyge fremman:
> næfre ic me ondræde domas þine,
> ne me weorce sind witebrogan,
> hildewoman, þe þu hæstlice,
> manfremmende, to me beotast,
> ne þu næfre gedest þurh gedwolan þinne
> þæt þu mec acyrre from Cristes lof.[106]

I will tell you the truth – as I live, I will not tolerate lies: I will never fear your judgments, nor are the terrors, the torments that you rashly, wickedly boast of to me distressing to me; nor shall you ever, through your folly, cause it to be that you draw me away from the worship of Christ.

Both father and daughter accuse each other of folly, though while Affricanus appeals to the wisdom of the community,[107] Juliana's replies are reiterations of personal conviction. Her rightness would likely be taken for granted by the poem's audience, obviating the need for elaborate arguments; but even within the poem, the justice of her cause is publicly vindicated by her survival of ordeals (lines 559–94).[108] It is the judge whose judgment is destroyed, for instead of acknowledging the clear proofs that Juliana was in the right, Heliseus 'wedde on gewitte swa wilde deor' ('raged in his mind like a wild beast', 597). Although as it survives the poem contains no dramatized conversions, her address to the heathen spectators before her execution appears to have been effective, because she is buried by 'micle mægne' ('a great host', 690a).[109]

In *Juliana*, then, judgment is a question of recognition: of seeing and adhering to truth. The result of this is an interestingly ambiguous picture of the individual's relation to the community. In the first part of the poem, Juliana's isolation in her adherence to the truth of Christianity, combined with her father's attempt to sway her by appealing to the 'judgment of wise men' (98a), would seem to portray the wider group as concerned mainly with preserving the status quo, and thus an obstacle to anyone seeking to find and present unheard-of truths. But Affricanus' dialogue makes clear that his real interest is *his* interest, and that his appeal to tradition is opportunistic. Moreover, when Juliana wrings a confession from the devil sent to mislead her, she learns that human error is grounded in malicious deceit – deceit to which people have been wrong to yield, no doubt, but which was unfairly practised upon them. The result is a partial exculpation of the heathen community, which proves the essential soundness of its judgment by recognizing Juliana's righteousness, heeding her words, and venerating her as a saint after her death.

Yet the poem's early picture of Juliana standing alone against the forces seeking her destruction is not entirely effaced by the triumphant conclusion. The poet's self-alignment with the saint in 695–6 and 717–19 seems to reflect an understanding of communal judgment which is simultaneously optimistic and defensive. It is optimistic in the sense that the poet trusts that the reader will appreciate the truth in his poem and act as his supporter after his death, much as Juliana's townspeople did for her; that through readers' just interpretation of his poem he will be justified, as she was by public ordeal. But the poem's attitude is also defensive, in that the wider community is imagined as always potentially hostile, and the strategies for managing its judgment are subtly coercive. First, *mis*judgment is not constructed as honest error; indeed, there is no honest error in the world of *Juliana*, for all such failure to recognize the truth stems from demonic promptings, and manifests itself as Affricanus' heartless venality, or Heliseus' bestial indifference to justice. Moreover, while the readership is invited to enter into solidarity with the poet, and to identify with the right-thinking Nicomedeans who venerated Juliana, its members are reminded in the poem's last lines that they too must be subject to God's judgment, and will require the same postmortem aid. Condemnation of the poem would seem to leave them in the company of the ruthless and unjust judge Heliseus and his followers, drowned and damned.

Scenes of judgment in Cynewulf's signed poems draw upon longstanding themes, but they are far from conventional gestures. Such instances are central to his strategy for interacting with his community. Particularly in the visions of postmortem judgment with which he concludes his poems, Cynewulf uses the idea of his own danger to bring his audience into solidarity with him. The device of the runes entices the readership to invest their energies in recalling Cynewulf's name from oblivion, while his studied control of personal pronouns shows a variety of methods for harnessing those readers' sympathies: often by yoking his own fate to theirs in the first person plural, but inevitably by reminding them that judgment comes to all. The result is an implied audience whose power the poet simultaneously desires, respects, and resents. It is, moreover, a perpetually present audience, one with a constant capacity to help (through prayer, appreciation, and recognition) or hurt (through scorn or neglect). Though his use of runes indicates his expectation of a readership, Cynewulf seemingly still imagines those readers engaging directly with *him*, rather than with an inanimate page. His community may include people whom he will never see, but he still composes for and with them.

'Us secgað bec': the companionship of books

Not just the books he composed, but also those he read, seem to have presented themselves to Cynewulf's imagination as active and embodied figures. In *Fates*, phrases like 'Hwæt, we þæt gehyrdon þurg halige bec' ('Lo, we have heard it from holy books', 63) present Latin literacy as essentially continuous with the oral tradition. The line is a close echo of an earlier invocation of sources:

Hwæt, we eac gehyrdon   be Iohanne
æglæawe menn   æðelo reccan![110]

Lo, we have likewise heard law-learned men recount a noble genealogy for John.

It is impossible to tell whether these 'law-learned men' are to be envisioned as recounting John's descent physically, or by means of books: perhaps there is no difference. The verb *gehyran* is common, and very often used as a marker of oral discourse, as in *Beowulf*'s 'ne gehyrde ic cymlicor ceol gegyrwed' ('I never heard of a ship adorned more beautifully', 38) or

welhwylc gecwæð
þæt he fram Sigemundes   secgan hyrde
ellendædum . . .[111]

He recounted most everything that he had heard tell about Sigemund's brave deeds . . .

Shared knowledge is crucial to any oral tradition, and Old English poetry is rich in phrases to invoke both such knowledge and the poet's reliance on it.[112] In Cynewulf's verse, books enter easily into this discourse of hearing and reporting; they seem foreign neither in language nor technology, and speak their parts as intelligibly as men.

In *Elene*, the boundary between human and book is disconcertingly permeable, though the poem's frequent invocation of books as authorities – particularly during Queen Elene's dispute with Judas – has perhaps led some scholars to perceive a greater divide between text and speech than actually exists within *this* text. The core of this apparent polarity is located in lines 627–84. Judas, threatened with death but intent on not divulging the secret of the Cross, denies the possibility of knowing the distant past:

Hu mæg ic þæt findan   þæt swa fyrn gewearð
wintra gangum?   Is nu worn sceacen,
CC oððe ma   geteled rime . . .
    Ic ne can þæt ic nat,
findan on fyrhðe   þæt swa fyrn gewearð.[113]

How can I discover that which has become so long ago with the passing years? Many have now passed, two hundred or more all told. . . . I cannot discover in my heart that which I do not know, that which happened so long ago.

Elene counters with the example of the Trojan War, which Judas' people 'geare cunnon' ('know well', 648b) since its events are things 'on gewritu setton' ('they set in writings', 654b). This Judas concedes, but adds that the Crucifixion is a different case, since

> We . . .
>   þis næfre
>   þurh æniges mannes   muð gehyrdon
>   hæleðum cyðan,   butan her nu ða.[114]

We never heard this made known to men through any man's mouth, except for those things here just now.

From this conflict, Schaefer speculates that *Elene* might be 'the depiction of the fight between two concurring modes of tradition, one oral (here depicted as 'heathen'), the other written (here shown as the only correct one, Christian)'.[115]

Such a reading, however, not only flattens the terms of Elene and Judas' immediate debate, but it neglects the close kinship between the acts of books and of people within the world of the poem. In the queen's response to Judas' denial, for instance, she conflates both kinds of source:

> Hwæt, we þæt hyrdon   þurh halige bec
> hæleðum cyðan   þæt ahangen wæs
> on Caluarie   cyninges freobearn,
> godes gastsunu.   Þu scealt geagninga
> wisdom onwreon,   swa gewritu secgaþ,
> æfter stedewange   hwær seo stow sie . . .[116]

Lo, we have heard it made known to men through holy books that the king's noble child, God's spiritual son, was hanged on Calvary. You will immediately reveal the knowledge, as the writings say, where through the land that place might be . . .

Lines 670–1a closely echo Judas' words, giving them the lie by suggesting that the *halige bec* are, in effect, *mannes muð*. Judas is not adhering stubbornly to an imperfect oral tradition; he is dissembling, and Elene's response is twofold. She first denies his facts (662–6) and then denies his distinction. Judas' implication in 656–61 is that an oral report must precede a written record, and he has neither; Elene's reply is that *she* knows *him* to possess one or both, and that moreover he knows there is no difference between the two. If the queen's intention were to assert the superiority of the written over the oral, she would not be interrogating Judas, but rather demanding that he produce his book. For her, however, the two are functionally identical: 'Þu scealt geagnunga / wisdom onwreon, swa gewritu secgaþ . . .'

Elene's immediate sources here happen to be books, but that does not make them intrinsically superior to people, either as informants or as guides for conduct. Just as Constantine earlier learned of the meaning of the Cross and the mysteries of the faith from Pope Sylvester's disciples (189–91), Elene's first action in the Holy Land is to seek out wise men capable of finding out the Cross. Her eventual source, Judas, is the offspring of a curiously textual family: which is to say, his father and brother exist mainly via stylized narrative. The Christian instruction by the dying Symon takes place, we are told, 'þurh leoðorune' (522b). This *hapax legomenon* seems to mean 'mysteries told in verse', though 'bodily mysteries' (alluding, perhaps, to the martyrdom of Stephen and the conversion of Paul) might also suit the context. Judas reveals his father's deathbed confidence with an odd paradox. It must be kept private, he tells his comrades,

> þy læs toworpen sien
> frod fyrngewritu   ond þa fæderlican
> lare forleten.   Ne bið lang ofer ðæt
> þæt Israhela   æðelu moten
> ofer middangeard   ma ricsian,
> æcræft eorla,   gif ðis yppe bið,
> swa þa þæt ilce gio   min yldra fæder
> sigerof sægde,   (þam wæs Sachius nama),
> frod fyrnwiota,   fæder minum . . .[117]

lest the aged ancient writings be broken and the teachings of our fathers be lost. If this becomes known, it will not be much longer that the descendants of the Israelites can rule longer over the world, or the law-learning of men, which is the very thing that my grandfather, a bold man (called Sachius) said, an aged ancient wise man, to my father . . .

Here Judas dramatizes a crucial irony in *Elene*. By privileging books over people – honouring the *frod fyrngewritu* over the *frod fyrnwiota* – he is guilty of the very crime he is trying to avoid: abandoning the fathers' teachings. By ignoring the *leoðorune* of his father and attempting to defy the prophecy of his grandfather, he shows that he imagines the authority of the past to be essentially disembodied, unconnected to present people and events. This is consistent with Anglo-Saxons' inherited construction of the Jews as people who clung to the letter of the Law, and refused to acknowledge its fulfilment in the incarnate Word.[118] Tellingly, therefore, Judas' conversion is accompanied by a fusion of man and book. In his prayer of thanks for the revelation of the Cross, he asks:

> Læt mec, mihta god,
> on rimtale   rices þines
> mid haligra   hlyte wunigan
> in þære beohrtan byrig,   þær is broðor min
> geweorðod in wuldre,   þæs he wære wið þec,
> Stephanus, heold,   þeah he stangreopum
> worpod wære.   He hafað wigges lean,
> blæd butan blinne.   Sint in bocum his
> wundor þa he worhte   on gewritum cyðed.[119]

Permit me, God of powers, to dwell in the number of your kingdom amid the portion of the saints in the bright city, where my brother is honoured in glory, since Stephen kept faith with you although he was crushed with stones. He has the reward of his victory, unceasing glory. In books his miracles, which he performed, are made known in writing.

The division between Stephen's unceasing glory in heaven and the immortality conferred by the textual recording of his miracles is entirely editorial.[120] For Judas, the two are contiguous, and the firm conviction of his brother's sanctity expressed here seems to stem from these writings as much as from his father's testimony. With this prayer, he shows that he has ceased to divide books from people.

Understanding this essential unity between written and spoken witness helps clarify many of the deeper assumptions of Cynewulf's verse. We have already seen how, in the *The Fates of the Apostles*, Cynewulf describes the testimony of books and people in the same terms; much of the strangeness of *Christ II* is also explained by the recognition that a book is no less direct a mode of witness than speech. The beginning of the poem, for instance, is addressed to 'ðu ... / mon se mæra' (440–1a, 'you, O renowned man'). George Hardin Brown has plausibly explained this as an invocation of Luke's Gospel.[121] The evangelist's voice, harmonized with those of Gregory and Cynewulf himself, creates a chorus in which the *bec* and *gewritu* of the first two speak through the Old English *boc* before *mon se mæra*.[122] They are also part of the dissemination of the Word invoked in the passage on the Great Commandment which Cynewulf added to his source material (lines 476–90): Luke as one of the evangelists of the gentiles; Gregory as apostle of the English (whose own influence was conveyed to his new flock through his books and his messengers); and Cynewulf himself, as creator of a poem of instruction and admonition. And just as Cynewulf fears judgment

> ðonne eft cymeð   engla þeoden,
> þe ic ne heold teala   þæt me hælend min
> on bocum bibead[123]

when the Prince of angels shall return, for I have not properly upheld what
my Saviour commanded me in books

he urges his readers (whom he exhorts as *us* in the conclusion) to save
themselves by affixing their hopes to Christ – by attending, in other words,
to what books say to them.

Books – whether in Latin or Old English – are for Cynewulf not inert
troves of words long since spoken; they remain active agents in the lives of
anyone who chooses to listen to them. To consider Cynewulf's poems
'written' rather than 'oral' is thus perhaps in one sense true, but also invokes
a set of assumptions that the poet himself evidently did not share. The
widespread association between writing and death, in other words, is not
the only or inevitable model of the relationship among author, book, and
audience. When Ricoeur wrote that 'to read a book is to consider its author
as already dead and the book as posthumous', he was extending an ancient
trope, in which books are cenotaphs and letters themselves are dead.[124]
This idea unquestionably had some valence in Anglo-Saxon England, as
Katherine O'Brien O'Keeffe has shown.[125] What Cynewulf shows us,
though, is that an Anglo-Saxon author need not consider himself condemned
to a twilit half-life through the medium of his work; indeed, Cynewulf's work
is not altogether a *medium*, but rather an alternative embodiment. Ricoeur's
sense that 'when we happen to encounter an author and to speak to him
(about his book, for example), we experience a profound disruption of the
peculiar relation that we have with the author in and through his work' would
have puzzled him.[126]

Cynewulf's sense of constant companionship in and through books was
not, I think, unique. Certainly other Old English poets considered it
possible to incarnate narrative. In *The Dream of the Rood*, for instance, the
narrator upends the entire notion of solitude with a single repeated phrase:
after the Cross of his vision has ceased to speak, he says,

> Gebæd ic me þa to þan beame   bliðe mode,
> elne micle,   þær ic ana wæs
> mæte werede.[127]

Then I prayed to the Cross with a joyful heart, with great zeal, there where I
was alone with a small troop.

The phrase that appears to be an exact variation upon *ana, mæte werede*, in
fact subverts it altogether, for we have encountered these words before, in
the Cross's narrative. When Christ's disciples have buried him and returned
home grieving,

> Reste he ðær mæte weorode.
> Hwæðere we ðær greotende   gode hwile
> stodon on staðole,   syððan stefn up gewat
> hilderinca.[128]

> He rested there with a small troop. But we stood there in that place for a good
> while, mourning, after the warriors' voice had departed upward.

While Christ appears to be alone, he is not; the Cross is with him, as it is
with the narrator when he prays *mæte werede*.[129] Absolute solitude, in short,
is impossible for the believer who understands the Cross's self-explication.
The same is true for Cynewulf: when he invokes the topos of composition
by night in his rhymed coda to *Elene*, he strips this convention of the
element of solitude which, in its Latin form, was essential, but which for
him had been removed through the *bocum* and *gewritum* (1254b, 1255b).[130]
For him, as for the poet of *The Dream of the Rood*, apparently inanimate
objects are living and ever-present companions endowed with the ability to
speak to, and advocate for, those who heed them.

Last words

When Cynewulf invokes the inevitability of death and judgment, he does so
in the knowledge that both take many forms. All people die and come to
God's judgment, to live or die again forever. And though an author might
live on through his books, he must still be continually subject to judgment
of another kind, by the people to whom he speaks. Yet a receptive audience
will gain in those books the gift of companionship: of advice and advocacy
to help them pass through their own judgment to come. Books and people
thus join together in a single community.

Cynewulf's dependence on his written sources, then, is less an act of
fealty than of friendship. They speak to him, and he tells his own readers of
the remarkable things they have said. Latin texts, with this introduction,
enter the English-speaking world as equals, not dictators. As for Cynewulf's
poems, they are equipped to hold their own in any company, and – like any
polite guest – will introduce themselves by name. Through his works, we
can enter into a community in which the distinction between writer and
speaker, and hearer and reader, was effectively null. How long, and how
widely, such a situation existed is hard to know. What Cynewulf shows us,
however, is yet another instance in which the habits of thought of an
oral culture – in which communication without personal proximity was
unthinkable – coexisted with written discourse. In this case, the idea that

books were, effectively, people, may have strengthened poets by allowing them to envision the world of manuscripts and their writers and readers as a community like their own, but extended across time and space. The use of writing, far from silencing Old English poets, allowed them to speak to anyone willing to listen to the voices of books.

Aldhelm's connections

So far in this chapter, I have dealt mainly with lost social groups: communities whose members are now unknown to us. But when we can reconstruct even part of an individual's social network, the imprint of the community's judgment becomes much clearer. A reconstructed network provides the skeleton around which to fit the skin of criticism: the result is not a substitute for the living organism, but nevertheless is capable of providing insight into its life functions. In this section, I use Aldhelm of Malmesbury as a test case. Because of the great quantity of recent work on his life and writings and his authoritative status among contemporaries and successors, Aldhelm is a perfect zero point for seventh-century literary-social networks. The pervasiveness of his influence on later Anglo-Latin verse has been thoroughly demonstrated, particularly by Michael Lapidge and Andy Orchard.[131] It is clear that Aldhelm's fame as a *littérateur* had spread beyond England during his lifetime, and indeed before his elevation to Sherborne's bishopric: the Irish monk Cellanus of Péronne, for instance, addressed him as *archimandrita* ('abbot') when requesting books.[132] Moreover, almost every Anglo-Latin poet in the eighth century read, and to some degree imitated, Aldhelm; his writings were known in Mercia and Northumbria as well as the southern kingdoms. What I hope to show here is how Aldhelm's connections can help explain how his verse became paradigmatic for others so quickly and persistently.

Knowledge of Aldhelm's life is based on a limited set of sources. Bede introduced him into the *Historia ecclesiastica* in Book v, at 705 when the bishopric of Wessex was divided and Aldhelm was appointed to the newly created see of Sherborne after many years as abbot of Malmesbury. In the précis he gave of Aldhelm's qualifications, Bede drew particular attention to the *Epistola ad Geruntium* and the *opus geminatum* on virginity.[133] Bede's brief account remained authoritative; while a book relating Aldhelm's life and miracles supposedly existed in the Anglo-Saxon period, it had been lost by the time Faricius of Arezzo and William of Malmesbury set out to compose lives of the saint in the late eleventh and early twelfth centuries.[134] William's account, though more dependent on Faricius than he cared to admit,[135] is much the more valuable of the two, since he includes a number of Aldhelm's letters which are otherwise unattested.[136] Other letters, along with poems in rhythmic octosyllables by Aldhelm and his student Æthilwald, are found only in the 'Codex Vindobonensis', a Continental manuscript associated with Boniface's mission.[137] Together these scattered witnesses permit the reconstruction of the general arc of Aldhelm's career, of which Michael Lapidge's is the most thorough and recent account.[138]

Drawing on these and other sources for seventh- and early eighth-century English culture, I examine three networks whose traces are still visible: the school of Theodore and Hadrian at Canterbury; Aldhelm's own school at Malmesbury; and the diffuse but densely interconnected world of seventh-century royalty. Each of these overlapping groups had different effects on the creation, dissemination, and absorption of Aldhelm's writings into the cultural world of early Anglo-Saxon England. Poetry was significant in cementing the bonds that held all these groups together, and my final case study will consider rhythmic octosyllables as a form of gift that helped to sustain social connections.

The mysteries of metre: Theodore, Hadrian, and the school at Canterbury

When Theodore of Tarsus arrived at Canterbury in 669, the southern Anglo-Saxon kingdoms had been without an archbishop for almost five years.[139] Along with his companion (and perhaps minder) Hadrian, who was appointed abbot of the monastery of SS Peter and Paul,[140] Theodore soon established in his new see a school which was – according to Bede – little short of paradise.[141] While recent research has revealed a good deal about the curriculum of the Canterbury school,[142] we can still be sure of only a few students' identities, mostly through the testimony of Bede. In the *Historia ecclesiastica*, he reports that Albinus, Hadrian's successor as abbot at Canterbury; Tobias, bishop of Rochester; and Oftfor, bishop of Worcester, all studied with Theodore, and he praises the immense learning they acquired from him.[143] Bede also relates an anecdote about John of Beverley, in which John mentions medical information which 'memini . . . beatae memoriae Theodorum archiepiscopum dicere'; Lapidge plausibly concludes that John had studied with Theodore as well.[144]

But though Bede does not mention it, Aldhelm, too, was a student at Canterbury, and his testimony has told us most about the non-biblical component of the curriculum there. Two surviving letters, one to Aldhelm's diocesan bishop and one to Abbot Hadrian, attest that Aldhelm spent time at the Canterbury school, though perhaps less than he wished.[145] The first of these letters indicates it was there that Aldhelm began to master the intricacies of quantitative metre. What seems to have excited him most about the discipline is its esoteric difficulty: he tells his bishop that he has been studying Roman law and

> quod his multo artius et perplexius est, centena scilicet metrorum genera pedestri regula discernere et ad musica cantilenae modulamina recto sillabarum tramite lustrare, cuius rei studiosis lectoribus tanto inextricabilior obscuritas praetenditur, quanto rarior doctorum numerositas reperitur.[146]

> what is far more difficult and convoluted than that, namely differentiating the hundred varieties of metre by the rules governing feet, and scanning the musical modulation of poems by the correct path of syllables – the more impenetrable this subject's obscurity becomes to dedicated readers, the smaller the number of teachers [*or*, those who have learned it].

The long list of metrical and rhetorical terms that follows shows how keenly Aldhelm wished to be one of these rare *docti*. He concludes it with the observation that

> Haec, ut reor, et his similia brevi temporis intercapidine momentaneoque ictu apprehendi nequaquam valebunt.[147]

> These and similar things, as I see it, will never be comprehended with short intervals of time or hasty glances.

Perhaps this was designed as a hint for more time at Canterbury. While it has previously been thought that Aldhelm could only have spent a brief period with Theodore and Hadrian – a couple of years in the 670s perhaps – before returning to Wessex to take up the abbacy of Malmesbury, Lapidge's recent redating of Aldhelm's appointment as abbot may allow for a much longer, if still interrupted, residence in Canterbury.[148] Aldhelm's undated letter to Hadrian indicates he had been forced to leave by illness and that ill health was still hindering his plans to return, but the fact of Aldhelm's authorship indicates that he did find time enough to master the *inextricabilis obscuritas* of quantitative metre, and his composition of a treatise on metre suggests that he wanted to increase the *doctorum numerositas*.

While Aldhelm's assertion of the esoteric nature of quantitative metre – and the difficulty of finding anyone competent in its mysteries – may have been self-glorifying, we have no reason to believe it was untrue. There is no evidence, in particular, that quantitative Latin verse was composed in Ireland at this time,[149] or written before Theodore's arrival at any of the northern English minsters founded under the influence of Irish missionaries.

This makes it plausible to begin with a hypothesis that Canterbury was the centre from which knowledge of, and enthusiasm for, composing quantitative Latin poetry first spread in Anglo-Saxon England.

If this hypothesis is correct, it suggests that another student may be added to our list of Canterbury alumni. In the anonymous *Vita Ceolfridi*, plausibly attributed to Bede, we are told that Ceolfrith, later abbot of Monkwearmouth-Jarrow,

> mox ordinatus ob studium discendi maxime uitae monasterialis et gradus, quem subierat, instituta, Cantiam petiit.[150]

> went to Kent as soon as he was ordained, out of eagerness for learning to the utmost about the monastic life and the institutes of the status which he had undertaken.

Brooks has suggested that Ceolfrith, therefore, may also have studied with Theodore.[151] Given Bede's closeness to the abbot and his great respect for the Canterbury school, it seems odd that he should not have mentioned his own teacher's connection with it, had such existed. It is possible, however, that silence in this case was politically expedient. Ceolfrith had been ordained by Wilfrid, and Theodore and Wilfrid came into conflict not long after the new archbishop's arrival in England. Yet we have testimony that Ceolfrith did go to Kent, and it is not at all implausible to think he may have joined Benedict Biscop, who after accompanying Theodore back from Rome was abbot *duobus annis* at SS. Peter and Paul, Canterbury, while Hadrian was delayed in Gaul.[152] If Ceolfrith studied with Theodore during this time, Bede might well have considered it best to elide the fact, so as to avoid presenting it as a partisan move.[153]

Ceolfrith, at any rate, is the only known or possible Canterbury alumnus besides Aldhelm to whom any surviving quantitative verse is attributed. In the *Vita Ceolfridi*, we are told that the pandects which the abbot presented as gifts to St Peter's at Rome were inscribed with these verses:

> Corpus ad eximii merito uenerabile Petri,
> Dedicat aecclesiae quem caput alta fides,
> Ceolfridus, Anglorum extremis de finibus abbas,
> Deuoti affectus pignora mitto mei.
> Meque meosque optans tanti inter gaudia patris
> In caelis memorem semper habere locum.[154]

> To the justly venerable body of the exalted Peter, whom lofty faith consecrates as head of the church, I Ceolfrith, abbot from the furthest borders of the Angles, send, out of love, tokens of my devotion, in the desire that I and mine might have a place eternally prepared in the heavens among the joys of the high father.

An altered version of the inscription survives in the Codex Amiatinus.[155] Although it is possible that this epigram was commissioned from someone else (say, Bede), there seems no strong reason to assume that these elegiac verses are not the work of Ceolfrith himself. The voice is insistently first person, and as the epigram was a favourite mode in early eighth-century England, the choice of form is plausible.

The metre is reasonably accomplished. There are four instances of elision, and none of hiatus. The only metrical licences are very common ones: short-ening the final syllable in *mittō* (line 4) and the medial *e* in *aecclēsiae* (2).[156] While the style is, for the most part, poles apart from Aldhelm's – the vocabulary is plain, and there is little alliteration – there are two significant points of similarity.[157] Ceolfrith's verse is extremely stichic; even within a couplet, each line forms a complete sense-unit. Aldhelm's quantitative verse shares the same quality, and Lapidge, who first pointed this out, hypothesized that 'The fact that nine out of ten lines in Aldhelm are end-stopped suggests that Aldhelm was able to think in terms of only one hexameter at a time. It is the mark of an inexperienced poet struggling to express himself in an unfamiliar medium.'[158] This explanation seems extremely likely. Very probably the end-stopping in Ceolfrith's epigram is due to the same cause: that he, like Aldhelm, was a 'first generation' poet, picking his way slowly across the rocky terrain of a quantitative line. The similarity, in other words, might be of situation rather than shared teaching. However, there is one other intriguing parallel between Ceolfrith's poem and Aldhelm's corpus. The scansion of the hexameter lines in the epigram can be described thus:[159]

DDDD
DSSS
DSSS

The first, entirely dactylic line displays a sort of metrical exuberance which Aldhelm rarely exhibits. The other two, however, conform precisely to Aldhelm's favourite metrical pattern – one which accounts for about 30 per cent of his hexameter lines.[160] Orchard has noted a marked preference for the DSSS pattern in a number of Anglo-Latin poets; but most of those can be proven to have been directly influenced by Aldhelm's work, which is not the case with Ceolfrith.[161] A six-line epigram is, of course, inconclusive as evidence of a poet's total metrical competence. But close analysis of Ceolfrith's epigram does not, at least, *preclude* the possibility that he and Aldhelm learned the art of verse in parallel, and developed some similar metrical tendencies while diverging in other aspects of their style.

Figure 3.1 maps the known or hypothesized Canterbury alumni across England: note that the kingdoms of Kent, Wessex, Mercia, and Northumbria

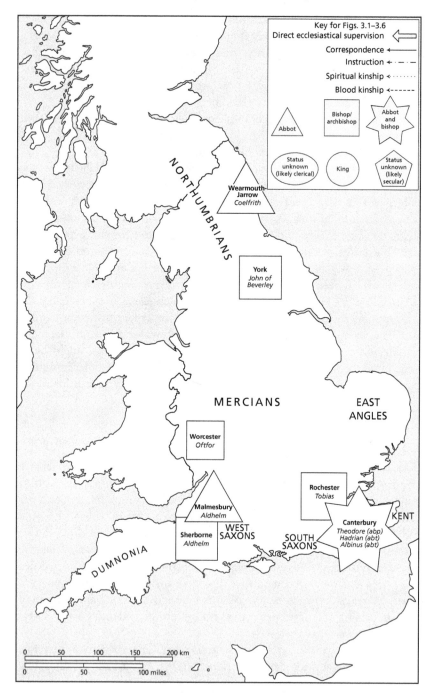

Figure 3.1 Map of Canterbury alumni

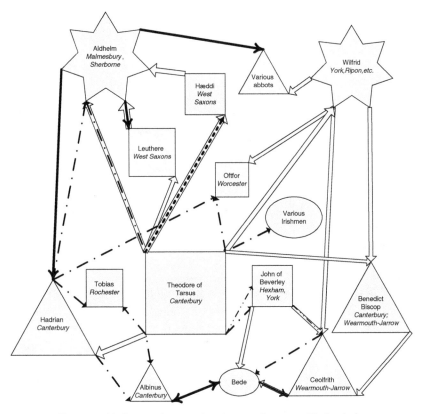

Figure 3.2 Ecclesiastical connections in seventh-century England: the
Canterbury school

are all represented. The fact that all these men were either bishops or abbots
of prestigious houses does not, I suspect, necessarily imply that Theodore
and Hadrian's school constituted 'a sort of Institute of Advanced Studies',[162]
but rather that we have only learned of their most distinguished pupils.
Figure 3.2 is an achronological illustration of the Canterbury school in the
ecclesiastical structure of its day, with a particular emphasis on mapping
Aldhelm's correspondence with members of the church hierarchy. Wilfrid's
relative importance in this network is interesting, though in part simply
reflective of his great power in late seventh-century church affairs. He and
Aldhelm seem to have had no direct correspondence, and there is no record of
their meeting, yet they are linked indirectly via a considerable number of
individuals. This indirect connection may explain some of the peculiarities
of Wilfrid's epitaph.

The epitaph, a twenty-line poem in hexameters, was recorded by Bede and apparently inscribed on the bishop's tomb at Ripon, and must thus have been composed between 711 and 734.[163] Nothing is known of its author, though the detail he devotes to Wilfrid's gifts to Ripon suggests he was a monk there. The metre of the poem is generally quite good;[164] it is notable for its accomplished use of elision – thirteen instances in twenty lines. The author seems to have deliberately worked towards metrical variety, since only one pair of consecutive lines shows the same metrical patterning. These – in lines 18 and 19 – immediately precede the poem's only verse with four consecutive spondees:

> Dona, Iesu, ut grex pastoris calle sequatur.[165]

The choice of a spondaic pattern in the epitaph's final, solemn prayer shows a sensitivity to the affective possibilities of quantitative metre that is extremely rare in Anglo-Latin verse. Aldhelm's poetry exhibits nothing like it. Yet, oddly enough, the epitaph is also permeated by Aldhelmian diction, and makes frequent use of a 'detachable' cadence – dieresis before the two final feet – which was a favourite technique of Aldhelm's when assembling a hexameter.[166] I note exact parallels with Aldhelm's *Carmina ecclesiastica* and *Enigmata*, and some less precise echoes of the *Carmen de uirginitate*; I suspect the author of Wilfrid's epitaph may have also used the word-lists in the *De pedum regulis*.[167] The use of cadences in particular indicates that Aldhelm's style is not merely a veneer pasted over a fundamentally differ-ent mode of versification. One might instead call this unknown poet's style essentially second generation: the offspring of Aldhelm's teaching and that of another master with a greater fondness for dactyls and a better understanding of elision. The characteristics of Wilfrid's epitaph, in other words, strongly suggest that Aldhelm could not have been the only Anglo-Saxon of his generation to conquer the mysteries of metre. It seems likely that his peers were also alumni of the Canterbury school, but it is now impossible to be sure.

Even with limited information, then, the network map of Theodore and Hadrian's school shows how the complex interconnections of the early Anglo-Saxon church enabled the teaching of two men to spread across the whole of England in a relatively short period of time. Despite differences of dialect and the probable difficulties of travel in the seventh century, we can see that individuals in different kingdoms had considerable intellectual contact: it is possible, therefore, to speak of an 'Anglo-Saxon literary culture'. The dispersal of Canterbury pupils throughout England may or may not have been a deliberate policy. As the next section indicates, however, it seems to have been consonant with educational practices in other parts of early northwest Europe, and it unquestionably helped perpetuate the teachings of Theodore and Hadrian for several generations.

The foster-children of wisdom: the disciples of Aldhelm and others

Abbot Hadrian outlived Theodore by nineteen years, and after his death in 709 was succeeded by Albinus, who had been at the abbey long enough to have studied with Theodore. How long Hadrian maintained the school at Canterbury after the great archbishop's death is difficult to say; even less clear is how or whether Albinus carried on his masters' teaching. In the preface to his *Historia ecclesiastica*, Bede speaks highly of Nothelm, a London priest who has brought letters and *viva voce* information to Northumbria from Albinus at Canterbury. It seems reasonable to infer from this that Nothelm was Albinus' protégé, and, probably, student: Nothelm went on to be archbishop of Canterbury from 735–9, so we must assume he was a man of education and ability. We know nothing, however, of his literary production, or whether metre was still taught at Canterbury.

Yet it must have still been possible to learn to compose quantitative verse in England after Theodore's death. By the second quarter of the eighth century, several Anglo-Latin poets can be identified, although their antecedents are often quite obscure. Bede is unquestionably the most distinguished of these, but his peculiar circumstances will be discussed in the next chapter.[168] Through Bede we know that Tætwine – Nothelm's predecessor – was elevated to the archbishopric of Canterbury from the monastery of Breedon-on-the-Hill in Mercia: but it is unclear where Tætwine was actually educated.[169] It has occasionally been speculated that he had studied in Canterbury before coming there as archbishop, but there is no external evidence to support this. He had access to Aldhelm's work, and to a reasonably good assortment of Late Antique grammarians,[170] but his library resources need not have been extensive. There were undoubtedly opportunities for learning Latin in the Midlands in the early eighth century; Oftfor, a Canterbury school alumnus, was bishop of the *Hwicce* at Worcester for about three years after Theodore's death, and Patrick Sims-Williams presents considerable evidence for Latin scholarship in the dioceses of Hereford and Worcester through the mid-eighth century.[171] Tætwine might have learned his art in any of a number of places, from teachers whose names may not have been preserved; his accomplishments, though, show that by the early eighth century Anglo-Saxon England had an educational tradition that included Latin verse.

Aldhelm's school at Malmesbury, therefore, may have been only one among many. Since it is one of the very few seventh-century monasteries for which we can identify a teacher, his pupils, and some literary productions

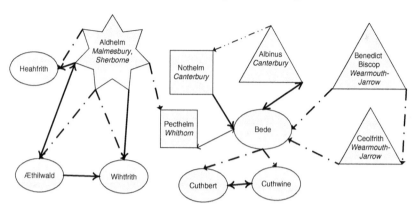

Figure 3.3 School networks (Malmesbury, Wearmouth-Jarrow)

of each, it may give us some idea of the nature of other schools for which evidence has not survived (see Figure 3.3). We fortunately possess some letters to and from Aldhelm's students, and a few poems by one of these students, named Æthilwald.[172] Even so, we know little of the next generation's attainments. One, Pecthelm, went on to become bishop of *Candida Casa* (Whithorn in modern Wigtonshire, Scotland); he was a correspondent of Bede's, and reported to him the vision of postmortem judgment seen by a Mercian soldier.[173] Of the subsequent careers of Æthilwald, Wihtfrith, and Heahfrith we know nothing.[174] We can, however, deduce from the surviving letters something of how they were educated.

The overall impression this correspondence gives is that teaching was personal, not institutional. Students sought out an individual because of his reputation, and maintained a connection with him afterwards, even if they left their former religious community. Aldhelm's admonitions to Heahfrith, Wihtfrith, and Æthilwald are all predicated on the assumption that his former students will still accept his spiritual and intellectual authority; those to Wihtfrith and Heahfrith also imply that Aldhelm has been making inquiries about them from correspondents abroad. Æthilwald calls himself Aldhelm's *alumnus* ('foster-son') and *adoptivus proles* ('adopted child'): this, I think, is not really a metaphor.[175] Monasteries very quickly became entwined in the complex systems of child-fosterage in Western Europe. In early Anglo-Saxon England, the practice of entrusting children or youths to abbots for education seems to have overlapped strongly with a tradition of fostering children with secular patrons.[176] This *commendatio* – as de Jong has shown – was significantly different from Benedictine child oblation; children given over for education were not permanently separated from their families, and although most went on to become monks or nuns, some seem to have re-entered the world. She cites an instance mentioned in Stephen of Ripon's *vita* of Wilfrid:[177]

> Principes quoque seculares, viri nobiles, filios suos ad erudiendum sibi dederunt, ut aut Deo servirent, si eligerent, aut adultos, si maluissent, regi armatos commendaret.[178]

> And also secular chieftains, noble men, gave him [Wilfrid] their sons to be instructed, so that they might serve God if they so chose, or, if they preferred, might be commended to the king as warriors when they were grown up.

The fact that the youths were given a choice to return to secular aristocratic pursuits marks this practice as essentially different from oblation. While it is difficult to know upon what terms Aldhelm received his students, the letter of admonition which he sent to Æthilwald seems to imply relations not altogether dissimilar to Wilfrid's:

> Quemadmodum te viva voce aliquotiens de aliquibus ammonere curavi, ita etiamnunc absentem paterna secundum Deum auctoritate fretus litteris exhortari non piget ... Itaque, fili mi carissime, licet adolescens aetate existas, vanissimis tamen oblectamentis huius mundi nequaquam te nimium subicias sive in cotidianis potationibus et conviviis usu frequentiore ac prolixiore inhoneste superfluis sive in equitandi vagatione culpabili seu in quibuslibet corporeae delectationis voluptatibus execrandis.[179]

> Although I have taken care to advise you in person to an extent about various things, I am not (despite my absence) reluctant to exhort you by letter, relying on my paternal authority under God ... So, my dearest son, though you are in the time of youth, nevertheless you should by no means subject yourself excessively to the utterly empty amusements of this world: either in daily drinking parties and feasts, which are excessive in their unwholesome over-frequency and too great length; or in blameworthy and pointless riding about on horseback; or in any detestable indulgence in fleshly pleasure whatsoever.

Even a young man like Æthilwald, who seems to have been keenly interested in study, evidently had opportunities for indulging in the usual amusements of aristocratic youth. Moreover, he must have either returned to his family, or travelled elsewhere for further training: his education by Aldhelm did not entail a permanent cloistered life at Malmesbury.

The parallel with Wilfrid's methods of educating noblemen's sons may suggest that Aldhelm was conforming to a common practice in the early Anglo-Saxon church. In the seventh century, however, one might reasonably question whether any practice for educating Christian youths (rather than converting

adult pagans) was long enough established to be considered standard or
common. I suspect that in the 'schools' of Wilfrid and of Aldhelm we see
not an indigenous system, but the overlap of two (and possibly three) similar,
but not identical, foreign educational systems. Wilfrid's close connection to
the Merovingian church is indicated in Stephen's *vita*, and echoed in many of
his practices in England.[180] The account of Wilfrid's early time in Gaul is
tinctured by folktale,[181] but there is no reason to doubt the fact of his
education in Lyons in the household of the bishop. Stephen refers
to 'Dalfinus' as 'patrem suum archiepiscopum Lugdunae' ('his [Wilfrid's]
father, the archbishop of Lyons').[182] Upon Wilfrid's return from Rome,

> episcopus gratias agebat Deo, quod filium suum incolumem pergentem et
> iterum revertentem Dominus custodivit. Nam et per tres annos simul cum
> eo mansit et a doctoribus valde eruditis multa didicit . . .[183]

> the bishop gave thanks to God, since the Lord had kept his son unharmed
> both in going forth and in returning again. So then for three years he [Wilfrid]
> lived with him, and was taught many things by very learned teachers . . .

The bishop is not himself a teacher, therefore, but rather the patron of
a school; and Wilfrid's attachment to him is to one who has been his
benefactor generally.[184] It seems likely that Wilfrid reproduced this model
in his own school, at least to some degree; the fact that his pupils were
permitted the choice of clerical or royal service implies the kind of semi-
secular orientation seen in the episcopal schools in Gaul.[185]

Aldhelm, however, seems to have been engaged in something closer to
the Irish tradition of consigning youths to the care of holy men (or women)
for education. This was akin to the native practice of child fosterage, but
while secular Irish foster-parents were customarily a rung below their foster-
children in the social scale, the abbots and saints who took in pupils were
conferring, rather than receiving, a favour.[186] The vocabulary, however, was
similar: masters were *nutritores*, and their pupils *alumni* – 'foster-parents'
and 'foster-children'.[187] Irish *alumni* of holy men seem to have been mainly
intended for the church, but not necessarily in the foundation of their
master; and they might have a succession of teachers.[188] This seems to have
also been the case with Aldhelm's students, some of whom travelled to
Ireland – much against Aldhelm's wishes – for further study.

Despite Aldhelm's expressed misgivings about the moral and intellectual
tenor of Irish teaching, it seems likely that the Irish model of schooling
affected him deeply. It may indeed have been his own first experience of
education, if the anonymous student who wrote to him noting 'quod a
quodam sancto viro de nostro genere nutritus es' ('that you were fostered by

a certain holy man of our race') was – as most scholars conclude – Irish.[189] If this is so, Aldhelm's self-description as Abbot Hadrian's *alumnus* offers a kind of epitome of his education: though his adult loyalties lay with Theodore and Hadrian – and through them with Rome – yet his vocabulary and the underlying framework of his thought was still imbued with the Irish tradition of education as fosterage. Æthilwald's letter, for instance, seems to confirm that he had been handed over to Aldhelm partly for instruction and partly for safekeeping:

> Aestivi igitur temporis cursu, quo immensis feralium passim congressionum expeditionibus haec miserrima patria lugubriter invidia vastatrice deformatur, tecum legendi studio conversatus demorabar.[190]

> Now in the summer season, when immense armies of bestial bands were everywhere lamentably scarring this wretched land with their devouring malice, I used to remain living with you in the pursuit of study.

As noted above, Æthilwald repeatedly describes himself as Aldhelm's foster-son, and his style as well as his letter confirms he was taught by Aldhelm personally. Yet the fact of his correspondence indicates he had left Malmesbury, probably for further study elsewhere.

Given his admiration for Theodore and Hadrian's school, it seems very likely that Aldhelm would have incorporated aspects of the *style* of their teaching – as well as the content – into his own school. We know little, though, about the formal arrangements of the Canterbury school, and in particular whether its students were expected to profess and remain as Canterbury monks. Of those whose names we know, only Albinus seems to have done so. Aldhelm left due to illness, and took up an abbacy in his native country; Oftfor and John of Beverley were promoted to bishop in different kingdoms; Ceolfrith, if he was a student, must have returned with Benedict Biscop to Northumbria. It may be that *stabilitas* was a rarity in early medieval monastic education generally. But what seems to have distinguished Theodore and Hadrian's school from its Irish counterparts is the assumption – seen often in Aldhelm's letters – that the Canterbury school is all its students will ever need. A certain transience in the student population at Canterbury is likely to have been the effect of circumstance, while it seems to have been a basic assumption in the Irish model of schooling.

Aldhelm may have deprecated the sort of restless quest for intellectual novelty which, he suggests, drove Irish scholars and their Anglo-Saxon imitators. But this very un-Benedictine model of education may have helped to spread his own influence abroad: the dispersal of his students brought their master's texts and style to new regions, even if we cannot be altogether sure where those were. We know that these *alumni* continued to correspond with their master, and each other; they maintained a network, in other words, that helped to stabilize a newly forged style of Anglo-Latin writing. In his surviving letter, Æthilwald indicates his esteem for the judgment of his teacher and a fellow pupil:

> Huic autem nostrae parvitatis epistulae trina cantati modolaminis carmina binis generibus digesta subdidimus, quorum primum dactilico heroici poe-matis exametro ac pedestri, ut autumo, regula enucleate trutinatum et in LXX coaeqantium vorsuum formulas, casu ita obtingente vel, ut verius dicam, supernae dispensationis nutu moderante, divisum; tertium quoque non pedum mensura elucubratum, sed octenis syllabis in uno quolibet vorsu compositis, una eademque littera comparis linearum tramitibus aptata cur-sim calamo perarante caraxatum tibi, sagacissime sator, transmittens dicavi; medium vero meo tuoque clienti Wihtfrido de transmarini scilicet itineris peregrinatione simillimis itidem vorsuum et syllabarum lineis confectum repraesentans porrexi. Haec idcirco vestrae beatitudinis venerandis obtut-uum luminibus repraesentanda fore necessarium duxi, quod nostrae parvi-tatis iudicio dignum esse visum est, ut omnem tibi, utpote patri, mearum litterarum editiunculam primum pandens propalarem, quatenus vestrae sublimitatis probabili rationis iudicio comprobata et ad aequitatis normulam derivata omnibus deinceps lectorum numerositatibus acceptabilis extet.[191]

> Also, to this letter from my unworthy self I have subjoined three poems of melodious measures constructed in two modes: of which the first, weighed out in the dactylic hexameter of heroic verse and (I hope) according to the correct rule of feet, is divided into seventy patterns of equally weighed verses, as permitted by chance or (as I should more truly say) by the approving intervention of supernal decree; the third – which is pieced out not according to the measure of feet, but arranged with eight syllables in each and every verse, and with swift-ploughing pen scratched out with one and the same letter adapted to the paired tracks of lines – I the sender dedicated to you, wisest father; while the second, about a journey of pilgrimage across the sea, and likewise composed in the very same lines of verses and syllables, I displayed before my and your companion Wihtfrith. I brought these things forward as necessary to be presented before the reverend vision of your blessedness's eyes, because it seemed fitting in the judgment of my unworthy self that I should first show the entire initial little draft of my writings to you, as to a father, so that having been tested against the laudable judgment of your lofty intellect and squared off to the standard of correctness, it would then be pleasing to all the congregation of readers.

Two of the poems Æthilwald describes have survived in the Vienna codex of Aldhelm's works.[192] While we cannot know what, if any, corrections his correspondents offered, the fact that Æthilwald valued their judgment enough to solicit it before 'publishing' his work demonstrates his continuing attachment to his teacher's style – shared, we must presume, by Wihtfrith. Orchard's analysis of Æthilwald's rhythmic octosyllables demonstrates that their style is, so to speak, more Aldhelmian than Aldhelm's: the alliteration, in particular, is even more mannered.[193] Moreover, Æthilwald's detailed description of each of his poems' metre suggests that the correction he sought was chiefly metrical in nature: this must have seemed to him an essential aspect of proper composition, and a distinctive mark of Aldhelm's style. Æthilwald's letter shows that the process of aesthetic judgment that forged 'poetic communities' could continue to operate at a distance. The ties created by the process of education endured like blood relationships, and were perhaps even more influential.

The 'Irish model' of education as fosterage, then, probably contributed significantly to the diffusion – and, thus, success – of Aldhelm's style. It is curiously difficult, though, to trace the influence of *particular* Irishmen on Aldhelm and his pupils. Figure 3.4 maps Aldhelm's known or probable Irish connections: he seems surrounded by Irish scholars, but most remain shadowy and nameless. Maildubh, Aldhelm's putative teacher and namesake of Malmesbury, is something less than a name, since his actual connection with Aldhelm (and indeed his existence) is difficult to substantiate.[194] Among the most plausible candidates for an actual Irish instructor is Adomnán, abbot of Iona, who was a close connection of Aldfrith, Aldhelm's godson and later king of Northumbria. Lapidge has traced some evidence that Aldhelm may have studied at Iona, and gained there a knowledge of Virgil and of the rhythmic octosyllabic verse form he passed on to his own students.[195] Study with Adomnán would help to explain Aldhelm's high reputation with some contemporary Irish scholars;[196] it may also indicate why Aldhelm seemed to have sources of information in Ireland, despite the dismissive posture he takes towards Irish scholarship in his letters to Heahfrith and Wihtfrith. If the style of education he provided to his own students was the sort he experienced himself, Aldhelm's Irish correspondents may have been his co-*alumni* from Iona: his foster-brothers. If Aldhelm was indeed educated at Iona, it would be interesting to know whether he maintained contact with Adomnán even after his time at Canterbury; but unfortunately no such evidence survives.

The descendants of kings: Aldhelm and royal kinship networks

As Wilfrid discovered during his exile, the royalty of seventh-century England was extensively intermarried, and seems to have bestowed feuds along with gold as wedding-gifts.[197] That Aldhelm was connected by blood

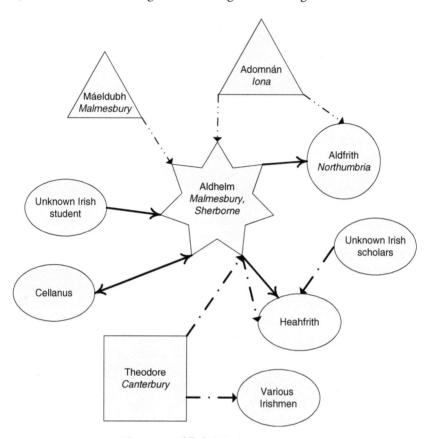

Figure 3.4 Aldhelm's Irish connections

to the royal house of Wessex has long been known; Lapidge has recently reconstituted the surviving evidence to suggest that Aldhelm's father – identified as *Kenten* by William of Malmesbury – was Centwine, king of Wessex from about 676–85.[198] Lapidge concludes that 'Aldhelm's relationship with the West Saxon royal family provides the key to understanding his career.'[199] Figure 3.5 maps Aldhelm's relations to seventh-century royal families.

Aldhelm's royal connections must certainly have been vital to ensuring the endowment of his monastery; grants from kings were the financial groundwork of most of the major seventh-century foundations.[200] But his aristocratic birth also shaped his literary career. His most important compositions were directed to kings, or to his relations and their connections.

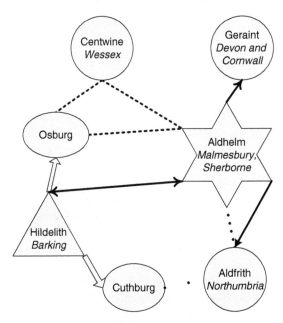

Figure 3.5 Aldhelm's royal connections

Thus, the *Epistola ad Acircium* (also containing his *Enigmata* and the metrical treatise *De pedum regulis*) was framed as a letter to Aldfrith, king of Northumbria, while the *Epistola ad Geruntium*, a treatise on the correct calculation of Easter, was directed to Geraint, king of Devon and Cornwall. Both parts of the *Opus de uirginitate* were addressed to Hildelith and her nuns at Barking: among them was one Osburg, who was Aldhelm's close kinswoman (his phrase is 'contribulibus necessitudinum nexibus conglutinata' ('closely conjoined [to me] with the shared tribal bonds of manifold relationship').[201] Lapidge has argued that the 'intimacy of the relation, indicated by the rare verb *conglutino*, may be best understood as meaning that Osburg was Aldhelm's sister'.[202]

In all these cases, Aldhelm's status and social ties seem to have been significant factors in the composition of the texts, not just the choice of dedicatees. Hildelith's community at Barking had evidently been in correspondence with Aldhelm for some time, and his somewhat unusual theorizing of virginity was well calculated to suit the interests and opinions of the women there.[203] That he chose to list the nuns by name suggests that he intended to express his regard for them as individuals, rather than as a corporation subsumed in the name of their abbess or house: he even mentions 'singulos epistolarum textus recitans' ('reading out the individual texts of the letters').[204] It is perhaps worth noting that only four of Aldhelm's addressees had taken names in religion – Justina, Scholastica, Eulalia and Thecla – and that the stories of every one of their namesake martyrs are recounted in the *Opus de uirginitate*. While the second person voice in this text is generally plural, then, that plurality is not undifferentiated. The fact that both parts of this treatise soon gained wide circulation should not blind us to the probability that the epistolary dedication of the *Prosa de uirginitate* is not just a formal convention, but a genuine expression of esteem for a group of people whose tastes and character significantly influenced the shape of Aldhelm's finished work. Kinship with Osburg would undoubtedly have given him some of the personal insight needed to assure his book's success with its recipients.

How much Aldhelm knew about the opinions of Geraint, king of Devon and Cornwall, is a different question. His letter dwells substantially upon the offences of the priests in Dyfed, as well as the deviations in tonsure and date of Easter promoted by the bishops in Geraint's kingdom: it may be that he was working from general assumptions about what the British believed, rather than specific local knowledge. Two points, however, suggest that Aldhelm might indeed have had personal knowledge of Geraint and his people. One is furnished by the *Carmen rhythmicum*, addressed to an unknown cleric named Helmgils:

> Quando profectus fueram
> Usque diram Domnoniam
> Per carentem Cornubiam
> Florulentis cespitibus
> Et foecundis graminibus . . .[205]

> When I had been travelling towards dreadful Devon through Cornwall, which lacks flowering fields and flourishing grasses . . .

The poem is undatable: it may be that it describes Aldhelm's first journey to the region, and that it postdates the *Epistola ad Geruntium*; though the reverse is also possible. All we can conclude is that Aldhelm did visit Devon and Cornwall at some point (and did not much like it). Why he might have been doing so is perhaps hinted at in some information furnished by Bede. As Lapidge and Herren pointed out, Bede knew the *Epistola ad Geruntium* only at second-hand.[206] But he does state that 'multos ... eorum, qui Occidentalibus Saxonibus subditi erant Brettones, ad catholicam dominici paschae celebrationem huius lectione perduxit' ('the reading of it guided many of those Britons who were subject to the West Saxons to the Catholic celebration of Easter').[207] If *Domnonia* were effectively a tributary province of Wessex at this time, Aldhelm may have encountered its people, and perhaps even its ruler, in the course of his interaction with his kindred in the West Saxon court. Whether this was the case or not, Bede's information explains why Aldhelm should have been chosen to write to Geraint: his connection with West Saxon royalty would have reinforced the authority of his own learning.

Aldfrith of Northumbria, by contrast, was evidently someone Aldhelm knew well, and from a time before either could have expected Aldfrith's accession to the throne.[208] They may, as Lapidge suggests, have been educated together on Iona;[209] certainly Aldhelm's status as Aldfrith's sponsor at confirmation connected the two men in a way considered as binding as blood-kinship.[210] This makes Aldhelm's choice of gift for Aldfrith all the more interesting. That the book was meant to rekindle old ties is stated outright at the end of the opening section:

> Haec idcirco tantis verborum ambagibus deprompsimus, ut pristini frater-nitatis affectus, quos praeteritorum evolutis annorum circulis conciliasse et copulasse denoscimur, recenti quodammodo memoria recuperentur et reca-lescant, ne rotante prolixi temporis diuturnitate torpescant aut longa loco-rum intercapidine refrigescant.[211]

> And so we have elaborated these matters with such verbal meanderings, so that the former feelings of brotherhood, which we are well known to have united and bound together in the rolling cycles of years gone by, might be revived in such manner by a fresh memory, and grow warm again, so that they might be neither dulled to sleep by the revolving days of a long stretch of time, nor chilled by a great separation of space.

The treatise on the number seven which begins the *Epistola ad Acircium* could perhaps be read as an oblique reminder of the force of the two men's spiritual bond, since the sequence of sevens is initiated by the reminder of the 'septiformi spiritalium charismatum munificentia' ('sevenfold munificence of spiritual gifts') conferred on Aldfrith by the bishop at his confirmation, when Aldhelm stood sponsor. But the bulk of the book is taken up with other matters: Aldhelm's *Enigmata*, and his treatise on metre. In his final exhortation, Aldhelm asks that 'hoc opusculum ... inexpugnabili metrorum pelta et grammaticorum parma protegere digneris' ('you will condescend to protect this little work with the impregnable shield of metres and the targe of the grammarians').[212] This *seems* to imply that he expects Aldfrith will learn to write verse himself, and thus 'defend' Aldhelm's work. It may be that his sponsor believed Aldfrith – who had a formidable reputation for learning in Ireland – would be pleased by the chance to learn quantitative metre, which the Irish could not teach.[213] If Aldfrith did learn the art of quantitative verse from Aldhelm's book, his compositions have since been lost. But the treatise Aldhelm sent him went on to be influential in the north, perhaps partly through his means.[214]

Abbots and bishops with kinship ties to royalty and aristocracy were the norm, rather than the exception, in Anglo-Saxon England.[215] But Aldhelm's particular connections within and through the Wessex royal dynasty seem to have enabled his reputation – and literary works – to spread beyond his native kingdom to Essex, Cornwall, and Northumbria. His birth probably enhanced the value his correspondents placed on his acquaintance and his writings, while in the cases of Aldfrith and of the nuns at Barking, the intimacy of Aldhelm's knowledge of people with significant cultural influence allowed him to shape his writings to suit their interests and needs. His success in doing so is reflected in the popularity and influence of his work.

Bonds of verse: octosyllabic poems as epistles and gifts

Bonds within the social networks of seventh-century England could be created in any number of ways. Some, as we have seen, were established at birth through blood-kinship; others, more or less involuntary, arose through participation in formal structures like the church. But individuals undoubtedly had a choice which ties to strengthen or maintain, even when circumstances disrupted a formerly close-knit network. Literature of various sorts, as we have already seen, was an important tool: along with ornate letters intended for preservation, entire treatises like the *Epistola ad Acircium* might be the means of cementing or reviving ties.

One particular mode of verse practised in early Anglo-Saxon England seems to have often functioned as a kind of social glue. Rhythmic octosyllables were a fairly popular form in the early Middle Ages: their flexibility fostered an array of local and individual variants.[216] As a hymnic metre, rhythmic octosyllables undoubtedly derived from the iambic dimeter of St Ambrose and his successors; but the Ambrosian form crossbred, so to speak, with other quantitative metres, including the anacreontic, which Prosper of Aquitaine had used for a long hortative poem, the *Carmen coniugis ad uxorem*.[217] Several variants arose in the British Isles; in Ireland, prayers and hymns were often written in rhymed rhythmic octosyllables, and it seems likely that these were an important influence on English authors.[218] The varieties and metrical underpinnings of Insular Latin octosyllables have been investigated thoroughly – though sometimes with contradictory results – by Lapidge, Herren, Howlett, and Orchard, among others.[219]

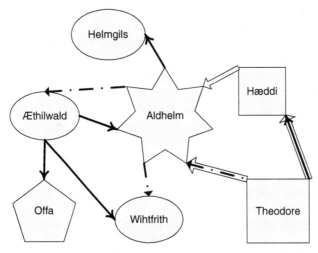

Figure 3.6 Octosyllabic exchanges in seventh-century England

What I shall examine here is the use of octosyllabic poems as gifts, and their role in cementing personal connections.

Only nine octosyllabic poems attributable to named authors survive from seventh-century England. Four have been assigned by Lapidge to Archbishop Theodore,[220] and four to Æthilwald;[221] the final poem is now usually credited to Aldhelm.[222] Three of Theodore's poems and one of Æthilwald's are prayers. The other five were exchanged among other named individuals: Figure 3.6 maps their connections.

Many of the recipients are known to us as bare names, but the poems themselves tell us something about them and their relationships with contemporaries. Hæddi, bishop of the West Saxons, for instance, is described by Bede as a man of more goodwill than learning,[223] but Theodore's opinion of him seems to have been higher, as we know from a poem preserved in CCCC 320:

> Te nunc, sancte speculator,
> uerbi Dei digne dator,
> Hæddi, pie presul, precor
> pontificum ditum decor:
> pro me tuo peregrino
> preces funde Theodoro.[224]

Now holy bishop, worthy bestower of God's word, pious prelate worthy of pontifical honours: I beg you, Hæddi, pour forth prayers for your pilgrim-exile Theodore.

As archbishop, Theodore outranked Hæddi, and moreover had confirmed
him as bishop, so Hæddi had reason to consider Theodore his patron.[225] Yet
this poem emphasizes the Wessex bishop's rank and his fitness to hold it,
while describing Theodore himself merely as a *peregrinus*, a 'pilgrim from
abroad'; the second person pronouns *te* (1) and *tuo* (5) are emphasized by
the trochaic rhythm, while *me* is unstressed.[226] Theodore's request for
prayers is designed to flatter and magnify its recipient. This would have
been unremarkable if sent from an inferior to a superior: but the reverse
situation implies a more genuine friendship, or at least a desire to maintain a
connection based more on esteem than on formal hierarchy.

The second person voice was an important device in Anglo-Latin octosyllabic verse: of the nine surviving poems, seven use the second person.[227]
Even at its least panegyric, the tone of these addresses is always respectful.
Aldhelm's opening lines to Helmgils, for instance, describe him with one of
Aldhelm's favourite adjectives for Christian warriors (*anthleticus*).[228] The
poem about three pilgrims that Æthilwald sent to Aldhelm and Wihtfrith
seems to use its second person passages as apostrophe, rather than addresses
to the reader, but the final lines can bear a double interpretation:

> Valetote felicibus
> Vitam clausuri calcibus![229]

Farewell, ye who will end your lives with a fortunate conclusion [*or*, on
fortunate shores]!

The *uos* addressed in these lines may be the pilgrim subjects (who are thus
apostrophized in lines 40–8); but the *felicibus . . . calcibus* are ambiguous
enough to include all readers attempting to live a virtuous life (or in a
monastery, depending on what we believe Æthilwald meant by the phrase).
A double meaning would also suit the semi-epistolary form of these poems,
closing it with a farewell to readers as well as subjects. Æthilwald's panegyric
on Aldhelm also bears an epistolary close:

> Tibi salus per secula
> Sospis et absque macula
> Maneat inmortaliter
> Fine tenus feliciter.[230]

To you may well-being remain unimpaired and without stain immortally,
abundantly, right to the end.

Effectively, this is *uale* exploded into a cloud of verbosity, but it does also
bring the celestial imagery of Æthilwald's praise back to a more concrete
wish to his master.

Æthilwald's final poem to an unknown Offa is even more clearly meant as both a letter and a flattering gift:

> Vale, uale fidissime
> Philochriste carissime,
> Quem in cordis cubiculo
> Cingo amoris uinculo.
> Haue, Houa altissime
> Ollim sodes sanctissime,
> Salutatus supplicibus
> Aethiluualdi cum uocibus.[231]

> Hail, hail, dearest and most faithful devotee of Christ, whom I bind tight with the chain of love within the inner chamber of my heart. Hail, most lofty Offa, formerly my most holy companion, you are greeted with Æthilwald's humble letters.

He goes on to praise Offa's birth, appearance, learning, and intellect, in terms that suggest his correspondent is a lay aristocrat.[232] There are interesting parallels here with the *Epistola ad Acircium* Aldhelm sent to Aldfrith. While *sodes* in Æthilwald's hands is an ambiguous word, and could mean anything from 'friend' to 'foster-brother', it implies the sort of youthful comradeship that Aldhelm once shared with Aldfrith – but without the hierarchical relation of sponsorship. Æthilwald's poem lacks the moral admonition and didacticism of Aldhelm's treatise: it closes, for instance, with a prayer that God might protect Offa, rather than with an injunction to Offa to serve God. Both texts, though, serve to remind their lay recipients of former friendship; both, too, combine elements of overt flattery with the assumption that poetry itself is a pleasing gift. Like the other Anglo-Latin octosyllabic poems addressed to known recipients, Æthilwald's verses to Offa are designed to renew and strengthen a tie attenuated by distance. That they are evidently addressed to a layman is further evidence that the social networks of seventh-century ecclesiastics were not confined within the church hierarchy, and that Latin poetry – far from being merely the toy of an exclusive coterie – could act as a tool for social cohesion across boundaries of space and social status.

Rebinding Aldhelm's connections

As a focal point for a snapshot of seventh-century elite society, Aldhelm's social network has revealed the intricacy of the ties that connected individuals within and across generations. The Canterbury school, Aldhelm's own school, and royal kin-groups were not separate spheres connected only by a single figure, but overlapping regions within a large and relatively closely-knit community. If more evidence survived, we could perhaps clarify some hazy spots on the map – the role of Wilfrid and his foundations in the training of poets and scholars in Mercia, for instance – but the overall outlines seem plain.

The interconnection of early Anglo-Saxon England had a major effect on the shape of early literary production in Latin. Letters and epistolary verse – especially, as we have seen, rhythmic octosyllables – were overtly intended to maintain social bonds. Most of Aldhelm's compositions were meant for particular people: his knowledge of these recipients shaped his writings in some still discernible ways, and the personalities of the nuns at Barking – and of Aldfrith and Helmgils – no doubt had effects on the works sent to them beyond what we can now perceive.

Understanding Aldhelm's social network also helps clarify how knowledge diffused across Anglo-Saxon England. Schools were not endpoints for people who sought education, but centres from which groups of people spread out, bearing their newly acquired information. Since we can be sure of the entry-point of one particular esoteric skill – the composition of quantitative Latin verse – we can map a few such trajectories. From Canterbury, Aldhelm returned to northern Wessex; through his teaching Æthilwald brought his knowledge to unknown regions, and Aldfrith received information about the new art in Northumbria. The author of Wilfrid's epitaph – whether a Mercian or Northumbrian – probably learned to compose partly through Aldhelm's means, perhaps at second-hand from the treatise on metre sent to Aldfrith, or from a now unknown pupil of the Malmesbury school. Meanwhile, Ceolfrith's knowledge of quantitative metre suggests a second vector outwards from Canterbury to Northumbria. The rapid diffusion of literary knowledge may have been an unintended and even unwanted byproduct of the early Anglo-Saxons' intellectual eclecticism – their receptivity to Irish and Gaulish as well as Roman styles of education and of monasticism. But the growth of far-flung networks of former friends and schoolmates undoubtedly contributed to the sudden vibrancy of Anglo-Latin literature in the seventh and early eighth centuries.

As Aldhelm took care to point out to Aldfrith when sending his *Enigmata* and textbook on quantitative metre, 'constat neminem nostrae stirpis prosapia genitum et Germanicae gentis cunabulis confotum in huiuscemodi negotio ante nostram mediocritatem tantopere desudasse' ('it so happens that no one born to the offspring of our race and brought up in the cradles of the Germanic people has so laboured in work of this sort before my humble self').[233] And indeed Aldhelm's individual labours were crucial to the future shape of Anglo-Latin literature. But they were thus successful because circumstances also placed Aldhelm at the nexus of several key social groups: he worked closely with the archbishop of Canterbury, with his royal kindred, with the aristocratic students entrusted to him, and even with the Irish scholarly community. Had Aldhelm's works not appealed to his contemporaries, his connections would probably not have saved them: but since he used his connections to anticipate the needs and tastes of his audience, his writings left a deep impress on Anglo-Latin literature for generations.

Conclusions

In the surviving traces of Anglo-Saxon England's poetic communities we can read something of the conditions in which much of the surviving verse was produced. The case histories explored here do not exhaust the variety of means poets had for interacting through their work with those whom they knew would read or hear it. I have concentrated on *The Battle of Maldon*, the works of Cynewulf, and the Latin poets of the late seventh century because they present different classes of evidence, and seem to contain the imprint of different kinds of community. Through Aldhelm's network, we can see in action some of the consequences of teachers becoming poets: epistolary verse, as well as gifts of his books to far-flung elite connections, helped him to maintain his ties to kinsfolk, fellow students, and former students across the Anglo-Saxon kingdoms. These connections increased his reputation and perpetuated his work, as well as widely propagating his style. While Aldhelm was unique in the magnitude of his personal influence, we must imagine other teachers – his contemporaries and successors – having similar effects on a smaller scale, and perhaps maintaining their own network through gifts of now lost verse. Teachers' ability to confer the art of poetry on their students enabled them to give such gifts in turn, and thus forge new poetic communities.

Given his choice of genre and his feelings towards books, Cynewulf may have been a teacher himself. He certainly seems to have shared many of Aldhelm's assumptions about poetry's ability to bridge gaps of space and time, and to speak through books directly to connections unseen. This may, perhaps, suggest that he too had a widespread social network. But in his focus on judgment, we can perceive that at least part of his community was immediately present to his imagination; that he expected and could anticipate certain reactions to his poems. This, to me, implies a long period of immersion in a living poetic community, though perhaps it need not have been fully intact when Cynewulf created his surviving poems. The coda to *Elene*, speaking as it does of the author *frod and fus* (1236a, 'old and eager [to depart]') and composing *nihtes nearwe* (1239a, 'anxiously by night'), draws upon longstanding tropes of composition, yet it need not therefore be untrue. Even if Cynewulf had outlived or separated from the community whose judgment left such striking traces in his work, he knew that some part of it, and some part of him, remained in the persons of books. Once detected, this sense of the indivisibility of written and spoken – of book and man – can be seen in some Latin epistolary verse, even including Aldhelm's and Alcuin's. It may also help to explain why certain oral literature was written down: the oral texts were *for* something, and they could still accomplish that purpose when speaking from parchment.

The Battle of Maldon may be an example of the latter phenomenon. Saturated in oral techniques and closely connected with a particular time and place, the poem seems to speak directly to one community. Its written form may have allowed it to address members of that community whom circumstances had taken elsewhere – making it a 'letter from home', rather than an attempt to find a wider audience. In *Maldon*'s case, it is impossible to verify this hypothesis; but while such a scenario runs counter to modern notions of the purpose of publication, it may be that Anglo-Saxon book production was a more personal affair.

Poets' relations to their communities could take many forms, and I should not wish to argue that those relations were always easy or amicable. Verse could and did act as a social bond, but as a medium it was not necessarily smooth or unambivalent. Indeed, I believe that a certain amount of anxiety often did accompany the creation of poetry, and that much of this anxiety stemmed from a sense of poetry's power to act in the real world – to further social goals of greater or lesser importance. Thus, Anglo-Saxon poets developed so many and such ingenious strategies for managing the judgment of others. Much could be accomplished if a poem worked: and so poets laboured mightily to forestall the possibility of it *not* working. The assurance of many of their techniques points to experience and, probably, the immediate force of example. For most Anglo-Saxon poets, the arbiter of success or failure was the community around them, the people they knew.

CHAPTER 4

The poet alone

If Anglo-Saxon poetry is chiefly a social phenomenon, what happens to those who are isolated? Though this question has shades of the 'Forbidden Experiment', it touches on an important aspect of poets' experience. It is easy to imagine divergent careers for people who had become poets in similar ways – say, three students at Malmesbury, of whom one re-entered secular life, another joined a mission field abroad, and the third became a bishop. In their different situations, these imaginary poets might compose quite different sorts of verse. Yet they would, as it were, have grown from the same stock, and therefore we would expect to find essential similarities in their work: perhaps most importantly, the imprint of the community in which they had learned their craft. In some cases, the effect of the new community would be so great as to efface most traces of the old. But a poet who became abbot of a remote monastery, or even a hermit, might continue to practise his art as he would have done had he remained with the people among whom he first learned to compose verse. Just as an adult stranded in a remote location does not lose language, a poet need not lose his skills when separated from a poetic community.

Suppose, however, he had never belonged to such a community in the first place. In an oral culture, such an individual would not become a poet: at least, he would not be able to produce anything recognized as verse by the wider society from which he was isolated. But the advent of writing made it possible to encounter poetry without a living human intermediary. A reader of verse might well be intrigued, and wish to emulate it. Would it be possible for such an individual to become a competent poet?

Evidence suggests that the answer to this question is a qualified 'yes'. Some Anglo-Saxon poets seem to have been autodidacts to a certain degree. In Chapter 2, I examined the metrical peculiarities of some scribes' colophons, and argued that these oddities stemmed from their authors' imitating verse without understanding its fundamental principles. Eadwig Basan, for instance, seems to have known what the rhythm and syllable count of a hexameter should look and sound like, but does not seem to have known about the rules for quantity. In the case studies in this chapter, I shall investigate the work of other Anglo-Saxon authors who operated on similar principles – who read a great deal of verse, and inferred from their reading what the rules ought to be. From a wider perspective, their conclusions were sometimes wrong. But such errors were also systematic, based on the same thought processes that often led them right. Such telltale patterns of error are one of the key diagnostic marks of the isolated poet.

I shall consider here two instances of isolated poets. Neither is the perfect specimen that Bard World might prefer, but each presents a set of characteristics which help us to form a model of how and why an Anglo-Saxon might become a poet without the guidance of a community. The first is the author of *Christ and Satan* as the poem now stands in Bodleian, Junius XI. *Author* is a problematic term, for, as I shall argue, this person actually expanded and revised someone else's poem, which had survived in an imperfect manuscript. But the poets' work can be distinguished at points, which helps us to identify some of the Junius poet's methods and (perhaps) motivations. My second case study is the Venerable Bede. This may seem a peculiar choice, given that Bede undoubtedly had teachers (such as Ceolfrith) and lived in a rule-governed monastery. Yet his work bears the signs of an individual relying principally on his own deductions from books, rather than the expertise of a poetic community. Whether this was the result of circumstances or of personal choice, Bede's poetic isolation at Jarrow demonstrates the hazard of a priori assumptions about the nature of Anglo-Saxon poets' experience.

Home renovations: *Christ and Satan*

'Liber II' in Junius XI seems something of an afterthought. The first 212 pages, containing *Genesis*, *Exodus*, and *Daniel*, were written by one scribe in a well-spaced vernacular book-hand, with blank half-sheets and pages left for a partially completed programme of illustration.[1] The final eighteen pages (of which the last one and a half are blank) were shoehorned into a single gathering beginning on page 211, with the aid of two added single sheets and a bifolium.[2] Two or three scribes filled most of this last gathering sometime in the early eleventh century.[3] The incompetence of the first of these scribes evidently irked a more or less contemporary reader, who made a number of additions and alterations to pages 213–15 particularly, though this corrector was also interested in making the poem conform generally to late West Saxon linguistic standards.[4]

Christ and Satan, however, does not conform well to any standards. Its style is repetitive, with many flaws in the metre – of which some but not all can be attributed to the text's poor state of transmission. As a poem on mainly apocryphal New Testament subjects, it seems ill-suited to the main Junius XI collection. As a narrative, its sequence is disrupted to no clear artistic purpose, particularly in its relation of Christ's temptation in the wilderness *after* the Harrowing of Hell. Critics have several times tried to justify the planned unity of *Christ and Satan* individually, and as part of a sequence in Junius XI; but their proposed thematic frameworks tend to be so broad as to encompass almost any Christian text.[5]

The question of unity has been taken up so often because doubt on this point is so easy to justify. The three main topics of *Christ and Satan* are very loosely connected thematically, chronologically, and within the text. In 1877, Ten Brink simply declared that there were three different poems, which he called 'Die gefallenen Engel' (lines 1–365), 'Christi Höllenfahrt und Auferstehung' (lines 366–664), and 'Christi Versuchung' (lines 665–733, using a slightly different lineation than the *ASPR*).[6] A few scholars adopted this division, but in the twentieth and twenty-first centuries most have been inclined to treat *Christ and Satan* as a single work, even if they harboured doubts.[7] The evidence of the manuscript tends to justify the 'unificationists'. Though the poem is divided into twelve (perhaps thirteen) fitts of varying lengths, the capital that begins Fitt 8 (at line 366, the beginning of Ten Brink's second division) does not differ from other fitt initials, and is certainly smaller than the poem's first initial on p. 213. The most elaborate initial in Liber II (a little zoomorphic **h** on p. 226, formed by a winged catlike creature intertwined with a bird of prey) begins Fitt 12 at line 597, and thus falls within Ten Brink's second poem. The fitt numbers are sequential and begin with the poem, though only numbers II, III, V, and VI were added to the manuscript.[8] It seems most likely, therefore, that *Christ and Satan* was intended to be read as a unit.

But the disjunctions in the text remain, and I believe that multiple authorship – or perhaps what might be better termed complex authorship – can explain the problematic texture of *Christ and Satan* as it now stands. The idea that the Junius XI text represents the redaction of an earlier work is not new. In 1883, for instance, Friedrich Groschopp argued that fragments of a longer epic on the life of Christ had been reassembled and patched together by a later author responsible for most of the homiletic passages in the current poem.[9] Variation in mode, however, is common enough in Old English poetry that it seems an unreliable test of multiple authorship. Assessing changes in versification techniques across the poem, however, can allow us to see where *Christ and Satan*'s internal seams actually lie.

Alliteration and poetic method

One simple test is to survey the patterns of alliteration in the poem. Since alliteration is structural in Old English metre, one could not be a poet without a basic grasp of its rules.[10] Beyond the fundamental requirement that it be present in each line, however, there seem to have been no wider constraints on alliteration. Poets vary substantially in deploying favoured letters, double alliteration, and ornaments such as extra, cross- or continuing alliteration.[11] Moreover, the test studies I have done suggest that individual poets' tendencies are relatively consistent, so that substantial variation within a poem is likely to be meaningful.

In order to gauge the internal consistency of alliterative practices, I chose three poems from the Exeter Book of similar length to *Christ and Satan*. Two of these, *Christ III* (798 lines) and *Guthlac A* (818 lines) I selected because Merrell Clubb had noted some striking similarities between these poems and *Christ and Satan*.[12] The third, *Juliana* (731 lines), bears Cynewulf's runic signature, and in the previous chapter I treated it as the unified work of a single author; it therefore represents a useful correlative. As internal units, I used fitts as indicated in the manuscript with enlarged capitals and line divisions. All longer Old English poems contain fitt divisions, and while in many cases they are certainly not authorial, they are at least a well-attested way of dividing up Old English verse.[13]

The metric itself is intended to assess the variation in poets' use of alliterative patterns by determining what percentage of a fitt is occupied by lines alliterating on the most common patterns. Because the particular letters preferred may (and do) vary from fitt to fitt, I have in each instance determined the alliterative patterns most common to each individual fitt – so that (for instance) if 25 per cent of the lines in Fitt 2 alliterated on **h**, this would be functionally identical to 25 per cent alliterating on **g** in Fitt 3. Because there is some reason to believe that Old English poets favoured variety in alliterative patterns as a stylistic principle, this test may also have some validity as a measure of poetic skill.[14]

Tables 4.1–4.3 list the test poems' four most common alliterative patterns by fitt. These patterns are graphed cumulatively in Figures 4.1–4.3, so that the rightmost point in the series indicates the total percentage of the fitt's lines occupied by the four most-favoured patterns. We can see from these figures that, within poems, the correspondence between fitts in overall patterns of variation is relatively close. In *Juliana*, as expected, the correspondence is *extremely* close, with no outliers and a standard deviation of less than 2 across the series.[15] Cynewulf's tendencies towards metrical variety

Table 4.1 *Alliterative preferences as percentages in* Juliana

Fitt 1		Fitt 2		Fitt 3		Fitt 4		Fitt 5		Fitt 6		Overall	
a[a]	15.4	a	18.3	a	14.2	s	13.7	a	13.7	a	15.2	a	14.9
f	13.5	g	11.7	f	12.5	a	12.8	w	13.1	s	12	s	11.1
h	11.5	f	10.8	h	12.5	m	11.0	f	11.1	w	12	w	11.1
w	11.5	w	10	s	11.7	w	10.1	h	11.1	h	10.4	f	10.3

[a] a in these tables represents vowel alliteration: by Old English metrical convention, any vowel may alliterate with any other vowel.

Table 4.2 *Alliterative preferences as percentages in* Guthlac A

Fitt 1		Fitt 2		Fitt 3		Fitt 4		Fitt 5		Fitt 6		Fitt 7		Fitt 8		Overall	
a	16.3	a	16.9	a	22.8	a	19.0	a	19.0	a	13.6	a	14.4	g	15.5	a	17.2
w	13.0	g	14.3	g	13.0	w	14.1	m	11.9	g	12.5	w	13.5	a	14.4	w	10.5
h	13.0	h	10.4	f	9.8	m	11.3	g	9.5	h	11.4	d	9.6	s	12.4	g	10.1
g	7.6	l	10.4	w	7.6	l	9.2	s	8.7	s	10.2	l	8.7	w	10.3	h	8.6

Table 4.3 *Alliterative preferences as percentages in* Christ III

Fitt 1		Fitt 2		Fitt 3		Fitt 4		Fitt 5		Fitt 6		Fitt 7		Overall	
a	21.9	a	16.5	a	19.5	a	26.6	a	25.7	a	18.6	s	14.8	a	19.9
m	12.4	h	14.7	h	11.9	w	14.1	f	11.9	h	13.7	a	11.9	s	10.9
s	12.4	w	13.8	s	11.9	s	10.9	h	10.9	s	12.7	f	11.1	h	10.7
h	9.5	f	11.0	f	9.3	l	7.8	m	9.9	f	9.8	h	11.1	w	10.3

remained stable throughout the poem, with less than 15 per cent of his lines overall alliterating on vowels, and a fairly equal ratio of his next most preferred letters. *Guthlac A* also demonstrates a fairly close correspondence between fitts in the amount of variety shown; the standard deviation is less than 3, and initial outliers (such as Fitts 3 and 6) tend to converge. *Christ III* is a more complex case. Its seven fitts fall into a more or less normal distribution, but one more widely dispersed than the other two test poems. The standard deviation is about 4, and Fitts 4 and 5, and Fitt 7, differ markedly from the poem's overall tendencies. The former two sections have a relatively high percentage of vowel alliteration, while Fitt 7's vowel alliteration is much lower than that due to chance.

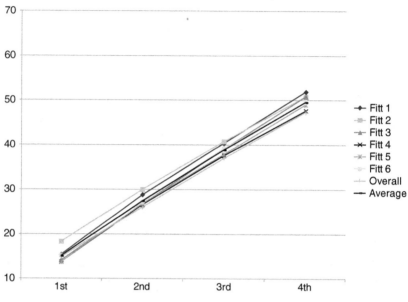

Figure 4.1 Alliterative preferences in *Juliana*

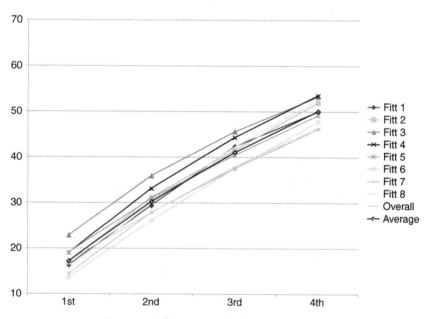

Figure 4.2 Alliterative preferences in *Guthlac A*

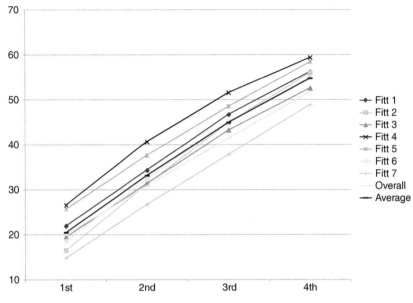

Figure 4.3 Alliterative preferences in *Christ III*

The vowel alliteration patterns in *Christ III* raise an important stylistic question: are the particular letters favoured by authors of any significance? In some cases, the answer must be 'yes' – witness *Guthlac A*'s marked preference of its hero's initial. The letter **g** certainly becomes the poet's metrical keynote far more often than would be due to chance, judging by the statistics in Ross's 'Philological Probability Problems'. Ross's sample has **g** occupying the first stressed syllable in only 3.3 per cent of Old English words likely to bear metrical stress: Table 4.4 gives the six most common initial letters. This sample is not without its problems – it is taken, first of all, from prose, and Old English poetry had a distinct vocabulary. However, the favoured alliterative patterns in all three poems do seem to track the most common initial letter-sounds, with readily explicable exceptions such as **g** for Guthlac. Yet in *Christ III* – and particularly in Fitts 4 and 5 – vowel alliteration is notably more common than a random dip into the *wordhord* would seem to dictate. Here too, though, Ross's statistics provide some guidance. Alliterative choices were not independent: when Old English poets selected a word to form the core of their alliterative line, that decision radically limited the possibilities for the other alliterating stressed word. When a word beginning with a vowel was chosen, any other word with an initial vowel could licitly pair with it: and so

Table 4.4 *Expected chance*
percentages of stressed initial letters[a]

a	17.0
w	10.1
s	9.4
h	8.5
f	7.3
m	7.3

[a] Derived from the prose-derived sample of 4,406 words given in Table 9 of Ross, 'Philological Probability Problems', p. 32.

Table 4.5 *Alliterative preferences as percentages in* Christ and Satan

Fitt 1		Fitt 2		Fitt 3		Fitt 4		Fitt 5		Fitt 6		Fitt 7	
a	25.7	a	26	a	25	h	25.7	a	33.3	a	23.0	a	16
s	13.5	w	20	w	15.6	a	17.1	w	13.3	h	13.1	h	16
h	12.2	f	12	h	14.1	w	14.3	s	10	f	8.2	w	14
w	9.5	h	12	b	7.8	b	11.4	b	6.7	g	8.2	f	10

Fitt 8		Fitt 9		Fitt 10		Fitt 11		Fitt 12		Fitt 13		Overall	
a	32.9	a	19.7	a	17.8	a	17.5	a	15.1	x[a]	35.7	a	21.9
h	18.4	f	11.3	d	11.1	h	17.5	h	14.3	a	14.3	h	13.7
w	9.2	w	11.3	g	11.1	s	12.5	w	11.8	b	7.1	w	11.4
s	6.6	h	9.9	s	11.1	w	10	s	9.2	h	7.1	s	8.4

[a] x denotes a line with no alliteration.

forming a vowel-alliterating line was about 60 per cent easier than one beginning with **w**, and about eight times easier than one alliterating on **r**. It is not surprising, therefore, that vowel alliteration should be more common in poetry than the actual number of Old English vowel-initial words would imply. Cynewulf's relatively low percentage of vowel-alliterating lines suggests he was actively choosing more difficult alternatives.

Christ III, then, seems to contain some fairly striking variability in technique, especially when compared to *Juliana* and *Guthlac A*. The variation across *Christ and Satan*, however, is substantially larger. Most of the fitts in *Christ and Satan* are shorter than those in the test poem: the longest, Fitt 12, is 119 lines, while Fitt 13 is only 14, and the average is about 56 lines. Table 4.5 lists the poem's most common alliterative patterns. Fitt 13, the shortest, is so

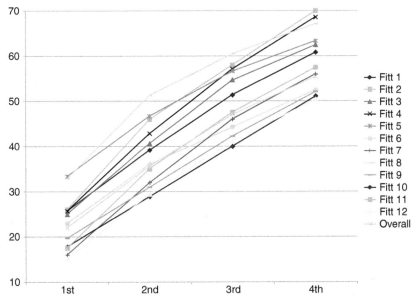

Figure 4.4 Alliterative preferences in *Christ and Satan*

anomalous that I have not included it in Figure 4.4.[16] As can be seen, the variation among fitts is extremely large, with a standard deviation between 6 and 7 for the second through fourth points in the series. What is particularly noteworthy for our purposes is the gap visible between the upper and lower clusters: the average (seen in Figure 4.5) divides Fitts 1–5 plus 8 from Fitts 6, 7, and 9–12. These two clusters have significant shared characteristics. The upper set (1–5, 8), which we will call α, has extremely high rates of vowel alliteration and a restricted number of alliterative patterns overall. On average, 65 per cent of the lines of fitts in α alliterate on one of their four preferred letters, while only 53 per cent of those in the lower cluster β do. The average difference between α and β is greater than that between *Christ III*'s most distant outliers, and the gap between *Christ and Satan*'s outliers is more than 20 points. It seems, therefore, that the variation in poetic technique within *Christ and Satan* is substantial enough to – at very least – require explanation.

Disassembling Christ and Satan

The discrepancies between fitts in *Christ and Satan* are not themselves sufficient to prove separate authorship, nor should they lead us to assume

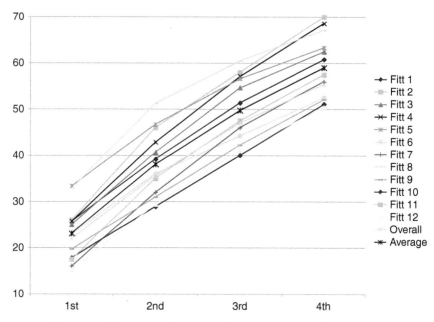

Figure 4.5 Alliterative preferences in *Christ and Satan*, including average

that the poem's seams run neatly along section boundaries. However, the statistics on alliteration do point to likely sites of disjunction. Fitt 8, falling within the stylistic parameters of group α but adjacent to β, seems a prime candidate – especially since the Harrowing of Hell sequence begins within this fitt. The shift from the laments of the fallen angels to the liberation of the patriarchs begins in a textually problematic passage, which I present here without emendation, but with a brief commentary on the metrical and syntactic difficulties:

> Sātanus   swearte geþohte   370
> þæt hē wolde on heofonum   hēhseld wyrcan
> uppe mid þām ēcan.   Þæt wæs ealdor heora,
> yfeles ordfruman.   Him þæt eft gehrēaw,
> þā hē tō helle   hnīgan sceolde,
> and his hired mid hine,   in tō geglīdan,   375
> nergendes nīð,   and nō seoððan
> þæt hī mosten in þone ēcan   andwlītan
> buton ende.   Þā him egsa becōm,
> dyne for dēman,   þā hē duru in helle
> bræc and bēgde.[17]   380

370a: line lacks a syllable. *ASPR* adds initial *Þā*, which is metrically unsatisfactory. *373a*: syntax unclear, since *ordfruman* is in exact apposition neither to *ealdor* nor *heora* (*ASPR* emends to *ordfruma*). *375b*: No alliteration (the a-verse requires a stress on **h**). *ASPR* emends *tō* to *hynðo*. *377b*: The verse is short, and the clause lacks a main verb. *ASPR* supplies *sēon*. *378a*: Though technically metrical, this is the only instance of the common 'X butan ende' formula to lack a second stress.[18] *379b*: The line is unmetrical, though removing *in* and construing *helle* as genitive would solve this.

Satan darkly intended that he would establish a throne in the heavens on high with the Eternal One. That was their lord, the chief of evil's. He came to regret that when he had to sink down to hell, and his retinue with him, slide in, the saviour's enmity, and never afterwards that they might forever in the eternal countenance [??]. Then terror came upon them, a clamour before the judge, when he broke and cast down the doors in hell.

Krapp's edition in *The Anglo-Saxon Poetic Records* remains standard: he tends to make the minimal emendations necessary for sense and – usually but not invariably – alliteration. That emendations for sense are necessary points to one of the complicating factors in any study of this poem: the recorded text of *Christ and Satan* is disrupted, and sometimes nonsensical. Line 7a, for instance, contains the word *ybmlyt*, which (besides being meaningless) is impossible in Old English phonology.[19] Flaws in the metre, therefore, may be due to problems in transmission, and should not be automatically ascribed to misunderstanding on the part of the poet. Identifying an anomalous metrical feature in *Christ and Satan* thus requires finding a pattern.

Fortunately (at least for our present purposes), the poem is repetitive enough that many comparisons are possible. So, for instance, the parallel passage at 463–6 tells us several things:

> Þis wæs on uhtan   eall geworden,
> ær dægrede,   þæt se dyne becom,
> hlud of heofonum,   þa he helle duru
> forbræc and forbegde . . .

This fully came to pass in the time before daybreak, before dawn, that the sound came loud from heaven when he broke and cast down the doors of hell. . .

These lines are metrically unexceptional: even the *Beowulf*-poet would not have objected to the anacrusis in 466a.[20] The passage shows us that the words *helle* and *duru* were treated elsewhere in the poem with their normal metrical values, and it also demonstrates the close verbal similarity between parts of Fitt

8 and Fitt 9. Earlier in Fitt 9, we find the line 'þær nu Satanus swearte þingað' (445: 'where Satan now broods darkly'), also a metrically normal treatment of *Satanus*. *Christ and Satan* is the only Old English poem to use the Latin form of this name, so this in itself links these two passages closely. The differences between Fitt 8 and the β sections of the poem are not, in short, differences of lexis. Rather, they show radically different metrical treatments of the same words. Some of this discrepancy is undoubtedly due to textual corruption, as the lack of an infinitive in line 377 indicates. But similarities between another passage in Fitt 9 and other parts of the poem suggest that not all the differences are necessarily due to scribal error.

In Christ's speech to the liberated patriarchs near the end of the fitt, we come across the following lines, which again I present without emendation:

> Gemunde ic ðæs mænego   and þa minnan ham
> lange þæs ðe ic of hæftum   ham gelædde
> up to earde,   þæt heo agan
> drihtnes domas   and duguðe þrym;
> wuniað in wynnum,   habbað wuldres blæd
> þusendmælum.[21]

> I remember this multitude and far from my home which I led up from captivity to their homeland, so that they [?] to possess the joys of the Lord and glory with the host; they will dwell in joy, they will have the splendour of glory a thousandfold.

There are many textual problems here. Line 502b (*and þa minnan ham*) does not seem to fit into the sentence: though *and* suggests it is in apposition with *ðæs mænego*, it is in the wrong case. Krapp emends *and* to *on*, which is probably right.[22] The cross-alliteration in line 503, together with the long sequence of unstressed words in 503a, is a little suspicious but not absolutely unmetrical, though *lange* is somewhat awkward in context. The real problem is in line 504b, where the infinitive *agan* requires a modal verb. The *ASPR* (and other editions) add *sceolon*, which is quite unobjectionable.[23]

However, some parallel passages should give us pause. The most striking of these is in Fitt 10:

> Forþon men sceolon   mæla gehwylce
> secgan drihtne þanc   dædum and weorcum,
> þæs ðe he us of hæftum   ham gelædde
> up to eðle,   þær we agan
> drihtnes domas,
> and we in wynnum   wunian moton.[24]

And so at all times people should give thanks to the Lord with deeds and acts, because he brought us home out of captivity up to the homeland, where we [may] possess the joys of the lord and we may dwell in joy.

This second passage exactly repeats part of the first, together with the unmetrical and apparently ungrammatical sequence *agan drihtnes domas*. In Fitt 10, however, the following line – which is in exact apposition – supplies the necessary modal verb *moton*. The metrical flaw is repeated, but the syntactic problem is mended. There are similar lines earlier in the poem:

> Ðæs ic wolde of selde   sunu metodes,
> drihten adrifan,   and agan me þæs dreames gewald,
> wuldres and wynne,   me þær wyrse gelamp
> þonne ic to hyhte   agan moste.[25]

Because I wanted to drive the Lord, the Creator's son from the hall, and possess for myself the control of that joy, the glory and bliss, it turned out worse for me there than I could have hoped.

> Þær heo sceppend seolf
> friðe befæðmeð,   fæder mancynnes,
> ahefeð holdlice   in heofones leoht,
> þær heo mid wuldorcyninge   wunian moton
> awa to ealdre,
> agan dreama dream   mid drihtne gode,
> a to worulde   a buton ende.[26]

There the Creator himself embraces them, the Father of mankind, and faithfully raises them up into heaven's light, where they will be able to live forever with the King of glory, possessing the joy of joys with the Lord God, forever and ever.

The first of these passages is in Fitt 3, and the third comes at the end of Fitt 6. Both are unproblematic syntactically, but metrically something of a mess. As an infinitive, *agan* normally ought to bear metrical stress; however, 'colourless' words like *beon* 'to be' and *habban* 'to have' are sometimes demoted, so 173b ('and agan me þæs dreames gewald') and 313a ('agan dreama dream') could be considered more or less normal. But the alliteration and lineation of the passage from Fitt 6 are badly disrupted, and that the problem lies in a line with vowel alliteration, plus *agan*, plus a line alliterating on **d**, looks remarkably suspicious.

We can, of course, simply decide that all these passages are irredeemably corrupt. However, we can also make sense of most of them by hypothesizing that the poet has extrapolated an unusual metrical value for *agan* in certain contexts. This can be seen by relineating the relevant verses:

up to earde,   þæt heo agan drihtnes domas and duguðe þrym (504–5)

up to eðle,   þær we agan drihtnes domas
and we in wynnum   wunian moton (552–5)

þær heo mid wuldorcyninge   wunian moton
awa to ealdre   agan dreama dream mid drihtne gode (311–13)

From the syntax, of course, we know that the relineation of 504–5 cannot be correct. *We*, however, have the benefit of the *Dictionary of Old English Web Corpus* and Bruce Mitchell's two-volume work on *Old English Syntax*. It may seem peculiar to suggest that a native Old English speaker might have been less confident in the verse of his own language than modern scholars. But Old English verse had its own grammar and its own vocabulary, both differing substantially from written prose – and, most likely, from normal spoken Old English. A reader who didn't know the rules, but who saw there *were* rules, would be forced to make deductions from the poetry he had – much like a visitor to a foreign country attempting to make do with a phrasebook. If the phrasebook is right, then all is well; if it is damaged or badly printed, then confusion will undoubtedly ensue, and the foreigner may never find out where things went wrong.

This, I suggest, is what has happened with *Christ and Satan*. The miscopied or damaged reading *þæt heo agan drihtnes domas* . . . at what is now 504–5 has misled a would-be poet into believing this is a correct line, perhaps a peculiar form of hypermetric verse. He has replicated part of it almost exactly in 552–3, and generated a similar verse from the underlying structure at 312–13. Believing by this point that *agan* can be used with considerable latitude before alliterating phrases in **d**, he also generates the quasi-correct 173b (*and agan me þæs dreames gewald*).

This is an odd pattern: but if we accept the premise that an Old English speaker did not necessarily know the rules of Old English verse, it is hardly an irrational one. It also has some striking implications for our understanding of *Christ and Satan* and its poet. First, the poem as it stands must preserve intact at least part of an earlier text. This is implied by the wide metrical differences across the poem, but the propagation of the error in 504–5 indicates that this passage must have been copied at least once (and either damaged or miscopied in the process) before reaching the *Christ and Satan* poet. However, the distribution of the anomalous *agan* passages across Fitts 3, 6, and 10 tells us that the whole poem was reworked to some extent: at least, fitt boundaries do not necessarily demarcate separate poets' work.

Table 4.6 *Verses in* ham

Fitt	Line	Full verse
Fitt 1	25	ða heo in helle **ham** staðeledon,
	38	Þis is ðeostræ **ham,** ðearle gebunden
	49	bidan in bendum, and me bættran **ham**
Fitt 2	88	þe ic hebbe to helle **ham** geledde
	91	Nu ic eow hebbe to hæftum **ham** gefærde
	95	agan moten. Is ðes atola **ham**
	99	Is ðæs walica **ham** wites afylled
	110	deofla menego to ðissum dimman **ham**
Fitt 3	147	þa ic mot to hæftum **ham** geferian
	177	alæded fram leohte in þone laðan **ham**
Fitt 4	215	hyhtlicra **ham** in heofonrice
	218	drihten hælend, in ðæm deoran **ham,**
Fitt 6	255	drihten adrifan of þam deoran **ham,**
	275	þonne ic on heofonum **ham** staðelode
	277	on heofona rice **ham** alefan
	293	Tæceð us se torhta trumlicne **ham,**
Fitt 7	336	dracan and næddran and þone dimman **ham**
	344	þa heo on heofonum **ham** staðelodon,
	361	a to aldre, uplicne **ham,**
Fitt 8	413	haligne **ham,** heofon to gewalde
	425	**ham** to helle; is nu hæftum strong,
	429	wolde helwarum **ham** gelihtan
Fitt 9	502	Gemunde ic ðæs mænego and þa minnan **ham**
	503	lange þæs ðe ic of hæftum **ham** gelædde
Fitt 10	551	þæs ðe he us of hæftum **ham** gelædde
Fitt 11	566	to þam halgan **ham** heofna ealdor
Fitt 12	657–8	engla ordfruma, and eorðan tudor to þissum eadigan **ham**

From these sets of passages, we can also tell that the *Christ and Satan* poet had a reasonably good grasp on basic principles of formulaic variation. He could make changes within a system (e.g. *up to eardel up to eðle*), but does not seem to have had a very large set of systems to vary. Thus, similar phrases are repeated (and repeated), often in very close sequence. We see a good example of this in a set of formulas clustered around a single word: *ham*. All the instances of this word in *Christ and Satan* are listed in Table 4.6, and classified by formula type in Table 4.7.

Christ and Satan accounts for more than a quarter of all uses of uninflected *hām* in the Old English verse corpus: the idea of 'home' must represent an important theme in the poem. Yet the way that theme is developed – the cluster of words used in conjunction with it – is remarkably

Table 4.7 *Types of* ham *formulas*

Type 1a (Bliss 1A1a)

α	88b	ham geledde
α	91b	ham gefærde
α	147b	ham geferian
β	277b	ham alefan
α	429b	ham gelihtan
β	503b	ham gelædde
β	551b	ham gelædde

Type 1b (Bliss 1D1)

α	25b	ham staðeledon
β	275b	ham staðelode
β	344b	ham staðelodon

Others (Bliss 1A1)

| α | 425a | **ham** to helle |

Type 2a (Bliss 3E2)

α	215a	hyhtlicra **ham**
β	293b	trumlicne **ham**
β	361b	uplicne **ham**
α	413a	haligne **ham**

Type 2b (Bliss 3B1)

α	38a	Þis is ðeostræ **ham**
α	49b	and me bættran **ham**
α	95b	Is ðes atola **ham**
α	99a	Is ðæs walica **ham**
α	110b	to ðissum dimman **ham**
α	177b	in þone laðan **ham**
α	218b	in ðæm deoran **ham**
β	255b	of þam deoran **ham**
β	336b	and þone dimman **ham**
β	502b	and þa minnan **ham**
β	566a	to þam halgan **ham**
β	658b	to þissum eadigan **ham**

static. The first type of formula, which pairs initial stressed *ham* with a verb, expresses only a very narrow range of concepts. Most formulas of type 1a mean 'bring home'; the only exceptions are *ham alefan* ('abandon home') and *ham gelihtan* ('illuminate the home'). Because these b-verses all alliterate on **h**, the poet could have chosen a verb in any other letter for the final non-alliterating stress: all these, however, alliterate on either **l** or **f**, as if the poet did not feel at liberty to stray beyond well-attested sound patterns. The second type of formula, in which *ham* forms the second stress and thus need not alliterate, shows a little more variety. Even here, though, three of the four type 2a formulas consist of *ham* paired with adjectives in –*lic*, and a third of the type 2b formulas have either *dimman ham* or *deoran ham* as their main stresses.

This cautious adherence to rule is perhaps most visible in Fitt 2, where every single verse-form is attested elsewhere. The first two and last of the *ham* formulas in Table 4.6 differ only in metrically invisible detail from verses in Fitts 3, 7, 9, and 10. The pair 95b and 99a echo each other in very short sequence, and both rely on a metrical template attested across the poem. Interestingly, 99a seems to incorporate *two* common formulas, slotting type 2a's basic pattern of alliterating –*lic* adjectives paired with *ham* into the flexible matrix of type 2b. The close repetition is inelegant, but metrically safe. This contrasts strikingly with the formulas we find in Fitt 8. Here we find *ham to helle*, the only use of *ham* which is not formulaic within the poem – though it should be noted that the underlying metrical template is probably the most common one in Old English verse. This fitt also employs the only type 2a formula that does not use an adjective in –*lic*, and a type 1a formula that expresses not a journey to hell, but the illumination of it during the Harrowing. Where Fitt 2 is cautiously conventional, Fitt 8 is innovative: and this pattern of difference may help us to trace more clearly the current poem's seams.

Constructing Christ and Satan

The substantial differences of metrical style between parts of *Christ and Satan* apparently stem from the working practices of at least two poets. The earlier of these probably had a more or less normal experience, and acquired knowledge of Old English poetic language within a community. But the latest (and perhaps most interesting) of these poets seems to have relied mainly on written texts and his own powers of induction to create a different text out of part-salvaged and part-new verse. Focusing on his contributions should, therefore, give us a better idea of how and why the extant poem was created: what we want from this study of the Junius XI text is not the dissected corpse of a poem, but rather a sense of the processes by which it was assembled.

Fitt 2, given its frequent and conservative use of formulas, seems to be a good candidate for attribution to the 'Renovator', as we might call him. This fifty-line section is explicitly an extension of Satan's speech in Fitt 1: it begins 'Eft reordade oðre siðe / feonda aldor' (75–6a: 'The chief of the devils spoke again a second time'). It recapitulates the themes of the earlier lament, touching on the Devil's sin of rebellion (84–7: cf. 50), the lost joys of heaven (81–3, 92–5, 104–6: cf. 36–7, 44–5), and the present misery of hell (89–104, 107–24: cf. 38–42, 48–9). Fitt 2 introduces additional tropes from the poetry of exile:

> Forðon ic sceal hean and earm   hweorfan ðy widor,
> wadan wræclastas,   wuldre benemed,
> dugdðum bedeled . . .[27]

Therefore I, abased and wretched, must wander the further, tread the paths of exile, deprived of glory, cut off from the hosts . . .

This resembles God's curse on Adam in *Genesis B*:

> Þu scealt oðerne   eðel secean,
> wynleasran wic,   and on wræc hweorfan
> nacod niedwædla,   neorxnawanges
> dugeðum bedæled;   þe is gedal witod
> lices and sawle.[28]

Thou must seek out another home, a more joyless dwelling, and go forth as a naked beggar into exile, cut off from the hosts of paradise; for thee the parting of soul and body is decreed.

There are also close similarities to other Old English poems, such as *The Wanderer* and *Guthlac A*.[29] What this knowledge of literary convention must indicate is that the Renovator had read or heard other Old English poems, and that he was familiar enough with themes like 'exile' to be able to employ them when needed. He was not, in other words, entirely a 'man of one book'. And yet Fitt 2 also shows us that the Renovator's tendency towards exact repetition carries over to the large scale as well as the small. Just as he prefers to hew closely to established metrical patterns, he also constructs Satan's second lament very much on the template of the first.

Our understanding of the Renovator's intentions and capacities depends, then, partly on where his templates come from. When we think about the purpose of the Junius XI text, it does matter whether the poem's overall contours were already present in a text he chose to fix, or whether he augmented one or more fragments into a new poem. Since I have argued that most of Fitt 2, whose style is characteristic of the α group, is the work of the Renovator, the practical question therefore is: did the Renovator decide to add the 'Laments of the Fallen Angels' to the poem himself, or was there a pre-existing template in the earlier poem?

The answer must lie in Fitt 1, which frames the fall of the angels as part of the story of Creation. After God has given glory to the chief rank of angels,

> Ðuhte him on mode þæt hit mihte swa,
> þæt hie weron seolfe swegles brytan,
> wuldres waldend. Him ðær wirse gelamp,
> ða heo in helle ham staðeledon,
> an æfter oðrum in þæt atole scref,
> þær heo brynewelme bidan sceoldon
> saran sorge, nales swegles leoht
> habban in heofnum heahgetimbrad,
> ac gedufan sceolun in ðone deopan wælm
> niðær under nessas in ðone neowlan grund,
> gredige and gifre. God ana wat
> hu he þæt scyldige werud forscrifen hefde![30]

It seemed to them in their heart that it might so be that they were themselves the rulers of heaven, the lords of glory. It turned out the worse for them there, when they established a home in hell, one after the other in that dreadful cavern, where they would have to endure burning surges, agonizing sorrow, and have none of the high-built light of heaven, but must plunge into the deep surge, down under the headlands into that deep abyss, greedy and famished. God alone knows how he has condemned that guilty host!

This passage is significant not only because it establishes a paradigm for the various laments of the devils in *Christ and Satan*, but because it has close parallels in *Guthlac A*.[31] The relevant parts appear in the course of Guthlac's altercation with the devils, who first drag him to the mouth of hell:

> Hwæðre hine gebrohton bolgenmode,
> wraðe wræcmæcgas, wuldres cempan,
> halig husulbearn, æt heldore,
> þær firenfulra fæge gæstas
> æfter swyltcwale secan onginnað
> ingong ærest in þæt atule hus,
> niþer under næssas neole grundas.[32]

But the cruel outcasts, enraged, brought the warrior of glory, the holy son of sacrifice [i.e., communicant?] to the doors of hell, where the condemned spirits of the sinful first seek entry after their death into that terrible house, the deep abyss down under the headlands.

The demons then tell him they are going to shove him in:

> Nu þu in helle scealt
> deope gedufan,   nales dryhtnes leoht
> habban in heofonum,   heahgetimbru,
> seld on swegle,   forþon þu synna to fela,
> facna gefremedes   in flæschoman.[33]

Now you must plunge deep into hell, and have none of the Lord's light in high-built heaven, the hall in the skies, because you have committed far too many criminal sins in the flesh.

Guthlac, however, will have none of it, and reproaches his assailants:

> Wendun ge ond woldun,   wiþerhycgende,
> þæt ge scyppende   sceoldan gelice
> wesan in wuldre.   Eow þær wyrs gelomp,
> ða eow se waldend   wraðe bisencte
> in þæt swearte susl . . .
>   Swa nu awa sceal
> wesan wideferh,   þæt ge wærnysse
> brynewylm hæbben,   nales bletsunga.[34]

You expected and believed, traitorous plotters, that you could become like the Creator in glory. It turned out the worse for you there, when the Ruler in wrath cast you into that dark torment . . . Thus it shall ever be that you evil ones shall have burning fires, not blessings.

Several of these parallels are unique in Old English verse.[35] The question is what they mean: do they indicate a direct literary relationship between these two poems, common dependence on a lost source, or simply adherence to traditional formulaic diction? The unique whole-line parallels would seem to make the third option – coincidence – improbable.[36] Clubb believed that either the poet of *Guthlac A* borrowed from *Christ and Satan*, or both were derived from a common source.[37] On the whole, though, what we have seen of the Renovator's working methods points towards the opposite conclusion: wholesale borrowing either from *Guthlac A* in very close to its current form, or from another poem also used by the *Guthlac A* poet. Close study of the *Guthlac* poet's working methods would probably indicate which is more likely.

If much of the 'Fall of the Angels' passage near the beginning of Fitt 1 of *Christ and Satan* is indeed cribbed from *Guthlac A* (or perhaps an ur-*Guthlac*), this means that the Renovator is responsible for creating most of the 'Laments of the Fallen Angels' portions of the poem, and that he probably did not feel himself bound to the overall purpose of the earlier texts he had before him. Though he hewed close to his sources in terms of style, word choice, and the structure of elements like speeches, the Renovator seems to have assembled the text as a whole as he wished. Though much of the Harrowing episode may have existed earlier, the Renovator's decision to frame it with the devils' laments indicates the tone he intended for the piece. Hell is very much the poem's keynote.

Significantly, the Renovator's hell is attained through false judgment. Beginning with 'Ðuhte him on mode . . .' in the passage from Fitt 1 quoted above, Satan and his followers reproach each other with mutual deceit and self-delusion. After their chieftain has lamented his new surroundings, the lesser devils reply:

> Þu us gelærdest   ðurh lyge ðinne
> þæt we helende   heran ne scealdon.
> Ðuhte þe anum   þæt ðu ahtest alles gewald,
> heofnes and eorþan,   wære halig god . . .[38]

With your lies you convinced us that we should not praise the Saviour. It seemed to you that you alone had power over everything – heaven and earth – that *you* were the Holy God . . .

The impersonal voice of *ðuhte* lends Satan's conceit a disembodied tone. No one persuaded him of his delusion; it simply came to him, and he has been led astray by the thoughts of his own mind. The potential of the mind to deceive itself and others layers more meaning upon the already freighted word for Lucifer's sin, *oferhygd*.[39] In his thoughts he got above himself, and through his uncontrolled mind he was damned. For those mortals contemplating his fate, there is not much to do except to maintain vigilance over their own minds:

> Forþon mæg gehycgan,   se ðe his heorte deah,
> þæt he him afirre   frecne geþohtas,
> laðe leahtras,   lifigendra gehwylc.
> Gemunan symle on mode   meotodes strengðo;
> gearwian us togenes   grene stræte
> up to englum,   þær is se ælmihtiga god.[40]

Therefore every man living who is steady in heart ought to recall that he should put far from himself wicked thoughts, hateful sins. We should always remember the Creator's power in our hearts; we should prepare for ourselves the green path up to the angels, where is the Almighty God.

For the poet here, controlling sin is a matter of banishing wrong thoughts and retaining right ones. It is an internal process, one of *self*-judgment. That this can go badly wrong is attested by the example of Lucifer and his angels. One may hope to join a collective – the *us* travelling the *grene stræte* to the dwelling of the angelic host – but this communal reward springs from a lifetime of inward vigilance.[41]

The danger of judgment which we see in *Christ and Satan*, then, is quite different from the perils found in (for instance) Cynewulf's verse. In both, individuals may be externally condemned by an all-knowing God. But the emphasis in *Christ and Satan* is on the hazards of inward misjudgment: of individuals leading themselves astray through the thoughts of their own minds. The Renovator's Devil is an object lesson in the potential pitfalls of contemplation, and as such he was probably created for – and by – those who spent much of their time in solitary thought.

Patchwork and the style of Old English verse

As a complex composite poem, *Christ and Satan* is thus somewhat similar to *Genesis*, its companion in the Junius XI manuscript. Moreover, the Renovator's recreation of a text from a damaged exemplar strongly resembles the textual history which Remley has constructed for *The Canticle of the Three Youths (Azarias)*, a revised descendant of a passage from *Daniel*.[42] Patchwork itself, therefore, must be recognized as a literary phenomenon in Old English verse. In *Christ and Satan*, however, we see the conjoined work of two kinds of poet: one indistinguishable from poets working within a community, and the other displaying very striking differences. In the Renovator's work – which occurs throughout the Junius XI text of *Christ and Satan*, but is particularly prevalent in the early fitts – we see someone tiptoeing among rules he does not quite understand, clinging to the guideline of repeatable formulas. In some cases, as we saw with his deductions about how *agan* could work, his sources led him astray; but on the whole he was able to use pre-existing material to piece together a poem of respectable length, and on a theme of his choosing.

The Renovator's self-taught version of Old English metre poses critical problems for both metrists and editors. The style of *Christ and Satan* is eccentric, and by the standards of the *Beowulf*-poet it is bad – but the Renovator clearly had no one like the *Beowulf*-poet to hand. For modern scholars, there is no benefit to deciding that the idiosyncratic metre of the Renovator is wrong and needs fixing, because doing so would efface the traces of his work process and the idiosyncrasies which make his poetry unique. This does not, however, mean that an editor should simply reproduce the Junius XI text, which (as the contemporary corrections partly indicate) was poorly copied. Instead, the ideal editor of *Christ and Satan* would have the difficult task of retracing the Renovator's steps, and working out what his idea of metre actually was. The Renovator believed in rules and tried to find them out; it would be a disservice to his efforts not to attempt to understand them. *Christ and Satan* needs a new edition, emended to conform to the Renovator's idea of Old English metre.

Such a suggestion raises the depressing prospect of a fragmented corpus of Old English poetry, each poem a law unto itself, and bookshelves full of metrical treatises applicable only to *Beowulf.* I do not think, however, that the situation is quite so bad as that. Just as communities of native speakers conform to shared grammatical rules, the accepted forms of Old English poetry will be shared among communities of poets. There may be metrical subdialects, but for most poets – poets within communities – metrical conventions will be standardized. It is mainly for isolated poets that scholars will have the necessity of reconstructing anomalous metres. This labour, however, may also have its benefits: poems in which we find strange individual laws are likely to be the work of poets who had libraries, not communities, and through them we can learn more about the range of Anglo-Saxons' reactions to literacy.

It is impossible to know if the Renovator of *Christ and Satan* ever had the opportunity to join in a poetic community, and to learn the conventions of Old English verse from living practitioners. It is certainly easy to imagine situations – child oblation among them – which would involuntarily separate would-be poets from communities. But we must not begin with the assumption that all isolated poets were necessarily victims of circumstance, for our next case demonstrates that some had a large share in creating the conditions in which they worked.

Bede's poetry: reconsiderations

As a monk, a teacher, and a man with an apparently large network of personal connections across England, the Venerable Bede seems at first glance anything but isolated. As we saw in Chapter 2, Bede's teacher Ceolfrith was a competent poet who may have studied at Canterbury, and Bede possibly had other teachers who were trained in England or abroad.[43] He himself was certainly in correspondence with Canterbury alumni such as Albinus of Canterbury, and the dedications of his works reveal a variety of contacts with bishops, kings, and minor clergy. Though he spent many of his working years at Jarrow – certainly the younger and perhaps the lesser of Benedict Biscop's monasteries between the Wear and Tyne – Bede was

certainly not cut off from the civilization of his time.[44] Judging by the range
of informants he quotes in his *Historia ecclesiastica*, he must have been
exceptionally well-connected.

At the same time, though, Bede seems curiously detached from the often
bloody and venal world of early Northumbria. Part of this impression, we
know, is a function of the rhetoric of his best-known work, the *Historia
ecclesiastica gentis Anglorum*, a masterpiece of controlled disbursement of
information.[45] But the impression of Bede's uniqueness – of the incom-
mensurability of his particular achievement with his surroundings – is a
common one among scholars. George Hardin Brown describes him as 'an
autodidact', and Patrick Wormald cites his 'lack of contact with the tastes of
the Northumbrian world outside the monastery'.[46] Responses like these
stem, I think, not from the forced conversion of Bede into an eighth-
century avatar of the modern scholar (though such notions do also occur),
but from the perception of a real and peculiar tendency in his work.

Bede's relationship to authority was complicated, and ranged from
deference to scepticism through a broad mid-spectrum of *apparent* submission masking a striking originality. The humble compiler *patrum uesti-
gia sequens* is the same man who from his deathbed called Isidore of Seville a
liar; and his apparent aversion to contradicting others in writing can give a
very misleading impression of his attitude towards his sources.[47] Recent
work on Bede's biblical commentaries has gone a considerable way towards
demonstrating his independence of thought within a genre framed around
submission to one's predecessors.[48] It should be remembered, too, that
Bede appears to have invented a new form of marginal source-notes as a way
of defending himself from accusations of heresy: he was quite prepared to
use written authority as a rhetorical weapon.[49] Though his tone of disinterested inquiry after truth can seem strikingly modern, it arises from a
tendency that in his own day may have appeared strange and, perhaps,
arrogant. Bede seemingly only trusted conclusions he had reached himself,
through his own research. This preference for working from first principles
is what allowed him to revolutionize the *computus*, the teaching of metre,
and the writing of history, but it probably annoyed those of his contemporaries whose work he ignored into oblivion.

Whoever his teachers may have been, therefore, Bede had the tempera-
ment of an autodidact, and this affects his work even when it is apparently at
its most cautiously conservative. Indeed, his cautious conservatism is quite
often a symptom of a radical scepticism about received opinion. We can see
a good example of this in the *Retractatio* to his commentary on the Acts of
the Apostles. In the period between his earlier and later works on Acts, Bede

had acquired a Greek text and taught himself a little of the language. He used this knowledge to create a sort of conditional-tense textual apparatus for his updated commentary:

> In quo etiam quaedam quae in Graeco siue aliter seu plus aut minus posita uidimus, breuiter commemorare curauimus; quae, utrum neglegentia interpretis omissa uel aliter dicta an incuria librariorum sint deprauata siue relicta, nondum scire potuimus. Namque Graecum exemplar fuisse falsatum suspicari non audeo; unde lectorem admoneo ut haec ubicumque fecerimus gratia eruditionis legat, non in suo tamen uolumine uelut emendaturus interserat, nisi forte ea in Latino codice suae editionis antiquitus sic interpretata reppererit.[50]

> And so wherever I have seen that the Greek has either different words, or more or fewer, I have tried to note it briefly; whether such readings were left out through the translator's negligence, or differently expressed, or whether they were corrupted or left out through the carelessness of scribes, I cannot presently say. For I do not dare to suspect that the Greek exemplar had been corrupt; therefore I advise the reader that he take all my readings as for the sake of scholarship, and not to incorporate them into his own volume as emendations – unless he should happen to find them thus interpreted in a very early Latin manuscript of his text.

The divergence between the Greek and Latin texts of Acts is a problem, but one that Bede considers soluble. He seems confident that he can eventually ascertain whether the difference stems from the original translation or from progressive scribal corruption ('*nondum* scire potuimus'), and even proposes a test that would confirm his readings: the corroboration of a very old Latin manuscript. But he also entertains a possibility he immediately denies: that the original translation might have been based on a faulty exemplar. Given the far-reaching consequences for every interpretation of Acts based on the Latin, rather than the Greek, he says that such a thing 'suspicari non audeo' ('I do not dare to suspect'). Except, of course, that plainly he has. Bede is willing to consider that much of Western biblical criticism might be based on weak foundations, but he believes that he knows how to shore those foundations up. All he would need is more books.

Bede's attitude might be characterized as 'fundamentalist', in the sense of believing that uncritical reliance on tradition is likely to mislead; for the truth, one must return to the tradition's origin. But his notions of the originary are different from modern ones, and this fact is particularly relevant to our understanding of his verse. In his *De arte metrica*, Bede distinguishes the practices of *antiqui poetae* – which is to say, pagan – from *moderni*, in a chapter on the metrical flaws of Classical verse. As to ancient poets' attitude towards the positioning of syllables in the final feet of a hexameter, he says,

> Qui et aliis in metrico opere regulis multum libere utebantur, quas moderni poetae distinctius ad certae normam definitionis obseruare maluerunt.[51]

> These and other rules in metrical construction they would treat with great freedom, which modern poets have preferred to observe more carefully according to the standard of an established definition.

Here we can see the equation Bede makes between rules of metre and of life. Just as the Christian Latin poets have preferred the *certae norma definitionis* of the Christian religion over that of the heathens, they are stricter about observing the true laws of verse construction, and are therefore a better model for imitation. Accordingly, Bede has replaced most of the Classical examples he found in the works of the Late Antique grammarians whose textbooks he drew upon with quotations from Christian Latin poets.[52] Yet he was not blind to the metrical faults or licences which he discovered in his reading, and so he wrote a chapter to explain 'Quod et auctoritas saepe et necessitas metricorum decreta uiolet' ('The fact that authority and necessity will often violate the rules of the metricians').[53] Most of the ancient grammarians who wrote on metre were themselves pagans, and this, by a rhetorical twist, allowed Bede to explain the licences of Christian Latin poets as deliberate, rather than merely licentious. So, for instance, he explains Sedulius' verse

> Clārīfĭc|ā dīx|ĭt nō|mēn tŭŭm. | Māgnĕquĕ |cāelō,

> In quo, ut ueritatem Dominici sermonis apertius commendaret, postposuit ordinem disciplinae saecularis.[54]

> in which he disregarded the rule of worldly art in order to more clearly praise the truth of the Lord's speech.

The final syllable of *tuum* is long by position, but Bede has construed Sedulius' metrical infelicity as a triumphant privileging of the divine over the worldly. The difference between the Christian poets' calculated defiance of grammarians' rules and the pagans' mere indifference seems clear enough in spirit, though rather hard for students to cope with in practice. There is perhaps some shade here of the fraught relations between the Old Law and the New.

What these examples from *De arte metrica* chiefly indicate is that for Bede, metre and verse style are not neutral phenomena. Once 'rule' and 'authority' in the composition of verse have been laden with religious and historical significance, a poet's formal choices take on profound meaning. In reading Bede's own verse, therefore, we must pay close attention to his use of – and divergence from – poetic models, in order to understand how he came to forge his own path as a poet. As in his commentaries and textbooks, Bede in his poetry often uses authoritative example as a doorway to deliberate originality.

The Aldhelm years

While we lack materials for a full reconstruction of Bede's career as a poet, recent work – particularly that of Michael Lapidge – has made it possible to sketch a general arc encompassing most of the surviving major poems.[55] The discovery that an early redaction of the *Vita metrica S. Cuthberti* still survives has helped illuminate the development of his skill during the early decades of the eighth century.[56] It seems likely, however, that some other poems of Bede's date from quite early in his career, perhaps even before the *c.* 705 date Lapidge gives the Besançon redaction of the *Vita metrica S. Cuthberti*, and these give us a remarkable insight into his formative influences. The hymn to St Æthelthryth included in the *Historia ecclesiastica* and the *Versus de die iudicii* are strikingly more ornate and more obviously indebted to Sedulius and Aldhelm than Bede's later works, and in them we can see the identifiably early English style that he went on to reject.

We do not know the exact date of *Alma deus trinitas*, the poem forming most of Book III, chapter 20 in the *Historia ecclesiastica*. In his brief prose introduction, he states that

> ante annos plurimos in laudem ac praeconium eiusdem reginae ac sponsae Christi ... elegaico metro conposuimus, et imitari morem sacrae scripturae, cuius historiae carmina plurima indita et haec metro ac uersibus constat esse conposita.[57]

> I composed [it] in elegiac metre many years ago in praise and commendation of this same queen and bride of Christ ..., and in imitation of the practice of the holy Scripture, in whose narrative many poems are inserted, which are composed in conformity with metre and verses.

The phrase *ante annos plurimos* would seem to suggest a date of composition much earlier than that of the *Historia ecclesiastica* (which was completed in 731), but not *how* much earlier. However, Bede's enthusiasm for St Æthelthryth seems to have been sparked by conversations with Wilfrid, which must have taken place before the bishop's final departure for the Continent in 709.[58] We can reasonably hypothesize that the poem dated from around this time; twenty or thirty years would certainly amount to *anni plurimi*.

Alma deus trinitas is formally ornate, as the opening couplets show:

> Alma Deus Trinitas, quae saecula cuncta gubernas,
> adnue iam coeptis, alma Deus Trinitas.
>
> Bella Maro resonet; nos pacis dona canamus,
> munera nos Christi; bella Maro resonet.[59]

> O God, Holy Trinity, who rules all ages: favour now my endeavours, O God, Holy Trinity. Let Maro chant of wars, I will sing the gifts of peace: mine be Christ's rewards, let Maro chant of wars.

The poem goes on through all twenty-three letters of the Latin alphabet (including K, Y, and Z), and concludes with AMEN as an acrostic. In each of the elegiac couplets the first half of the hexameter is repeated at the end of the pentameter. The name for this form is 'epanaleptic abecedary', and it appears to be Bede's own contrivance. In it he combines the structures of Sedulius' two hymns, *Cantemus socii Domino* (in epanaleptic elegiac couplets) and *A solis ortus cardine*, an abecedary. Abecedarian poems are also found in the Bible (in Psalms 36 and 118, for instance, and the Book of Lamentations), and it may be this that prompted Bede's prefatory remarks.

Metrically, the poem is very accomplished. There are no errors, and only a few licences.[60] The pattern of feet in the hexameters is more rigid than Bede's normal practice: owing to the demands of the epanaleptic form, all twenty-seven begin with two dactyls. His favoured patterns in *Alma deus trinitas* are:

DDSS (56 per cent)
DDSD (22 per cent)
DDDS (15 per cent)
DDDD (7 per cent)

Given the requirement for two initial dactyls, this list tracks with Bede's usual preferences in hexameter structure.[61] The poem's diction, too, is carefully wrought, and rarely formulaic. We can, however, see traces of Bede's reading in his phraseology, and it reveals an interesting set of connections. The collocation *alma ... trinitas* in line 1, for instance, is startlingly rare: in the 'Library of Latin Texts' it occurs only here and in chapter 60 of Aldhelm's *Prosa de uirginitate*.[62] There is another echo of this last chapter of Aldhelm's work in line 27 (*regali ... stemmate*). The list of virgin martyrs in lines 17–22 may be partly indebted to Aldhelm's treatise, which discusses five of the six saints Bede names.[63] The first line of *Alma deus trinitas* also incorporates an echo of one of Aldhelm's *enigmata*:

> Ni soror et frater uaga saecula iure gubernent,
> heu! chaos immensum clauderet cuncta latebris ...[64]

> Did not this brother and errant sister rule the ages with their law, alas! vast chaos would smother all things in obscurity ...

Note particularly how instead of simply adopting a complete cadence from a single verse, Bede creates a new phrase from a combination of two lines. Even so, this couplet is far more obvious in its literary indebtedness than is usual in his verse. In an examination of the influence of Aldhelm's diction on the *Vita metrica S. Cuthberti*, Orchard has shown that Bede habitually varies both his own favourite phrases and the phrases he has derived from his models, and that

> synonym-substitution ... largely obscures his reliance on the borrowed phraseology of previous poets, and gives what I suggest is the false impression that Bede relies less on the words of his predecessors than other Anglo-Latin authors.[65]

In *Alma deus trinitas*, however, we hear some fairly clear echoes of Aldhelm's words, and – in the poem's ornate structure, diction, and Classical allusions – of Aldhelm's aesthetic. The epanaleptic abecedary form is reminiscent of the elaborate acrostic prefaces to the *Enigmata* and *Carmen de uirginitate*, and the invocation (and rejection) of Virgil is remarkably like Aldhelm's rejection of the Muses in these same verse prefaces.[66] Embedded in the magnum opus of his last years, this early poem shows the extent to which Bede was indebted to his Anglo-Latin predecessor at the beginning of his career, and makes the later divergence of his style all the more interesting.

The Aldhelmianism of *Alma deus trinitas* is shared by another work which Bede probably wrote early in his career. Though popular in the early Middle Ages, the *Versus de die iudicii* have not yet appeared in an adequate edition, and this complicates assessments of their style and diction.[67] However, Lapidge's study has shown that *De die iudicii* contains several metrical flaws of the sort that Bede worked hard to expunge from his later poetry; he concludes that the work 'may be an early composition of Bede, and one to which he did not return when he had acquired a more perfect command of Latin prosody'.[68] Orchard has identified a number of verbal parallels the poem shares with Aldhelm's verse.[69] There are also other stylistic similarities. Like Aldhelm's work, *De die iudicii* is highly end-stopped, and this, combined with its high percentage of 'golden lines', gives it a static, ornamental quality quite different from the fleeter, enjambed verse of the *Vita metrica S. Cuthberti.*[70] Lines like

> Inter apostolicas animis laetantibus arces
> Atque inter roseis splendentia castra triumphis,
> Candida uirgineo simul inter agmina flore[71]

> among the apostolic citadels with the rejoicing souls, and among the shining cities with rose-red banners, and among the bright throngs in the flower of virginity

are very carefully wrought: 147 is a 'golden line' with two pairs of interlaced adjectives and nouns, and the two verses preceding it contain a chiastic pattern of hyperbaton that in 146 also generates internal rhyme. Note too that all three lines are in exact syntactic parallel: this kind of apposition is very characteristic of *De die iudicii*, and also of Aldhelm's poetry.[72]

The particular kind of poetic beauty which *De die iudicii* displays is one that Bede himself endorsed in the *De arte metrica*. Neil Wright has discussed Bede's championing of enjambment, and of what Dryden called the 'golden line', in the textbook chapter titled *Quae sit optima carminis forma.*[73] Of these two, only the golden line plays a significant part in the style of *De die iudicii*. However, Bede also describes another device which he does put into practice:

> Aliquando uersum nominibus tantum perficere gratum est, ut Fortunatus:

> > Lilia, narcissus, uiolae, rosa, nardus, amomum,
> > oblectant animos germina nulla meos. . . .

> Fecit et in uerbis:

> > Blanditur, refouet, ueneratur, honorat, obumbrat,
> > et locat in thalamo membra pudica suo.[74]

> Sometimes it is pleasing to form the entire verse out of nouns, as Fortunatus does [from *De uirginitate* 237–8] . . . and he also made one from verbs [from *De uirginitate* 127–8].

This is called 'verse-filling asyndeton',[75] and the *De die iudicii* uses it frequently. Nouns are most common, for instance:

> Taedia, tristitiae, trux, indignatio, languor[76]

> Weariness, sorrows, savagery, indignation, depression

In one passage, though, Bede uses verbs, and is clearly thinking of the same example from Venantius Fortunatus cited in *De arte metrica*:

> Semper adest praesens, cunctos *fovet*, implet, *honorat*,
> Glorificat, seruat, *ueneratur*, diligit, ornat,
> Col*locat* altithrona laetosque in sede polorum . . .[77]

> He is ever present, and everyone he soothes, fills, honours, glorifies, protects, cherishes, loves, adorns, and places the joyful ones in the high-throned seat of the heavens . . .

Characteristically, he rearranges his borrowings from the earlier author, but *un*characteristically indulges in an even longer and more ornate passage than his source.

The particular stylistic embellishments of *De die iudicii*, then, are in keeping with Bede's own advice. But the poem is also very much of the school in which 'more is more', and in this respect it departs from *De arte metrica*. There, after giving an account of the golden line, Bede says that

> Nec tamen hoc continuatim agendum, uerum post aliquot interpositos uersus. Si enim semper uno modo pedes ordinabis et uersus, tametsi optimis sit, status statim uilescit.[78]

> But this should not be done continuously, only every few verses. For indeed if you always arrange your feet and verses in the same way, even if it is the best way, that mode will immediately be degraded.

Wright suggests that this statement 'could be taken as a criticism not only of Aldhelm's repeated golden lines but also of his repetition of his favourite patterns of dactyl and spondee'.[79] I would agree; but I would also argue that the style Bede is here deprecating is not just Aldhelm's, but that of his own early work. Perhaps the reason that he did not return to the *Versus de die iudicii* was that they were too thoroughly, incorrigibly Aldhelmian: too mannered, too end-stopped, perhaps even too alliterative.[80] Though also ornate, *Alma deus trinitas* is not as plainly indebted to Bede's predecessor, and revisiting it *post annos plurimos* was perhaps less trying to the spirit. Together, though, these two early poems show how close to Aldhelm and his tradition Bede's poetry had once been.

Reactions and redactions: *the* Vita metrica S. Cuthberti

Bede's most significant poetic work – the hexametrical life of St Cuthbert – is in some ways in keeping with the then-short history of Anglo-Latin literature. As a hagiographic poem highly indebted to the models of Late Antique

Christian verse, and conceived of in symbiotic relation to a prose text, the *Vita metrica* shares some significant qualities with Aldhelm's *Carmen de uirginitate*.[81] But as Orchard and Wright have demonstrated, the texture of Bede's verse 'seems almost deliberately contrived to contrast with that of his predecessor'.[82] Highly dactylic in its measure, variable in its diction, and inclined towards frequent enjambment and elision, the *Vita metrica* sounds quite unlike any of Aldhelm's poems. This was an effect Bede worked for, as Lapidge has shown by comparison of the two extant versions of the poem.

Michael Lapidge's discovery that the text of the *Vita metrica* in Besançon, Bibliothèque municipale, 186, represents a first redaction of the poem provides a remarkable window into Bede's priorities as a poet.[83] The revisions between the earlier (c. 705) and later (sometime before 721) forms of the *Vita metrica* were not wholesale or structural; rather, individual lines were recast or rewritten for reasons that were usually stylistic. Improving the metre, as Lapidge has demonstrated, was one of Bede's principal concerns. He corrected a number of false scansions throughout the poem;[84] so, for instance,

> Casta ferit, tandemque gemens erumpit in istam
> Oblitus lacrimis post maesta silentia vocem[85]

> he bore a chaste [heart], and finally, sighing and stained with tears, he burst out into this speech after a sorrowful silence

has had *oblitus* altered to *perfusus*, which clarifies the sense and removes the false quantity in *oblĭtus*.[86] More interestingly, however, Bede also revised many lines in order to introduce elision. For instance,

> Illud ovans fesso direptum tegmine velum

> Requesting the hanging taken from the wall-coverings for the sick man

has become

> Illud ovans fesso dirept(um) a pariete velum[87]

> Requesting the hanging taken from the wall for the sick man . . .

There is no real change in sense: evidently Bede considered elision desirable in itself.[88]

He also tinkered with his text's borrowed diction. Lapidge has discussed one instance in which Bede altered a borrowing from Arator – partly perhaps for the sake of emphasizing parallel syntax through alliteration, but likely partly also for the sake of not quoting directly from a predecessor.[89] This happens elsewhere: at line 728, for example, what appears to be a close echo of

Ausonius is obscured, and at 834 he alters an apparent allusion to Cyprianus Gallus.[90] There seem to be far fewer instances of the reverse process, though these do exist – as in line 850, where the change of *lamentans busta* to *rogitans sacra busta* adds a reminiscence of Arator 1.186. It should be noted, however, that this alteration also turns a highly spondaic line into a more dactylic one (DSSS becomes DSDD), so it may be that Bede's metrical priorities won out over his desire for original diction.

The changes Bede made between the Besançon and 'vulgate' redactions of his text do not represent a revolution in his aesthetics or metrical practices, but rather an intensification of the preferences evinced in the earlier version. When he returned to the poem, he wanted it to be more correct to be sure. But he also made it more dactylic and (through the incorporation of elision) more varied and difficult in its rhythms, as well as more original in its diction through the erasure of close borrowings from earlier texts. These purely stylistic tendencies all contrast sharply with the practices of Aldhelm, and they point to a profoundly significant aspect of Bede's poetic sensibility: his passion for uniqueness. Bede did use earlier texts as models, so that the bent of his writings cannot exactly be called originality in the modern sense. But the *Vita metrica S. Cuthberti* reveals that he consciously avoided replication in his poetry – of others, and of himself.

A look at Bede's use of one particular poeticism, the passive infinitive in *–ier*, will illustrate more clearly what 'a passion for uniqueness' entails. Table 4.8 lists all instances of this archaism in the *Vita metrica* and in Aldhelm's poetry. What should be instantly visible is that the two authors were quite similar in their habits – preferring, for instance, to locate the verb in the fifth foot. This is an exaggeration of a tendency in most earlier hexameter poets; Prudentius, for instance, also greatly prefers the *–ier* passive infinitive to complete the fifth foot. It is also clear that this similarity is not coincidental. Aldhelm seems to have invented *famularier* as a poetic version of the deponent verb *famulor*'s infinitive, and he uses it several times in a formulaic collocation meaning 'to serve Christ/the Lord'. Bede adopts the form, but not the phrase, and he never conjugates the same word in *–ier* twice. He is even careful to vary the conjugations of the verbs he uses: where eight of Aldhelm's ten examples are from the first conjugation, only four of Bede's nine are. Bede seems to value variety for its own sake, both within his own poem and in comparison with earlier works (like those of Aldhelm) which he had certainly read.

This profound reluctance to simply adopt the words or style of earlier poets is of a piece with Bede's complicated relationship to authority. Aldhelm is by no means his only elided source; Lapidge, for instance, has

Table 4.8 *Poetic passive infinitives in* –ier *in Aldhelm and Bede*

Aldhelm's poetry	*Vita metrica S. Cuthberti*
Humana specie vidit signarier olim, CE IV, x, 17	Se que suos que rogans precibus tutarier almi. 147
Quam summo spolier capitis de vertice rubra. En 24, 5	Supplice tum nutu sese benedicier orant. 231
Imperio terrente iubet venerarier omnes: CdV 371	Laudis ab humanae liber munirier aura. 376
Dum contempserunt Christo **famularier** uni CdV 549	Quid referam aequoreas iusto **famularier** undas 451
Possent et iugiter domino **famularier** alto CdV 759	Vilibus et mavis secretus condier antris, 524
Dum solus soli Christo **famularier** optat CdV 945	Pectora et ignivomas baratri sub cogier umbras 604
Aut mortis valeat clades effarier atras, CdV 1746	Absentis que etiam poenis se plectier atris. 605
Nonnulli iuvenum thalamis adsciscier optant, CdV 1785	Se cupiens solitis sacri firmarier horsis. 630
Omnibus, integre qui conversarier optant CdV 2053	Malebat satanae tetricis pulsarier armis, 684
Mallet et immunis regi **famularier** alto CdV 2072	

recently demonstrated how deeply indebted Bede was to a close study of Virgil, although the chapter from *De arte metrica* explaining 'Ut prisci poetae quaedam aliter quam moderni posuerunt' is in large part devoted to criticizing Virgil as a poetic model.[91] But the studied avoidance of self-repetition which we see in the *Vita metrica* points towards an active aesthetic principle which – as Orchard's work suggests – Bede simply did not share with most Anglo-Latin poets.[92] His value for variety – for uniqueness – sets his work apart, as does his intense self-scrutiny.

Self-judgment

Bede's poetic isolation was quite different from that of the Renovator of *Christ and Satan*: it is not marked by errors, but by a peculiar hypercorrectness. There are obvious reasons for this difference. Unlike any Old English poet, Bede had access to explicit written analyses of the rules governing Latin poetry: Late Antique metrical treatises made it possible to be an autodidact, and Bede's own *De arte metrica* made it even easier for later generations. He had a fixed standard, therefore, against which to measure the peculiarities he encountered in the texts available to him. As we have seen in his explanations for metrical flaws in Classical and Christian Latin poets, Bede understood deviations from the norm through an ideological lens. Interestingly, though, when he examined his own work, it was by a stricter measure than he applied to the *moderni*. The changes he made to the *Vita metrica S. Cuthberti* demonstrate that his standard for himself was extremely high; he required not simply metrical correctness, but also a degree of variety and difficulty that went well beyond that of many of his models.

Bede is a poetic isolate, then, because the judgment to which he conformed was entirely his own. The process by which he formed the criteria for his judgment was evidently protracted, as we can see by the difference between his earliest, 'Aldhelmian' work and the *Vita metrica*. It also seems to have been a curious mixture of imitation and rejection. Though his metrical treatise suggests a profound ambivalence towards the Classical poets generally and Virgil in particular, Lapidge has shown that Bede's use of caesurae in his verse is strikingly Virgilian, and that he skilfully employs 'features which are not discussed in *any* metrical treatise – ancient, late antique, or early medieval – and which could only have been learned from the minute study of an excellent poet such as Virgil'.[93] His early poetry, and even his later use of passive infinitives in –*ier*, shows Bede also devoted close attention to the work of his predecessor Aldhelm. Here we can see most clearly how he deliberately distinguished his style from that of others, pursuing a standard that was his own because it was specifically un-Aldhelmian. Bede's ambiguous notice of the Wessex bishop in the *Historia ecclesiastica* has been discussed elsewhere.[94] Given the rapid and widespread dissemination of Aldhelm's writings discussed in Chapter 3, I would suggest that Bede's early embrace and later rejection of Aldhelm's style is a reaction to a more general current in Anglo-Latin literature. The moment at which Bede decided to differentiate his work from the prevailing standard of his times is difficult to pinpoint, but it must have been quite early in his career; certainly before 705, and probably before his ordination as a priest. Aldhelm would have still been alive.

The idiopathic standards of Bede's verse are reflected in his images of the process of judgment. Like Anglo-Saxon poets of all stripes, Bede was obsessed with judgment. But characteristically, it appears in his poetry in the form of solitary introspection. Even in the early *Versus de die iudicii*, collective judgment is framed in terms of silent self-examination:

> Arboris umbriferae maestus sub tegmine solus
> Dum sedi, subito planctu turbatus amaro
> Carmina prae tristi cecini haec lugubria mente
> Utpote commemorans scelerum commissa meorum,
> Et maculas uitae, mortisque inamabile tempus . . .
> Haec memorans mecum, tacito sub murmure dixi . . .⁹⁵

> While I sat alone and sorrowful beneath the cover of a shady tree, suddenly tormented by a bitter lament, I sang these gloomy songs from a sad heart, since I was remembering the sins I had committed, and my life's stains, and the dreadful hour of death . . . Recalling all these things within myself, I said under my breath . . .

The speaker goes on to think of the general *Dies iudicii*, but he approaches it in terms of his personal fate and his private fears and sins. The poem is inward-directed, imagined as uttered 'tacito sub murmure' for the speaker's own benefit. Though his *maculae uitae* are not particularized – so that the poem, with the feelings of penitence it dramatizes and inspires, is generalizable to all sinners – they are contemplated *solus*.

In his metrical version of Psalm 41, the process of introspection seems a painful and dangerous one. As Lapidge points out of Bede's selection of psalms, these works 'are concerned with that moment in life when the soul is separated from the body and travels to see the face of God'.⁹⁶ The contemplation of death provokes a turn inwards, and the speaker envisions himself as wholly isolated except for whatever help God may choose to give:

> Haec labiis clausis, sed cordis uoce frequenti
> Deprecor implorans tete, spes unica uitae,
> Qui me, inquam, solus sueras defendere ab hoste
> Solarique pius maestum. Nunc quare repente
> Oblitus miseri uultus auertis egenti,
> Soliuagusque gemo, dirus dum praeualet, hostis?⁹⁷

> With sealed lips but with the heart's constant voice I plead these things, imploring Thee, sole hope of life, who alone made me, to defend me against the enemy and to comfort me in my sorrow. Why now am I suddenly forgotten, your countenance turned from one in wretched need, and I cry out wandering alone, while the cruel enemy prevails?

The silence of the prayer, and the solitude of the speaker, are additions to the Psalm's text. The *dirus hostis* is the Psalmist's, but the 'Oratio Bedae Presbyteri' may help to explain how Bede understood this danger:

> O Deus aeternae mundo spes unica uitae,
>   fida manens miseris solus in axe salus,

Da mihi suffragium in tanto discrimine firmum
et famulum a nece, rex magne, tuere tuum:
ne caro succumbat ualidis infirma tyrannis,
si sola innumeris obuia tela paret.[98]

O God, the world's sole hope of eternal life, abiding as the faithful for the wretched in the world, give me steadfast aid in such a crisis, and save, O mighty King, your servant from destruction, lest the weak flesh should fall before the uncounted mighty enemies if left to face the opposing weapons alone.

He goes on to invoke Christ as a victorious battle-leader against the Devil (11–18), in the familiar transformation of martial imagery into a metaphor for spiritual struggle. The process by which an individual comes to judgment, then, is through a difficult inward war against sin and despair. No help can be hoped for but God's.

The interiority of Bede's prayers flows from a long tradition of Christian self-examination, but it also reflects the mental process that shaped his work as a poet. The penitential sense of his work is of one agonizingly conscious of imperfection, and in search of the inner light that only God can bestow. Other people are not, ultimately, a source of aid or consolation. Though Bede's hagiographical poems display the virtues of the saints, their footsteps do not seem to provide *him* with the instant power of the man healed by St Cuthbert's sandals.[99] Instead, we see in Bede's works an ongoing struggle with the very idea of example and authority, and a determination to seek his own path.

Conclusions

Isolation from a poetic community is not necessarily a matter of physical solitude. Rather, it stems from the inability to submit one's work to the judgment of others. In the case of the Redactor of *Christ and Satan*, this isolation probably was inadvertent; it certainly led to an uncertainty about the rules of verse, a cautious approach to replicating them, and an acute consciousness of the dangers of relying too much on the thoughts of one's own mind. Bede's circumstances seem to have been more complicated. He may have had several teachers, and probably knew others who understood Latin poetry; he was certainly well provided with a set of guidebooks and exemplars. Yet the trajectory of Bede's poetic career is *away* from the standards of his age, and towards an idea of perfection which was largely self-devised.

When considering the experience of Anglo-Saxon poets, then, it is clear that external circumstances were critical to the eventual form of their work. But the example of Bede in particular shows that poets were not inevitably bound by the conditions in which they found themselves; they also shaped their own ideas of poetry. In the next chapter, I shall examine some further instances in which the distinction between 'community' and 'isolation' was blurred, and in which we see Anglo-Saxons redefining poetry, and using their creations to reconstitute their social worlds.

CHAPTER 5

Spectral communities

Neither 'community' nor 'isolation' can exist in elemental purity. A total community, in which each individual conformed wholly and voluntarily to the standards of the group, would have to somehow purge itself of the differences in status and personality intrinsic to human society. If it did so, it would probably be static, its members disinclined to produce new poetry at all. The same result would almost certainly attend pure isolation: a true isolate would be unlikely to have language, much less art. I believe that the experience of most Anglo-Saxon poets was one of community with an admixture of isolation, but in proportions diverse enough to produce a very broad range of results. Historical circumstance, the alembic in which these compounds were distilled into individual lives and groups, moreover varied so much that the result is a wide spectrum of poetic experience.

This chapter presents three case studies examining certain types of hybrid states: isolated communities, individuals isolated within communities, and communities in the process of formation. Each offers a different perspective on how poets' experience and practice could be affected by those around them, and on the forms of poetry that such circumstances tend to encourage. In isolated communities, for instance, the group often seems to become more homogeneous over time, even as it diverges from the wider culture in which it originated. The group of English missionaries who travelled to Germany in the eighth century under St Boniface's direction provides one striking example of this. Boniface's verse style, which was heavily influenced by Aldhelm to begin with, grew more and more reliant on a limited set of phrases and tropes, while that of his followers seems to have mirrored his. This relatively closed community entered a literary feedback loop as its members reinforced each others' stylistic tics: Boniface's circle is perhaps the nearest we come in the Anglo-Saxon period to a pure community, and the trajectory of its style helps trace the life cycle of localized aesthetic standards.

The tendency of isolated groups to become, as it were, more and more like themselves, is also apparent in the work of individuals isolated within communities. Wulfstan Cantor, precentor of Winchester Cathedral around the year 1000, is a prime example of this. Wulfstan had been a child oblate and a student of the reforming bishop Æthelwold, and as an adult he held a position of considerable authority within his monastery. He lived virtually all his life, therefore, within a closely knit community bound by multiple, overlapping allegiances. Wulfstan, however, had remarkable talents as a musician and a metrist; he revolutionized church music in Winchester, and in his time was probably the only man in England capable of composing quantitative Latin lyrics. His position as precentor testifies to the recognition his abilities received from his brothers. Wulfstan also produced a substantial body of accomplished but idiosyncratic Latin verse, whose form and subject matter suggest he was under some pressure to compose texts that were not only valuable to the community, but characteristic of himself. Though parallel with Bede's situation in some regards, Wulfstan's isolation as a poet was probably not self-chosen, and its effects shed light on what happens to a poet when a community recognizes him as somehow pre-eminent.

Finally, we shall examine intriguing traces of what appears to be a new poetic community in the late Anglo-Saxon period. The style of verse known with debatable degrees of accuracy as 'Alfredian' defies traditional (or rather, Beowulfian) rules in regular ways. These poems – of which the *Metres of Boethius* and the *Paris Psalms* are the pre-eminent examples – seem to have created a new mode of verse, one designed to provide readers of English with a convincing simulacrum of the experience of reading Latin texts. Poets who worked in this 'Southern mode' often presented their texts as collective creations, or mere versions of pre-existing texts. But though this mode imposed restrictions on both style and voice, it offered compensation in the form of extended community and intellectual prestige for vernacular poets. Though often taken as a sign of Old English verse's decline, the Southern mode represents a high-water mark in Anglo-Saxon poets' achievements.

The three hybrid modes of community explored here do not and cannot represent the full range of poets' experience in the Anglo-Saxon period. It is my hope, however, that by further investigating the circumstances of poetic creation – and the traces these circumstances leave in verse – we may better understand the processes that gave rise to poems of whose historical externals we know nothing.

The echo chamber: eighth-century verse on the periphery

Anglo-Saxon history is haunted by the remnants of communities that must once have had distinct identities. But while the absence of records prevents us from understanding the particularities of such experiences, study of the life cycles of community identity can nevertheless present a range of probabilities for the fates of these lost groups, even those isolated on the borders of the Anglo-Saxon world. Such isolation is a curiously complex phenomenon; it is both physical and mental, and its effects can manifest themselves in surprising ways. Linguistically and culturally, isolated communities are often associated with extreme conservatism. Separation has undoubtedly helped many groups to preserve modes of language – and ways of life – abandoned by the larger communities whence they originally came.[1] In the Anglo-Saxon period, for instance, the Isle of Wight was the last bastion of paganism in southern Britain until it was conquered by the West Saxon king Cædwalla. Bede makes a special point of mentioning the strong tidal currents clashing in the Solent, the three-mile-wide strait that separates the island from the Hampshire coast: this is an explanation, not just a point of geographical interest.[2] A far greater degree of physical separation enabled Icelandic to retain linguistic features closer to Old Norse than to modern Norwegian. From the beginning, however, Iceland's separateness was as much ideological as geographical; Icelanders' self-conception as inheritors of a unique destiny permeated their early literature and their relations with mainland Scandinavia.[3] Such a sense of identity seems to be crucial to the development and fate of isolated communities.[4] But while Icelandic language and culture endured centuries of foreign rule, this is hardly an inevitable outcome for isolated communities. Small enclaves may be absorbed into a more dominant culture, or may simply ebb and fail as their members leave or die.

Levelling – the loss of local particularity as smaller groups accommodate themselves to the dominant culture – is the more common paradigm for dialect loss,[5] and it seems not unreasonable to extrapolate this tendency to poetic style. In such a scenario, as members of a poetic community tried to assimilate their work to the judgments of influential new members they would tend to jettison the features separating them. The resulting poems would be more homogeneous, more like those of poets in the dominant culture. One could see early Middle English poets' adoption of rhyming octosyllabic couplets – a favourite form of French poets, who probably in turn modelled it on Latin verse – as an example of such aesthetic accommodation. In some cases, though, the effect on a community is exactly the opposite: its distinctive traits grow exaggerated as it maintains its separateness from the wider culture.[6]

We see precisely this 'concentration' (as Schilling-Estes and Wolfram call it) in the works of one well-known small community, the Anglo-Saxon missionaries who followed St Boniface (Wynfrith) to Germany in the mid-eighth century. Boniface's English coadjutors – mainly West Saxons like him, or Mercians – were usually connected by blood or by longstanding associations.[7] The missionaries' letters – to each other, to secular magnates in England or on the Continent, to bishops and popes – show that in addition to bonds of kinship or friendship they shared a relatively restricted set of literary referents, among which Aldhelm's works were the most important.[8] These letters, as Orchard puts it,

> apparently developed what is effectively almost a private language, deliberately echoing and reshaping the same words and the same themes. It is as if a group of individuals had read precisely the same handful of books, from which they endlessly (and progressively loosely) quote, until they end up quoting not the original texts, but their own quotations. The overwhelming impression to be derived from these texts is the profound sense of exile and of isolation . . .[9]

As a sub-language shared by a close-knit community physically separated from its origin, then, the peculiar Latinity developed by Boniface and his correspondents had many characteristics of an isolated dialect.

From Boniface's writings, it seems he regarded himself as sojourning in a linguistic as well as doctrinal wilderness, and this self-image as a defender of true Latinity most likely helped reinforce the inward-looking character of his circle's writings. The best-known (and funniest) example of Boniface's war against *illiterati* is probably his rebaptism of children whom a poorly educated priest had christened 'in nomine patria et filia et spiritus sancti'.[10] But one of his riddles also points to such an attitude:

> Iam dudum 'nutrix errorum' et 'stulta' uocabor:
> Germine nempe meo concrescunt pignora saeclis
> Noxia peccati late per limina mundi,
> Ob quod semper amauit me Germanica tellus,
> Rustica gens hominum Sclaforum et Scythia dura.
> Adsum si gnato, genitor non gaudet in illo.
> Non caelum terramue, maris non aequora salsa
> Tranantem solem et lunam, non sidera supra
> Ignea contemplans quaero, quis conderet auctor.
> Altrix me numquam docuit, sapientia quid sit.
> Altera sordidior saeclis non cernitur usquam.
> Idcirco 'inuisam' uocitat me Grecia prudens,
> Tetrica quod numquam uitans pecamina curo.[11]

I shall be called 'nursemaid of error' and 'fool' for a long time now: for from my seed the noxious offspring of transgression flourish through the ages widely throughout the boundaries of the world – which is why the Germanic land has always loved me, along with the peasant race of Slavic men, and stern Scythia. If I dwell with a son, his father has no joy in him. Heaven and earth, sun and moon sailing over the salty plains of the sea, the fiery stars above – I think of none of them, nor contemplate who could be their Maker. No foster-mother ever taught me what wisdom is; you'll never see a more contemptible one than me throughout the ages. The prudent Greeks called me 'purblind', because I never try to avoid black sins.

Boniface depicts the barbarian tribes of central Europe not as Ignorance's unwilling captives, but her devoted friends (*semper amauit me*, 4). Moreover, while his conception of ignorance evidently includes incuriosity – a lack of that spirit of inquiry about the natural world that could bring gentiles to a recognition of the divine principle – his synonyms for the vice imply a profoundly philological understanding of her opposite, *sapientia*. The phrase *nutrix errorum*, for instance, derives from Isidore's *Synonyma*: 'Ignorantia mater errorum est, ignorantia uitiorum nutrix' ('Ignorance is the mother of error, ignorance is the nursemaid of vice'); Boniface's definition collapses Isidore's rather than truncating it, leaving room for knowledgeable readers to substitute the whole.[12] Such an allusive, metonymic method depends on author and reader having absorbed the same books: we must presume the sister to whom he directed his riddle-poems had also read the *Synonyma*.[13]

The poem on 'Ignorantia' demonstrates that a set of shared texts was part of what Boniface saw as separating him – and the community of those who read and replied to his work – from the barbarians. In such a group, poetry helped emphasize and reinforce the strength of extant ties, and it was often explicitly presented as a gift. Boniface's circle is in this respect clearly contiguous with Aldhelm's. As we saw in Chapter 3, Aldhelm and his correspondents exchanged poems as a means of maintaining social bonds, and their favourite, idiosyncratic form of rhythmic octosyllables was practised by Boniface and at least two of his fellow missionaries, Lull and Beorhtgyth.[14] But what is particularly remarkable about the verse of Boniface and his correspondents is how Aldhelm features as a kind of touchstone for poetry: he was not *a* model, but *the* model. The letter of Leofgyth, which Orchard has comprehensively analysed, is an excellent example of this.[15] Seeking the patronage of her kinsman Boniface, she sent him the 'paruum munusculum' of a (prose) letter concluded by a four-line hexametrical prayer, assembled mainly out of Aldhelmian phrases. Leofgyth asserts her connection to Boniface in multiple ways: outright in her reminder of their blood relationship and her training by Boniface's friend Eadburg, and more subtly by her demonstration of shared knowledge of Aldhelm's work and the 'poeticae artis disciplinam' ('discipline of poetic art'). She was showing her kinsman that she spoke his language: persuasively, we must presume, since she travelled to Germany to become abbess of Tauberbischofsheim under his influence.

Another epistolary poem – anonymous in the manuscript, but which Tangl plausibly attributes to Lull – seems to use quotation for the same purpose of demonstrating solidarity.[16] Directed to Boniface and requesting his permission to remain in Thuringia to pursue studies that had been interrupted by illness, the letter is clearly intended to convey Lull's continued loyalty to his master. As part of this strategy, the twenty-line poem (which, Lull claims, 'correctionis causa direxi', 'I sent to be corrected') demonstrates his stylistic affinities: like much of Boniface's correspondence, the verses are a salad of biblical and Aldhelmian discourse. Under its dressing of hexameters, the parallel diction is not always readily visible, but can usually be picked out. For instance, these two and a half lines are modelled on one of Aldhelm's:

> Pectoris obtusi tenebras sed gratia dempsit
> Saluantis Christi, gratis pia sensibus augens
> Dona meis stolidis.[17]

> But the grace of the saving Christ removes the shadows of a dull heart, freely heaping holy gifts upon my coarse senses.

In the prologue to the *Enigmata* we find:

> Inspirans stolidae pia gratis munera mentI[18]

> Freely inspiring holy gifts in my dull mind

Lull has augmented his source in several Aldhelm-approved ways: in line 16, for instance, he constructs a new cadence from words used separately (but in identical metrical positions), and begins the verse with a fairly rare participial adjective used by Arator in an example scanned in *De metris*.[19] With the aid of synonym substitutions, such as *dona* for *munera*, he has contrived lines that express the recurrent Bonifatian theme of gift-giving – combined with Aldhelm's particular variant on divine inspiration – in language that is simultaneously unique and derivative. Lull's epistolary poem is in this sense perhaps the best extant example of the kind of poetry Aldhelm's *De metris* was designed to produce. It is original – it contains very few of the whole-line pastiches that Leofgyth and indeed Boniface often used – but it is also wholly familiar in thought, and pervaded by an Aldhelmian tone that is difficult to pinpoint because it exists at the level of verse structure and diction rather than phrase.

In his poem, then, Lull was not merely demonstrating his esteem for his mentor despite their separation, but also the essential and unchanged nature of his thought. Despite his study in Thuringia, he still wrote letters and composed poems like an Englishman. Not much more of Lull's verse has survived,[20] but that which has suggests that the phatic aspects of his style were indeed characteristic. Another letter attributed to him contains twelve lines in hexameters together with six octosyllabic couplets; although the recipient's name has been deleted, she was clearly a nun of English origin.[21] The hexameters are more obviously Aldhelmian than those directed to Boniface, with several cadences from the *Carmen de uirginitate* used verbatim. Most interesting, though, is the poem's final line:

> Crede mihi, quia te summo conplector amore.[22]

> Believe me, for I embrace you in the greatest love.

This line, as Tangl notes, echoes not other verse, but a line from Ecgburg's letter to Boniface: 'Idcirco crede mihi Deo teste, quia te summo complector amore' ('And so believe me, as God is my witness, for I embrace you in the greatest love').[23] Addressed to 'Abbot Wynfrith', this epistle was evidently sent before Boniface received his new name and papal mandate. But Ecgburg's former teacher must have valued her letter, since it appears in all three major codices of his correspondence.[24] While Lull may or may not have expected his addressee to know this particular letter, it is very striking that he chose to echo an English nun's language in writing to an English nun. The epistolary poem is a particularly clear example of the inward-looking nature of the literary dialect of Boniface's circle: not only does it invoke the group's touchstone texts, but it rehearses the diction of Boniface's own correspondents. Lull makes it very apparent that he and the recipient are speaking the same language.

The characteristic style of Boniface's circle can be summed up as a kind of exaggerated Anglo-Latinity: no one who was not a Christian trained either in England or by the English could have composed in this way. Circulating as it did among a group already closely connected by kinship and religious commitment, the verse further signalled their commitment to each other. Given the self-reinforcing nature of the 'Bonifatian style' and the fact that most of its practitioners were teachers, it would therefore seem potentially durable as a literary dialect. Yet it died out relatively quickly, even in monasteries founded by Boniface or his immediate followers. Beyond the correspondence, only a few poems can be persuasively attributed to disciples of Boniface or his students. The *Enigmata Laureshamensia* – so called because they are found only in Vatican, Palat. lat. 1753, a Lorsch manuscript probably written there in the late eighth or early ninth century – have perhaps the best claim to a Bonifatian heritage.[25] Along with several other important grammatical texts, the manuscript contains a full text of Aldhelm's *De metris* (including the *Enigmata*), and Boniface's own tract *Caesurae uersuum*, which bears his name only in this manuscript: the first four riddles seem to have been put into the middle of Boniface's text.[26] The Lorsch riddles are thus physically embedded in the context of early English poetic education. Not only do all twelve of the poems share a thoroughly Aldhelmian diction, but many of their riddle subjects are modelled on Aldhelm's to the extent that some are little more than a rephrasing of his texts.[27] Even when their central conceits vary, they still lean heavily on his work. *Enigma* V is a good example of this:

> Lucidus et laetus quinis considere ramis
> Saepe solent pariter splendentes, laeta iubentes
> Aedibus in mediis fieri non tristia corda.
> Dumque simul ludunt ramisque tenentur apertis,
> Dulcia quin bibulis tradunt et bassia buccis,
> Mulcifer egreditur tantumque remanet adhaerens
> Lucidus in ramis, quibus antea sedit uterque.[28]

A shining one and a happy one often sit on five branches, equally magnificent, bidding hearts in the midst of the hall to be happy, not sorrowful. And when they sport together and are held in the splayed branches, why they press sweet kisses on moistened lips, the Softener [or perhaps *Multifer*, 'Fruitful'] departs, and only the shining one remains stranded in the branches in which they had both sat before.

The Lorsch riddles are untitled, but the author's source material gives the game away:

> Sed mentes muto, dum labris oscula trado
> Dulcia compressis impendens basia buccis,
> Atque pedum gressus titubantes sterno ruina.[29]

But I change minds when with my lips I give kisses, pressing sweet kisses on pursed mouths, and the feet's tottering steps I cast down to ruin.

Aldhelm's *Enigma* LXXX, 'Calix uitreus', has a more aggressive tone than the cheery glass from Lorsch, but the idea of the glass's lip giving kisses has been taken over along with the words. More creatively, the description of the wine as *Mulcifer* apparently derives from a reading of *Enigma* XXVII, 'Coticula':

> Mulcifer annorum numerum ni dempserit igne;
> Mox rigida species mollescit torribus atris.[30]

unless Mulcifer takes away the number of my years with fire; he quickly softens a rigid nature with his terrible heat.

It is not clear whether the author of the Lorsch poem knew Mulciber was the god of fire, but as an epithet for wine it is both clever and apt.

Judging by their content, style, and manuscript context, then, the Lorsch riddles may well have been composed on the Continent by students of one of Boniface's compatriots, though it is not impossible that they were imported along with other texts in the manuscript.[31] But though they seem to be the work of one or more people learning to compose verse in the English manner taught and practised by Boniface, they have no apparent successors. A companion of theirs in the manuscript points towards one possible reason. An epitaph for a priest named Domberht, the poem describes the dead man's birth and education:

> Artibus et meritis fulgens Bonifatius almus,
> Pro Christo gladiis qui sua membra dedit,
> Hunc magno studio docuit, nutriuit, amauit,
> Complens quod sonuit uatis in aure pium.
> Francorum ad patriam tremulas uenere per undas
> Anglorum pelagi germine de nitido.[32]

The holy Boniface, resplendent with learning and virtues – he who for Christ submitted his body to the sword – taught, nurtured, and loved this man with great zeal, fulfilling what the prophet spoke in his ear. From a distinguished lineage, they came across the turbulent waves of the English sea to the homeland of the Franks.

Though a memorial for a student of Boniface's, the poem's form and diction bespeak the influence of a different English exile: Alcuin. While Aldhelm and Boniface did both compose elegiac couplets, they preferred hexameters; elegiacs, however, were the characteristic form of the early Carolingian poets, especially for occasional poems.[33] Moreover, the phraseology of Domberht's epitaph is heavily indebted to Alcuin.[34] The poem's stylistic orientation is not, in short, towards the 'facta priorum' ('deeds of our forebears') invoked in its first line, but towards contemporaries in Aachen and the great monasteries of the 'Francorum patria'. A telling sentence is copied at the end of the epitaph: 'Rogo te, domine pater, ut emendes et corrigas' ('Revered father, I beg you will emend and correct this').[35] Much though the author respected Domberht, he considered someone else – perhaps Alcuin's student Ricbod, abbot of Lorsch? – to be his master and the arbiter of his work.

The replacement of Boniface's successors with clerics trained at Charlemagne's court spelled the end of the English-oriented poetic style on the Continent. The death of this literary dialect must therefore be considered, in the main, a side-effect of the success of Boniface's overall goal: the establishment of a series of stable, well-organized monasteries, diocese, and archdiocese serving the needs of the German countryside and attracting local residents to the service of the church. As more and more native Germans were trained to serve in and lead Boniface's foundations, the poetry they composed was naturally reoriented towards locally relevant preferences. But the fragmentation of Boniface's immediate circle following his death must also have played a part in the end of the literary style he taught. After his martyrdom at Dokkum, for instance, an unseemly squabble over his remains developed between two of Boniface's students and chosen successors: Lull, then archbishop of Mainz, and Sturm, a native Hessian and abbot of Fulda. The early ninth-century life of Sturm asserts that this developed into a power struggle over Fulda itself, resulting in the abbey's permanent independence from the archbishopric.[36] Moreover, though Lull became the primary custodian of Boniface's 'literary estate', he does not himself appear to have attracted many followers, and his immediate successors at Mainz seem to have felt, at best, ambivalent towards his legacy.[37] Boniface himself was the keystone of his coadjutors' sense of group identity, and without him their motive for stylistic cohesion collapsed. While Lull carried on the literary dialect, he evidently lacked the personal qualities that might have persuaded others to perpetuate it or transform it from a coterie style to a dominant aesthetic.

The 'Bonifatian style' was thus at its peak during the relatively brief period in which the English missionaries felt themselves alone under a kind of cultural siege; their private dialect died when the community fragmented and ceased looking inward for support. As we learn more about the histories of local aesthetic modes, we may come to discern other patterns of change besides this one of concentration followed by extinction. Moreover, the degree to which communities are isolated, or perceive themselves as such, is not always easy to define. The rare survival of personal correspondence allows a glimpse into the self-conception of Boniface and his fellow missionaries; but in less well documented communities, the study of communities' poetic dialects may perhaps provide insight into their psychological state.

Northumbria in the late eighth and ninth centuries would be an interesting test case for this, though the question of what became of its literary
culture may not bear a simple answer. Carver, in his survey of the remains of
Northumbrian cultural communities, has pointed out the substantial
degree of local difference, which often seems to have stemmed from
informed choice among a range of known practices.[38] It is important to
recollect this local particularity in any attempt to understand the poetic
survivals of this period, which include the *Metrical Calendar of York*, the
Miracula S. Niniae, and Æthilwulf's *De abbatibus*. A particular community's orientation may not result from physical isolation or force of circumstances, and it need not reflect the practices of people twenty miles away.
Both the *Miracula S. Niniae* and *De abbatibus* show close familiarity with
Alcuin's writings, and one could read this in a variety of ways: as a turn
inward spurred by a sense of abandonment or danger, the sort of stylistic
self-devouring that Boniface's circle shows; or, conversely, an internation-
alization of perspective. Further study of the poetic sub-dialects of this
period may thus help us understand the complexities of how Anglo-Saxon
communities reacted to changes in their world.

'Ultimus Anglorum seruulus ymnicinium': Wulfstan Cantor, England's ultimate hymnodist

Extraordinary competence is sometimes recognized in surprising ways. In
his survey of British writers, the sixteenth-century scholar John Leland
included a remarkable panegyric to Wulfstan, a student of Bishop
Æthelwold of Winchester:

> Deum immortalem! Quantum ille religionis infucatæ, quantum pietatis,
> quantum nervosæ eruditionis sub tanto hausit præceptore ... Dicite igitur,
> felicis memoriae musæ, quibus animum præcipue studiis intenderit. Nam,
> uobis dictantibus, sermo quovis melle dulcior instar torrentis defluet.
> Carmen præter cætera juvenis coluit, cujus illecebris captus, ægre aliquando
> liberiorem dicendi campum ingrediebatur: tentavit tamen, idque cum felic-
> itate aliqua. At ut maxime aptus erat ad numeros, ita ad illos, tanquam ad
> delicias suas, semper recurrebat. Nec defuit vox bene canora, ut neque
> summa canendi peritia; quo utroque nomine collegianis suis ter charus
> erat. Unde tamen et præcentor factus, quod genus magistratus apud mon-
> achos in magno olim pretio.[39]

> Immortal God, how much unfeigned devotion, how much piety, how much
> vigorous learning did he imbibe under such a teacher ... Say then, O muses
> of happy memory, to which pursuits in especial he directed his heart: for, at

your telling, discourse sweeter than any honey shall torrent-like flow forth. The youth cultivated song above all other things; ensnared by its delights, he would at any time but with reluctance enter into the broader field of discourse – though he indeed made such forays, and with some success. But as his greatest talent was for verse, so he invariably returned to it as if to his darling. He lacked neither a melodious voice nor the highest degree of erudition in singing: for both of which capacities he was greatly valued by his collegians. For this reason he was also made precentor, an office which among monks was formerly held in high esteem.

Leland's glowing account grows rather more muted as he turns to specifics: in his discussion of the metrical *Life of St Swithun* he concedes that 'carmen tamen, ut ingenue fatear, subinde impar et inæquale' ('indeed to be quite honest the poem is often patchy and uneven'), but that 'quod vitii in carmine est, adscribat candidus lector barbaro sæculo, in quo mirum certe *Wolfstanum* potuisse aliquid præstare, quod nostra hac aurea ætate attentum mereatur lectorem' ('what faults there are in the poem, the candid reader will ascribe to the barbarous age, in which it is certainly remarkable that Wulfstan could produce something that does merit an attentive reader in this Golden Age of ours').[40]

In commenting on this passage, Lapidge notes that Leland's own skill as a Latin poet certainly fit him to pass judgment. After an intensive study of Wulfstan's technique as an author of hexameter verse, Lapidge himself echoes the Tudor antiquary's tone: 'he was a Latin poet of outstanding calibre whose verse bears comparison with that of any early medieval Latin poet and even, in some small ways, with the poets of classical antiquity'.[41] The sense that there was something extraordinary and unaccountable about Wulfstan's skill is one that few commentators on his work seem to escape.[42] Leland's poetical vision of the Winchester monk's love for his art – and of the esteem in which his community held him – sounds the keynote for this section because it pinpoints a crucial question about poets working within a community: what happens when someone's talents really are unique?

With Wulfstan Cantor, scholarship has been impeded less than usual by the fact that only one work has been transmitted under his name. Until recently, indeed, *no* texts were known to name him as author: his composition of the (prose) *Vita S. Æthelwoldi* was attested first by William of Malmesbury, and Leland himself deduced that Wulfstan must have written the *Narratio metrica de S. Swithuno*; it was through comparison with the poem on Swithun that François Dolbeau realized that the *Breuiloquium de omnibus sanctis*, a poem preserved in Brussels, Bibliothèque royale, spelled out VVLFSTANUS in an acrostic.[43] Between the tenth century and the

1980s (when Dolbeau made his discovery), several other works have been attributed to Wulfstan, including a series of hymns and a substantial amount of liturgical material. Curiously, even when these identifications are based on mistaken assumptions, they tend to receive substantial credence. A good example is Blume's attribution of three hymns on St Augustine of Canterbury to Wulfstan, on the basis of his belief that their manuscript – the 'Durham Hymnal', Durham Cathedral, B.III.32 – originated in Winchester.[44] The Durham Hymnal is now known to have been written in Canterbury, yet Blume's attribution still seems plausible.[45] One reason for this is the hymns' range of metrical forms: Ambrosian;[46] epanaleptic elegiacs; and – most remarkably – the second asclepiadic stanza,[47] which no other Anglo-Saxon seems to have attempted. As Lapidge points out, the author of these works would have to be 'familiar with Horace and ... a thoroughly accomplished metrician', two requirements which radically restrict the list of potential candidates.[48] Wulfstan must stand high on that very short list. Now it may justly be objected that attributing poems in difficult quantitative metres to Wulfstan Cantor because Wulfstan Cantor was presumed to have written in difficult quantitative metres is egregiously circular. But the conviction that the hymns to Augustine sound like Wulfstan's is, nevertheless, not an irrational one. Before investigating their Wulfstanianness, however, it is worth sounding deeper into the corpus of lyric and liturgical verse attributed to him.

In almost all cases, evidence for Wulfstan's authorship rests on a very similar combination of circumstantial evidence and stylistic similarity. The *Analecta hymnica*, for instance, ascribes four hymns to Wulfstan because they appear in Rouen, Bibliothèque municipale, 1385, in a booklet that also contains Lantfred's prose account of St Swithun's miracles; the hymns, moreover, are devoted to Swithun, Æthelwold, and Birinus, whose cults – like the manuscript itself – all date to late tenth-century Winchester.[49] The voice of the poem to Æthelwold is that of one who knew him personally: as in

> Hausimus omne bonum cuius ab ore sacro

From whose holy mouth we imbibed all righteousness

or

> Transfer ad alta poli pueros quod ipse nutristi:
> Nos prece continua transfer ad alta poli.[50]

Bring to heaven's heights the children whom you yourself brought up: with continuous prayer bring us to heaven's heights.

In the *Narratio metrica*, Wulfstan speaks of 'Noster Aðeluuoldus, pastor, pater atque magister' ('Æthelwold, our pastor, father, and teacher'), and mentions that he was among the 'pueri ... pusilli' ('young boys') when Æthelwold elevated Swithun's relics in 971.[51] We know, too, from the very existence of the *Vita S. Æthelwoldi* and the *Narratio metrica* that Wulfstan composed material for the cults of Winchester's saints; and from chapters 42 and 43 of the *Vita Æthelwoldi*, it seems he personally instigated the translation of Æthelwold's remains.

The circumstantial evidence for Wulfstan's authorship of the four Rouen lyrics is strong, then, and reinforced by certain peculiarities of form and presentation. As we know from the *Breuiloquium de omnibus sanctis*, Wulfstan certainly practised acrostics: not only do the hexameter lines of the elegiacs prefacing the main poem spell his name, but the work concludes with a remarkable hexametrical passage spelling NUNC ET IN AEUUM DEO GRATIAS AMEN in acrostic, and NUNC ET IN AEUUM SIT DEO LAUS AMEN in telestich. The concluding 'Amen' is also a signature of the four elegiac poems, which are all epanaleptic abecedaries; the *Breuiloquium* and the hymns also share some similar diction.[52]

Moreover, the poems in the Rouen manuscript are accompanied by lengthy, rather peculiar *incipits* and *explicits* in prose. For instance:

> Incipit hymnus in honore sancti patris et gloriosi pontificis Adelwoldi, elegiaco et paracterico carmine per Alphabetum compositus

> Here begins a hymn in honour of the holy father and glorious bishop Æthelwold, composed in elegiac paracteric verse according to the alphabet

or

> Finit hymnus vili quidem poemate, sed pia devotione editus in honorem sancti Birini episcopi.[53]

> Here ends the hymn which, though in contemptible verse, was written with sincere devotion in honour of St Birinus, bishop.

Only the final hymn to St Swithun is not introduced with a *titulus* identifying the metrical form as elegiac and 'paracteric' – evidently the technical term for epanaleptic; the oddly deprecating tone of the Birinus hymn's *explicit* indicates that these paratexts are authorial.

The *Breuiloquium de omnibus sanctis* and the *Narratio metrica* are both provided with an apparatus of prose *tituli*, though after Arator this was a not uncommon feature of longer narrative poems.[54] An even closer analogue to the Rouen poems' *tituli* can be found in the 'Winchester Troper', CCCC

473.[55] A small-format book intended for a cantor's use, the Winchester Troper was probably written sometime in the 1020s or 1030s, and thus almost certainly well after Wulfstan's death; but much of the original material contained in it has traditionally been traced back to his influence.[56] Among this book's many intriguing features are a set of quirky *tituli* for a range of the liturgical material. Variants on the *Kyrie eleison*, for instance, are enumerated in deliberately varied language (as, 'Item deus scit hic sunt kyrriele', 'Here again, God knows, another *Kyrie*').[57] Rubrics for some of the *organa* display a memorably charming enthusiasm for the music: for example,

> Laus amoenissima per sacra dulciter reboanda sollenia

> A most beautiful praise resounding sweetly through the holy rites

or the hexametrical

> Organa dulcisono docto modulamine compta
> Ut petat altare resonat laus iste sacerdos.[58]

> *Organa* learnedly arranged in sweet-sounding measure, that the priest might approach the altar with this praise resounding.

Comptus, which means 'adorned' or 'well-arranged', is not an especially common word, particularly when applied to music; Rankin comments that 'Its use thus conveys not only the quality of elegance, but also the fact of having been made that way through rhetorical art.'[59] It should be noted that Wulfstan himself seems to use the word to denote a particular kind of sacred beauty. In the *Narratio metrica*, the word occurs twice, first in Book 1, when St Swithun first appears to a layman:

> tempore nocturno cuidam per somnia fabro
> sanctus adest, nitidis perfusus uertice canis,
> angelico uultu niueoque decorus amictu,
> undique bissini comptus uelamine pepli,
> aurea perspicuis et habens sandalia plantis.[60]

> In the nighttime the saint appears in a dream to a certain smith, his head flowing with shining white hair, splendid with an angelic face and snowy garments, adorned with the covering of a long linen mantle, and with golden sandals visible on his feet.

The other occurrence of the word is also in a vision of the saint, whom another layman sees after entering a marvellous church in his dream:

> stantem conspexit et illic
> quendam pontificem, miro decoramine comptum,

> ante altare sacrum, ueluti celebrare paratum
> missarum domino sollempnia . . .[61]

he saw a bishop, adorned with marvellous ornaments, standing before the
holy altar, as if about to celebrate the holy rites of Mass before the Lord . . .

In this second instance, the phrase 'miro decoramine comptum' ('adorned
with marvellous ornaments') can modify either the bishop or the altar before
which he stands, blurring man into artifact. It is particularly striking that, like
the *organa* rubric, this use of *comptus* occurs in the context of a priest before
the altar: in all these uses of the word, we can perceive connotations of the
labour needed to elevate the paraphernalia of the Mass – vestments, music,
celebrants – to the degree of beauty suited to their purpose.

The common ascription of the Rouen hymns and much of the original
material in the Winchester Troper to Wulfstan Cantor rests, in other words,
on more than chronological plausibility: these works share a sensibility as
well as distinctive stylistic peculiarities. The tone of the rubrics – enthusi-
astic, technically precise, seemingly fond of words for their own sake – is not
unlike that of the author who could spend three hexameters introducing a
two-line quote from Sedulius.[62] The works also share a penchant for
difficulty: a tendency to clothe material in technically virtuosic, though
not always flamboyant garb. The hexametrical form of the rubric 'Organa
dulcisono' is one example of this impulse; so is the arbitrarily imposed
constraint of the epanaleptic abecedary. Though the author could have
achieved his ends with infinitely less effort, it was essential to him that his
material be *compta*. The same drive reveals itself in the form of many of
Wulfstan's verses. Dolbeau and (especially) Lapidge have analysed
Wulfstan's prosodic practices in detail, drawing attention to his metrical
variety and mastery of techniques like elision and the placement of mono-
syllables in the sixth foot.[63] In several cases, a verse's effect depends on
acute sensitivity to quantity, as in

> Et solo sermone solo dant largiter imbrem . . .[64]

And with a bare word they grant rain plentifully to the earth . . .

Here, the play on *sōlus* 'alone' and *sŏlum* 'earth' is oddly reminiscent of
Britten. Occasionally Wulfstan will even draw attention to his metrical skill,
as in the *Epistola specialis* to Bishop Ælfheah prefixed to his *Narratio metrica*:

> post alii septem, quos nunc edicere promptum est
> carmine uersifico, cum pede dactilico:
> Ælstan, Æþelgarus rursumque Ælfstanus et Æscuuig,
> Ælfheah, Æþelsinus, hic et Adulfus erant.[65]

Then seven more [bishops], who can readily be enumerated in measured dactylic verse: Ælfstan, Æþelgar, and then Ælfstan and Æscwig; Ælfheah, Æthelsige, and Adulf were there too.

Ovid (or a somewhat more culturally open-minded version of him) might well have been proud of such a catalogue.

Wulfstan was also extremely fond of complex aural devices, and his manipulation of rhyme is unusually sophisticated for tenth-century England. Internal or leonine rhyme is common in his hexameters, but so are more intricate or larger-scale patterns. The spectacular chapter of the *Narratio metrica* in which an unfortunate Wintonian is pursued by Furies is a wellspring of such passages:

> Quae cum uidissent quod iussis nollet earum
> auditum prebere suum, sed calle citato
> arripuisse fugam, rabidarum more luparum
> insectantur eum perniciter, atque malignum
> uirus ab ore uomunt misero cum talia promunt ...[66]

When they saw that he would not give their commands a hearing, but was hastily taking flight along the road, they swiftly pursued him like rabid she-wolves, and belched an evil poison from their mouths as they said ...

Here, sound binds and recombines sense units across and within verses. Many of Wulfstan's effects are achieved by manipulating homeoteleuton, especially in the placement of nouns and adjectives of identical declensional endings (e.g., *rabidarum* ... *luparum*). Here, homeoteleuton works to subdivide verses, balancing (for instance) the rejected act *auditum prebere suum* against the chosen alternative *sed calle citato*, which is enjambed with the next line. Full rhyme links paired actions, as with *more* (the wolflike pursuit) and *ore* (the spit poison), or *uomunt* (again, the poison) and *promunt* (implying the Furies' speech *is* the poison). Consonance and assonance link *uidissent*, *iussis*, and *arripuisse*: Wulfstan seems to have been bound by no Classical strictures on tense, and his verbs' conjugation often reflects aesthetic considerations. In this case, the hissing pluperfect and perfect infinitive combine with *iussis* to suggest the supernatural creatures' snakelike qualities (described earlier in the passage: *gelido serpentino-que ueneno*, 510, 'with icy snakelike venom'), and to separate the dependent temporal clause from the main clause. Yet of these effects, perhaps only the leonine rhyme in 527 can be described as instantly obvious: the passage's enjambment creates a forward impetus that conceals its highly wrought nature. The aural effects combine with sense rather than distracting from it, and as a result it is surprisingly easy to overlook the verse's extraordinary artistry.

Yet despite his enthusiasm for intricacy and difficulty, Wulfstan, as Dolbeau observed, 'succombe parfois à la facilité'.[67] In particular, he tended to repeat words and phrases, and to permanently pigeonhole words into one part of a verse: Lapidge has documented the considerable extent of Wulfstan's formulaic usage and of his tendency to 'lexical localization'.[68] Both these tendencies, it should be noted, are common to other Anglo-Latin authors (and indeed to many medieval poets); but Wulfstan's habit of reusing his own phraseology verbatim, or with minimal modification, nevertheless gives his verse a familiar flavour, especially when taken in any quantity.

As a poet, then, Wulfstan Cantor had a very distinctive individual style. This does not make him unique in the Anglo-Saxon period: others like Cynewulf, Frithegod, Alcuin, Bede, and Aldhelm had defining traits of diction, metrical practice, and other features that have made their work recognizable to (at very least) modern commentators. In Aldhelm's case, we can make a plausible argument that the distinctiveness of his technique was deliberate, and intended to be associated with him personally. His treatise on metre, after all, contains an assertion of his status as the first English author of quantitative Latin verse, and his exemplary collection of *enigmata* is prefaced with an acrostic bearing his name, so that learning the art of composition from the *De metris et enigmatibus et de pedum regulis* was not a matter of abstract absorption of rules, but of learning to compose verse like Aldhelm's.[69] That his successors recognized this is strongly implied by the evidence of the 'Bonifatian' style just discussed – while the trajectory of Bede's career suggests that conscious rejection of Aldhelm's style was for him a necessary precursor to developing an independent voice. To an Anglo-Saxon, then, associating a style – perhaps especially a Latin style – with an individual was not inconceivable, and it is therefore worth considering whether Wulfstan Cantor's idiolect would have been recognizable as such to contemporaries.

That Wulfstan *himself* was well known during and after his lifetime is as thoroughly attested as such facts can be a millennium later. As Leland deduced, appointment as precentor indicates that he was held in esteem within the community of Winchester's Old Minster. But a small array of surviving material suggests that Wulfstan was unusually closely identified with this office: as when the Old English *Rule of Chrodegang* gives 'Wulfstan cantor' as part of an exemplary list of ecclesiastical officers.[70] Indeed, through the original material in the Winchester Troper, Wulfstan's sensibilities must have continued to permeate the music of his successors as precentor, so that his accomplishments as a cantor would have been perceptible long after his death.[71] Moreover, the *Vita* of Æthelwold suggests Wulfstan may have been known as 'the cantor' beyond his monastic community. When Ælfhelm, a blind layman from Wallingford, experiences a miraculous vision of the not-yet-canonized Æthelwold, he is told:

> Cum festinus Wintoniam perueneris et Veteris Coenobii ecclesiam intra-ueris, accersiri fac a te monachum quendam Wulfstanum, cognomento Cantorem.[72]

> When you have got quickly to Winchester and entered the Old Minster's church, have summoned to you a certain monk Wulfstan, called the Cantor.

Wulfstan wrote this himself to be sure, but given what we are told in the *Narratio metrica* of the Old Minster organ's domination of the city's sound-scape, it is hardly unlikely that Wintonians and their neighbors in the surrounding countryside would know who he was.[73]

As a musician and liturgist, then, Wulfstan was undoubtedly someone to be asked for by name. What, though, of his poetry? As we have seen, his skill in versification was distinctive, but many of Wulfstan's techniques are quite subtle. Mastery of quantitative metre especially is often only perceptible to those who have mastered it themselves. Yet an understanding of, and value for, Latin poetry may have been ingrained in the Winchester community; certainly an unusually high percentage of its tropes are in hexameters.[74] Moreover, many of Wulfstan's characteristic formal devices must have been easily recognizable: rhyme, probably, and certainly his 'paracteric' verse. The UULFSTANUS acrostic in the *Breuiloquium de omnibus sanctis* is epanaleptic, literally fusing the technique with his name: the Rouen hymns to Winchester saints compound this association. Epanaleptic verse may then have been something of a signature form for him; it is worth noting that it seems well calculated for performance by a double choir.

As a poet, then, too, Wulfstan had a voice that his contemporaries could plausibly have found distinctive. He seems himself to have had a strong sense of responsibility for Winchester's sacral power, as seen in his work to create Æthelwold's cult and support the cults of Swithun and Birinus with suitable liturgical material. His self-designation as 'Wulfstanum cogno-mento cantorem' indicates that he identified himself with his office as least as strongly as others did. This peculiar status within the community also left a strong impression on his work. In Chapter 3, we saw how Wulfstan pre-emptively deflected his brothers' judgment on the *Narratio metrica* into the channel of intercessory prayer.[75] Intercession, indeed, is a central theme of Wulfstan's. While imploring patron saints' prayers (and praising their efficacy) is a common element in hymnody, in these works the convention gains fresh power as we see the saints' actions habitually and reflexively yoked with the hymn itself. Wulfstan, in other words, presents the making of a poem as an intercessory act.

This connection is elegantly dramatized in several of the Rouen texts. The hymn to Æthelwold, for instance, fuses song and intercession:

> Transfer ad alta poli pueros quos ipse nutristi,
>   Nos prece continua transfer ad alta poli,
> Vocibus angelicis ibi quo psallamus ovantes
>   Laudemusque Deum vocibus angelicis.
> Xristus ut hic faveat votis, sis fautor opimus,
>   Sis pius auditor, Christus ut hic faveat.
> Ymnifer iste chorus resonat tibi carmina laetus,
>   Sit iugiter gaudens hymnifer iste chorus.[76]

> Bring to heaven's heights the children whom you yourself brought up: by your continuous prayer bring us to heaven's heights, there where with angelic voices we may sing psalms in prayer, and shall praise God with angelic voices. That Christ may here favour our prayers, be our generous patron: be our kindly hearer, that Christ may favour us here. Your joyful hymn-singing chorus resounds verses to you: may your hymn-singing chorus be forever joyous.

The couplets in this passage alternate between intercession by the saint and song by his servants. The causal connection between the two is deliberately blurred by the complication of tense: in the T and V couplets, Æthelwold's prayers *will* enable his flock to sing in heaven. But in the second paired set of lines, the saint is entreated to be an 'auditor' to an ongoing act, the chorus's song; he is asked not merely to *hear* 'ymnifer iste chorus' ('your hymnic chorus'), but to be its judge and advocate.[77] By passing favourable (*pius*) judgment upon the songs and advocating with God for their singers, Æthelwold will ensure their perpetual continuance. The temporal switch, from future to present and back again, renders the link between hymnody and intercession not simply linear (the song prompting the saint's prayer) but cyclical and indivisible; the two acts are fused as heavenly and earthly time unite. The connection between the creation of the hymn and the act of intercession is seen even more clearly in the poem to St Birinus:

> Magne patrone, tuus nos traxit ab hoste triumphus,
>   Nos labor eripuit, magne patrone, tuus.
> Nostra camena tibi canit haec, pia carmina patri
>   Intonat et iubilat nostra camena tibi.[78]

Great patron, your triumph seizes us from the enemy: your labour, great patron, delivers us. This our poem sings to you: to you, father, our poem chants and for joy sings pious verses.

In the second couplet of this passage, the actor is the poem itself ('Nostra camena'). Its labours, as it sings in various modes to Birinus (here, *pater* 'father'), are juxtaposed with those of the *patronus* ('patron') as he works for his devotees' salvation. In celebrating the saint's efforts, the hymn reflects, complements, and augments them: it speaks for the congregation to St Birinus as he speaks for them to God.

In the *Breuiloquium de omnibus sanctis*, Wulfstan's own position as poetic intercessor is perhaps most explicit. The opening prefatory acrostic presents the work as the fulfilment of a personal pledge:

> Vota serena tibi, Ihesu bone, reddere uoui;
> Offero nunc eadem uota serena tibi.[79]

I vowed to bring you fair offerings, kind Jesus: and now I present those same bright offerings to you.

The acrostic continues in the first person, exhorting Christ's forgiveness and intercession on Wulfstan's behalf. It concludes with a turn back to the work itself, and an explicit link between the poem and its author's salvation:

> Versibus ecce cano, scriptis quę tradita legi,
>   Et dominum in sanctis, uersibus ecce cano.
> Soluite uincla meae, sancti, rogo, tarda loquelę,
>   Post mortemque animę soluite uincla meę.[80]

See, I sing in verses the things I found handed down in writing: and the Lord in his saints, behold, I sing in verses. Break, O saints, the leaden chains upon my tongue: and after my death break the chains upon my soul.

But though the prologue is personal, the voice of the main text is not. Wulfstan has preserved the hortative plural of the sermon source, 'Legimus in ecclesiasticis historiis', which occasionally looks outward to 'fratres' (218, 310, 633, 642, 676). The final section, lines 633–89, speaks directly to a congregation:

> Nos igitur, fratres, alacri pietate fideles,
> Intercessorum suffragia tanta piorum,
> De quibus exiguo sumus hęc sermone locuti,
> Queramus toto cordis meditamine puro . . .[81]

Let us too, faithful brothers, seek out with ready faith and pure intention of heart the advocacy of these holy intercessors, of which we have been speaking in this little discourse . . .

The saints' intercession is not limited to an individual, but besought for a community encouraged to follow their example. The final acrostic, too, is in first person plural:

Nunc quia permodicum Christi iuuamine carmen
Versifico soliti finiuimus ordine canu . . .[82]

Now, since with Christ's help we have finished, with metrical song in accustomary order, our little poem . . .

The shift from *ego* to *nos* is central to the poem's action. Though it begins as an act of personal devotion, the *Breuiloquium de omnibus sanctis* transforms itself into a channel for the voices of a group. By the epilogue, the poet is speaking not for himself, but for his community: the solo has swelled into a chorus.

In Wulfstan's verse, the boundary between his voice and the group's is removed. The immediate result is not the dissolution of his poetic individuality. Instead, the community has elected to speak through the words and music he produced as precentor and chief poet of Winchester's cults. This unquestionably gave Wulfstan a real, if somewhat peculiar, power in (and perhaps beyond) the Old Minster. As for the effects of this status on him, from what we have seen in his work, Wulfstan came to identify closely with intercessory powers of saints, perhaps especially those of Æthelwold, whom he had known in life as a teacher, leader, and priest. As cantor, Wulfstan evidently perceived himself as a similar intermediary figure, providing an artistic channel through which the community could address their saints. But as his own writings indicate, intercessors had a responsibility to the needs of their congregations. His surviving work demonstrates that Wulfstan took this seriously: it is striking how entirely his substantial output serves the liturgical and hagiographical requirements of late tenth-century Winchester. I would argue too that Wulfstan's stylistic idiosyncrasies are also, at least in part, a response to his position within his community. The peculiarities that make his work recognizable are also a sign of his investment in its production: of its 'genuine Wulfstanness'. Along with his position of authority may have come an expectation of the total service of his talents; this would certainly have accorded with the ethos of reformed Benedictine monasticism. Someone like Wulfstan, whose skill as a musician and poet was genuinely extraordinary, could effectively demonstrate his acquiescence to his group's needs by producing consistently recognizable material. A 'signature style' would enable Wulfstan to show that he continued to speak for Winchester.

All this makes the Wulfstanian flavour of the Durham Hymnal poems to St Augustine the more intriguing. These poems share some verbal parallels with his known work, particularly in the dactylic 'Summa Dei bonitas': in the second couplet, the phrase 'laudibus eximiis' echoes two of the L couplets in the Rouen hymns ('Laudibus innumeris' in the Æthelwold hymn, and 'Laudibus angelicis' in the first hymn to Swithun).[83] Likewise, *commoda quaeque* (10) appears in just this fixed form in the *Narratio metrica* (I.1612; II.89), and six of the seven times Wulfstan uses the adjective *salutifer–* in the *Narratio metrica* it is also (as in 'Summa Dei bonitas', line 5) fixed in the first half of the hexameter and preceded by a dissyllable.[84] But such similarities in diction are not the most compelling reason for associating the Augustine hymns with Wulfstan. Rather, the poems' unusually difficult metrical forms and stylistic unity harmonize them with Wulfstan's distinctive practice.

All three are technically accomplished and make complicated use of aural effects, especially rhyme, as the first stanza of the matins hymn demonstrates:

> Aveto, placidis presul amabilis,
> aveto, cẹlebri laude notabilis,
> aveto, salubri luce capabilis
> Augustine placabilis.[85]

Hail, bishop friendly to the meek; hail, man renowned in frequent praise; hail, you who are filled with salvific light: merciful Augustine!

Anaphora, rhyme, alliteration, and syntactic parallelism interlink the lines: the same strategy recurs in stanza three. The latter four of the poem's seven stanzas are incrementally less aurally spectacular, but the sixth serves to connect the entire hymn sequence:

> Exhinc subveniat digna precatio
> in sublime tuis prepete servulis
> quos nutrire studes fastibus aetheris
> Augustine placabilis.[86]

Then fitting prayer swiftly assists into the heights your poor servants, whom you labour to support into the heavenly feasts, merciful Augustine.

Here alone in the cycle are Augustine's devotees pictured in heaven; this joins them to the chorus invoked in the first stanza of the hymn for vespers:

Caelestis aule nobiles
mundique recti principis
concorditer ferant deo
laudum trophea precluo[87]

> Let the noble ones belonging to the heavenly hall and to the world's true
> Prince together bring praise to the renowned God for his victories.

The hymn sequence forms a unified structure; as the singers progress
towards its end, they return in spirit to its beginning. Along the way, they
have rehearsed Augustine's journey from Italy to England, and besought his
intercession for his congregants: though relatively short, the cycle is an
efficient work of hagiography as well as liturgy.

Perhaps the most striking aspect of the hymns is their combination of
professional efficiency with great technical difficulty: they are manifestly the
work of someone who knew exactly what a confessor-saint's praises ought to
include. The second, epanaleptic hymn is a microcosm of the Rouen
abecedarian poems: an invocation with praise is followed by a biographical
note; the saint is translated to heaven; his protection is besought, along with
forgiveness for the community's sins, and the poem concludes with a hope
of salvation, partly through his means. The hymn to Birinus takes the same
course, but in twenty-seven couplets instead of seven. Where Wulfstan's
works habitually concluded with an acrostic AMEN, the Augustine hymns
all contain compressed doxologies, all in different words.

The Durham Hymnal poems for St Augustine leave us with two questions: if they are not Wulfstan's works, why do they sound so much as if
they were? Or if they *are* his, how did he come to compose hymns for the
cult of Canterbury's patron saint? Hypothetical answers to both questions
can, I think, be found in Wulfstan's status within the Winchester community. As a poet, musical innovator, and liturgical standard-bearer for
Æthelwold's cult, it is likely that Wulfstan's accomplishments would have
been known outside Winchester, and they must have been known in
Canterbury after Ælfheah – the bishop to whom he addressed the *Epistola
specialis* – was made archbishop in 1006. According to Eadmer, Ælfheah
brought St Swithun's head to add to Canterbury's relics, and he may
likewise have brought textual materials to support the saint's veneration.[88]
Some at least of Wulfstan's writings reached Canterbury, since an excerpt
from the *Narratio metrica* (and an abecedarian epanaleptic hymn for all
saints) appears in the St Augustine's, Canterbury manuscript, CUL
Gg.5.35.[89] Whether or not Ælfheah took Wulfstan with him to Kent – as
Lapidge suggests[90] – the St Augustine hymns demonstrate that someone in

early eleventh-century Canterbury saw the need for work of exactly the kind Wulfstan produced. Augustine's cult needed an advocate to match Æthelwold's and Swithun's. Perhaps they managed to find a local poet – one of great technical skill, and who took Wulfstan for a stylistic model – who restricted his output to these three hymns. However, I think it unlikely that one could find a substitute for Wulfstan himself.

The Southern mode: regeneration

Hardly anyone sets out to degenerate. In general, it is supposed to be what happens while one isn't looking: while focused on success or survival or pleasure, one ignores something else, some essential standard, until it has slipped irrecoverably away.[91] In such cases, attempts to recover the old standard serve only as signs of how utterly it is gone, and how unequal successors are to their forebears. The art of Constantine's reign used to be considered a perfect example of this phenomenon. Though he attempted to rival the early emperors with a grand programme of imperial art, the earlier sculpture incorporated into new works like the Arch of Constantine laid bare the Christian empire's lack of the skill and discernment of former days.

The story of 'The Decline and Fall' is too drearily familiar to medievalists to require rehearsal, except to point out that in most cases those telling it believe themselves to have escaped or reversed that historical trend: if one wishes to be considered a shining light, it helps to have darkness whence to emerge. Anglo-Saxon history has many such lights, and the tenth century especially is a veritable Perseid shower of them: Wulfstan Cantor's account of Æthelwold, for instance, makes the most of the incompetence and moral turpitude of the unreformed cathedral chapter at Winchester before his hero's advent.

But the chief and brightest of our Anglo-Saxon lights, especially to modern times, is Alfred of Wessex. Simon Keynes has given a splendid account of his mythos.[92] For literary scholars, many of the most important recent controversies about Alfredian literature have had to do with the exact degree of prior darkness,[93] and with the candlepower that the king – personally or by proxy – actually managed to shed on the intellectual landscape of England.[94] A remarkable thing about the literary programme associated with Alfred is that it is traditionally linked with both creation and degeneracy. Though there unquestionably was a body of Old English prose literature before the tenth century, it was during the reigns of Alfred and his descendants that the vernacular was made a suitable medium for history, philosophy, and religious discourse at all levels.[95] However, with a very few exceptions, the verse associated with Alfred and his court has been considered decadent, a sign of the ebb of the Old English poetic tradition.[96] The king, it seems, was an Augustus for prose and a Constantine for verse.

The coincidence of these qualities is probably not accidental. It is not simply prejudice to assert that the *Metres of Boethius* are qualitatively different from *Exodus*, say, or the works of Cynewulf, and Griffith's detailed analysis has shown that much of the difference between the *Metres* and more paradigmatic verse like *Beowulf* stems directly from their author's very close adherence to the prose source.[97] Other features point to numerous secondary phenomena also at work: for instance, the innovative verse type xx//, resembling Bliss's light a2 verse, but with two consecutive stressed words at the verse's end in place of a single compound.[98] This new form is probably related to the scarcity of poetic compounds in the *Metres* and in other later verse. Fulk has presented an array of evidence indicating that the three gradations of stress underlying earlier Old English metre were no longer perceptible by the mid-tenth century.[99] With the metrical force of compounds in flux, reanalysis of some patterns was inevitable.

Linguistic change, then, accounts for some of the difference between late Southern verse and more classical Old English poetry. But it does not explain the radical differences in style and subject. Since its earliest recorded period, Old English verse drew on Latin texts, but works like the *Metres of Boethius*, *Judgment Day II*, the so-called *Benedictine* (or *Junius*) *Office* and others present themselves as faithful representations of their sources in ways that *Andreas*, Cynewulf's *Christ II*, or even *Genesis A* do not. Through techniques like end-stopping, new structural mechanisms, and the use of a deliberately restricted vocabulary, later poets created a new register for Old English verse.[100] In its divergence from classical poetry, the new Southern mode provided a conspicuously non-nativizing medium for representing foreign texts. The 'decadence' of the verse style – which is to say, its avoidance of many of the standard signifiers of poetic register in Old English – enabled its users to create texts that functioned not as commentaries or retellings, but as simulacra.[101] The Southern mode, in other words, represents the apotheosis of Old English verse, not its downfall.

I connect this new form of verse with the hegemony of the Wessex kings for reasons that are ideological as well as chronological. The courts of Alfred and his successors welcomed foreigners, and their re-envisioning of the English monarchy and church during the tenth century drew extensively on Frankish and German models: tenth-century modernity had a distinctly international tone.[102] At the same time, there was a new emphasis on the provision of authoritative texts in Old English: not just law codes, but religious guidelines, Scripture, and history.[103] This seems a curious combination, but it evidently reflects a series of pragmatic accommodations reached by secular and ecclesiastical powers during the course of the century. The turn to monastic, rather than secular, religious foundations during Edgar's reign did not reverse the profound interest in church governance shown by Alfred and Athelstan.[104] The new poetic mode served to cement the bonds between ecclesiastical and secular power by giving laypeople a functioning equivalent of sacred texts, and by enabling the clergy to demonstrate how church ritual was compatible with a mainly vernacular public discourse. The Southern mode succeeded by *not* adapting Latin materials to earlier poetic conventions: by defamiliarizing vernacular poetry, it constructed an illusion of foreignness and, thus, authenticity.

My definition of the Southern mode would thus require it to be (a) distinctively different in form from 'normal' or 'classical' verse, and (b) connected in its subject matter with the sphere of Latin culture. The stylistic differences must be deliberate, not purely a function of language change: end-stopping of lines and reduced use of marked poetic vocabulary would be two important elements, though particular poets might also use devices like rhyme or Latinate diction to this end. As for choice of subject, in most cases poems in the Southern mode will depend directly on Latin texts, though this need not be true in all instances. The essential criterion is that a poem sound as if it might have a Latin original.

Though the timeline and geographical scope of the development of this mode of poetry are still somewhat obscure, we can nevertheless establish some broad parameters. Table 5.1 gives a (very conservative) list of poems of this sort. The Southern mode was embraced in Kent, as we see from the *Kentish Hymn* and *Psalm 50*. These texts, written in a very distinctively Kentish dialect, are preserved in Cotton Vespasian D.vi, a mid-tenth-century book from (probably) St Augustine's, Canterbury. The prosimetrical version of the *Old English Boethius* may also have been copied in Kent or its near environs, or by someone from the region.[105] Wessex itself is represented by several manuscripts, including poems in the second part of CCCC 201, Lambeth 427, and (most likely) the Exeter Book. The mid-eleventh-century Worcester book Junius 121, which preserves a bilingual text sometimes called the *Benedictine Office*, takes the Southern mode as far north as the old territory of the Hwicce. Though the composition of most of these texts can only be localized to a dialect region, the manuscript evidence indicates that the Southern mode was indeed widely distributed across the south of England, and that its poems were valued enough to be copied

Table 5.1 *Manuscripts containing late Southern verse*

Manuscript	Date and site of origin	Southern mode contents
Cotton Otho A.vi G 347; K 167	*s.* x(mid); SE England	*OE Boethius* (prosimetric)
Cotton Vespasian D.vi G 389; K 207	*s.* x (mid/2nd half); St Augustine's, Canterbury	*Kentish Hymn* *Psalm 50*
Exeter 3501 G 257; K 116	*s.* x(2); SW England (?)	*Riddle 40*
BN lat. 8824 **G 891; K 367**	*s.* xi(med); **Canterbury?**	*Paris Psalms*
Junius 121 **G 644; K 338**	*s.* xi(mid); **Worcester**	'Benedictine Office'
CCCC 201 (1) G 65; K 49A	*s.* xi in.	*Judgment Day II* *Rewards of Piety*
CCCC 201(2) G 65.5; K 49B	*s.* xi(1/mid); Winchester or Exeter	*Lord's Prayer II* *Gloria I* (shared with J 121)
Cotton Tiberius B.i (2) **G 370.2; K 191**	*s.* xi(med); **Abingdon**	*Menologium*
Lambeth 427 G 517; K 280	*s.* xi(1); Winchester?	*Prayer* (1st 15 lines)
Cotton Julius A.ii (2nd part) K 159	*s.* xii(med)	*Prayer*
Trinity College Cambridge **R.17.1**	*s.* **xii; Christ Church** **Canterbury**	**Excerpts from** *Paris Psalms* (Eadwine Psalter)
BL, Additional 43703	(Nowell's transcript)	*Seasons for Fasting*

through the tenth, eleventh, and even (in the case of *A Prayer* in Cotton Julius A.ii) into the twelfth century.

By working backward through the manuscript tradition, we can catch some glimpses of how the Southern mode spread and how it worked. *A Prayer* is preserved in full only in the twelfth-century booklet that forms folios 136–44 of Cotton Julius A.ii, but the fragmentary portion in Lambeth Palace 427 is nearly identical except in spelling: the text, then, existed by the late eleventh century. In the earlier manuscript, *A Prayer* was one of several texts of practical devotion added to a psalter whose continuous interlinear gloss allowed it to be read and used by English-speakers: others include a glossed prayer and glossed confession. Julius A.ii is more grammatically oriented: it also contains the *Adrian and Ritheus* dialogue and an English version of the *Distichs of Cato*. In both books, *A Prayer* participates in a vernacular version of a Latin-dependent tradition. Though it is the only text in the Lambeth manuscript unaccompanied by a Latin base, *A Prayer*'s content and style are saturated in biblical language that points towards a Latin original. Consider lines 8–20:

> Æla, frea beorhta, folkes scippend!
> Gemilsa þyn mod me to gode,
> sile þyne are þynum earminge.
> Se byð earming þe on eorðan her
> dæiges and nihtes deofle campað
> and hys willan wyrcð; wa him þære mirigðe,
> þonne he ða handlean hafað and sceawað,
> bute he þæs yfeles ær geswyce.
> Se byð eadig, se þe on eorðan her
> dæiges and nyhtes drihtne hyræð
> and a his willan wyrcð; wel him þæs geweorkes,
> ðonne he ða handlean hafað and sceawað,
> gyf he ealteawne ende gedreogeð.[106]

O radiant Lord, Creator of the people! Let your heart have pity on me to my good; give your grace to your wretched one. Wretched is he who here on earth fights day and night for the Devil and does his will; woe will come upon him for that pleasure, when he has and sees his reward, unless he has turned from that evil. Blessed is he who here on earth heeds the Lord day and night and always does His will; good will come upon him for that labour, when he has and sees his reward, if he faithfully endures to the end.

The *æla* (*eala*) at the beginning of the passage invokes a variety of liturgical texts, including the O Antiphons and several of the Canticles; Psalm 50:3 provides a close parallel for lines 8–10.[107] The carefully balanced contrast between the *earming* and *eadig* both elucidates the opening plea and echoes the structure of Proverbs (for instance, 'abominabile Domino pravum cor et voluntas eius in his qui simpliciter ambulant', 'The depraved in heart are an abomination to the Lord, but those who walk blamelessly are his delight'), while the exact repetition invokes passages like the Commandments and Beatitudes.[108] Though *A Prayer* has no actual Latin source, its style conveys a reassuring sense of precedent. Its self-constructed authority thus allows it to function as a devotional text alongside the psalms and canticles in Lambeth 427, and as a work of moral instruction in Julius A.ii; in both instances, monoglot audiences could feel as if they were authentically engaging with Latinate culture.

The Old English Metrical Psalms, which interlink a wide range of eleventh- and twelfth-century books, seem to have enabled a similar sense of active participation in high culture. Four manuscripts contain excerpts of the metrical psalms (in **bold** in Table 5.1). The best-known and most complete of these, the Paris Psalter (Paris, Bibliothèque nationale, lat. 8824), contains the complete psalter in parallel with a Latin text, prefaced by explanatory *tituli*.[109] The compiler of the Paris Psalter drew on two different English versions of the Psalms: 1–50 are in prose, and 51–100 are metrical. It seems almost certain, however, that a metrical version of the full psalter once existed. Bodleian, Junius 121 contains metrical psalm excerpts that are so similar to the Paris version in the last hundred psalms that its quotations from the first fifty most likely derive from one full translation, copies of which were available to the scribe of the Paris Psalter and to the author of the Old English office in Junius 121.[110] This metrical version of the Psalms was also used by the glossator of the Eadwine Psalter, and by the author of the *Menologium*.[111] We know of no other surviving work of Old English poetry that was so widely quoted.

Gretsch in particular has demonstrated how central psalter-glossing was to late Anglo-Saxon intellectual culture, and she is probably right that that the Metrical Psalms 'would have held no attraction for the Royal Glossator', or for many English scholars of comparable Latinity.[112] It is noteworthy, then, that the Eadwine Psalter, a splendid twelfth-century book from Christ Church Canterbury containing three versions of the Latin Psalms together with a full English gloss on the *Romanum* version, twice quotes the Metrical Psalms, incorporating verses from Psalm 90 into the running gloss and a fragment of Psalm 142 into the marginal commentary.[113] The preference for the metrical version at these points, O'Neill has suggested, may well have been on aesthetic grounds.[114] As the Eadwine Psalter substantially postdates the Norman Conquest, there may perhaps have been a nostalgic component to the continued reading of the Psalms in Old English verse.[115] Given the small scale of the excerpts, though, it is difficult to be sure of more than that the Metrical Psalms were still read by monks or clerks in twelfth-century Canterbury.

The Paris Psalter, our most important source for Old English psalm texts, is an even more eccentric book than its post-Conquest cousin. Its physical format is peculiar, with its text fitted to an extremely narrow area of the already tall, narrow pages: Toswell has compared it to the books held by figures in late Anglo-Saxon biblical illustrations.[116] But the Psalter was unquestionably assembled with great care. Most of its text is written in two columns to the page, with the left-hand column presenting the Latin, and Old English on the right. Each verse is carefully aligned and supplied with a coloured initial, so that one may see at a glance how the Latin and English correspond; as the vernacular text is generally somewhat longer than the Latin, the scribe had to measure precisely to coordinate the layout.[117] The first fifty psalms are also prefaced with prose explanations in English that extend across both columns. Visually, then, the book emphasizes the physical equivalence of the Latin and vernacular. Users of the manuscript could read the English with the comforting sense that they were receiving everything the Latin had to offer, and perhaps a bit more. If Toswell is right in thinking the Paris Psalter was a formal experiment, it may be that the *Wulfwinus cognomento Cada* whose name appears in the colophon on fol. 186[r] was responsible for the innovative bilingual layout.[118] Emms has identified Wulfwine Cada with a *Wulfwinus scriptor* in an *obit* list from St Augustine's, Canterbury, and Canterbury is perhaps the most plausible place for the manuscript's production.[119] Since the Eadwine Psalter text cannot have been copied directly from the Paris Psalter, there must have been at least one other copy of the Metrical Psalms available there.[120]

The Paris Psalter contains no lection marks or monastic pressmarks, and it may well have been designed from the beginning for a lay owner.[121] This would connect it with a much broader cultural trend in late Anglo-Saxon England towards allowing laypeople access to religious texts in the vernacular. Ælfric of Eynsham's participation in translating the Old English Hexateuch, and the English *vitae* he wrote to give the noblemen Æthelweard and Æthelmær a better knowledge of the saints venerated by monks, are perhaps the most famous examples. In most cases, the manuscripts actually owned by laypeople have been lost; but some texts that survive in institutional copies indicate that the Paris Psalter may not have been alone in using the Metrical Psalms to open the world of professional religious practice to vernacular readers. The *Junius Office* is a bilingual, prosimetric text preserved in Junius 121, a late eleventh-century book devoted mainly to texts associated with Wulfstan, bishop of Worcester and later archbishop of York.[122] Junius 121 was almost certainly written at Worcester, though the colophon of *Wulfgeatus scriptor Wigornensis* was probably copied from its exemplar.[123] The *Junius Office* itself is a complex text that seems to have been constructed and reconstructed out of a variety of materials; but as an English exposition of liturgical ritual, it is thoroughly in line with what we know of Wulfstan's intellectual preoccupations, and may have been intended for the secular clergy or laity.[124]

The prose framework of the *Junius Office* is an explanation of the daily office based ultimately on excerpts from Hrabanus Maurus' *De clericorum institutione*. Judging by its style, Wulfstan himself seems to have revised the text, though he may not have originally translated it.[125] The embedded poetry, on the other hand, appears to have been gathered from several different sources. The Metrical Psalms, as we have seen, must have circulated separately: from a full text, the compiler of the *Office* has excerpted particular Old English verses and paired them with their Latin antecedents. But the compiler also incorporated a series of poems based on the Gloria, Lord's Prayer, and Apostles' Creed, whose method of rendering the Latin into Old English is entirely different from that of the Metrical Psalms. The Old English *Gloria* is also preserved in CCCC 201 (though separate from the prose explanation), together with a different version of the Lord's Prayer: these two poems are similar enough that common authorship seems plausible. It seems most likely, therefore, that at least three different poets were responsible for the verse in the *Junius Office*, and this variation gives the text something of the heterogeneous feel of the Latin services.

Latin is the backbone of these texts, as Junius 121 and CCCC 201 demonstrate visually.[126] In these books, the Old English *Creed, Gloria,* and both versions of the *Lord's Prayer* are segmented into verse paragraphs. The Latin phrase that forms the core of each paragraph is copied along with it, often tucked into the blank space at the end of the preceding paragraph of Old English. Each unit – both Latin and Old English – begins with an enlarged capital; in CCCC 201, these are picked out in alternating red and green. Both books tend to align the Latin phrases with the outer margin of the page, as if for ease of reference, and since the Old English expands greatly upon the Latin, the latter recedes into a sort of running title rather than continuous text. In Junius 121, the quotations from the Psalter alternate between Latin and Old English. Most can be found in the service for Prime and Chapter, just after the versified Creed, on fols. 47–50.[127] In this sequence of quotations, there is little visual distinction between the Latin and Old English: with script and capitals of roughly equal size, it would be impossible to perceive that an Old English verse depends on the preceding Latin one without either knowledge of the language, or recognition that the sequence is following a particular convention. Not all the Latin material in the *Junius Office* is provided with an English apparatus – repetitions are not glossed, and 'interpreter's fatigue' seems to have set in towards the end of the daily cycle – but the vernacular text is not graphically subordinated to the Latin in the way that glosses are. In many of the prose and verse textual units, the Latin seems to function as an organizing principle: it provides a name for the Old English content, rather than appearing as the content itself.

The various manifestations of the Old English Metrical Psalms thus fall along a continuum of visible relations to the Latin text: the vernacular is clearly subordinate in the Eadwine Psalter, but equal or primary in the Paris

Psalter and Junius 121. In the *Menologium*, the Old English has simply become the text:

> þænne dream gerist
> wel wide gehwær,   swa se witega sang:
> Þis is se dæg   þæne drihten us
> wisfæst worhte,   wera cneorissum,
> eallum eorðwarum   eadigum to blisse.[128]

> then joy arises far and wide, as the prophet sang: 'This is the day that the wise Lord has made for us, the children of men, as a joy to all the blessed inhabitants of the earth.'

Though the lines describing the Easter feast are not quite identical with Psalm 117:22 in the *Paris Psalms*, they are similar enough to make it clear that the *Menologium* poet is quoting the Metrical Psalter.[129] As presented here, the verses simply are the words of the prophet, in much the same way that the Old English version of Bede's *Historia ecclesiastica* seamlessly incorporates the vernacular text of *Cædmon's Hymn*. The *Menologium* necessarily includes many foreign names and technical terms like *kalends*, and this, together with lines like 'þæt man reliquias ræran onginneð' (73, 'on which relics are elevated') makes the foreign origin of the subject matter impossible to overlook. Yet the poem seems designed to convey the English nation's successful amalgamation of Latinate religious culture, as the final lines explicitly declare:

> Nu ge findan magon
> haligra tiida   þe man healdan sceal,
> swa bebugeð gebod   geond Brytenricu
> Sexna kyninges   on þas sylfan tiid.[130]

> Now you can ascertain the holy festivals that must be celebrated, as the command of the king of the Saxons extends throughout the realm of Britain in this very season.

Remarkably, the imperative force behind the *Menologium*'s sacred calendar is connected not to the archbishop or pope, but to the Saxon king whose hegemony extends across Britain. Without actually asserting that the king is responsible for the calendar, its sway is made coterminous with his. These lines make clear the *Menologium*'s relation to the *Anglo-Saxon Chronicle*, its companion in Cotton Tiberius B.i,[131] and they also help construct a larger narrative in which speakers of English attain a progressive mastery over areas once dominated by Latin culture (history, *computus*, *Britannia*). The inclusion of the quote from the Metrical Psalms contributes to this narrative by providing the illusion of unmediated access to the Bible, just as the poem as a whole tells its readers that they 'nu. . .findan magon' their place in the Christian year.

The *Menologium* thus gives us a particularly vivid insight into the rhetorical potential of late Southern verse. Its inelegant metre and the foreign flavor of its lexis make it slightly alien, but this controlled element of otherness makes the poem's claim to convey mastery of Christian calendrics all the more persuasive. We often assume that a nationalistic cultural agenda is accompanied by a preference for traditionalism, or nativist purity, in cultural products. But what the *Menologium* and its manuscript demonstrate is that a display of the assimilation of foreign elements can also act as proof of a nation's confidence. In Cotton Tiberius B.i, a reader of English can see the dominion of the vernacular extend to new regions of knowledge, just as the power of the Saxon kings has expanded across Britain. It is profoundly ironic that the Southern mode has been taken as a sign of the decline of the Anglo-Saxon poetic tradition, when both context and content indicate that it represents the apex of Old English as a language of high culture.

Though the Southern mode was closely tied to the West Saxon hegemony, one of its most interesting features is its dialectal range. In Kent, the tradition of vernacular psalmody evidently spanned many decades, and (as the Eadwine Psalter shows) outlasted the Wessex kings. If, as seems plausible, the Paris Psalter was intended for a lay owner, the Metrical Psalms may have helped the monks – and possibly even the archbishops – of Canterbury to engage their secular contemporaries more closely with the church. Moreover, two poems preserved in Cotton Vespasian D.vi demonstrate that Canterbury poets were creating devotional poetry in the Southern mode by the mid-tenth century. The *Kentish Hymn* is a praise-poem deeply imbued with Biblical language: for instance, its first lines,

> Wuton wuldrian   weorada dryhten
> halgan hlioðorcwidum,   hiofenrices weard,
> lufian liofwendum,   lifęs agend,
> and him simle sio   sigefęst wuldor
> uppe mid ænglum,   and on eorðan sibb
> gumena gehwilcum   goodes willan[132]

We must praise the lord of hosts, heaven-kingdom's guardian, with holy voice, ardently honouring life's ruler: and may the victorious glory be to him always up among the angels, and on earth peace to all men of good will.

invoke the angels' salutation to the shepherds in the Gospel of Luke.[133] In the manuscript, the *Hymn* is followed by a prose chronology of the Old

Testament, and then by *Psalm 50*, which frames its poetic version of the penitential psalm with a biographical account of David's sin and repentance. The final lines of the poem exhort *us* the audience (154b, 157a) to emulate David and seek God's forgiveness: as in the *Hymn*, the voice impels readers towards active devotion.

Both the *Kentish Hymn* and *Psalm 50* are written in a strongly Kentish dialect, but they contain some hypercorrective forms which suggest an attempt to put the poems into West Saxon.[134] When writing poetry, it seems, either the scribe or the author was thinking beyond the walls of Canterbury. The poems themselves indicate that their authors were familiar with some literary touchstones. The first two lines of the *Kentish Hymn* echo the first line of *Cædmon's Hymn*, while the verse biographical framework of *Psalm 50* corresponds to Metre 1 in the prosimetrical *Old English Boethius*. Like Metre 1, *Psalm 50* draws upon a commentary tradition to create an historical and interpretive context for the translation proper.[135] While it is more difficult to assert that the author of *Psalm 50* must have known the *Boethius* than that the author of the *Kentish Hymn* knew Cædmon's poem, it is still hardly implausible, especially given that Christ Church Canterbury did own a copy of the text.[136] The local dialect, in other words, is not a sign of a provincial mindset; the poets looked for inspiration to literature both classical and contemporary, and tried to make their works conform to a broader literary standard. While there are many possible reasons for later Canterbury scholars' preference for the Metrical Psalms over home-grown versions, that text's wide distribution may itself have justified its use. Though evidently composed by a Mercian, the Metrical Psalms have been much more thoroughly West Saxonized than *Psalm 50*, making them more suitable for an audience who considered themselves English rather than specifically Kentish.[137] The verse in Vespasian D.vi is a sign that the Southern mode was valued in Canterbury from at least the mid-tenth century, even if these particular Kentish poems seem to have left no immediate descendants.

Psalm 50 may not have become the paradigm for vernacular psalmody, but its form points towards a likely site of origin for the Southern mode. The prosimetrical version of the *Old English Boethius* represents an ambitious attempt to recreate the formal effect of *De consolatione philosophiae*. Though the innovative strangeness of Boethius' metrical variety was irreplicable in English, a late ninth- or early tenth-century versifier still succeeded in creating an Old English text that alternated verse with prose as the Latin did.[138] The justification offered for the versification is oddly passive-aggressive: King Alfred, we are told, wanted to recount the book in poetry

þy læs ælinge   ut adrife
selflicne secg,   þonne he swelces lyt
gymð for his gilpe.[139]

lest boredom drive away the self-regarding man, when for his pride he
reckons such things of small account.

This explanation has something in common with the traditional view of
poetry's *dulcedo* in comparison to prose, but the suggestion that people who
demand poetry are probably arrogant and lazy adds a peculiar tang of
bitterness. What it also tells us, though, is that the poetry was intended to
produce a particular sort of feeling in the book's readers: interest, certainly,
but also respect. The prologue's implication is that the more judgmental
sort of reader will not take unadulterated prose seriously.

Yet the versifier of the *Old English Boethius* has not resorted to converting
the entire text into poetry; instead he has affixed a biographical framework
in verse, and converted most, though not all, of the passages corresponding
to Latin metres.[140] His interest in keeping the *Old English Boethius* analogous to the Latin must therefore have superseded any desire to win over
sceptics in the audience. It may be, however, that many of these hypothetical snobs would have been satisfied by the text's new alignment with
the embedded genre labels. The prose version diligently signals the Latin's
shifts between prose and verse (for instance, 'Þa se wisdom þa þis spell areht
hæfde, þa ongan he giddian and þus singende cwæð . . .', 'When Wisdom
had made this speech, then he began to chant and thus singing said . . .'[141])
while the Old English continues along the same grade. These reminders of
the distance between the Latin and vernacular – signals that the Old English
text is not self-sufficient – all correspond to actual formal changes in the
prosimetrical version. In the few instances in which the *metra* have been left
as prose, the genre tags are absent in the parallel passages in Bodley 180,
which may well explain why the versifier overlooked these passages. What
the prosimetrical *Old English Boethius* allows readers to do – as the all-prose
version did not – is to forget that they are reading a translation. One can see,
then, why it might have appealed more strongly to such *selflice secgas* as
disliked being reminded that they were not, in fact, reading a Latin book.

While much of the stilted peculiarity of the *Metres of Boethius* stems from
the text's fidelity to the Old English prose, rather than to the Latin, its
differences from 'Classical' verse make it a paradigmatic example of the
Southern mode. The avoidance of traditional markers of poetic register –
such as compounding, and the displacement of particles from their prose
placement – together with the frequent incorporation of exotic Greek and

Latin names give the *Metres* a very different sensibility from more or less contemporary poems like *The Battle of Brunanburh* and (probably) *Judith*. The latter forms a particularly striking contrast: brilliant and accomplished though *Judith* is, it would be impossible for a reader to imagine that he or she was experiencing the actual apocryphal text – nor indeed is that the poem's point. But it is the point of the versimetrical *Boethius*. Conforming in structure to the Latin, but lacking the obviously vernacular bravura of *Judith*, it enabled readers to enjoy the illusion that they were themselves reading an important and difficult work of Latin literature.

If the prose and verse prefaces to the *Old English Boethius* are at all accurate, the verse was a retrofit designed to solve a problem of reception. Even as an afterthought, though, it may well have become a paradigm. We have already seen *Psalm 50*'s structural similarity to the *Metres*' integration of a translated text into a biographical framework, while most poems listed in Table 5.1 share the *Metres*' avoidance of poetic compounds, frequent incorporation of foreign words, tendency towards end-stopping, and use of a syntax midway between that of prose and 'Classical' verse. It is still too early to write a full history of the Southern mode, but the evidence of manuscript date and formal influence suggests that the *Old English Boethius* probably stands at or near its foundation. From it we can trace a vector to Canterbury, where poets evidently recognized the Southern mode's potential for creating devotional texts. Kentish productions of psalm texts, however, were supplanted by the Metrical Psalms. Though we cannot now say where this ambitious recreation of the psalms was written, it had been disseminated across southern England by the beginning of the eleventh century, and became the engine for a variety of innovative vernacular versions of important Latin texts. Though the *Old English Boethius* could conceivably have led to the production of vernacular counterparts of more secular texts, its mode seems to have been co-opted entirely for religious verse. Much of the demand for these English simulacra, though, may have come from laypeople.

The Southern mode, then, was in many ways strikingly and rapidly successful as a literary style. Judging by the number of works associated with it, it must have been popular with poets as well: nine different poets, at minimum, must have produced the works in Table 5.1. Given its plausible connection with lay piety, one can see several possible attractions of the Southern mode both for monks and secular clerics. Old English had a respectable place in professional religious discourse, and fellow clerics may well have found these texts useful and enjoyable.[142] But by giving laypeople the chance to feel that they were directly experiencing Latin texts, the authors of such poems could also help build ties beyond cloister or cathedral walls. It is even possible that some authors in the Southern mode were themselves laypeople who wanted to participate in Latinate high culture: even a poet with 'small Latin' or none could create verse that sounded as if it had a Latin antecedent. Much of the power of this form of verse rested, then, in its ability to create a new kind of poetic community.

The tariff for entering this new community was quite often, it seems, a submersion of personal voice. Though devotional poetry does have room for the idiosyncratic *I*, as Cynewulf's signatures (for instance) show, poems in the Southern mode tended to cede control of voice to the source text. Thus, the Metrical Psalms replicated the Latin's complex fluctuation between the second person and singular and plural first person. With the exception of the prologue (whose voice is discussed in Chapter 1 above), the versifier of the *Metres of Boethius* maintained the *dramatis personae* of his source. Liturgical texts like the *Credo* and *Lord's Prayer* were necessarily constrained by the Latin's use of singular or plural first person, which was essential to each text's function and identity.[143] Though *Judgment Day II* apparently presents a particular penitential voice, the manuscript's rubricated ascription of the poem to 'Bede presbiter' makes the Old English *ic* a ventriloquist, one who goes on to offer general Christian instruction in the homiletic verse that follows.[144] Though it is not clear that *Judgment Day II* and *The Rewards of Piety* are by the same author, they are presented in CCCC 201 as part of a coherent sequence of devotional poetry. A reader could easily transfer some of Bede's authority to the *ic* that speaks in the next lines: what the poet would lose in individual credit he would gain in moral force. We see another canny manipulation of ventriloquism in *Psalm 50*, where the historical framework makes it clear that *ic* must be understood as King David, while the closing turn to a homiletic plural opens up the possibility that the reader too might speak with David's voice. In all these cases, we see poets embracing strong restrictions on voice imposed by source and genre: and in all cases, there also seems to be a clear reward in the form of increased authority or efficacy for the text. Poetry of the Southern mode had a strong pragmatic bent.

Most likely, not everyone in the tenth and eleventh centuries embraced this new mode of verse. Especially at the beginning of its course, in the early to mid-tenth century, one can imagine practitioners of other styles – like the poets of *Judith* and *The Battle of Brunanburh* – feeling with many modern critics that the Southern mode was poor, degenerate stuff. But the wide geographical range of this style, and its survival well into the eleventh century, show that many Anglo-Saxons valued it. The books that preserve this style of poetry help us see how it could forge cultural bonds between clerics and laypeople by giving readers of the vernacular a sense of ownership of the Latin tradition. The peculiarities of voice in the Southern mode indicate its strong functional character. The tendency towards ventriloquism, and towards an illusion of mimetic fidelity to the source, would work to deflect judgment away from the poets and, indeed, the texts: a reader who found the style peculiar or content difficult would be prompted, often by cues in the manuscript, to ascribe these features to the text's Latinity. Some poets no doubt used this as a cover for lazy workmanship, but others did labour to create a new form of verse that was simultaneously English and foreign.

The Southern mode demonstrates that Old English verse cannot be considered monolithic in style or purpose. Accidents of preservation have made the tenth and eleventh centuries better known to us than earlier ones: but there is no reason to believe that late Anglo-Saxon England was alone in having multiple poetic modes simultaneously available. The Southern mode's own multiple affiliations – the differences we can see in preoccupations at Kent, or in texts linked to the West Saxon court – show us how crucial particular communities were to forming poets' work. The more we learn about the Southern mode, the more we shall learn about the immediate experience of life in late Anglo-Saxon culture: and vice versa.

Conclusions

Difference is sometimes better exemplified than explained. The purpose of this chapter's heterogeneity is to show how various the experience of Anglo-Saxon poets really was, and how this has left its mark in the variety of Anglo-Saxon verse. Certain modes of community may have predictable effects, as in the case of Boniface's small, inward-looking group of disciples and correspondents. But in other instances – such as Wulfstan Cantor's intense sense of responsibility for Winchester's communal voice, or the ramifying set of groups that adopted and adapted the Southern mode of Old English poetry – the results depended on factors that could not necessarily have been foreseen, even by the people involved. Time and chance have thus helped to bring about a corpus of verse that can still challenge and surprise.

All three of these case studies emphasize how very strongly embedded Anglo-Saxon verse was in the work of its creators. Disinterested, autotelic verse was probably thinkable during the Anglo-Saxon period, especially after the advent of literacy; but it is hard not to conclude that Anglo-Saxon poets would have seen such an attitude towards art as a waste of an opportunity. Practicality was not necessarily limiting: the superfluity of ornament that we see in Wulfstan Cantor's liturgical compositions is an excellent example of how beauty could perfect function. In Wulfstan's particular case, he viewed his work as an offering to God and his community, and while two mites were acceptable from a poor widow, Dives had to do better. The same, one can imagine, would be true in less charged circumstances. The judgment of the community may well have rewarded those who honoured it by showing they were striving for more than mediocrity: perhaps the Anglo-Saxons' love for complex surface patterning is a reflex of this. Technical difficulty may have been a sign of respect for one's audience, making very ornate texts more, rather than less, functional. By further pursuing how poets shaped their texts for particular purposes in a community, we may gain a better understanding of many aspects of their style, both foreign and familiar.

Afterword
A way of happening

The inefficacy of art – especially of poetry – is something of a trope in modern discourse, one that even many of poetry's defenders have embraced.[1] This notion would have puzzled Anglo-Saxons, who became poets in order to do something: often, to be what they were, but better.[2] While their unenchanted view of poets' work is not very conducive to grand historical paintings like John Martin's *The Bard*, it opens up new ways of seeing how a great many different kinds of people went about the business of living in their world. Poetry, for the Anglo-Saxons, was not something that separated them from others, but was a way of being in society, 'a way of happening, a mouth'.[3]

In *Becoming a Poet in Anglo-Saxon England*, I have traced a few of the many paths by which people came to compose verse in Old English or Latin, as well as some of the purposes that drew them on. As we saw in the first two chapters, the Anglo-Saxons did not use words for 'poet' to describe a particular career path or separate caste; poets were those who excelled in the art of making verse. For them, becoming a poet was a matter of practice, a continuous action rather than a status. This was paradoxically liberating: while it might generally be left to posterity to decide who merited the name of *scop* or *poeta*, the practice of poetry was left open to those willing and able to learn. These practising poets were a varied group. Prosopographical evidence shows that teachers, scribes, musicians, and courtiers were most often among those who had the means and motivation to become poets; it is certainly no coincidence that most of these roles often surrounded their occupants with written, spoken, or sung verse, and with others who knew poetry or wished to know it – with, in other words, poetic communities. Many of these groups and communities probably overlapped: we know of teachers of the liberal art of *musica*, of bishops who copied books and attended on kings. Yet certain broad classes of occupational experience seem to have given rise to certain broad classes of verse. Some of these are predictable – teachers' didactic verse, scribes' colophons, musicians' hymns, and courtiers' panegyrics. Other associations are less expected, but nevertheless arose from the nature of poets' daily experience: courtiers who wrote prayers, for instance; musician-hagiographers; even teachers who composed epics. Anglo-Saxon verse was 'socially engaged' in the sense that much of it was created in service of its makers' social roles. Continued research into secular and ecclesiastical labour, governance, and education in Anglo-Saxon England will therefore have the side-benefit of illuminating the history of its poetry.

Though Society sometimes presents itself as a grand abstraction with equally grandiose demands, people more often experience it in the less Platonic, more comprehensible form of particular interactions with particular people. In the same way that we do not learn Language, but the languages of our parents and friends, Anglo-Saxons learning Old English and Latin poetry responded to the knowledge and idiosyncrasies of those around them. As the three latter chapters of *Becoming a Poet* variously demonstrate, such poetic communities shaped the thought and work of poets in both their presence and absence. The key mechanism, the intermediary between the community and the individual, is judgment – thought about what others would think. Such judgment operates at multiple levels within poetry: it enables one to decide if a line is metrically correct, just as it helps one decide on the ethics of a character's action (or the poet's portrayal of that action). When poets work within communities, the response of those around them provides a ready means of calibrating their judgment: such poetry bears the imprint of the community in the form of its author's anticipation of others' judgment. The examples of Cynewulf and Aldhelm show that the written word could extend, rather than impede, poetic communities, but the advent of writing also made it possible to become a poet alone. Books enabled readers to deduce the rules of verse without recourse to the thoughts of living practitioners or audiences. Relying solely on their own judgment, however, made the work of poetic isolates as peculiar as the speech of those on the borders of linguistic communities. That these idiosyncrasies are the product of isolation, rather than literacy, is demonstrated by the way they are replicated on a larger scale when a community itself becomes isolated. It thus seems likely that poets' social circumstances were among the most important determinants of the kind of verse they could produce.

But as the last chapter illustrates, the difference between poets working in communities and isolated poets is not exclusive or dichotomous. I believe that social judgment, whose pervasive influence is outlined in Chapter 3, is akin to a fundamental force in human society: its action is especially visible in the arbitrarily rule-governed art of verse, but (like any other fundamental force) judgment's influence can be countered by other, stronger forces, or attenuated by distance. I expect, therefore, that my analytical paradigm can be extended beyond poetry, to prose and to other arts; though the special characteristics of these different forms would cause the effects of a community's judgment, or the lack of it, to manifest differently. But even within the realm of poetry, I have left unexplored many ways in which historical circumstance or ideology might affect the basic polarity of community and isolation. Poetic expressions of the eremitic ideal would form one especially interesting permutation, but there are, I hope, many other ways of building on my basic framework.

The writing of this book has changed my thinking about Anglo-Saxon literature and society in countless ways. It has, for one, brought home to me the magnitude of our losses: the hazy spot in Figure 3.2, where Bishop Wilfrid's correspondence ought to be, is a visible manifestation of many vanished archives. We know when the library of Christ Church Canterbury burned, and when that of Malmesbury was sold to a pastry-cook, but the book collections of most smaller houses and nunneries have sunk without ripples. As for the possessions of laymen, we can be sure of even less: aristocrats like Æthelweard could be poets, and some doubtless owned books containing verse, but what became of those books (or the other movable goods of the men who died at Ashingdon or Hastings) we do not know. So even the written record of Anglo-Saxon poets' work is hopelessly imperfect; of the poetry that was heard, not written, we naturally have only rumours and echoes. Our knowledge of this period, therefore, has limits that can never be more than partially shifted.

And yet, at the same time, it has become clear to me that we have inherited more than we think, and that the Anglo-Saxons' Latin literature especially holds a great deal that is unexplored. But even if we never discovered another word from an Anglo-Saxon's pen, the assembly and interpretation of what we do have is still the work of lifetimes. I do not in the least imagine that I have exhausted the possibilities even of the few poets and poems I have discussed here: I should be sorry if I had. There is much to be done, and of the topics treated briefly in this book, many deserve their own monographs. I am particularly conscious that the literature of the Danelaw and of Scandinavian-speakers in England, Anglo-Latin hymnody, and the Southern mode of Old English verse merited far more extensive discussion than I could provide them here. I hope, however, that *Becoming a Poet* can help others in giving such works and poetic communities their due. What is called for, in these and all other cases, is attention to the evidence – the evidence for how and by whom these genres and arts were practised, for what contemporaries believed them to be – and to the contents of the works themselves.

When a great cache of burial-urns was turned up in Norfolk in 1657, Thomas Browne was struck that something so ancient could at the same time be new. As he wrote in *Hydriotaphia*,

> Time hath endlesse rarities, and shows of all varieties; which reveals old things in heaven, and makes new discoveries in earth, and even earth itself a discovery. That great antiquity *America* lay buried for thousands of years; and a large part of the earth is still in the Urne unto us.[4]

Though so many of the remnants of Anglo-Saxon culture have been excavated and laid out to our gaze, a great deal of their meaning is yet in the urn. But continually trying to see the things that survive for what they are, we can perceive somewhat of what they were before they were buried. Much of the past is still to come.

A handlist of named authors of Old English or Latin verse in Anglo-Saxon England

Abbreviations

GSc Gameson, *The Scribe Speaks* (item number)
LH Lapidge, 'Hermeneutic Style' (appendix number)
LP Lapidge, 'Some Latin Poems' (page range)
LR Lapidge, 'Some Remnants' (item number)
MD Stubbs (ed.), *Memorials of Saint Dunstan* (page range)
S Sharpe, *Handlist* (item number)
T Tangl (ed.), *Briefe des heiligen Bonifatius* (item number)

* = no surviving works in verse
** = attribution questionable
<u>Name</u>: composed in Old English
<u>Name</u>: reported to have composed in Old English; attribution questioned, or no verse survives

1. **Abbo of Fleury** (S 1). †1004. Francia; worked in Ramsey (East Anglia). Abbot of Fleury. Teacher; musician. *Works*: Acrostic verse (hexameter) (ed. S. Gwara, 'Three Acrostic Poems', *JML* 2 (1992): 203–35; M. Lapidge and P. Baker, 'More Acrostic Verse', *JML* 7 (1997): 1–27); dedicatory poem to Ramsey monks (elegiacs)(*PL* 139, col. 534); probably hymns (see pp. 78–80).
2. **Alcuin of York** ('Flaccus'/'Albinus') (S 87). †804. Northumbria; worked in Francia. Abbot of Tours. Teacher. *Works*: *The Bishops, Kings, and Saints of York* (hexameter)(ed. Godman); *Vita metrica S. Willibrordi* (elegiacs, hexameter)(ed. Dräger); many occasional and epistolary poems and *tituli* (hexameter, elegiacs, rhythmic metres)(ed. Dümmler).
3. <u>**Aldhelm of Malmesbury**</u> (S 89). †709. Wessex. Abbot of Malmesbury; bishop of Sherborne. Teacher. *Works*: *Enigmata*; *Carmen de uirginitate*;

Carmina ecclesiastica (hexameter); *Carmen rhythmicum* (rhythmic octosyl-lables)(ed. Ehwald). Probable author of epitaph for Theodore in *HE*.

4. **Aldred.** *s.* x. Northumbria. Provost of Chester-le-Street. Glossator and scribe. *Works*: Metrical colophons in the Lindisfarne Gospels (hexam-eter, rhyming couplet) (ed. L. Nees, 'Reading Aldred's Colophon for the Lindisfarne Gospels', *Speculum* 78 (2003): 333–77).

5. **<u>Alfred</u> (S 106). †899. Wessex. King of Wessex. *Works*: Reputed to have composed the *Metres of Boethius* (*ASPR*; also *OEB*).

6. **Ædeluald.** *s.* viii or ix? Northumbria or Mercia? Bishop. *Works*: Acrostic prayer (rhythmic hexameter) (ed. A. Kuypers, *Prayer Book of Aedeluald the Bishop, Commonly Called the Book of Cerne*. Cambridge University Press, 1902. p. 41).

7. **Ælfric Bata** (S 54). *s.* xi. Kent. Monk. Teacher. *Works*: *Incipit* and *explicit* to *Colloquies* (hexameter, elegiac) (ed. S. Gwara, *Anglo-Saxon Conversations*. Woodbridge: Boydell, 1997).

8. **Ælfweard of Glastonbury** (S 57). *s.* x/xi. Wessex. Abbot of Glastonbury. *Works*: Epistolary verse to Sigeric, archbishop of Canterbury (elegiacs) (MD 403).

9. **Æthelweard** (S 67). *s.* x^{ex}. Wessex. Ealdorman of Dorset. *Works*: Poems (in eccentric forms) embedded in his *Chronicon* (ed. Campbell).

10. ***Æthelwold** (S 68). †984. Wessex. Bishop of Winchester. Teacher. *Works*: Reported by his student Wulfstan Cantor to have taught Latin metre, but none of his own verse is known to survive.

11. **Æthilwald** (S 66). *s.* vii/viii. Educated in Wessex. Probably an ecclesiastic, but his later career is unknown. *Works*: *Carmina rhyth-mica* (rhythmic octosyllables) (ed. Ehwald, Miles); now-lost poem in hexameters.

12. **Æthilwulf** (S 69). *s.* ix. Northumbria. Priest and monk; possibly also scribe. *Works*: *De abbatibus* (hexameter, elegiacs) (ed. Campbell).

13. **B (Byrhthelm?)** (S 175). *s.* x. Probably Wessex; worked in the Low Countries. Clerk, probably in secular orders. *Works*: Three poems embedded in his *Vita Dunstani*; an epistolary poem (hexameter) (MD 8–9; 16–17; 20; 375–6).

14. **Bald.** *s.* x(?). Probably Wessex. Doctor? *Works*: Colophon to 'Bald's Leechbook' (quasi-hexameter) (GSc 12). Someone else (the scribe Cild?) may have composed the verses.

15. <u>**Bede the Venerable**</u> (S 152). †735. Northumbria. Priest and Monk. Teacher; likely also scribe. *Works*: *Vita metrica S. Cuthberti* (hexameter) (ed. Jaager); embedded verse in *HE* (elegiacs); hymns and prayers

(iambic dimeter, elegiacs, hexameter) (ed. Fraipont); epigrams (hexameter, elegiacs) (LR 2, 10); attributed *Bede's Death Song* (*ASPR*).

16. **Berhtgyth**. *s*. viii. Probably Wessex; worked in Germania. *Works*: Two epistolary poems (rhythmic octosyllables) (T 147, 148).

17. **Boniface (Wynfrith)** (S 166). †755. Wessex; worked in Germania. Archbishop of Mainz. Teacher. *Works*: *Enigmata* (hexameter)(ed. Glorie); metrical prefaces to *Ars Grammatica* (elegiac, hexameter, rhythmic octosyllables) (ed. Gebauer and Löfstedt); epistolary verse (hexameter, rhythmic octosyllables) (T 9, 10, 50).

18. **Byrhtferth of Ramsey** (S 174). *s*. x/xi. East Anglia. Teacher. *Works*: 'Cum nu halig gast' (rhythmic hexameter) (ed. P. Baker and M. Lapidge, *Byrhtferth's Enchiridion*, EETS SS 15. 1995).

19. **Cædmon**. *s*. vii. Northumbria. Layman, later monk. *Works*: *Hymn* (*ASPR*, also ed. O'Donnell).

20. **Cenwald**. †958. Mercia and Wessex. Bishop of Worcester. *Works*: Inscription in the MacDurnan Gospels (rhythmic octosyllables) (ed. Keynes, 'Books', pp. 156–9).

21. **Ceolfrid of Wearmouth-Jarrow** (S 183). †716. Northumbria. Abbot. Teacher. *Works*: Epigram on the Codex Amiatinus (elegiacs).

22. **Cumma of Abingdon**. *s*. viii. Wessex. Abbot of Abingdon. *Works*: Epigram on a bowl (LR 22).

23. ****Cunneah** (S 214). *s*. viii. Irish? Abbot. *Works*: Epigram to Colmán (para-metrical) (LR 23). 'Cunneah' (Cyneheah?) may be the addressee of this epigram; see Sims-Williams, *Religion and Literature*, pp. 355–6.

24. **Cuð**. *s*. viii. Worcester? *Works*: *Versus de sancta trinitate* (hexameter) (BL, Royal 2.A.xx, 40ʳ) (ed. Sims-Williams, *Religion and Literature*, pp. 358–9).

25. **Cuthbert of Hereford** (S 211). †760. Mercia; Kent. Bishop of Hereford; archbishop of Canterbury. *Works*: Epigrams on a cross-cloth and a tomb (hexameter) (LR 20, 21).

26. **Cuthbert of Wearmouth-Jarrow** (S 212). *s*. viii. Northumbria. Abbot of Wearmouth-Jarrow. *Works*: Epistolary verse (hexameter) (T 116). Also recorded *Bede's Death Song*.

27. **Cynewulf**. Likely *s*. ix. Mercia? Probably an ecclesiastic, but his career is unknown. *Works*: *The Fates of the Apostles*; *Elene*; *Christ II*; *Juliana* (*ASPR*). Other works, including *Guthlac B*, have also been attributed to him.

28. **Dunstan of Glastonbury** (S 245). †988. Wessex; worked in Kent. Abbot of Glastonbury; archbishop of Canterbury. Teacher; scribe.

Works: Epigram; Acrostic (hexameter) (LH IV); distichs on an organ, font, and bell (hexameter) (ed. Lapidge, 'St Dunstan's Latin Poetry').

29. *Eadburg of Thanet. †751. Kent. Abbess of Minster-in-Thanet. Teacher. *Works*: None survive, although Leofgyth (41) attributes her knowledge of metre to Eadburg's instruction.

30. **Eadwald.** *s.* ix? Scribe. *Works*: Acrostic colophon to a copy of Felix's *Vita Guthlaci* (pseudo-metrical) (CCCC 307, 52^{r-v}). Errors indicate that the poem was badly copied from an exemplar.

31. **Eadwig Basan.** *s.* xi. Kent. Monk of Christ Church Canterbury. Scribe. *Works*: Colophon to Eadwig Gospels (rhythmic hexameter) (GSc 29).

32. **Eusebius (Hwætberht?)** (S 287, 534). *s.* viii. Northumbrian, if he is to be identified with the abbot of Jarrow, though this connection is by no means certain (see pp. 57–8). *Works*: *Enigmata* (hexameter) (ed. Glorie).

33. **Frithegod (Fredegaud of Brioude)** (S 301). *s.* x. Francia; worked in Canterbury. *Works*: *Breuiloquium vitae beati Wilfredi* (hexameter) (ed. Campbell); hymn (rhythmic stanzas) (ed. R. Love, 'Frithegod of Canterbury's Maundy Thursday Hymn', *ASE* 34 (2005): 219–36).

34. **Godemann** (S 387). *s.* x. Wessex. Monk at Winchester. Scribe. *Works*: Colophon to Benedictional of Æthelwold (BL, Add. 49598) (hexameter) (LH II).

35. **Hæddi** (S 418). †705. Wessex. Bishop of Wessex. *Works*: Dedicatory epigram (rhythmic octosyllables) (LR 25).

36. **Herbertus.** *s.* x/xi. Francia; worked in Wessex? Monk. *Works*: Poem to Abbot Wulfgar of Abingdon (elegiacs) (BL, Add. 32246).

37. **Israel the Grammarian** (S 540). *s.* x. Brittany; worked in Wessex. Teacher. *Works*: *De arte metrica* (hexameter) (ed. Strecker, MGH PLAC 5, pp. 501–2); various didactic verse (see Sharpe, p. 194).

38. **John the Old Saxon** (S 825). *s.* ix. Germania; worked in Wessex. Abbot of Athelney. Teacher. *Works*: Three acrostic poems for Alfred and Athelstan (pseudo-hexameters) (LP 60–71).

39. **Koaena.** *s.* viii. Northumbria. *Works*: Epistolary verses (hexameter) (T 124).

40. **Lantfred of Winchester** (S 1001). *s.* x. Francia?; worked in Wessex. Monk of Winchester. *Works*: Embedded verse in *Translatio et miracula S. Suithuni* (ed. in Lapidge, *Cult of St Swithun*); attributed two satiric poems (hexameter; adonics) (ed. Lapidge, 'Three Latin Poems').

41. **Leofgyth (Leoba).** *s.* viii. Kent; worked in Germania. Abbess of Tauberbischofsheim. Teacher. *Works*: Epistolary verse (hexameter) (T 29).

42. **Lull ('Lytel')** (S 1025). †786. Wessex; worked in Germania. Archbishop of Mainz. *Works*: Epistolary verse (hexameter, rhythmic octosyllables)

(T 103, 140); *Carmen de conuersione Saxonum* (ed. Hauck, 'Karolingische Taufpfalzen', pp. 62–5).

43. **Milred of Worcester** (S 1064). †775. Mercia. Bishop of Worcester. *Works*: Epigram (hexameter) (LR 1).

44. ****Osbern of Canterbury** (S 1141). †1094(?). Kent. Precentor of Christ Church Canterbury. Musician. *Works*: His lost earlier work on St Ælfheah was intended to be sung, and may have been in verse.

45. **Oswald of Ramsey** (S 1149). *s.* x/xi. East Anglia. Monk. Teacher. *Works*: Poem on retrograde verse (LH III). Oswald also wrote a now lost collection of prayers and treatise on composition.

46. **Owun.** *s.* x. N or W England? Scribe. *Works*: Colophon to the MacRegol Gospels (Bodleian, Auct. D.2.19, 168ᵛ–9ʳ) (GSc 16).

47. **Peter.** *s.* x. Worked in Wessex. *Works*: Circular poem for Athelstan (rhythmic iambic dimeter catalectic) (LP 86).

48. **Tætwine** (S 1681). †734. Mercia; worked in Kent. Archbishop of Canterbury. Probably a teacher. *Works*: *Enigmata* (hexameter) (ed. Glorie).

49. **Theodore of Tarsus** (S 1686). †690. Asia Minor; worked in Kent. Archbishop of Canterbury. Teacher. *Works*: Four epistolary poems and prayers (rhythmic octosyllables) (ed. Lapidge, 'Theodore and Anglo-Latin').

50. **Wulfstan Cantor** (S 2229). *s.* x/xi. Wessex. Precentor of Old Minster, Winchester. Musician. *Works*: *Narratio metrica de S. Swuithuno* (elegiacs, hexameter) (ed. in Lapidge, *Cult of St Swithun*); *Breuiloquium de omnibus sanctis* (elegiacs, hexameter) (ed. Dolbeau); various hymns and metrical tropes (hexameter, elegiacs, iambic dimeter, various stanzaic metres) (*AH et al.*).

Skalds working in Anglo-Saxon England

I. Pre-Cnut poets and their patrons

1. Egill Skalla-Grímsson
   a. *Aðalsteinsdrápa* (Athelstan)
   b. *Hǫfuðlausn* (Eiríkr blóðøx)
2. Gunnlaugr ormstunga
   a. *Aðalráðsdrápa* (Æthelred)
3. Þórleifr Rauðfeldarson
   a. *Sveinsdrápa* (Sveinn Haraldsson)
4. Anonymous
   a. *Eiríksmál* (Eiríkr blóðøx)

II. Poets patronized by Cnut

A. With surviving works
   1. Sigvatr Þórðarson
      a. *Knútsdrápa*
   2. Óttarr svarti
      a. *Knútsdrápa*
   3. Hallvarðr háreksblesi
      a. *Knútsdrápa*
   4. Þórarinn loftunga
      a. *Hǫfuðlausn*
      b. *Tøgdrápa*
B. Works lost, but names attested in *Skáldatal*
   1. Arnórr jarlaskáld
   2. Bersi Torfuson
   3. Steinn Skaptason
   4. Óðarkeptr

III. *Poets with other patrons in eleventh-century England*

1. Þórðr Kolbeinsson
   a. *Eiríksdrápa* (Earl Eirik, a follower of Cnut: delivered at court)
2. Anonymous
   a. *Liðsmannaflokkr* (Cnut/Emma?)
3. Thorkell Skallason
   a. *Valþjófsflokkr* (Earl Waltheof)

Sources: Campbell, *Skaldic Verse*; Townend, 'Pre-Cnut'; *Skaldic Poetry* (http://skaldic.arts.usyd.edu.au)

Notes

INTRODUCTION: HOW CAN WE KNOW ABOUT ANGLO-SAXON POETS?

1. Wright, *Womankind*, p. 67.
2. Nagel, 'What is it Like to be a Bat?', p. 439.
3. On the problem of defining verse, see pp. 35–6.
4. *HE* IV.24. All translations are mine unless noted otherwise.
5. *Ibid.*
6. The literature on the story and hymn is vast: see Caie, *Bibliography*; and O'Donnell (ed.), *Cædmon's Hymn*.
7. E.g., 'in quibus [carminibus] cunctis homines ab amore scelerum abstrahere, ad dilectionem uero et sollertiam bonae actionis excitare curabat' ('in all of which songs he laboured to draw men away from the love of sin, and to incite them to delight in and to practise good works').
8. *HE* IV.24.

1 WHAT WAS A POET?

1. Turner, *History*, vol. II, pp. 338–9 (Book IX, ch. 1).
2. Besides drawing attention to *Beowulf* before Thorkelin's publication of the poem, Turner's history was a standard reference for early literary scholars like Conybeare. Walter Scott drew upon it for the historical background to *Ivanhoe*, perpetuating Turner's work in the popular consciousness.
3. Turner, *History*, vol. II, p. 345 (Book IX, ch. 1).
4. Frank, 'Search', pp. 14–28.
5. *Ibid.*, p. 11; Turner, *History*, vol. II, p. 338.
6. On this problem, see further the Introduction.
7. Malone and Baugh, 'Old English Period', pp. 45–6.
8. Bloomfield and Dunn, *Role of the Poet*, p. 101.
9. Opland, *Oral Poetry*, p. 261.
10. Frank, 'Search', p. 12.
11. Greenfield and Calder, *New Critical History*, esp. pp. 122–302.
12. Greenblatt and others (eds.), *Norton Anthology*, vol. I, p. 5.
13. *Ibid.*, pp. 30, 52, 55.
14. Niles, 'Myth', p. 39.

15. *Wid* 88–102. (Old English verse, except *Beowulf*, quoted from *ASPR* unless noted otherwise, though I have occasionally altered punctuation.) Ealhhild was identified earlier in the poem (ll. 5–9) as the wife of Eormanric: this knowledge clarifies the referent of *operne* (97b), as Ealhhild's gift echoes her husband's.

16. *Deor* 35–42.

17. See Opland, *Oral Poetry*, pp. 216–17.

18. See, e.g., Klinck, *Elegies*, p. 168; and Malone, *Deor*, pp. 16–17, 39.

19. Heorrenda is probably the Old English reflex of Hôrant, the persuasive minstrel in the Middle High German romance *Kudrun*: see Klinck, *Elegies*, pp. 167–8.

20. Niles, 'Myth', p. 31.

21. *Beo* 89b–92. *Beowulf* text from Fulk, Bjork, and Niles (eds.), *Klaeber's Beowulf*, 4th edn, unless otherwise noted.

22. *Beo* 867b–76a.

23. See Opland, 'Beowulf'; Eliason, 'Improvised Lay'.

24. *Beo* 1063–8a (I here prefer the text of Klaeber's third edition, which treats *healgamen* as an object).

25. *Beo* 2105–10.

26. Opland, *Oral Poetry*, pp. 199–201, collects and discusses alternative readings (which depend a great deal upon how one chooses to punctuate the passage).

27. *Beo* 312a, 834a, 1646a, 1816a, 2183a (Beowulf); 3111a (Wiglaf); 3169b (Beowulf's twelve mourners).

28. Niles, 'Myth', p. 12.

29. Opland, *Oral Poetry*, p. 257.

30. This was Cameron *et al.*, *DOE Corpus in Electronic Form* (1981). The first concordance made with the full corpus was published in 1980 (Venezky and Healey, *Microfiche Concordance*). Opland notes the difficulties the lack of such tools posed for studies of common words like *song* (*Oral Poetry*, p. 246).

31. Zupitza (ed.), *Grammatik*, p. 302.

32. *ClGl* 1, 3943; on Old English loan-formations see Gneuss, *Lehnbildungen*.

33. *Poeta: ÆGl* 302, 8–9; *AntGl* 6, 728 (with *uel uates* after OE); *melopius: ClGl* 1, 4013; *ClGl* 2, 885 (misspelled *leohtwyrhta*).

34. B: VII.117; C: Pr. 5, 114 (*OEB*, vol. 1, pp. 255, 398).

35. *OEB*, vol. 1, p. 384.

36. Earl, *Thinking*, pp. 87–99.

37. *Met* 17, 21b; 22, 53b; 30, 8b. As O'Brien O'Keeffe has noted ('Listening', p. 34), it would also be strange for the book to consider itself plural.

38. Godden, 'Editing', pp. 164–6.

39. O'Brien O'Keeffe, 'Listening', p. 35.

40. Frantzen, 'Preface', pp. 132–4.

41. On voice in Alfredian texts, see Godden, 'Player King'; on Cotton Otho A.vi, and Junius's transcripts, see *OEB*, vol. 1, pp. 18–34.

42. See further below, pp. 90–1.

43. Robinson, 'Rewards', pp. 196–8, demonstrated the inseparability of this poem from the surrounding Latin text, particularly for understanding the syntax of

the final lines, not quoted here, which depend on the following Latin salutation for their sense. I would argue, though, that *Þus me gesette* refers back to the contents, rather than forward to the treatise (cf. Robinson, 'Rewards', p. 196).

44. *Aldhelm* 1–5a. On the poem, see further Whitbread, '*Aldhelm*'.

45. Virgil and Homer: *Boethius*, B: XLI.1–2; C: met. 30, 1–4 (*OEB*, vol. 1, pp. 374, 533); Homer: *Orosius* 1.xi.31; Terence: *Orosius* 1v.x.28 (Bately (ed.), *Orosius*, pp. 31, 107).

46. vi.v.24; 1.xiv.14 (Bately (ed.), *Orosius*, pp. 137, 35).

47. *AntGl* 6, 729; *scopas* are responsible for the *sceandlice leoðas* that afflict Mary of Egypt (*LS* 23, 627), and *leaspellunge* in the *Orosius* (iii.i.16–17, Bately (ed.), p. 53).

48. *Vates*: *HyGl* 2, 47.1, 99.3; *comicus* or *comedus*: *AntGl* 4, 307, 741; *AntGl* 6, 729; *ClGl* 1, 1155; *ClGl* 2, 884; *HlGl* C1206, C1256; *tragedus*: *AntGl* 4, 741; *AntGl* 6, 729; *lyricus*: *AntGl* 4, 725; *ClGl* 1, 3816.

49. E.g., *ÆGl* 299.14; *AntGl* 2, 906.

50. *KtPs* 6a. This is the only instance of this word in verse.

51. Liebermann (ed.), *Gesetze*, vol. 1, p. 472. *Grið* 21, 2.

52. See below, pp. 77–8.

53. *ChristA* 302b–3.

54. *DEdg* 29–33b.

55. *Rid* 80 9–10a; *Gifts* 35b–6a; *OrW* 2. *Gied*'s exact connotations are still unclear, but it sometimes denoted prose.

56. Opland, *Oral Poetry*, p. 250; cf. also pp. 251–3; and Hollowell, '*Scop and Woðbora*', and the references there given.

57. Opland, *Oral Poetry*, pp. 243–6; see also above, p. 20.

58. *Wid* 136a (+139a); *Max I* 166a; *Beo* 1160a.

59. *Beo* 1159b–60a.

60. E.g., the Old English *Historia ecclesiastica*'s 'buton Iacobe þæm songere' ('except for James the Cantor'), iv.2.27 (ed. Miller, vol. 1.2, p. 258).

61. For instance, Catullus, Virgil, Propertius, and Ovid all described themselves as *poetae*. On the social and economic status of Roman poets through the second century AD, see White, '*Amicitia*'.

62. If Lapidge is correct in attributing the 'Altercatio magistri et discipuli' and 'Responsio discipuli' from CUL Kk.5.34 to Lantfred (see his 'Three Latin Poems'), this omission is particularly striking, since much of the mock-rancour in these poems turns on versification. See further Chapter 2 below.

63. The adoption of *uates* as a word for a saint is perhaps to be attributed to Paulinus of Nola's application of it to John the Baptist in his *Carmen* vi. Bede's designation of St Cuthbert as *uates* in his metrical *vita* was influential.

64. The literature on early Carolingian court poets is vast: for selected references, see below, pp. 85–9. On Alcuin's career and its historical background, see Bullough, *Alcuin*.

65. XVI, 3–4 (Dümmler, p. 239). 'Samuel' was the by-name of Beornrad, bishop of Sens and abbot of Echternach.

66. II, 6–10 (Dümmler, p. 360).

67. xxv, 131–2 (Dümmler, p. 486).
68. xxxix, 1–4 (Dümmler, p. 252).
69. cviii.i (Dümmler, p. 334). *Albinus* was another of Alcuin's by-names; he used it more often in his writing than *Alc(h)uinus*.
70. Garrison, 'English and Irish', p. 105.
71. On Venantius Fortunatus' career and the influence of his example on Carolingian poets, see Godman, *Poets and Emperors*, pp. 1–39.
72. On what little is known of Æthilwulf's monastic house and his career, see Campbell (ed.), *De abbatibus*, pp. xxi–xxxv; Lapidge, 'Aediluulf'; Thornbury, 'Æthilwulf *poeta*'.
73. *De abbatibus* 796–9.
74. Ehwald, p. 524. The lines 'Lector, casses catholice / Atque obses anthletice' identify his correspondent as Helmgisl. Aldhelm's student Aethilwald did the same in his *Carmen* iv, Latinizing his teacher's name as 'cassem priscum' (l. 15).
75. Godman (ed.), *Bishops, Kings, and Saints*, p. 2 (ll. 1–6).
76. See Thornbury, 'Aldhelm's Rejection'.
77. Campbell (ed.), *Chronicle*, p. 55, ll. 5–7. NB *ventis* is Campbell's emendation from MS *vestri*.
78. Several of Æthelweard's phrases echo Alcuin's (e.g., *tingere . . . calamum*: xvii, xviii; *proprium . . . carmen*: xxvi; references from Dümmler's edition). It seems likely to me that there was some direct influence, but the question deserves further investigation.
79. Glorie (ed.), CCSL 133, p. 208.
80. *Ibid.*
81. Thanks to an anonymous reader for this suggestion. Both manuscripts attest the reading *uatem*, so a misreading would have to date back to their common source.
82. Ehwald, p. 96.
83. Ehwald, p. 93.
84. Ehwald, pp. 485, 314, 68.
85. *CE* i, 6 (p. 11); *CE* iv.i.2 (p. 19).
86. For the line and its source, see Lapidge and Rosier, *Poetic Works*, p. 233, n. 3. As Lapidge and Rosier note, a copy of *Carmen ecclesiasticum* i was preserved at Malmesbury, and the poem may also have been inscribed in a church, though there is no record of where and when it was visible (p. 38).
87. See above, pp. 27–8.
88. Lapidge, 'Three Latin Poems', pp. 230–4, 270 (the phrase is in l. 58).
89. Lapidge and Winterbottom (eds.), *Life of St Æthelwold*, pp. lxxxvi–lxxxvii, and chapters 9, 31 (pp. 14, 48).
90. Lapidge, 'Three Latin Poems', p. 270 (lines 65–6).
91. On which see n. 61 above.
92. Kant, *Critique of Judgement*, p. 18. See further Chapter 3 above (and Chapter 2, since I suspect that in practice quantitative Latin verse was often understood through reflective judgment).

93. *Fates* 1; *Epistola specialis* 6. On Cynewulf, see below, pp. 120–35, and on Wulfstan, pp. 209–23.

2 WHO BECAME POETS?

1. Wilson, *Lost Literature*, remains the classic study of vanished texts, but the degree to which medieval textual survivals are or are not representative should be periodically revisited. New statistical techniques, and a better understanding of how older texts were re-used, could still prove revelatory.
2. See below, pp. 210–11.
3. Strecker, 'Quellen'.
4. On attributions of Old English verse to King Alfred, see *OEB*, vol. 1, pp. 146–51.
5. These are Tiberius A.xv and Vespasian A.xiv (the latter known as 'the letter-book of Archbishop Wulfstan').
6. Sims-Williams, *Religion and Literature*, pp. 328–59; Lapidge, 'Some Remnants'.
7. For the methods and difficulties of interpreting the evidence of surviving books, see Gneuss, *Handlist*, pp. 1–21; and Lapidge, *Anglo-Saxon Library*, pp. 63–90.
8. The *Colloquy*'s first line establishes its dynamic: 'Nos pueri rogamus te, magister, ut doceas nos loqui latialiter recte' ('We children ask you, master, to teach us to speak correctly in Latin'): Garmonsway (ed.), *Colloquy*, p. 18. In chapters 77–9 of the *De rebus gestis Ælfredi*, Asser of St David's (who includes himself in the list) enumerates the learned clerics whom Alfred of Wessex gathered as his teachers and advisors: see Stevenson (ed.), *Asser's Life of Alfred*, pp. 62–6, and Keynes and Lapidge, *Alfred the Great*.
9. Anderson, 'Medieval Teaching Texts', pp. 182–5; Leonhardt, *Dimensio*, esp. pp. 24–71.
10. Ruff, 'Place of Metrics', pp. 151–2; Anderson, 'Medieval Teaching Texts'. On the form and use of Late Antique grammars in Britain, see Law, *Insular Latin Grammarians*, esp. pp. 13–29.
11. Bede's hymns in iambic dimeter are ed. Fraipont. His 'Librum hymnorum diuerso metro siue rithmo' (*HE* v.24) has not survived intact; he probably wrote others, which may have been preserved anonymously.
12. On the quantitative lyrics of Wulfstan Cantor and Abbo of Fleury, see below, pp. 78–80 and 211. Rhythmic lyric verse was somewhat more common: see pp. 81–3.
13. *DAM* §10, p. 108: 'ceteris omnibus pulchrius celsiusque'. Bede's phrase is taken from Mallius Theodorus, but given his free use of multiple sources and tendency towards rewording, it may be taken as indicative of his sentiments. On Bede's working methods, see Chapter 4, pp. 183–97.
14. Aldhelm writes that his treatise will focus on 'praestantissimas dactilici exametri regulas, quod ceterorum omnium arcem et infulas possidet' ('the most outstanding rules of the dactylic hexameter, which among all the other [metres] holds the citadel and honours': *De metris*, in Ehwald, p. 82). Boniface quotes Isidore: 'Hoc autem [heroicum] metrum auctoritate cetera metra praecedit: unum ex omnibus tam maximis operibus aptum apparuisse grauitatisque ac dulcedinis aeque capax'

('This [i.e., heroic] metre excels all others in dignity; being uniquely fit for the greatest works, and equally capable of seriousness and charm': Gebauer and Löfstedt (eds.), *Ars metrica*, p. 111); cf. *Etymologiae* 1.xxxix.9. Interestingly, Boniface omits Isidore's 'quam paruis' after 'tam maximis', and has *grauitas* in place of Isidore's *suauitas*. It is not clear if this reflects his source manuscript, or if he was deliberately emphasizing the impressiveness of heroic metre.

15. Ruff, 'Place of Metrics'.
16. *Ibid.*, p. 170.
17. See Kendall's list (which is fuller than that of Laistner and King, *Hand-list*, pp. 132–6): *DAM*, pp. 60–74.
18. *DAM* §iv, p. 95.
19. Ruff, 'Place of Metrics', pp. 166–9.
20. *DAM* §xvi, p. 129. On his theory of historical development, see Chapter 4 below.
21. *DAM* §xxiv, pp. 138–9. For discussion of these 'vulgares poetae', see Thornbury, 'Anglo-Saxon Poetics', pp. 92–4.
22. *DAM* §xxiv, pp. 138–9.
23. Tangl 116, p. 252. Technically, the long final syllable of *tētē* is a false quantity. Bede himself, however, seems to have scanned it long (see, e.g., 'Deprecor implorans tētē spes unica uitae', *Soliloquium de psalmo XLI*, l. 31). The few instances of this word in Classical verse potentially available at Wearmouth-Jarrow (e.g., *Aeneid* xii.891) are elided. Despite its extreme rarity elsewhere, Bede uses *tete* three times in his own verse, making Cuthbert's couplet distinctively Bedan.
24. Laistner and King list fifty-five manuscripts of the *De arte metrica* (either separately or together with *De schematibus et tropeis*), plus two excerpts, with examples from France, Germany, Switzerland, and Spain, as well as England (*Hand-List*, pp. 131–5). Conversely, Ehwald notes eight extant copies of *De metris*, all Continental. The metrical portions of the *Epistola ad Acircium* are translated and discussed by Neil Wright in Lapidge and Rosier, *Poetic Works*, pp. 183–219; the treatise on the number seven can be found in Lapidge and Herren, *Prose Works*, pp. 31–47.
25. Ruff, 'Place of Metrics', p. 169.
26. Ehwald, p. 163.
27. Lapidge, 'Aldhelm's Latin Poetry', p. 251.
28. *Ibid.*; Orchard, *Poetic Art*, and 'Old Sources'; and see below, pp. 201–8.
29. Ehwald, p. 77.
30. See the *apparatus fontium* in Gebauer and Löfstedt's edition; on the grammatical texts' currency in Anglo-Saxon England, see Law, *Insular Latin Grammarians*, pp. 14–29.
31. This is an early ninth-century manuscript from Lorsch; for a brief description, see Finch, 'Symphosius', pp. 6–8. Lapidge has argued that it is derived from a Canterbury exemplar ('Rufinus', pp. 127–8).
32. Wieland, 'Glossed Manuscript'; Robinson, 'Syntactical Glosses'; Irvine, *Textual Culture*, pp. 334–404.

33. Lapidge, 'Study of Latin Texts'; and see also Page, 'Feasibility of a Corpus'.
34. Lendinara, 'Instructional Manuscripts', p. 105; the handlist of manuscripts occupies pp. 105–13.
35. *Ibid.*, pp. 71–9 at 75. See also in the same volume Rumble, 'Palaeographical Aspects', pp. 128–30, who points out several classes of (non-didactic) notation in manuscripts which can confuse descriptions of medieval reading apparatus.
36. There do, however, seem to be instances of the *glossa ipsae gratia* – Aldred's gloss to the Lindisfarne Gospels would be a prime example. For these see below, p. 244.
37. G 538: *s.* ix–x, Brittany and Wales. See Gneuss, 'Dunstan'; Budny, 'Frontispiece'. Oxford maintains a full digital facsimile at http://image.ox.ac.uk/show?collection=bodleian&manuscript=msauctf432.
38. G 12: *s.* xi^med, prob. St Augustine's, Canterbury. For the structure and contents, see Rigg and Wieland, 'Canterbury Classbook'.
39. Lapidge, 'Study of Latin Texts', pp. 494–5; Lendinara, 'Instructional Manuscripts', pp. 60–5, 72.
40. Cf. (respectively) Wieland, 'Glossed Manuscript'; Lendinara, 'Instructional Manuscripts', p. 72; and Lapidge, 'Study of Latin Texts', pp. 495–8.
41. Page provides an example of such a 'second career' from the Parker Library: the second part of CCCC 173 (G 53), an eighth-century manuscript of Sedulius' *Carmen Paschale* (with a few other poems), was patched up for further use in the tenth century, with the addition of several leaves and a prefatory poem ('Feasibility of a Corpus', p. 92; see also Wieland, 'Glossed Manuscript', pp. 171–2).
42. Lapidge, *Anglo-Saxon Library*, pp. 335–6, 'Study of Latin Texts', pp. 458–9; Orchard, *Poetic Art*, pp. 130–5.
43. For overviews of changes in reading habits between the Anglo-Saxon and Norman regimes, see Lendinara, 'Instructional Manuscripts', pp. 92–104; Thomson, 'Norman Conquest'; Webber, *Scribes*, pp. 31–43.
44. Lendinara, 'Instructional Manuscripts', p. 71.
45. Orchard, *Poetic Art*, pp. 126–238, esp. 140, 200–12.
46. The publication of Toronto's Anglo-Saxon Formulary Project will, one hopes, forward this considerably, as will further volumes of the *Sources of Anglo-Saxon Literary Culture*.
47. On Ogilvy, *Books Known to the English*, see the detailed and scathing reviews of Gneuss and Wallach.
48. Roberts, *Biblical Epic*; Herzog, *Bibelepik*; Green, *Latin Epics*; Wilcox, 'Vernacular Biblical Epics', pp. 63–85.
49. Roberts, *Biblical Epic*, esp. pp. 5–106; Lapidge, 'Study of Latin Texts' and 'Versifying the Bible'; Wilcox, 'Vernacular Biblical Epics', pp. 86–104.
50. Roberts, *Biblical Epic*, pp. 67–92.
51. Paulinus of Périgueux (*s.* v) and Venantius Fortunatus (*s.* vi) both constructed their works in four books, to echo the structure of Sulpicius Severus' prose *vita*.
52. Wieland, '*Geminus stilus*'; Godman, '*Opus geminatum*'; Thornbury, 'Anglo-Saxon Poetics', pp. 25–39. The wide variety of relationships between verse and

prose 'twins' in Anglo-Latin suggests that the *opus geminatum* was a mode, not a genre, and that its characteristics were never codified.

53. Dräger (ed.), *Vita Willibrordi*, p. 12.
54. See Roberts, *Biblical Epic*, pp. 73–4, n. 47.
55. See Lapidge, 'Versifying the Bible'; Wilcox, 'Vernacular Biblical Epics'; and the sources there cited.
56. The most salient difference is that neither *Christ and Satan* nor *The Fates of the Apostles* depends upon a single source-text. For the construction of these works, see below, pp. 121–3 and 162–83.
57. Wilcox demonstrates how *Exodus* deploys the epic norms of Alcimus Avitus, Cyprianus Gallus, and Prudentius ('Vernacular Biblical Epics', pp. 206–93).
58. Lapidge, 'Versifying the Bible', pp. 25–8; Wilcox, 'Vernacular Biblical Epics'; though see Remley, 'Aldhelm', for a connection between *Exodus* and Aldhelm himself.
59. On the Anglo-Saxon riddle tradition generally, see Orchard, 'Enigma Variations'.
60. For the place of the *Enigmata* in Aldhelm's career, see Lapidge and Rosier, *Poetic Works*, p. 61.
61. Of the five manuscripts with Anglo-Saxon provenance containing Aldhelm's *Enigmata* separately from the *Epistola ad Acircium*, four have strong claims to be considered classbooks. Of these, two (Bodleian, Rawlinson C.697 [G 661] and BL, Royal 15.A.xvi [G 489]) apparently originated in France. The Rawlinson manuscript also contains the *Versus cuiusdam Scotti de alphabeto* together with Aldhelm's *Carmen de uirginitate* and Prudentius' *Psychomachia*; the Royal manuscript contains Juvencus' *Libri euangeliorum* and a short excerpt from Bede's *De arte metrica*, together with a Greek–Latin glossary added in Canterbury (on which see Lendinara, 'Scholica').
62. On Gg.5.35, see above, n. 38. On Royal 12.C.xxiii (G 478), a book from Christ Church Canterbury of *s*. x/xi, see Stork, *Through a Gloss*, pp. 5–10, for a description; the excerpt from *Epistola ad Acircium* (titled 'Prologus Aldhelmi super enigmata Simphosii uersificus') is edited pp. 81–93.
63. Orchard, 'Enigma Variations', p. 284.
64. Riddle topics are listed in Ehwald, pp. 59–60; see further Lapidge and Rosier, *Poetic Works*, pp. 61–9.
65. Ehwald, p. 111.
66. See John 4:34–8.
67. Howe, 'Aldhelm's *Enigmata*' (see pp. 54–5 for *Enigma* XXXVII).
68. Ehwald, p. 113.
69. For the oyster in l. 6, see Isidore, *Etymologiae* XII.51. In earlier Latin, *nepa* more commonly means *scorpio*, though Plautus certainly intends 'crab' by it in *Casina* 443: this line is quoted by Pompeius Festus in *De uerborum significatu epitome*, where *nepa* is indeed equated with *cancer*. Aldhelm's positioning of *nepa* in the first foot must have been intended to make the unfamiliar word's scansion absolutely transparent to readers, but the first syllable of *nepa* should be short. If Pompeius Festus was indeed Aldhelm's source, he may have

assumed that the example from Plautus was in dactylic hexameters, and that the first syllable of the final word must be long.

70. Aldhelm's *Enigmata* were frequently glossed, and lexical and explanatory glosses on the vocabulary were among the more common forms of annotation: see Stork, *Through a Gloss*, for an unusually thoroughly glossed text. Stork provides an overview of types of glosses on pp. 27–78, though no global statistics.

71. Lapidge and Rosier, *Poetic Works*, pp. 64–6.

72. Only two surviving manuscripts of the *Enigmata* contain the prose 'prologue', but they are not closely related, and one, Karlsruhe, Badische Landesbibliothek, Aug. LXXXV, is quite early: see CCSL 133, pp. 360–5 (ed. Glorie, who also notes a now lost manuscript from Liège that apparently contained the prologue); Stork, *Through a Gloss*, pp. 10–13; and on the fraught relations between the *Enigmata* manuscripts, O'Brien O'Keeffe and Journet, 'Numerical Taxonomy'.

73. Tætwine's riddles are ed. Glorie, pp. 165–208. Bede notes his consecration as archbishop in *HE* v.23.

74. For specific echoes of Aldhelm, see Orchard, *Poetic Art*, pp. 242, 286–7; and the source notes in Glorie's edition.

75. The *Ars Tatuini*, which focuses on the morphology of the eight parts of speech, survives in four Continental manuscripts, one of which (Vatican, Pal. lat. 1746) begins *Incipit Ars Tatuini*: see De Marco (ed.), CCSL 133, pp. vi–xii; Law, *Insular Latin Grammarians*, pp. 64–7.

76. De Marco (ed.), CCSL 133, p. 183.

77. *Ars Tatuini* 1.54 (De Marco (ed.), CCSL 133, p. 22). The definition is modified from Pompeius' (Keil, *Grammatici Latini*, vol. v, p. 171).

78. Cf. the riddles on the bell (vii), altar (viii), cross (ix), raised lectern (x), and paten (xii).

79. Glorie (ed.), CCSL 133, p. 170. I have slightly repunctuated Glorie's text.

80. Irvine, *Textual Culture*: see esp. p. 364.

81. Lapidge, 'Anglo-Latin', pp. 9–10; Orchard, *Poetic Art*, p. 242; see also Bolton, *History*, p. 222, although note that Eusebius' riddles *precede* Tætwine's.

82. Hurst (ed.), CCSL 119, p. 212. See Bolton, *History*, pp. 219–23.

83. *Historia abbatum* 11.18, in Plummer (ed.), *Opera historica*, p. 383.

84. Lapidge and Rosier, *Poetic Works*, p. 245, n. 29 (and p. 66); Lapidge, 'Present State', p. 52.

85. Orchard, *Poetic Art*, p. 254.

86. Lapidge has previously pointed out this attempt at an overarching theological schema: see Lapidge and Rosier, *Poetic Works*, p. 67.

87. Glorie (ed.), CCSL 133, p. 239.

88. Ehwald, p. 76.

89. See Bayless, 'Alcuin's *Disputatio Pippini*'.

90. Trautmann, 'Zeit, Heimat und Verfasser', p. 372. 'Wenn man dann noch die verschiedenheit der einzelnen rätsel in stil, ton, können und sprache erwägt, so kommt man bald zu der überzeugung, daß die ER nicht nur keine einheitliche und gleichartige sammlung sind, sondern daß sie von verschiedenen dichtern

herrühren müssen.' Trautmann provides an overview of early authorship theories in this article; Tupper, *Old English Riddles*, pp. liii–lxii, gives a detailed survey of the rise and fall of the 'Cynewulf theory'.

91. See Fulk, *History*, pp. 404–10; note though his comment that given 'the reasons offered above to doubt the unity of the collection, it is remarkable how uniform these [linguistic] features are in their indication of a particular date and dialect. The riddles seem close in date to *Beowulf* and the early biblical narratives' (p. 408).

92. Smith (ed.), *Three Northumbrian Poems*, pp. 26–37; Fulk, *History*, pp. 404–5. On the *Leiden Riddle*'s manuscript, see Parkes, 'Leiden Riddle', who argues for a tenth-century date.

93. O'Brien O'Keeffe, 'Text of Aldhelm's *Enigma* no. C'.

94. Irvine, *Textual Culture*, p. 360; Lerer, *Literacy and Power*, pp. 103–6.

95. On the translation strategy and rhetorical techniques of *Riddle 40*, see Steen, *Verse and Virtuosity*, pp. 98–109.

96. Bitterli, *Say What I am Called*: see esp. pp. 35–79.

97. See Larrington, *Store of Common Sense*, pp. 120–60; Hansen, *Solomon Complex*; Shippey, *Poems of Wisdom*.

98. *Carmen* cxix (Dümmler, p. 347).

99. On Israel's sojourn in England, and the manuscripts of his *De arte metrica*, see Lapidge, 'Israel the Grammarian'. For the medical poems (found, *inter alia*, in CUL Gg.5.35), see Lapidge, 'Hermeneutic Style', pp. 141–3. The mnemonic poems' origin is obscure, though they may possibly be English; see Cameron, 'Sources of Medical Knowledge', p. 154, n. 8.

100. Oswald of Ramsey, 'On composing verse', ll. 1–5, 9, ed. in Lapidge, 'Hermeneutic Style', pp. 144–5.

101. See Lockett, 'Oswald's *uersus retrogradi*'.

102. It is undoubtedly relevant that Oswald himself studied at Fleury: see *ibid.* for his Continental stylistic affiliations.

103. Asser, *Gesta Ælfredi* §22–3, in Stevenson (ed.), p. 20.

104. See, e.g., O'Brien O'Keeffe, *Visible Song*, pp. 81–4; Brown, 'Female Book-Ownership', esp. p. 47; Dockray-Miller, *Motherhood*, pp. 44–7.

105. Asser, *Gesta Ælfredi* §75, in Stevenson (ed.), pp. 58–9. By *libris utuntur*, Asser may well mean they had books read to them.

106. On Aldhelm's student Æthilwald, see below, pp. 147–9, 156–7.

107. On Wulfstan, Æthelwold, and his school, see below, pp. 102–4, 211–12.

108. Lapidge, 'Three Latin Poems'; and see above, p. 33.

109. See Lapidge, 'Hermeneutic Style' and 'St Dunstan's Latin Poetry'.

110. Tangl 29, pp. 52–3: 'Istam artem ab Eadburge magisterio didici.'

111. On the poetry of Boniface's circle, see below, pp. 200–9.

112. Stevenson, 'Women Poets', presents the available evidence.

113. Gameson, *The Scribe Speaks*, pp. 8–11.

114. On Eadwig Basan's script and career, see Bishop, *English Caroline Minuscule*, nos. 24–5; Dumville, *English Caroline Script*, pp. 111–40; Rushforth, 'Prodigal Fragment', pp. 138–40; Gameson, 'Colophon of the Eadwig Gospels'; Pfaff,

'Eadui Basan'. Pfaff's suggestion (p. 282) that Eadwig might have been the author of the colophon in the twelfth-century 'Eadwine Gospels' (Cambridge, Trinity College, R.17.1/987) beginning 'Scriptorum princeps ego', is appealing, but unlikely: regular Leonine hexameters were rare in pre-Conquest England, but very common in the twelfth century.

115. Hanover, Kestner Museum, WM XXIa 36, fol. 183ᵛ (abbreviations silently expanded). For an image, see Gameson, 'Colophon of the Eadwig Gospels', plate v.

116. 'The colophon is written in the elegant Caroline Minuscule of the single scribe responsible for the Anglo-Saxon stratum of the book but is done in coloured inks (the four lines being blue, green, red and blue respectively)': Gameson, *The Scribe Speaks*, p. 45.

117. Dumville, *English Caroline Script*, p. 121. He adds that we 'must allow that 'Eaduuius cognomento Basan' may not have been the name of the scribe of the Hannover gospel book' (pp. 121–2); Gameson, however, sees 'no reason to doubt that "Eadwig Basan" was indeed the name of the scribe of our manuscript' ('Colophon of the Eadwig Gospels', p. 202, n. 6; on the book's history, see pp. 221–2). Lapidge concurs with Dumville: 'Autographs', p. 104, n. 4.

118. On the rhythmic hexameter, see Norberg, *Introduction*, pp. 102–6. I use Norberg's notation for rhythmic verse here.

119. It *would* be possible to divide the middle portion into three rhymed verses, with an extrametrical insertion: 'Librum istum mónachus / scripsit Eaduuíus (cognomento Basan) / Sit illi longa sálus', i.e., 7p+5p+7p. But this pattern might be coincidental.

120. Bodleian, Auct. D.2.19, 168ᵛ–9ʳ, in Gameson, *The Scribe Speaks*, no. 16, p. 39. The shift from prose to verse occurs at the page break, as Gameson notes (pp. 15–16).

121. *MEp.*

122. Robinson, '"Bede's" Envoi': both prose and verse prayers are edited, translated, and discussed pp. 12–19.

123. The manuscript is now viewable via Parker Library on the Web: http://parkerweb.stanford.edu. The metrical colophon begins p. 483.

124. Robinson, '"Bede's" Envoi', p. 9.

125. See above, p. 24.

126. On the text and its history, see Ronalds and Ross, '*Thureth*'.

127. The text is on fol. 31ᵛ. For images, see Ronalds and Ross, '*Thureth*', p. 364; and Stanley and Robinson, *Old English Verse Texts*, no. 10.

128. Bitterli, *Say What I Am*, pp. 135–93; see also Shook, 'Anglo-Saxon Scriptorium'.

129. Shook, 'Anglo-Saxon Scriptorium', p. 218.

130. Riddles are numbered as in the *ASPR*. *Speop*: 42, l. 4; *hwilū mon*: 49, l. 4. For a facsimile and concise account of the book's compilation, see Muir (ed.), *Exeter DVD*.

131. On the *ic seah* formula, see Orchard, 'Enigma Variations', pp. 289–90.

132. Bitterli, *Say What I Am*, pp. 146–50 (with discussion of this riddle).

133. BL, Royal 6.A.vi, fol. 109^r, in Gameson, *The Scribe Speaks*, no. 20. This is a late tenth-century copy of the *Prosa de uirginitate* from Christ Church Canterbury (G 464).
134. Gameson, *The Scribe Speaks*, p. 8.
135. DiNapoli, 'Kingdom of the Blind'; and cf. Bitterli's analysis in *Say What I Am*, pp. 151–69.
136. On use of gold in early Anglo-Saxon manuscripts, see Brown, *Lindisfarne Gospels*, pp. 277–80; and (for the full period) Dodwell, *Anglo-Saxon Art*, esp. pp. 98–108.
137. Bitterli, *Say What I Am*, pp. 170–90, esp. 178–88.
138. O'Brien O'Keeffe, *Visible Song*.
139. On Bede's prayers, see Robinson, '"Bede's" Envoi', pp. 4–5; on biographies of Boethius and their use in Anglo-Saxon England, see Discenza, 'Unauthorized Biographies'.
140. Hatton 20, the copy sent to Bishop Wærferth of Worcester, dates from 890–7 (Ker 324). On the manuscripts of the *Pastoral Care*, see Horgan, 'Relationship', with stemma at p. 169; on witnesses of the metrical preface specifically, see O'Brien O'Keeffe, *Visible Song*, pp. 88–94.
141. *ASPR*, vol. VI, p. 110, ll. 11–16. On the text of this poem (which is more complicated than the *ASPR* indicates), see O'Brien O'Keeffe, *Visible Song*, pp. 77–107.
142. On the proem to the *Boethius*, see pp. 22–3.
143. The psalter and hymns were used for teaching basic literacy: see, e.g., Boynton, 'Training'; Contreni, 'Pursuit'.
144. None of Osbern's poetry survives, so far as I can ascertain, but his statement in the preface to his prose *Vita S. Ealphegi* that 'musica virum modulatione dudum extulimus' ('I previously set forth [a version] in men's musical modulation', *Anglia Sacra* II, 122) suggests that his (now lost) previous life of Ælfheah was intended to be sung, and thus was possibly in verse: though the text may have consisted of liturgical material in prose, with accompanying music.
145. *Fort* 80–4.
146. Opland, *Oral Poetry*, esp. pp. 230–56; see also above, pp. 19–20.
147. See William of Malmesbury, *Gesta Regum* II.138–9.
148. Ziolkowski, *Nota Bene*, pp. 109–72.
149. Judging by Hartzell's *Catalogue*, there are thirteen surviving non-liturgical manuscripts containing neumed verse. Besides CUL Gg.5.35, there are six copies of *De consolatione philosophiae* containing neumed metra (Cambridge, Trinity College, O.3.7 [G 193]; El Escorial, Real Biblioteca, E.II.1 [G 823]; BN, lat. 6401 [G 886]; Vatican, lat. 3363 [G 908]); four of Prudentius (CCCC 223 [G 70]; Durham, Dean and Chapter, B.IV.9 [G 246]; BL, Cotton Cleopatra C.VIII [G 324]; Bodleian, Auct. F.3.6 [G 537]); a neumed copy of the pseudo-Virgilian 'Ut belli sonuere' (Edinburgh, National Library of Scotland, Advocates 18.7.7 [G 253]: also neumed in Gg.5.35); and the 'Versus de sideribus' attributed in the manuscript to Priscian (BL, Additional 11034 [G 280]).

150. Ziolkowski, *Nota Bene*, pp. 126–43. The relation between neumes and spoken accent, however, seems to have been much closer.
151. G 72. *S.* x^2 or x^{ex}. Contains the 'Excerptiones Hogeri abbatis' (from Boethius' *De musica*); *Musica enchiriadis*; *Scolica enchiriadis*; and *Commemoratio breuis de tonis et psalmis modulandis*.
152. Contains Hucbald of Saint-Amand's *De harmonica institutione*, fols. 263^r–76^r.
153. G 784. It contains the full text of Boethius' *De musica*, followed by extensive excerpts from Bede's *De arte metrica* and *De temporum ratione*, as well as other scientific material. A facsimile and discussion of this book, which was owned by the abbey of Mont-Saint-Michel, can be found in Santosuosso (ed.), *Music Theory in Medieval Normandy*. Masi, 'Manuscripts Containing the *De musica*', attributes it to *s.* xi; Santosuosso, on the basis of the Easter tables on fol. 96^v, prefers 'the last decade of the tenth century' (p. xvi). There are two main scribes in this book; the first wrote *De musica* (fols. 1^r–82^r); the second completed the Bedan and miscellaneous texts. On fol. 83^v there are some marginal scribbles in Old English (in a hand that resembles the second scribe's): 'ge æt beo'; something I cannot make out from the facsimile; and 'þaþa'.
154. The title of Wulfstan's treatise, and the commentator's quotations from it, were identified and printed by Michael Lapidge in his Introduction to Lapidge and Winterbottom (eds.), *Life of St Æthelwold*, pp. xvi–xvii.
155. *HE* IV.18. John, as Bede tells us, was abbot of St Martin's in Rome as well as precentor at St Peter's; as a papal legate, his duties included inquiry into the orthodoxy of the English church and establishment of proper liturgical observance. But it seems to have been his knowledge of chant that was remembered: Bede says that 'uerum de omnibus pene eiusdem prouinciae monasteriis ad audiendum eum, qui cantandi erant periti, confluebant' ('indeed those who were skilled in music crowded in from practically all the monasteries of the entire province in order to hear him').
156. On the transition from oral to partly written musical tradition, see Treitler, 'Oral, Written, and Literate Process'; and Rankin, 'Memory to Record'.
157. Boethius, *De institutione musica* I.xxxiv (Friedlein (ed.), pp. 224–5). The final words are not an afterthought: Boethius considered an understanding of poetry as intrinsic to the work of a *musicus*.
158. Boynton, 'Sources and Significance'.
159. Contreni, 'Pursuit', pp. 125–6; Riché, *Écoles*, pp. 274–6.
160. Fassler, 'Office of the Cantor', esp. pp. 37, 42.
161. Rubenstein, 'Life and Writings', esp. pp. 28–31. Lanfranc's *Decreta* specify that the cantor has authority over rehearsals and performance of the liturgy, and that 'De uniuersis monasterii libris curam gerit, et eos in custodia sua habeat' ('He takes care of all the monastery's books, and should keep them in his custody'): *Decreta Lanfranci* §86, in Knowles and Brooke (eds.), *Monastic Constitutions*, pp. 118–23 at 122.
162. Aimo, *Vita S. Abbonis*, cap. iii (*PL* 139, col. 390C): 'Inde Aurelianis regressus, musicae artis dulcedinem, quamvis occulte, propter invidos, a quodam clerico non paucis redemit nummis' ('Returning thence [i.e. from Paris and Rheims]

to Orléans, he paid a not inconsiderable sum of money to a certain cleric for the sweetness of the art of music – though secretly, because of envious men'). Boynton considers the implications of the curious qualifier *occulte, propter invidos* in 'Sources and Significance', p. 72. On Abbo's career generally, see Mostert, *Political Theology*, pp. 40–64; Gransden, '*Passio Sancti Eadmundi*', pp. 20–2. Lendinara, 'Abbo of Fleury', provides a useful summary of Abbo's works in relation to Anglo-Saxon literature.

163. Winterbottom (ed.), *Three Lives*, pp. 67–87.
164. Winterbottom notes the following parallels: §3, 6 (p. 70): *Carmen* 1.1.1; §8, 17 (p. 75): *Carmen* 1.3.8; §8, 26 (p. 75): *Carmen* 3.2.13; §11, 3/6 (p. 79): *Carmen* 1.22.1. Abbo's *Quaestiones grammaticales*, written perhaps during his English exile, contains echoes of virtually all Horace's major works: see Guerreau-Jalabert (ed.), *Questions grammaticales*, p. 320. See also Lapidge, *Anglo-Saxon Library*, pp. 244–5.
165. Gneuss's *Handlist* notes only two: an excerpt from the *Carmina* in the 'Cambridge Songs' portion of CUL Gg.5.35 (*Carmen* 3.12: no. 46 in Ziolkowski (ed.), *Cambridge Songs*, pp. 122–4, and notes pp. 301–2), and excerpts from the *Epistolae* in Edinburgh, National Library of Scotland, Advocates 18.6.12 (G 252), a late eleventh-century verse miscellany from Thorney. See Lapidge, *Anglo-Saxon Library*, pp. 307–8, for a somewhat more inclusive list, encompassing early Norman-era manuscripts.
166. See Lapidge, *Anglo-Saxon Library*, p. 308 (and cross-references).
167. The Vespasian hymnal (Ker 208; G 391) is discussed in Gneuss, *Hymnar*, esp. pp. 98–101. The Lambeth manuscript (G 514), containing the earliest known text of the *Vita*, is a *libellus* of only twelve folios; it also contains a mass for St Edmund. On Lambeth 362 in the textual tradition of Abbo's *Vita S. Eadmundi*, see Gransden, '*Passio Sancti Eadmundi*', pp. 63–4.
168. Milfull, *Hymns*, nos. 153–5 (pp. 457–61). *Laurea regni* is no. 154. My discussion here is much indebted to this indispensable edition.
169. *Ibid.*, p. 458.
170. *Ibid.*
171. Borzsák (ed.), *Q. Horati Flacci Opera*, p. 23.
172. Winterbottom (ed.), *Three Lives*, p. 79.
173. For instance, eighteen texts in Milfull, *Hymns*, are in quantitative Sapphic stanzas: 5, 6, 47, 62, 63, 86, 88, 97, 100, 123, 125, 127–9 (a three-part hymn for a church dedication), 130, 131, 132, 160.
174. See Lapidge and Winterbottom (eds.), *Life of St Æthelwold*, p. xxv; and below, p. 211. A Worcester hymn for St Oswald (Milfull, no. 157) is in rhythmic Sapphic stanzas.
175. See above, p. 41.
176. See Gneuss, *Hymnar*, esp. pp. 194–206; Boynton, 'Didactic'.
177. G 765. Among the volume's other contents are Bede's *De arte metrica* and *De schematibus et tropis*, as well as Israel's versified *De arte metrica*. The table of metrical feet is at the end of the volume, from 74^v–7^v. The book has been severely damaged by damp, and the table's rubric is now illegible.

178. For instance: 'Spondeus cum tribracho – – u u u' (fol. 75ᵛ). The lists are arranged according to the first foot, and cycle regularly through each combination.

179. Ruff, 'Place of Metrics'.

180. St Ambrose famously composed hymns for the besieged citizens of Milan to sing (see Augustine's *Confessiones* 9.7.15), and Augustine wrote his *Psalmus contra partem Donati* in rhythmic rather than quantitative metre 'lest the requirements of the metre force me to use words unfamiliar to the common folk' (*Retractiones* 1.xx).

181. Above, p. 43.

182. Gneuss, *Hymnar*, pp. 239–45 at 244. This could conceivably make them the work of Osbern – an avenue perhaps worth pursuing.

183. Lines 9–16 (Gneuss, *Hymnar*, p. 242).

184. Gneuss, *Hymnar*, p. 244.

185. Norberg, *Introduction*, pp. 106–9.

186. On the verse of the office, see below, pp. 229–30. Most of the late Old English liturgical poetry, including versions of the Lord's Prayer, Creed, and *Gloria*, has been edited in Keeffer (ed.), *Liturgical Verse*; and Jones (ed.), *Shorter Poems*.

187. G 389; Ker 207. On the hymn's place in the manuscript, see Keeffer, 'Respect for the Book'; and below, pp. 232–3.

188. For overviews of the status and activities of court poets, see for Ireland: Mac Eoin, 'Poet and Prince', and Williams, 'Court Poet'; for Wales: Jarman and Hughes (eds.), *Guide to Welsh Literature*, pp. 51–156, and Lloyd-Jones, 'Court Poets'; for Scandinavia, especially Norway and Iceland: Davíðsdóttir, 'Old Norse Court Poetry', and Gade, 'Poetry and its Changing Importance', esp. pp. 70–84. See also Bloomfield and Dunn, *Role of the Poet* (which combines Anglo-Saxon and Celtic evidence).

189. See especially Opland's series of articles titled 'Scop and Imbongi' as well as his *Oral Poetry*.

190. See above, pp. 14–19.

191. Chapter 1, pp. 11–12; Turner, *History*, vol. II, p. 345.

192. Earle, *Deeds of Beowulf*, p. xcvii. On Earle's career, see the *DNB* entry by Charles Plummer (revised by John Haigh).

193. Cook, *Possible Begetter*, esp. p. 343.

194. Whitelock, *Audience of Beowulf*, esp. pp. 29, 89–105.

195. For an overview of current theories, see Fulk, Bjork, and Niles (eds.), *Klaeber's Beowulf*, pp. clxxii–clxxiv. (For the East Anglian hypothesis, see Newton, *Origins of Beowulf*.)

196. The bibliography on Alcuin is vast. For his career, I have relied most on Bullough, *Alcuin*; and Godman's Introduction to *Bishops, Kings, and Saints*.

197. See especially Bullough, *Alcuin*, pp. 236–8 (and also 304–8), who points out how unusual such a cathedral school actually was in the mid-eighth century.

198. For Alcuin's encomium on Ælberht, see Godman (ed.), *Bishops, Kings, and Saints*, ll. 1395–1596. On the books, see Lapidge, 'Surviving Booklists', pp. 45–9.

199. Cf., for instance, Godman (ed.), *Bishops, Kings, and Saints*, pp. xxxvi–xxxvii, and Bullough, *Alcuin*, pp. 336–46.

200. See Bullough, 'Charlemagne's "Men of God"', pp. 138–42, for his account of Alcuin's actual influence.

201. Schaller, 'Vortrags- und Zirkulardichtung'; Bullough, *Alcuin*, pp. 316–18; and Sinisi, 'York to Paris', who modifies Schaller's account of the poem's genre.

202. *Carmen* IV, ll. 36–44 (Dümmler, pp. 221–2).

203. Godman, *Poets and Emperors*, pp. 44–6; Sinisi, 'York to Paris'.

204. Of the 124 separate poems in Dümmler's edition, 53 seem to have been intended as epistles or as gifts for particular recipients (not counting epitaphs or *tituli* for books); 35 of the 53 are entirely or primarily in elegiacs.

205. *Carmen* XXIII, ll. 1–6 (Dümmler, p. 243).

206. Ovid, *Amores* II.16, II.9a; Tibullus II.3; *DDI* 1–3.

207. On the poem, see Orchard, 'Wish You Were Here', pp. 39–41; Godman, 'Poetic Style'; Newlands, 'Poem of Exile'.

208. *Carmen* XXXVII, ll. 7–12 (Dümmler, p. 252). On the by-name 'David', see Garrison, 'Social World'.

209. Garrison, 'English and Irish', pp. 104–5, and 'Emergence'.

210. Godman, *Poets and Emperors*, pp. 38–9, 45–6, 48.

211. See, e.g., Garrison, 'Alcuin and Tibullus'; Lendinara, 'Mixed Attitudes'; Whitta, 'Ille ego'.

212. Tangl 124, p. 262.

213. Orchard, 'Wish You Were Here', pp. 24–7 at 26–7.

214. See below, pp. 154–7.

215. For an edition and detailed study of the epitaph, see Wallach, *Alcuin and Charlemagne*, pp. 178–97.

216. The poems in Charles's name include two addressed to the Italian deacons Peter and Paul (Dümmler, pp. 69–70; see Godman, *Poets and Emperors*, p. 55). With regard to the York poem, contrast the encomiastic tone of *Karolus Magnus et Leo Papa* (on which see Schaller, 'Aachener Epos'; Godman, *Poets and Emperors*, pp. 82–91).

217. First published in 1981, and reprinted 1993 in Lapidge, *Anglo-Latin Literature, 900–1066*.

218. Lapidge, 'Some Latin Poems', pp. 60–71, at 60–1; cf. Wieland, 'New Look', who dates the poem to Athelstan's reign.

219. Lapidge, 'Some Latin Poems', pp. 69–71. The poems are found in Bern, Burgerbibliothek, 671.

220. Lapidge, 'Some Latin Poems', pp. 71–81, 86.

221. Godman, *Poets and Emperors*, pp. 56–9.

222. See Keynes and Lapidge, *Alfred the Great*, pp. 26–7; cf. though Bately, 'Grimbald', p. 2.

223. Lapidge, 'Israel the Grammarian'.

224. For an overview, see Frank, *Old Norse Court Poetry*, pp. 21–33.

225. The *Skáldatal* is in Jónsson (ed.), *Edda*. For the prose narrative tradition, see Ross, 'Skald Sagas as a Genre'. On the portrayal of England in *Egilssaga*, see

Fjalldall, *Icelandic Medieval Texts*, pp. 69–82 (and pp. 101–12 for thoughts about the literary function of Anglo-Saxon royal courts in saga narrative).

226. See Poole, 'Skaldic Verse'; and especially Townend, 'Contextualizing the *Knútsdrápur*'.

227. See Frank, 'Skaldic Tooth', and 'Skaldic Verse'.

228. Townend, 'Pre-Cnut'.

229. See, e.g., Whitelock, *Audience of Beowulf*; Clemoes, 'Style', p. 185; Jacobs, 'Anglo-Danish', pp. 41–2.

230. Thomas, *Augustan Reception*, pp. 93–121. In England, Servius' commentaries on Virgil seem to have been known in both the early and later periods: see Lapidge, *Anglo-Saxon Library*, p. 332.

231. Scharer, 'Writing of History'; Bredehoft, *Textual Histories*; Parkes, 'Parker Manuscript' (who associates the early compilation with Alfred's advisor Grimbald of Saint-Bertin).

232. See, e.g., Opland, *Oral Poetry*, pp. 161–78 (esp. 172); Niles, 'Skaldic Technique', p. 363; Townend, 'Pre-Cnut'; Carroll, 'Concepts'.

233. See Elias, *Court Society*, esp. pp. 45–72 (as well as 113–16 for some reflections on literature's function in such a society). Nelson applied this test to Charlemagne's court, in 'Was Charlemagne's Court a Courtly Society?', and answered in the affirmative.

234. For an overview of both the physical form and institutions, see Campbell, 'Anglo-Saxon Courts'.

235. Scharer, 'Writing of History', p. 190.

236. On the extensive parallel households of late Anglo-Saxon queens, see Stafford, *Queen Emma and Queen Edith*, pp. 107–22. We know much less about the organization of the earlier periods, but women certainly could own – and thus probably commission – books. The Book of Nunnaminster itself (BL, Harley 2965) dates from the early ninth century and cannot have been commissioned by Ealhswith, though she may have given it to the Winchester foundation along with other gifts recorded on the manuscript's final leaves: see Michelle Brown's description of the book in Webster and Backhouse (eds.), *Making of England*, pp. 210–11 (no. 164) and in her 'Female Book-Ownership'; on the prayers themselves see Raw, 'Alfredian Piety'. On lay patronage and consumption of verse in the later period, see further below, pp. 228–37.

237. Keynes and Lapidge, *Alfred the Great*, pp. 26–8.

238. See Foot, *Æthelstan*, esp. pp. 91–3, 99–107.

239. See esp. Niles, 'Skaldic Technique'; Townend, 'Pre-Cnut'.

3 THE POET IN THE COMMUNITY

1. See Anderson, *Imagined Communities*, pp. 6–7; and Elias, *What is Sociology?*, pp. 122–8.

2. In *Traditionen der klassischen Rhetorik*, Knappe demonstrated the Anglo-Saxons' lack of systematic training in the Classical rhetorical tradition (for an English adumbration see her 'Classical Rhetoric'). However, Steen points out that the

Anglo-Saxons did absorb many Roman rhetorical techniques at second-hand, via the Christian Latin poets in particular (*Verse and Virtuosity*, pp. 7–20).

3. See Richards, *Practical Criticism*, esp. pp. 182–3.
4. The critical literature on this subject is vast; for a condensed overview, with essential references, see Orchard, 'Oral Tradition'.
5. Russom elegantly demonstrates this in 'Artful Avoidance'.
6. See Riedinger, 'Old English Formula'. This important article makes a strong case for a dictionary of formulas, since (as she demonstrates) the poetic meaning cannot necessarily be extrapolated from the words composing the formula. It is to be hoped that Toronto's 'Anglo-Saxon Formulary' project will lead to such a guide.
7. See Labov and Waletsky, 'Narrative Analysis'; and also Labov, *Language in the Inner City*, pp. 354–96.
8. Milroy, *Language and Social Networks*, esp. pp. 139–76.
9. Lenker, 'Benedictine Reform'. One might also see Drout, *How Tradition Works*, which is largely focused on the Benedictine reform era; Drout's focus on 'memes' (= word-collocations, ideas, bits of information or behaviour) could be inverted into an examination of the networks by which these memes are presumably spread.
10. Lenker, 'Benedictine Reform', esp. pp. 233–5.
11. What I mean by sustaining a connection across *temporal* distance is that letters were frequently used to perpetuate the effects of past interactions or instigate future ones. In the early Middle Ages, epistolary correspondence was less likely to constitute the sole medium of a current connection – i.e., to form a connection in itself (though counterexamples might well be possible).
12. *De oratore* 3.50 (ed. Kumaniecki, p. 345).
13. Kant, *Critique of Judgement*, Part 1, §40, p. 151. My understanding of Kant's view is essentially informed by Arendt, *Lectures*.
14. See, e.g., Labov, *Language in the Inner City*, pp. 256–7 (and for that matter Mitford (ed.), *Noblesse Oblige*, esp. Ross, 'U and Non-U').
15. Festinger, 'Theory of Social Comparison', outlines processes by which people form opinions of their own standing in relation to others.
16. In terms of speech as a marker of group solidarity, see especially the foundational studies of Labov, 'Social Motivation' (on the dialect of Martha's Vineyard, MA; recast within a larger argument in his *Sociolinguistic Patterns*, pp. 1–42); Milroy, *Language and Social Networks*, esp. pp. 207–12 (on neighbourhoods in Belfast, Northern Ireland); Trudgill, *Social Differentiation* (for Norwich). On emulation of other groups, see esp. the chapter 'Hypercorrection by the Lower Middle Class' in Labov, *Sociolinguistic Patterns*, pp. 122–42.
17. Horace's *Ars poetica* brilliantly exemplifies this with revealing examples of how literary judgment might work (or fail) among Roman poets and their friends and patrons; its form – as an epistle to a consul and his aspiring-poet sons – in itself gestures to a broad and long-established network of poets and critics. Research on modern oral cultures has also provided many examples of poetic forms that are inseparable from their social context.

18. *Max* I.A, 1–4b. On the force of *hygecræft* (which may imply learned arts) see Discenza, 'Power, Skill and Virtue', pp. 82–9.

19. Scholarship has long been divided as to whether *Maxims I* represents one poem or three; three sections are distinguished with the same spacing and large initial capitals the Exeter Book scribe used to separate individual poems, but they are clearly of the same genre, and all individually lack the sort of clear ending that structures the other surviving verse maxims (*Max II*, in BL, Cotton Tiberius B.i, fol. 115a–b). Both the *ASPR* and Muir's editions split the difference by setting the verses out with a single title, but in sections lettered A, B, and C.

20. See Hansen, *Solomon Complex*, pp. 157–62 (and 147–52).

21. *Vain* 15–18a. See Magennis, *Images of Community*, pp. 99–101, for further comment on this passage.

22. *ES* 27–34.

23. See esp. *ES* 11–26. On the 'humility topos' – part of the ancient rhetorical technique often called *captatio benevolentiae* – see esp. Curtius, *European Literature*, pp. 83–5, 407–13.

24. *Epistola generalis* 35–40.

25. On Wulfstan Cantor's unique position in his community, see further below, pp. 209–23.

26. Others can be seen in pp. 143–9, 203–5.

27. The bishop is thought to have been Æthelwold of Winchester: see Lapidge, 'Three Latin Poems'; and above, p. 33.

28. Lines 63–8 (ed. Lapidge, 'Three Latin Poems', p. 270).

29. Campbell (ed.), *De abbatibus* 800–11; for textual difficulties see Campbell.

30. A sustained study of voice and modes of religious discourse in Old English poetry is still needed; but on various aspects of the first person in some devotional poems, see especially Keeffer, '"Ic" and "We"', and Randle, 'Homiletics' (esp. pp. 194–5). Zacher, *Preaching*, pp. 273–4, points out the poems' striking use of *second* person singular; and Orchard, 'Cross-References', traces the literary ramifications of *Dream of the Rood*'s hortative phrasing.

31. See further pp. 200–9.

32. The bibliography on voice and perspective in this poem is substantial; see especially Isaacs, *Structural Principles*, pp. 3–18; Irving, 'Crucifixion Witnessed'; Pasternack, 'Stylistic Disjunctions'.

33. *Dream* 144b–8a.

34. The Rood does gesture outwards to its fellow crosses on Golgotha in lines 70–5a, but these companions disappear as silently as they arrive.

35. Schlauch, 'Prosopopoeia'; Orton, 'Object-Personification'.

36. *Enig* C 80–3.

37. The speaker is feminine, corresponding to the grammatical gender of *creatura*: it is not clear how far this should be pressed.

38. *Enig* XL 5.

39. *Rid* 1, 1–3a.

40. *Rid* 2, 12b–15. I use the *ASPR* lineation and numbering, but accept Williamson's arguments that *Riddles* 1–3 are in fact a single text (*Old English Riddles*, pp. 127–33).
41. *Rid* 42, 5b–17.
42. Lerer, 'Riddle and the Book'; Bitterli, *Say What I am Called*, pp. 120–4.
43. On the unequal dynamics of riddling, see also Hansen, *Solomon Complex*, pp. 131–2.
44. Until recently, the transcript was considered the work of John Elphinstone: see Rogers, 'David Casley's Transcript'. For a facsimile, see Scragg (ed.), *Battle of Maldon*, pp. 2–14.
45. Scragg (ed.), *Battle of Maldon*, pp. 3–4.
46. *Ibid.*, p. 4.
47. O'Brien O'Keeffe (ed.), *ASC: MS C*, p. 86. The A text, which records the event under 993, names Unlaf (Olaf Tryggvason, later king of Norway) as leader of the Viking army (Bately (ed.), *ASC: MS A*, p. 79).
48. See especially Blake, 'Genesis'; and McKinnell, 'Date'.
49. See Campbell, 'England, c. 991'; Davis, 'Cultural Historicity'; Niles, *Heroic Poems*, pp. 203–52; Trilling, *Aesthetics of Nostalgia*, pp. 157–73.
50. In calling *The Battle of Maldon* a simulacrum, I would point out that Casley's transcript was written in an 'Anglo-Saxon' script which purports to, but does not, represent a source (Rogers: 'Casley's 'imitative' Anglo-Saxon hand has no certain value as a facsimile. One suspects he would write much this same hand, whether he was copying vernacular text from the tenth or the twelfth century': 'David Casley's Transcript', p. 150). Likewise Scragg has drawn attention to the 'sense of realism and immediacy' used within the poem to represent events that could not have taken place as represented (*Battle of Maldon*, p. 36).
51. For the poet's oblique invocation of the royal decision to pay Danegeld following the defeat at Maldon, see Tyler, *Old English Poetics*, pp. 157–71; Niles, *Heroic Poems*, pp. 203–52.
52. Labov, *Language in the Inner City*, pp. 354–96 at 366. For various forms of evaluation in narrative, see pp. 370–5.
53. *Beo* 38–9.
54. *Beo* 980–4a.
55. Fleischmann, 'Evaluation in Narrative'.
56. *Mald* 5–10. On the cultural significance of the hawk, see Owen-Crocker, 'Hawks'.
57. *Mald* 239–43.
58. This corresponds closely to Byrhtferth's statement in the *Vita S. Oswaldi* that 'Byrihtnoðus cecidit, et reliqui fugerunt' ('Byrhtnoth fell, and the rest fled'). Though the poem is concerned to show that some few did stand and fight to the end, apparently the panicked retreat of most of the English army after their leader's death was generally known, and perhaps generally considered the cause of the defeat. For Byrhtferth's text as a source on the battle, see Lapidge, '*Life of St Oswald*' (with the quotation taken from p. 54).
59. *Mald* 72b–3.

60. Even modern readers tend to grasp this instinctively. Thus Niles's note: 'Curiously, students of mine who have never read the *Liber Eliensis* have referred to Byrhtnoth as being outnumbered at Maldon. They have been surprised to discover that there is no basis for this idea in the poem' (*Heroic Poems*, p. 218, n. 36). While doubtless a cultural template for the 'last stand' is, as Niles argues, also in operation, I suspect these students are not misreading the poem, but rather are swayed by the poet's use of oral narrative techniques still found in modern discourse.
61. *Mald* 134–7.
62. *Mald* 149–51.
63. *Mald* 89–90.
64. Samouce, 'General Byrhtnoth'; Abels, 'English Tactics', p. 148.
65. Gneuss, 'Byrhtnoð's *ofermod*'.
66. See Abels, 'English Tactics', pp. 149–52, for a reading of analogous examples of blame assignment from various contemporary texts, including the *Anglo-Saxon Chronicle*; see also Szarmach, '(Sub-)Genre', p. 59. Trilling, *Aesthetics of Nostalgia*, pp. 151–69, explores the wider implications of this historiography in search of heroes in *Maldon* and the *Chronicle*, and contrasts it with an Orosian framework of divine retribution.
67. *Mald* 220–3a.
68. *Mald* 249–52a.
69. Woolf, 'Ideal'; Frank, 'Anachronism'; Niles, *Heroic Poems*, pp. 224–35; Trilling, *Aesthetics of Nostalgia*, esp. pp. 169–73.
70. See, e.g., Bloomfield, 'Beowulf, Byrhtnoth'; Blake, '*Battle of Maldon*'; Robinson, 'God, Death, and Loyalty'; Niles, *Heroic Poems*, p. 247.
71. See, e.g., Irving, 'Heroic Style'; John, *Reassessing*, p. 143 (esp. n. 7); and cf. Scragg, 'Fact or Fiction', pp. 21–4.
72. See above, p. 115.
73. Locherbie-Cameron, 'Men Named in the Poem'. See also Stafford, 'Kinship and Women', for an examination of naming patterns and kinship identification in the minor nobility.
74. See, e.g., Blake, '*Battle of Maldon*', pp. 337–8; Robinson, 'God, Death, and Loyalty', pp. 116–20; Kightley, 'Communal Interdependence'.
75. Phonological and lexical evidence on this question is sparse; see Scragg (ed.), *Battle of Maldon*, pp. 23–8. A few words and spellings suggest an East Anglian dialect, but in the main the poem is in standard late West Saxon.
76. I use the masculine pronoun for simplicity. I think a male author more probable, but by no means a certainty.
77. Labov, *Language in the Inner City*, p. 373 (and 393–5).
78. Stafford, 'Kinship and Women', p. 227.
79. Robinson, 'Some Aspects', pp. 122–4.
80. Scragg (ed.), *Battle of Maldon*, pp. 28–33.
81. See Fulk, *History*, pp. 251–68, esp. 259–60 and 265–6.
82. See, e.g., Scragg, 'Battle', p. 33, on the poem's social anachronisms; and Tyler, *Old English Poetics*, pp. 160–71, on invocation of gold treasure. Many who see

archaisms in the poem would nevertheless agree with Frank ('Anachronism') and others who argue for the poem's ideological modernity.

83. Scragg (ed.), *Battle of Maldon*, pp. 31–2.

84. Out of 325 verses, 167 B-verses end in a finite verb, 40 in infinitives, and 9 in past participles.

85. *Brunanburh* (73 lines): 23 B-verses end in finite verbs, 3 in infinitives, and 3 in past participles. *Seasons for Fasting* (230 lines): 75 B-verses end in finite verbs, 24 in infinitives, 1 inflected infinitive, 11 past participles. On the date of *Seasons for Fasting* (which, like *Maldon*, survives only in an early modern transcript), see Richards, 'Old Wine', esp. pp. 362–3.

86. This has given rise to a curious subgenre of literature review, which laments the misdirection of Cynewulf studies while recounting it.

87. The deciphered name in *Jul*, *ChristB*, and *El* was published near-simultaneously in 1840 by John Mitchell Kemble, 'Anglo-Saxon Runes', pp. 360–4, and Jakob Grimm, *Andreas und Elene*, pp. L–LI. It seems, however, that Kemble had worked this out in 1836 or 1837 and communicated his discovery to Grimm by letter, and that Grimm had forgotten about it: see Grimm's letter to Kemble published in Dilkey and Schneider, 'Kemble and the Brothers Grimm'. Arthur Napier discovered that the verse on the Vercelli Book's badly stained fol. 54a contained the name 'Cynwulf' in runes, adding *Fates* to the 'signed works' in 1889 ('Collation der altenglische Gedichte').

88. Sisam, 'Cynewulf and his Poetry', pp. 2–7, surveys the problem and relevant evidence. As Fulk notes ('Canon, Dialect', pp. 3–4), the current state of scholarship differs little from that presented in Sisam's 1933 British Academy lecture.

89. The only poem whose source remains controversial is *Fates*, since it is not yet clear whether it derives from a single work (whether martyrology or passional) or from separate lives which Cynewulf *samnode wide* ('gathered from far and wide', *Fates* 2b). For a cross-section of current positions see Cross, 'Cynewulf's Traditions'; Conner, 'On Dating Cynewulf'; and McCulloh, 'Did Cynewulf Use a Martyrology?'. For *Jul*'s source see Lapidge, 'Cynewulf and the *Passio S. Iulianae*'; for those of *El* and *ChristB* see Calder and Allen, *Sources and Analogues*, pp. 59–69 and 78–83 respectively.

90. Butler, 'Cynewulf Question Revived', forcefully critiqued the metrical analysis of Das, *Cynewulf and the Cynewulf Canon*, which had been thought to have finally limited the canon to the four signed poems. Her conclusion 'that the entire question of the authorship of the Cynewulf group should be reopened' (p. 23) has been taken up periodically, with very mixed results: Donoghue, *Style in Old English Poetry*, concluded through syntactic analysis that the style of *Jul* and *El* differs significantly from that of *Fates* and *ChristB*, and that most likely 'the same Cynewulf put his signature to four poems but was not the author – in the modern sense of the word – of all four' (p. 115). Conversely, Orchard argues from his study of shared formulaic diction 'that the four signed poems are indeed what they appear to be: the finished products of a single poet', and further that 'on the basis of the existing evidence the notion that

Cynewulf wrote *Guthlac B* is an attractive one' ('Both Style and Substance', p. 294). So far, however, the 'Cynewulf Question' has not been reopened in an integrated fashion, through combined analysis of metrical, lexical/formulaic, syntactic, and source-critical evidence.

91. A chemical reagent has rendered part of fol. 54a nearly illegible; see Muinzer, 'Maier's Transcript'.

92. *Fates* 88–95.

93. Frese, emphasizing unity rather than hierarchy, calls this 'a kind of poetic communion of saints' ('Runic Signatures', p. 330).

94. This point is controversial. Sisam's contention that 'a vernacular poet addressed himself primarily to the ear of a listener' and that Cynewulf was no different in this regard ('Cynewulf and his Poetry', p. 25) remains worth considering; but for further arguments that Cynewulf largely intended his works for readers, see Niles, *Enigmatic Poems*, pp. 285–6; and Ó Carragáin, 'Cynewulf's Epilogue'.

95. *Fates* 107–14.

96. *El* 1277–1321. Cynewulf's eschatology here resembles Alcuin's, but probably derives from his own reading of the Fathers, particularly Ambrose: see Brown, 'Cynewulf and Alcuin'. On the purifying flame of judgment, see Bedingfield, 'Anglo-Saxons on Fire'.

97. *El* 1309–14.

98. *El* 1316b–21.

99. *El* 1265b–6a: '[U] wæs geara / geogoðhades glæm' ('Ours long ago was the splendour of youth').

100. *El* 1236–7.

101. *Jul* 718b–29a.

102. See, e.g., *Sea* 1 and *Wife* 1; and elsewhere in Cynewulf's works, *ChristB* 633.

103. *Jul* 729b–31.

104. *Jul* 695b–6: 'Is me þearf micel / þæt seo halge me helpe gefremme' ('I am in great need of the saint's help'); 715b–17a: 'Þonne arna biþearf / þæt me seo halge wið þone hyhstan cyning / geþingige' ('Then was I in need of the mercies that the saint might beg for me from the highest King').

105. *Jul* 96b–100a.

106. *Jul* 132–9.

107. E.g., *witena dom* (98a); see also 123 and 146.

108. On Juliana's victory in the eyes of Anglo-Saxon law, see Abraham, 'Case at Law'.

109. Mass public conversions may well have been dramatized in one of the missing portions of text (between lines 558 and 559), caused by the loss of a folio. On the contents (which may have included the conversion and execution of Juliana's own proposed executioners) see Woolf (ed.), *Juliana*, pp. 47–8.

110. *Fates* 23–4.

111. *Beo* 874b–6a.

112. See esp. Parks, 'Traditional Narrator'.

113. *El* 632–4, 640b–1.

114. *El* 656a, 659b–61.

115. Schaefer, 'Hearing From Books', p. 130. DiNapoli, 'Poesis and Authority', frames the conflict as between a literate and specifically *poetic* oral culture, but largely agrees with this alignment of the characters and their loyalties.
116. *El* 670–5.
117. *El* 430b–8.
118. See Scheil, *Footsteps*, esp. pp. 219–28; and further Hill, 'Sapiental Structure'; Anderson, *Cynewulf*, pp. 121–5.
119. *El* 818b–26.
120. As seen in Sisam (ed.), *Vercelli Book*, on fol. 129^r *blinne* and *sint* are separated only by the normal space between words; there is no medial punctuation, and *sint* is not capitalized. (*Stephanus*, however, is marked by a very dark capital S, and is preceded by extra space and a *punctus*.)
121. Brown, 'Descent-Ascent Motif', p. 133.
122. Thus I think Clemoes's distinction between Gregorian *gewritu* as against biblical *bec* in l. 547 ('Image of the Ascension', pp. 120–1, n. 24) misses Cynewulf's point: that Gregory and Luke both relate the same message.
123. *ChristB* 791–3a.
124. Ricoeur, 'What is a Text', p. 137. Ong sketches the breadth and depth of this trope in his essay '*Maranatha*' (in his *Interfaces*, pp. 230–71, esp. 232–40); though he notes the physical potency of books in primarily oral cultures (p. 259), he does not deal with any instances in which this metaphor takes priority over that of death.
125. O'Brien O'Keeffe, *Visible Song*, pp. 51–4.
126. Ricoeur, 'What is a Text', pp. 136–7.
127. *Dream* 122–4a.
128. *Dream* 69b–72a.
129. I owe this reading to Andy Orchard; see his 'Cross-References', p. 232.
130. See Ziolkowski, 'Classical Influences'; and also Thornbury, 'Aldhelm's Rejection', pp. 88–9.
131. See especially Orchard, *Poetic Art*; and Lapidge, 'Hermeneutic Style'.
132. Lapidge and Herren, *Prose Works*, p. 149.
133. *HE* v.18.
134. On this alleged book, see Faricius, Prol. 5, in Winterbottom (ed.); this is probably what William was alluding to when he said 'Gaudeat aliquis de Aldelmi miraculis plura se legisse, quae uiuens dumtaxat fecerit. Ad me profecto nichil manauit . . .' (Winterbottom and Thomson (eds.), *Gesta Pontificum* v. Prol., p. 498).
135. See Winterbottom, 'Faricius's Life', pp. 111–12; and Thomson's notes to *Gesta Pontificum* v.
136. In Ehwald's numbering, these are *Epistolae* 2, 3, iii, 7, 8, 9, and 10; and see Lapidge and Herren, *Prose Works*, p. 136.
137. Vienna, Österreichische Nationalbibliothek, lat. 751 was written at Mainz in the mid-ninth century, and also contains Boniface's letters.
138. Lapidge, 'Career of Aldhelm'.
139. Brooks, *Early History*, p. 71.

140. See Lapidge, 'Career of Archbishop Theodore', pp. 25–6; and Bede, *HE* IV.1, pp. 328–32.
141. Bede, *HE* IV.2, pp. 332–4; on the imagery of Bede's description, see Thornbury, 'Anglo-Saxon Poetics', p. 65.
142. See Bischoff and Lapidge (eds.), *Biblical Commentaries*; Lapidge (ed.), *Archbishop Theodore*.
143. For Bede's testimony regarding Theodore's disciples, see *HE* V.20, p. 530 (Albinus); V.23, p. 556 (Tobias); IV.23, p. 408 (Oftfor); and see Brooks, *Early History*, p. 94.
144. *HE* V.3, p. 460: 'I remember archbishop Theodore of blessed memory saying . . .'. See Bischoff and Lapidge (eds.), *Biblical Commentaries*, p. 268.
145. *Epistola* I (to an unnamed bishop, presumably Leuthere, bishop of the West Saxons 670–6: see Ehwald, p. 475); *Epistola* II (to Hadrian). On the texts see also Lapidge and Herren, *Prose Works*, pp. 137–9.
146. *Epistola* I (Ehwald, pp. 476–7).
147. *Ibid.* (p. 477).
148. Lapidge, 'Career of Aldhelm', pp. 48–51. Aldhelm's appointment was customarily dated to 675 on the basis of the foundation charter of Malmesbury, preserved by William of Malmesbury and long known to have been at least partly forged, although its dating clause has usually been thought reliable. Lapidge proposes setting it aside entirely, in favour of more dependable charter evidence from 681 or 685.
149. Stevenson, 'Altus Prosator', p. 340.
150. *Vita Ceolfridi* §3, in Plummer (ed.), *Opera historica*, p. 389. On the attribution of the *Vita Ceolfridi*, see McClure, 'Life of Ceolfrid'.
151. Brooks, *Early History*, pp. 94, 347, n. 32.
152. *Historia abbatum* §3, in Plummer (ed.), *Opera historica*, p. 367. Closer examination of Ceolfrith's letter to King Nechtan of the Picts on the calculation of Easter (*HE* V.21) might also help to solve this question (though it may well prove to have been written by Bede, as is generally asserted).
153. There is not space here for a full consideration of the still controversial question of Bede's attitude towards Wilfrid; see Kirby, 'Bede, Eddius Stephanus'; Goffart, *Narrators*, pp. 235–328. I cannot agree with Goffart that Bede was unmixedly and steadily hostile to the quondam bishop of York; it seems to me rather that Bede was trying to negotiate a middle ground among partisan loyalties.
154. *Vita Ceolfridi* §37, in Plummer (ed.), *Opera historica*, p. 402.
155. On the alterations, see Marsden, 'Amiatinus'; for bibliography on the book (to 2001) see Gorman, 'Codex Amiatinus'. A third – and again, slightly different – text survived in the *Liber epigrammatum* compiled by Milred, bishop of Worcester: see Lapidge, 'Some Remnants', pp. 365–6, for an edition with variants.
156. Though technically a licence, *ecclēsia* was the normal scansion among Christian Latin poets.
157. On Aldhelm's style generally, see Orchard, *Poetic Art*, pp. 73–125.

158. Lapidge, 'Aldhelm's Latin Poetry', p. 255.
159. D = dactyl, S = spondee. (Each elegiac couplet consists of a hexameter and a pentameter line.) I leave out the final two feet, which – as with virtually all Anglo-Latin verse – form a fixed cadence of dactyl + spondee or trochee: see Lapidge, 'Aldhelm's Latin Poetry', p. 252; Orchard, *Poetic Art*, p. 85.
160. See Table 4 in Orchard, *Poetic Art*, p. 85.
161. See *ibid.*, pp. 239–83, and esp. Table A7, pp. 296–8.
162. Bischoff and Lapidge (eds.), *Biblical Commentaries*, p. 268.
163. *HE* v.19, pp. 528–30.
164. I note only one significant error: *tropăeum* (7).
165. *HE* v.19, pp. 528–30. Line 20: 'Grant, O Jesus, that the shepherd's flock may follow in his path.'
166. On Aldhelm's practice, see Lapidge, 'Aldhelm's Latin Poetry', pp. 252, 263–7; Orchard, *Poetic Art*, pp. 92–7. Thirteen out of twenty lines in Wilfrid's epitaph have diaeresis before the cadence.
167. Space does not permit a full account, but see, e.g., *CE* iv.v.17, 'Pausat in Effeso praefatus corpore praesul' (cf. 1, 'Uilfridus hic magnus requiescit corpore praesul'); *Enig* LXXVI, 7, 'Stipite de patulo dum penderet arbiter orbis' (cf. 3, 'Cui claues caeli Christus dedit arbiter orbis'). The epitaph's ll. 6–7, 'Quin etiam sublime crucis radiante metallo / Hic posuit tropaeum, nec non et quattuor auro', may have been partly modelled on *CE* iii, 77–8 ('Hic crucis ex auro splendescit lamina fulvo / Argentique simul gemmis ornata metallo'), combined with the word-lists in *De pedum regulis*: e.g., p. 167 ('Item neutralia: macellum, metallum, cilindrum, aratrum, sacellum, tropaeum . . .').
168. See below, pp. 183–97.
169. *HE* v.23, p. 558.
170. Sources noted in De Marco's CCSL edition include Donatus, Priscian, Charisius, Pompeius, Consentius, and Isidore.
171. Sims-Williams, *Religion and Literature*, esp. pp. 177–359.
172. The relevant letters are (in Ehwald's numbering): 3 (to Wihtfrith); 5 (to Heahfrith); 8 (to Æthilwald); 11 (from Æthilwald). The letters are translated in Lapidge and Herren, *Prose Works*, pp. 152–70 (with introductions at 136–51); Æthilwald's poems are now edited and translated in Miles, 'Carmina Rhythmica'.
173. For the vision, see *HE* v.13, pp. 498–503. Pecthelm was 'cum . . . Aldhelmo multo tempore adhuc diaconus siue monachus' (*HE* v.18, p. 512).
174. Æthilwald is sometimes identified with the bishop of Lindisfarne of the same name. This is chronologically plausible, but not otherwise substantiated: 'Æthelwold' and its variants was an extremely common name (see Prosopography of Anglo-Saxon England, www.pase.ac.uk, s.n.).
175. *Ep.* 11 (Ehwald, pp. 495, 496).
176. De Jong, *In Samuel's Image*, pp. 192–227; Parkes, 'Celtic Fosterage', esp. pp. 379–81, 370–2. Parkes's distinction between cliental and patronal fosterage is particularly important here.
177. De Jong, *In Samuel's Image*, pp. 198–213 at 209.

178. *VW* §xxi, p. 44.
179. *Ep.* 8 (Ehwald, pp. 499–500).
180. See esp. Wormald, 'Bede and Benedict Biscop', pp. 144–6.
181. On the historicity of Stephen's account of Wilfrid in Lyons, and especially the death of Aunemundus, see Nelson, 'Queens as Jezebels', pp. 63–7.
182. *VW* §v, p. 12. The character is evidently a conflation of Aunemundus, archbishop of Lyons, with his brother Dalfinus, the secular ruler of the city: see Colgrave in *VW*, p. 153; and Farmer, 'Saint Wilfrid', pp. 40–2.
183. *VW* §vi, p. 12.
184. On this institution in Merovingian France, see Heinzelmann, '*Studia sanctorum*', esp. pp. 124–9.
185. Riché, *Écoles*, pp. 39–41.
186. See Parkes, 'Celtic Fosterage'; and Kerlouegan, 'Mise en nourriture', esp. p. 136.
187. Kerlouegan, 'Mise en nourriture', p. 109.
188. *Ibid.*, p. 140.
189. *Ep.* 1 (Ehwald, p. 494); note the use of *nutrire* to mean 'taught'. Ehwald attributes the letter to 'Scottus ignoti nominis'; on the probable 'race' of the author, see Lapidge and Herren, *Prose Works*, pp. 146–7. On scholarly exchange between Anglo-Saxon England and Ireland in the seventh century generally, see Herren, 'Scholarly Contacts'; as well as Howlett, 'Aldhelm and Irish Learning'.
190. *Ep.* 7 (Ehwald, p. 495).
191. *Ep.* 7 (Ehwald, pp. 496–7).
192. See Miles, '*Carmina Rhythmica*', for a full account. It is not impossible that the seventy-line hexameter poem also survives, although it has as yet not been identified.
193. Orchard, *Poetic Art*, pp. 19–72, esp. 39–54.
194. See Lapidge and Herren, *Prose Works*, pp. 6–7; and Winterbottom and Thomson (eds.), *Gesta Pontificum*, II.257–8 (n. to §197.2).
195. Lapidge, 'Career of Aldhelm', pp. 22–30.
196. For the relevant *epistolae*: *Ep.* I (Ehwald, p. 464, from 'Scottus quidam'); and *Ep.* III and 7 (pp. 498–9, from and to Cellanus).
197. See, e.g., Wilfrid's troubles with the Mercian queen, who was the sister of his enemy Ecgfrith, and the West Saxon queen, the sister of Ecgfrith's wife Iurminburg: *VW* §xl, p. 80.
198. Lapidge, 'Career of Aldhelm', pp. 17–18.
199. *Ibid.*, p. 65.
200. On the general background of royal endowments of monasteries in the late seventh century, see Blair, *Church*, pp. 84–91; and Yorke, *Conversion*, pp. 163–70.
201. Salutation to the *Prosa de uirginitate* (Ehwald, p. 229).
202. Lapidge, 'Career of Aldhelm', p. 19.
203. The discussion in Lapidge and Herren, *Prose Works*, pp. 51–8, is fundamental, but see also O'Sullivan, 'Aldhelm's *De virginitate*'; Hollis, *Anglo-Saxon Women*, pp. 75–112; and Pasternack, 'Sexual Practices'.

204. *Prosa de uirginitate* §11 (Ehwald, p. 229). As he mentions *receiving* them at the same time in the previous paragraph, presumably a packet of individual letters was conveyed to Aldhelm.
205. Lines 8–12 (Ehwald, p. 524). On Helmgils's name (Latinized as *casses catholice / atque obses anthletice*, ll. 1–2), see Bradley, 'Some Poems', p. 292.
206. For the inaccuracies of Bede's description, see Lapidge and Herren, *Prose Works*, pp. 140–3. Bede may have assumed that the *Epistola ad Geruntium* was composed along the same lines as the *Epistola ad Acircium*, and thus qualified as a 'book' rather than a simple letter.
207. *HE* v.18.
208. On the complicated dynastic politics involved, see Moisl, 'Bernician'; and Higham, *Convert Kings*, pp. 133–267.
209. Lapidge, 'Career of Aldhelm', pp. 22–7.
210. On Aldhelm as Aldfrith's sponsor (rather than godfather) and the lasting implications of this relationship, see Lynch, *Christianizing Kinship*, pp. 110–16.
211. Ehwald, pp. 74–5.
212. Ehwald, p. 201.
213. On Aldfrith's fame as a scholar and philosopher in Irish, see Ireland, 'Learning of a *Sapiens*' and 'Irish Genealogies'; Herren, 'Scholarly Contacts', pp. 39–40.
214. *Fontes Anglo-Saxonici* records use of *De metris* by Bede and Felix (author of the *Vita Guthlaci*), as well as use of the *Enigmata* by Bede, Tætwine, Alcuin, the authors of the *Miracula S. Niniae*, and 'Eusebius' (who may not have been a northerner). The author of Wilfrid's epitaph probably also used the treatise: see above, n. 167.
215. See Blair, *Church* (esp. pp. 84–91); Yorke, *Nunneries*; Campbell, 'Elements'.
216. See Norberg, *Introduction*, pp. 106–10, 136–41, for the definition, development, and varieties of the form.
217. See *ibid.*, pp. 69–73.
218. Murphy, *Early Irish Metrics*, pp. 8–20; see esp. Orchard, *Poetic Art*, pp. 29–42.
219. Lapidge, 'Insular Latin Debate Poem' and 'Theodore and Anglo-Latin'; Herren, 'Stress Systems'; Howlett, 'Seventh-Century Texts', pp. 21–32; Orchard, *Poetic Art*, pp. 19–72.
220. Lapidge, 'Theodore and Anglo-Latin'. The poems are edited pp. 240–5.
221. In Ehwald, 'Carmina rhythmica', pp. 528–37; now edited and translated in Miles, '*Carmina Rhythmica*'.
222. For defences of Aldhelm's authorship, see Lapidge and Herren, *Prose Works*, pp. 16–18; and Lapidge and Rosier, *Poetic Works*, pp. 171–6.
223. *HE* v.18.
224. Lapidge, 'Theodore and Anglo-Latin', p. 240. I have followed Lapidge's interpretation of *speculator* (1); on the poem's manuscript contexts (in a collection of Theodore's canon judgments) see *ibid.*, pp. 225–6.
225. See *HE* iv.12.
226. On the trochaic rhythm of Theodore's verse, and potential links to Greek hymnody, see Lapidge, 'Theodore and Anglo-Latin'; on this poem's rhythm, see *ibid.*, p. 226.

227. This includes two of Theodore's prayers (II and IV in Lapidge's edition). Two other prayers – Theodore III and Æthilwald II – are in the first person, and address God in the third person.
228. See above, n. 205.
229. Æthilwald I, ll. 183–4 (Ehwald, p. 533). See Miles's (very plausible) metonymic interpretation of *calx* ('*Carmina Rhythmica*', p. 108).
230. Æthilwald III, ll. 75–8 (Ehwald, p. 535).
231. Æthilwald IV, ll. 1–8 (Ehwald, p. 536).
232. In particular, the mention of his hair (27–8) would be *extremely* odd if Offa were a monk.
233. Ehwald, p. 202 (part of the 'Allocutio excusativa ad regem').

4 THE POET ALONE

1. The Bodleian has published an excellent digital facsimile, edited by Bernard Muir, which includes commentary and bibliography on the texts and illustrations.
2. On the structure of the final gathering, see Raw, 'Construction' (with a diagram on p. 196).
3. Pp. 213–29 are written in Vernacular Minuscule; one scribe wrote pp. 213–15, and another 216–28. Ker (p. 408) attributed p. 229 to a third hand, but Muir, the editor of the most recent facsimile, follows Raw in attributing 229 to the second scribe (see n. 48 to his Introduction).
4. On the 'Late West Saxon Corrector', see Finnegan (ed.), *Christ and Satan*, pp. 59–60.
5. Isaacs, *Structural Principles*, pp. 127–44 (orchestration of speeches); Finnegan (ed.), *Christ and Satan*, pp. 10–11 (salvation history/'ages of man', with Christ as the fulfilment of Old Testament prefigurations); Sleeth, *Studies*, pp. 8–26 (Christ as Creator; 'abasement–exaltation' in the contrast between Satan and Christ).
6. Ten Brink, *Geschichte* vol. 1, pp. 102–5.
7. E.g., Muir: 'It seems to the present editor that the poem as it stands today was intended to be read as a continuous narrative, but that its three sections or movements were originally composed by three different Anglo-Saxon poets' (*MS. Junius 11*, 'Date, Texts, and Authorship'). Finnegan (ed.), *Christ and Satan*, pp. 12–17, provides a comprehensive critical history of this question.
8. These are at pp. 214, 215, 218, 219. Krapp (ed.), *Junius Manuscript* (*ASPR*), provides a convenient table of fitt divisions at p. xl.
9. Groschopp, '*Christ und Satan*'.
10. See Hoover, 'Primacy of Alliteration', for the most forceful statement of this, as well as Kendall, *Metrical Grammar*, pp. 13–26. Even metrists who see stress as the most basic element of Old English metre tend to consider alliteration as inseparable from metrical stress: see, e.g., Russom, *Old English Meter*, p. 2.
11. 'Double alliteration' is the employment of two alliterating stresses in the a-verse (AA/AX, where each capital represents a metrical stress and '/' the caesura). For a

snapshot of the range of double alliteration practices, see Hutcheson, *Old English Poetic Metre*, p. 271. Extra alliteration would be represented by the pattern AB/AB; cross-alliteration by BA/AB, and continuing alliteration a situation where the alliterative pattern of one line is picked up by the next (e.g., AA/AB//BB/BX, or AA/AX//AA/AY). For ornamental alliteration and its stylistic significance, see Le Page, 'Alliterative Patterns'; and Orchard, 'Artful Alliteration'.

12. Clubb (ed.), *Christ and Satan*, pp. xxvii–xxxix (and see also below).

13. See Fulk, 'Origin'.

14. This question still needs to be investigated thoroughly, but see Le Page, 'Alliterative Patterns', pp. 436–7, for a demonstration that the *Beowulf*-poet actively avoided consecutive lines with the same alliterative pattern.

15. This is particularly interesting, given that folios have been lost within Fitts 3 and 5 (so that there may originally have been up to eight fitts). That these 'composite' fitts are effectively indistinguishable from the others suggests a very high degree of consistency within, as well as between fitts.

16. It is possible that Fitt 13 was intended as a subsection of Fitt 12; the capital Ð on p. 229 is smaller than most of the other fitt initials, although it does project into the left margin. In any event, the text in this passage is severely disrupted.

17. *Sat* 370–80a.

18. The only possible exception is *JDay I* 27a, 'hū hī butan ende' (with vowel alliteration). However, the two additional initial syllables make this a normal light verse.

19. The usual emendation, *ymblyt*, is equally nonsensical; see Thornbury, '"Healing" Line 7'.

20. Cf. 'forgyteð and forgymeð', *Beo* 1751a.

21. *Sat* 502–7a.

22. In the manuscript *and* is abbreviated with the Tironian nota 7, but an earlier scribe could easily have misread *on* as *ond*.

23. Though *moton* is perhaps better; cf. 95a (and, e.g., *HomFr I* 45b, *Phoen* 559b).

24. *Sat* 549–54.

25. *Sat* 172–5.

26. *Sat* 308b–14.

27. *Sat* 119–21a.

28. *GenB* 927–31a.

29. *Wan* 5a; *GuthA* 454b. On the motif, see Greenfield, 'Formulaic Expression'.

30. *Sat* 22–33.

31. Various scholars have pointed this out; Clubb's 1925 edition provides a useful bibliography and set of parallels, though he comes to different conclusions from mine (*Christ and Satan*, pp. xxvii–xxx).

32. *GuthA* 557–63.

33. *GuthA* 582b–6.

34. *GuthA* 663–7a, 670b–2.

35. E.g., *þær wyrs gelomp*; *habban in heofnum heahgetimbr⟨ad/u⟩*; *niðer under næssas neole grundas*. The compound *brynewelm* is also rare; it only appears elsewhere in *Beowulf*.

36. The rarity, concentration in single passages, and order of shared formulas are all ways of differentiating literary borrowing from the shared use of an oral tradition: see Orchard, 'Computing Cynewulf' and 'Both Style and Substance'.
37. Clubb (ed.), *Christ and Satan*, p. xviii.
38. *Sat* 53–6.
39. *Christ and Satan* does not use the more famous term, *ofermod*. *Oferhygd* occurs at 50a, 69a, 113a, 196a, 226a, and 369a; and as the verb *oferhygan* ('scorn') at 250a and 304a (in a positive sense in the latter instance: meaning 'scorn sin').
40. *Sat* 282–7.
41. On the 'green street', see Keenan, 'Exodus 312'; and Doane, 'Green Street'.
42. Remley, *'Daniel'*.
43. For some suggestions, see Kendall, 'Bede and Education', pp. 102–3.
44. See Wood, 'Foundation', for a consideration of the houses and their connection.
45. On the biases and lacunae in the *Historia ecclesiastica*, see *inter alia* Howe, *Migration and Mythmaking*, pp. 33–71; Goffart, *Narrators*, pp. 235–328; Wormald, 'Bede, Beowulf'.
46. Brown, *Companion*, p. 1; Wormald, 'Bede and Benedict Biscop', p. 13 (and see also Wormald's 'Bede, *Beowulf* ').
47. Bede uses the phrase 'following in the fathers' footsteps' in the prologues to his 'Thirty Questions on the Books of Kings' and his commentary on 1 Samuel. His pupil Cuthbert reports that in his last days he worked at correcting Isidore's statements, saying that 'I do not want my children reading lies and wasting their time on this after my death' ('nolo ut pueri mei mendacium legant, et in hoc post meum obitum sine fructu laborent': *De obitu Baedae*, in Plummer (ed.), *Opera historica*, vol. 1, p. clxii). On anti-Isidoreanism in the *Historia ecclesiastica*, see Ray, 'Bede's *Vera Lex Historiae*'.
48. The originality and skill of Bede's work is eloquently described by Meyvaert in 'Bede the Scholar'; see also Ray, 'Who did Bede Think He Was'; DeGregorio, 'Footsteps of His Own'.
49. Stansbury, 'Source-Marks' and 'Early-Medieval Biblical Commentaries', esp. pp. 72–5.
50. Laistner (ed.), *Retractatio*, p. 93 (praefatio). On this passage see also Meyvaert, 'Bede the Scholar', p. 50; Bede's Greek manuscript is now Bodleian, Laud Gr. 35.
51. *DAM* §xvi, p. 130.
52. On the sources of the *De arte metrica*, see Kendall's detailed apparatus to his CCSL edition (in vol. 123A); on the (generally close) relation between its strictures and Bede's own practices, see Wright, 'Metrical Art(s)'.
53. *DAM*, title to §xv, p. 127.
54. *DAM* §xv, p. 129. The verse is *Carmen paschale* v, 8 ('He said, Glorify your name; and a great [voice] in heaven . . .').
55. In his colophon to the *Historia ecclesiastica*, Bede mentions his composition of a 'liber epigrammatum' and a 'liber hymnorum'; neither of these survive intact, but see Lapidge, 'Bede the Poet', pp. 314–32.

56. Lapidge, 'Bede's Metrical *Vita*'. See further below, pp. 191–4.
57. *HE* iii.20, p. 396.
58. Bede confirms the report of Æthelthryth's perpetual virginity in the first person: 'sicut mihimet sciscitanti ... beatae memoriae Uilfrid episcopus refer- ebat' (*HE* iii.19, p. 390: 'as Bishop Wilfrid of blessed memory related to me when I asked ...'). On Wilfrid's last departure from England, see Stephen of Ripon's account in Colgrave (ed.), *Life of Bishop Wilfrid*, §§LXIII–LXIV.
59. *HE* iv.20, pp. 396–8.
60. E.g., *productio ob caesuram* in 5 (*mihi*); a trisyllabic scansion of *diffugiunt* (44); a habitual shortening of the final syllable in *virgō* (11, 12, 25, 46, but not 17); also *credō* (33). All of these are quite licit.
61. See Lapidge, 'Versus de die iudicii', pp. 106–7. On the significance of the placement of feet within the hexameter for understanding Anglo-Latin metri- cal practice, see Orchard, *Poetic Art*, pp. 84–91, 239–80; and Lapidge, 'Aldhelm's Latin Poetry', pp. 251–5.
62. Statements are based on searches of the Library of Latin Texts – Series A, published by Brepols. For contents (which include all of the Corpus Christianorum Series Latina), see http://clt.brepolis.net/llta/pages/Toc.aspx.
63. Only Euphemia (20) is not in the *Prosa de uirginitate*; she is mentioned, however, in *Carmen* 27 of Paulinus of Nola, whose work Bede certainly knew: see Wright, 'Imitation of the Poems'.
64. Aldhelm, *Enigma* LXXIX, 'Sol et luna', ll. 9–10 (Ehwald, p. 134). For other echoes of Aldhelm's verse (including the *Carmen de uirginitate*), see Thornbury, 'Anglo-Saxon Poetics', p. 40, n. 88.
65. Orchard, *Poetic Art*, pp. 259–60 at 260.
66. See Thornbury, 'Aldhelm's Rejection'.
67. Fraipont's CCSL text is seriously flawed, and based on only seven manuscripts out of more than forty extant (see Lapidge, 'Versus de die iudicii', p. 103); it is not clear that Fraipont actually saw more than two of these manuscripts, both of which were relatively late (CCSL 122, p. 439). Lapidge's new edition of the poem has not been published as of the time of this writing. Many have (justifiably) doubted whether *De die iudicii* is in fact Bede's work: see, e.g., Lendinara, 'Translating Doomsday', p. 17. However, the manuscript attribu- tions to Bede are very common (see Whitbread, 'Study', pp. 195–207), and as the following pages indicate, the poem's divergence from Bede's mature style can be explained. But at the same time I do not think it impossible that *DDI* is the work of another Northumbrian poet; if this were the case, *Alma deus trinitas* may be Bede's only souvenir of his early style.
68. Lapidge, 'Versus de die iudicii', pp. 108–10 at 110.
69. Orchard, *Poetic Art*, pp. 257, 287.
70. In his study of Bede's metrical style in the *Vita metrica*, Wright contrasts Bede's 'carefully varied enjambment and internal pauses' and the care he took in constructing different patterns of 'golden symmetry' with Aldhelm's 'insist- ent repetition of similar (and end-stopped) golden lines' ('Metrical Art(s)', pp. 161, 167).

71. *DDI* 145–7.
72. See, e.g., *Enigma* C, 25–7, 40–4.
73. Wright, 'Metrical Art(s)'. The chapter (§XI) is found in *DAM*, pp. 111–16.
74. *DAM*, p. 114.
75. On this device in medieval literature more generally, see Curtius, *European Literature*, pp. 285–7.
76. *DDI* 115. Other examples: 118, 132–4, 136. In many other cases, the list does not quite fill the line, or conjunctions keep it from being asyndetic (e.g., 114, 119–20, 130–1, 135, 137).
77. *DDI* 139–41.
78. *DAM*, pp. 113–14.
79. Wright, 'Metrical Art(s)', p. 167.
80. At a conservative estimate, 57 per cent of the poem's 163 lines contain alliteration. If alliteration were measured according to Old English principles (equivalence of all vowels, of **f** and **v**, etc.; counting of stressed root of words with prefixes) the total would be much higher.
81. Lapidge demonstrated the *Vita metrica*'s significant debt to Arator: see 'Bede's Metrical *Vita*', pp. 348–52. On the Anglo-Latin tradition of paired verse and prose texts (derived from Late Antique practice), see also Godman, '*Opus geminatum*'; and Wieland, '*Geminus stilus*'.
82. Orchard, *Poetic Art*, p. 258.
83. Lapidge, 'Bede's Metrical *Vita*', esp. pp. 339–47.
84. *Ibid.*, p. 343.
85. *VC* 931–2.
86. Thanks to Frank Bezner for discussion on this point. The prevention of elision across the line-boundary, which Bede had identified as licit (see *DAM* §XIII, pp. 121–2), may have further recommended this alteration.
87. *VC* 951.
88. See Lapidge, 'Bede's Metrical *Vita*', p. 344, for a full list.
89. *Ibid.*, p. 344 (discussing line 7).
90. 728: *lumina pulsu* (cf. Ausonius, *Precatio* 2, 8) becomes the unique phrase *tempora pulsu*. 834: *signi uenerabilis index* (cf. Cyprianus Gallus, *Heptateuchos* (Exodus), 1104, *signum uenerabile regis*) becomes *signi memorabilis index*.
91. This is §XVI, discussed above. See Lapidge, 'Bede and the Poetic Diction'; on the citations of Virgil in *De arte metrica* – which are often based on faulty texts – see Heikkinen, 'Vergilian Quotations'.
92. See Orchard, *Poetic Art*, pp. 239–92.
93. Lapidge, 'Bede and the Poetic Diction', p. 741.
94. See Szarmach, 'Bede on Aldhelm'; Orchard, *Poetic Art*, pp. 2–3.
95. *DDI* 3–7, 12.
96. Lapidge, 'Bede the Poet', p. 318.
97. 'Soliloquium Bedae: Psalm 41', 30–5. Cf. Psalm 41:9–10.
98. 'Oratio Bedae' 1–6, in Fraipont (ed.), CCSL 122.
99. See the *Vita metrica* §XLIII, in *VC*.

5 SPECTRAL COMMUNITIES

1. Trudgill, 'Contact and Isolation', gives several such examples.
2. *HE* iv.16.
3. See O'Donoghue, *Old Norse-Icelandic*, esp. pp. 106–48.
4. Linguistically, this would correspond to Andersen's 'endocentric' orientation (which he compares to de Saussure's *esprit de clocher*): 'Center and Periphery', esp. pp. 39, 71–8.
5. See Campbell and Muntzel, 'Structural Consequences' (and other essays in the same volume).
6. See Andersen, 'Center and Periphery', pp. 54–73, and Schilling-Estes and Wolfram, 'Alternative Models', for dialectal parallels.
7. McKitterick, 'Anglo-Saxon Missionaries'.
8. Orchard, 'Old Sources'.
9. *Ibid.*, p. 20.
10. Tangl 68, p. 141. Roughly, 'in the name of the Fatherland and the Daughter and the Holy Spirit'. The quote is from a letter of Pope Zacharias, who asked Boniface to stop rebaptizing, since the priest was acting out of ignorance, not heretical intent. Boniface seems also to have been encroaching on the Bavarian district of the Irishman Virgil (afterwards bishop of Salzburg), whom he would later accuse of heresy (see Tangl 80, at pp. 178–9).
11. Glorie (ed.), CCSL 133, p. 339.
12. Elfassi (ed.), CCSL 111B, 11.65, p. 116. Isidore's *Synonyma* was among the books Boniface brought to the Continent, and one of the earlier copies may contain his handwriting: see Di Sciacca, *Finding the Right Words*, pp. 51–2, 72–5. I have been unable to ascertain the source of Boniface's final synonym, *inuisa*, but its attribution to *Grecia prudens* also suggests an etymological connection via a Greek synonym.
13. The *soror* is not named, and while it seems probable she was a fellow monastic, it is not clear whether she was also a blood- or foster-sister.
14. Orchard, *Poetic Art*, pp. 61–7. As mentioned above (p. 148), the octosyllabic poems of Aldhelm and Æthilwald were sent to the Continent, and are now uniquely preserved in a manuscript, Vienna 751, whose exemplars were probably assembled at Mainz under Lull's direction.
15. Orchard, 'Old Sources', pp. 29–32. The letter is Tangl 29, pp. 52–3.
16. Tangl 103, pp. 225–7.
17. Tangl 103, p. 227, ll. 15–17.
18. Ehwald, p. 98, l. 15.
19. *Sensibus*: *Enig* LXXII ('Colosus'), p. 130, l. 8; *augens*: *CdV*, p. 390, l. 861; *salvantis*: *De metris*, p. 93 (quoting Arator 1.883).
20. Hauck's attribution to Lull of the seventy-five-line *Carmen de conuersione Saxonum* is extremely persuasive; his case rests heavily on the intensely Aldhelmian diction of the poem ('Karolingische Taufpfalzen', pp. 56–74).

21. Tangl 140, pp. 279–80. Tangl dates the letter to the latter part of Lull's career; like many of the letters in Vienna 751, names have been replaced by .N. which, as Orchard points out ('Old Sources', p. 18), indicates the codex was intended as an epistolary pattern-book.

22. Tangl 140, p. 280, l. 25.

23. Tangl 13, p. 19, l. 11.

24. Tangl, p. 18.

25. On the manuscript, see Bischoff, 'Lorsch', esp. pp. 118–19.

26. See Gebauer and Löfstedt (eds.), *Ars metrica*, p. 105; and above, p. 45. I have not seen the manuscript, but Löfstedt gives the foliation of *Caesurae uersuum* as 114^{r-v}, 116^r, and Dümmler that of the riddles as 115, 117 ('Lorscher Rätsel', p. 262).

27. XI, on a bullock, is practically identical to *Enigma* LXXXII 'Iuuencus', but gauging from the many other parallels (on which see Lendinara, 'Aenigmata', pp. 84–7) the 'ox riddle' was known widely, and in a relatively fixed form.

28. Dümmler, p. 22.

29. Ehwald, p. 134, ll. 7–9.

30. Ehwald, p. 109, ll. 4–5. The f/b alternation is notably common in Old English.

31. See Dümmler, 'Lorscher Rätsel', p. 262. Lendinara ('Aenigmata', p. 74) suggests that the riddles may be a product of Alcuin's influence, but there are no striking similarities with his work: because of this, I tend to think they predate his fame, although I think it likely that Alcuin's student Ricbod, abbot of Lorsch, had a strong influence on the compilation of Palat. lat. 1753.

32. Dümmler, p. 20, ll. 23–8.

33. On Alcuin's preference for elegiacs, see above, p. 86.

34. Cf. the parallels to ll. 23–6: CX.xii.2, 'Exornat, meritis et praesul Hilarius almus'; IX.208, 'Qui se pro Christo subiciunt gladiis'; 1.1450, 'Hos sibi con-iunxit, docuit, nutrivit, amavit'; LXV.i.6, 'De quibus egregius vatis in ore canit.'

35. Dümmler, p. 20, l. 37. The line is unmetrical, and probably was not meant to be recopied.

36. Engelbert (ed.), *Vita Sturmi*, pp. 149–54.

37. See Palmer, 'Bishop Lull'.

38. Carver, 'Intellectual Communities'.

39. Leland, *Commentarii*, in Hall (ed.), vol. 1, pp. 164–5.

40. *Ibid.*, pp. 165–6.

41. Lapidge, *Cult*, pp. 341, 364.

42. Cf. also Dolbeau, on Wulfstan's adaptation of a prose source: 'Plus l'imitation est fidèle, plus remarquable est la prouesse technique, plus subtile la métamorphose du texte original. La chenille devient papillon en conservant beaucoup d'attributs de son état primitif ('*Breuiloquium*', p. 51).

43. Lapidge and Winterbottom (eds.), *Life of St Æthelwold*, pp. xv–xxii; Dolbeau (ed.), '*Breuiloquium*', pp. 37–44 (the manuscript is 11.984, catalogue number 3290), esp. at 38, where he notes how badly the scribe botched the acrostic.

44. *AH* 51, p. 165.
45. See Milfull, *Hymns*; the texts are edited pp. 320–4.
46. It is often difficult to be certain whether octosyllabic hymns are intended to be rhythmical or quantitative; Milfull (*Hymns*, p. 320) considers the poem in question, 'Caelestis aulae nobiles', to be rhythmical, while Lapidge (Lapidge and Winterbottom (eds.), *Life of St Æthelwold*, p. xxxvii) reads it as quantitative. If we concede that the author regarded all line-final syllables as *anceps* and that h was a full consonant (which would suit Old English phonology; see Lapidge, *Cult*, p. 349), there is only one error, *iŭgis* 'forever' (26). I think it must therefore be considered quantitative, especially since several lines contain paroxytonic (rather than proparoxytonic) stress, e.g., 3, 10, 19.
47. According to Milfull's notes (*Hymns*, p. 324), although classifications of Horace's metres differ. It consists of three lesser asclepiads and a glyconic.
48. Lapidge and Winterbottom (eds.), *Life of St Æthelwold*, pp. xxxvii–xxxviii, at xxxviii.
49. *AH* 48, pp. 9–18. The manuscript is G 927; see further Lapidge, *Cult*, pp. 238–9.
50. *AH* 48, p. 10, ll. 6, 37–8.
51. *ES* 273 (Lapidge, *Cult*, p. 394); 1.iv.889 (Lapidge, *Cult*, p. 454).
52. Cf., for instance, 'Nosque polo iungat Christus de lumine lumeN' (Dolbeau, '*Breuiloquium*', l. 716) and 'Nos super aethra poli cuneis adiunge supernis', l. 53 of the hymn to Æthelwold. The final N of the Swithun hymn is also provided by *nos*.
53. *AH* 48, pp. 11, 13.
54. See Lapidge, 'Bede's Metrical *Vita*', pp. 348–52.
55. G 116; there is now a colour facsimile with invaluable commentary: Rankin (ed.), *Winchester Troper*.
56. Rankin (ed.), *Winchester Troper*, pp. xi, 15.
57. The list of *Kyrie eleisons* comes at fols. 55ʳ–8ʳ; this one is at 57ᵛ. Rankin connects the studied variation in the rubrics to contemporary principles of rhetoric (*ibid.*, pp. 72–3).
58. Fols. 135ʳ and 138ᵛ. See Rankin (ed.), *Winchester Troper*, p. 63 for a list and analysis of these rubrics.
59. *Ibid.*, p. 63.
60. 1.7–11 (Lapidge, *Cult*, p. 412).
61. 11.954–7 (Lapidge, *Cult*, p. 540).
62. Dolbeau (ed.), '*Breuiloquium*', p. 65, ll. 82–4: 'Hoc sacer egregius, hoc uersificator et ille / Sedulius, noster nitido sermone magister, / Considerans scribit, iubilans qui talia dicit.' *Carmen paschale* 1.66–7 follows.
63. Dolbeau (ed.), '*Breuiloquium*', pp. 52–7; Lapidge, *Cult*, pp. 341–64, esp. at 343–52.
64. Dolbeau (ed.), '*Breuiloquium*', p. 73, l. 294.
65. *ES* 71–4 (Lapidge, *Cult*, pp. 376–8). Wulfstan's scansion of Æthelgārus is probably correct in late Old English: cf. *Maldon* 320a, and see Fulk, *History*, p. 256. Note also *rursumqu(e) Ælfstanus* and *prompt(um) est*.
66. 1.iii.523–7 (Lapidge, *Cult*, p. 436).

67. Dolbeau, '*Breuiloquium*', p. 50.
68. Lapidge, *Cult*, pp. 356–64.
69. See above, pp. 44–5.
70. Napier (ed.), *Rule*, ii.29, p. 9. Quoted Lapidge and Winterbottom (eds.), *Life of St Æthelwold*, pp. xiii–xiv at xiii.
71. Rankin (ed.), *Winchester Troper*, p. 15.
72. Lapidge and Winterbottom (eds.), *Life of St Æthelwold*, §42, p. 64.
73. Lapidge, *Cult*, pp. 382–6. E.g., *ES* 173–4: '*Musarumque melos auditur ubique per urbem / et peragrat totam fama uolans patriam*' ('And the instruments' music is heard throughout the city, and flying report of it passes through the whole country').
74. Rankin, 'Swithun in Music', p. 193, n. 9 (in Lapidge, *Cult*).
75. Above, p. 103.
76. *AH* 48, p. 10, ll. 37–44.
77. Though *auditor* did not denote a formal office at this period, it nevertheless pertained to legal or quasi-legal contexts: see Niermeyer, svv. *audire, auditor*, for a number of Carolingian attestations.
78. *AH* 48, p. 12, ll. 23–6.
79. Dolbeau (ed.), '*Breuiloquium*', p. 63, ll. 1–2.
80. *Ibid.*, ll. 17–20.
81. *Ibid.*, p. 84, ll. 633–6.
82. *Ibid.* p. 87, ll. 690–1.
83. Milfull, *Hymns*, p. 323; *AH* 48, pp. 10 and 15, l. 21.
84. *ES* 495; i.1235; ii.363, 846, 1004, 1037.
85. Milfull, *Hymns*, p. 322, ll. 1–4.
86. *Ibid.*, p. 323, ll. 21–4.
87. *Ibid.*, p. 320, ll. 1–4.
88. On the relics see Lapidge, *Cult*, pp. 38–40 (and the note by John Crook, pp. 61–5: the head is now in Évreux).
89. Lapidge and Winterbottom (eds.), *Life of St Æthelwold*, pp. xxix–xxx, xxxviii.
90. *Ibid.*, p. xxxviii.
91. E.g., Nordau, *Degeneration*, p. 57: 'the degenerate . . . suffer from weakness of will and defective attention.'
92. Keynes, 'Cult of King Alfred'.
93. See Lapidge, 'Latin Learning'; Dumville, 'English Script'; Gneuss, 'King Alfred', *vs* Morrish, 'King Alfred's Letter'.
94. See Godden, 'Did King Alfred', *vs* Bately, 'Did King Alfred'; Pratt, 'Problems of Authorship'.
95. See esp. Bately, 'Old English Prose'.
96. E.g., Sisam accepts Alfred's authorship of the *Metres of Boethius*, but emphasizes their 'prosy and often feeble expression' (*Studies*, p. 297); Griffith subtitled his article on the *Paris Psalms* 'The Decay of the Old English Tradition' ('Poetic Language').
97. Griffith, 'Composition'.

98. Fulk, *History*, p. 252. For a methodologically quite different approach to this period, see Bredehoft, *Early English Metre*.

99. Fulk, *History*, pp. 252–64. On the diction of the *Metres*, see *OEB*, vol. I, pp. 191–4; and Griffith, 'Composition'.

100. Cf. also Bredehoft, *Authors, Audiences*, who comes to somewhat similar conclusions, though via different methodology and with quite different assumptions about the scope and meaning of late verse style.

101. I use *simulacrum* to mean an entity that stands in place of another entity (which it purports to resemble) not in spite, but *because* of its difference from that other entity: translations, idols, and coin or paper currency thus would all be forms of simulacra. My definition draws on Deleuze's idea of the 'reversed Platonic' simulacrum (see esp. Deleuze, 'Simulacrum', pp. 253–66).

102. See, e.g., Bately, 'England and the Continent'; Leyser, 'Ottonen'; Bullough, 'Continental Background'; and above, pp. 89–94.

103. Whitelock, 'Prose', is still a helpful survey.

104. Stafford, *Unification*, pp. 180–200.

105. *OEB*, vol. I, p. 153.

106. *Pr* 8–20.

107. 'Miserere mei Deus secundum misericordiam tuam: iuxta multitudinem miserationum tuarum dele iniquitates meas' ('Have mercy on me, O God, in your goodness; in the greatness of your compassion wipe out my offence').

108. Proverbs 11:20. For the Psalm-derived resonance of *eadig*, see Harris, 'Happiness'.

109. The Latin text is not, however, that from which the Old English was translated: see Sisam and Sisam, 'Psalm Texts', in Colgrave (ed.), *Paris Psalter*, p. 15.

110. Krapp (ed.), *ASPR*, vol. v, pp. xix–xx.

111. Baker, 'Little-Known Variant'; Toswell, 'Metrical Psalter'.

112. Gretsch, *Intellectual Foundations* (quotation at p. 82).

113. Baker, 'Little-Known Variant'; O'Neill, 'Fragment'.

114. O'Neill, 'Fragment', p. 436.

115. There is good reason to think the Eadwine Psalter was designed as a kind of *summa* of psalter scholarship: see Gibson *et al.* (eds.), *Eadwine Psalter*, esp. Gibson's 'Conclusions', pp. 209–13; and Treharne, *Living Through Conquest*, pp. 167–87.

116. Toswell, 'Format', p. 132.

117. For facsimiles see Colgrave (ed.), *Paris Psalter*; and online via the Bibliothèque nationale de France: http://gallica.bnf.fr/ark:/12148/btv1b8451636f.

118. Toswell, 'Format', p. 133; on the colophon see Gameson, *The Scribe Speaks*, p. 46. 'Cada' appears as part of a place-name in charters from Worcestershire (S 786, 1599), Hampshire (S 693, 1007), and Oxfordshire (S 217). Tengvik considers the by-name to mean 'lumpish', though the later reflexes he cites would point towards 'small' (*Bynames*, p. 297).

119. Emms, 'Scribe'.

120. Baker, 'Little-Known Variant'.

121. Emms, 'Scribe', p. 182. Jean, duc de Berry, was the book's first identifiable medieval owner, though how he acquired it is unknown. On lay ownership and reading of the Psalms in Carolingian Europe (especially by women), see Garver, 'Learned Women', pp. 131–3.
122. I adopt the title suggested by Jones in his new edition (Appendix B in *Shorter Poems*, pp. 284–343 at 285).
123. Gameson, *The Scribe Speaks*, p. 47.
124. See Jones, 'Liturgical Interests', esp. p. 347.
125. Jones (ed.), *Shorter Poems*, pp. 284–90; Ure (ed.), *Benedictine Office*, pp. 15, 25–46. The textual variants between Junius 121 and CCCC 201 (the other surviving manuscript of the prose) are quite substantial; separate (or parallel-text) editions would be valuable.
126. A (black and white) facsimile of Junius 121 can be found in Pulsiano, Doane, *et al.* (eds.), *Anglo-Saxon Manuscripts in Microfiche Facsimile*, vol. VI; a digital colour facsimile of CCCC 201 is now available at Parker Library on the Web: http://parkerweb.stanford.edu.
127. Jones (ed.), *Shorter Poems*, p. 286.
128. *Men* 58b–62.
129. On the variants, see Toswell, 'Metrical Psalter'.
130. *Men* 228b–31.
131. Bredehoft, *Authors, Audiences*, pp. 113–30, ascribes the *Menologium* and the four earlier *ASC* poems to a single author, whom he identifies with Æthelwold of Winchester or his circle: however, the commonalities he adduces are not especially close. However, the *Menologium*-poet need not have written any part of the *ASC* to find it rhetorically useful.
132. *KtHy* 1–6.
133. Lc 2:13–14. 'et subito facta est cum angelo multitudo militiae caelestis laudantium Deum et dicentium: gloria in altissimis Deo et in terra pax in hominibus bonae voluntatis.' ('And suddenly there were with the angel a multitude of the heavenly host praising God and saying, "Glory to God in the highest, and on earth peace among men of good will."')
134. Fulk, *History*, pp. 285–6.
135. On Metre 1 and the tradition of Boethian biography, see Discenza, 'Unauthorized Biographies'.
136. *OEB*, vol. I, pp. 42–3; though it is now unknown whether this version was prose or prosimetric.
137. Fulk, *History*, pp. 410–14.
138. See Griffith, 'Composition'; and *OEB*, vol. I, pp. 146–51.
139. *Met Proem* 5–7a. For the full preface, see above, p. 22; on the complexities of the vocabulary – which draws heavily on the prose – see O'Brien O'Keeffe, 'Listening'.
140. Griffith, 'Composition', pp. 81–2, n. 5.
141. *OEB* §19, vol. I, p. 282; corresponding to Book II, pr.9/met.9.
142. On the 'perfectly normal' use of the vernacular in English liturgical books, see Gittos, 'Evidence', esp. pp. 75–82 (at 80).

143. Junius 121 does, however, provide one intriguing exception to this in the first line of its version of the Lord's Prayer: 'Fæder manncynnes, frofre ic þe bidde' ('Father of mankind, I pray you for mercy'). Though the voice switches within a few lines to the canonical plural, the use of the singular may indicate this version's original purpose was individual devotion.

144. See Robinson, 'Rewards'.

AFTERWORD: A WAY OF HAPPENING

1. It is hard to imagine a film critic titling his book *Beautiful and Pointless*, as David Orr did his 2011 *Guide to Modern Poetry*.

2. On Anglo-Saxons and the proleptic injunction to 'be what you are', see O'Brien O'Keeffe, *Stealing Obedience*, pp. 94–150.

3. Auden, 'In Memory of W. B. Yeats', p. 94.

4. Murison (ed.), *Hydriotaphia*, p. 1.

Bibliography

FACSIMILES

Colgrave, Bertram (ed.). *The Paris Psalter*. EEMF 8. 1958.

Muir, Bernard J. (ed.), with Nick Kennedy. *A Digital Facsimile of Oxford, Bodleian Library, MS. Junius 11*. Bodleian Digital Texts 1. Oxford: Bodleian Library, 2004. CD-ROM.

The Exeter DVD: The Exeter Anthology of Old English Poetry. University of Exeter Press, 2006. DVD.

Pulsiano, Phillip, A. N. Doane, *et al.* (eds.). *Anglo-Saxon Manuscripts in Microfiche Facsimile*. 20 vols. (ongoing). Tempe, AZ: ACMRS, 1994–present.

Rankin, Susan (ed.). *The Winchester Troper*. Early English Church Music 50. London: British Academy, 2007.

Santosuosso, Alma (ed.). *MSS Avranches, Bibliothèque municipale, 236, 237: Music Theory in Mediaeval Normandy. Vol. 1: Boethius' De institutione musica*. Publications of Mediaeval Musical Manuscripts 24/1. Ottawa, ON: Institute of Mediæval Music, 1999.

Sisam, Celia (ed.). *The Vercelli Book (Vercelli Biblioteca Capitolare CXVII)*. EEMF 19. 1976.

Stanley, E. G., and F. C. Robinson (eds.). *Old English Verse Texts from Many Sources: A Comprehensive Collection*. EEMF 23. 1991.

REFERENCE TOOLS

Early Manuscripts at Oxford University. http://image.ox.ac.uk.

Fontes Anglo-Saxonici Project. *Fontes Anglo-Saxonici: World Wide Web Register*. http://fontes.english.ox.ac.uk.

Gneuss, Helmut. *Handlist of Anglo-Saxon Manuscripts*. Tempe, AZ: ACMRS, 2001.

Hartzell, K. D. *Catalogue of Manuscripts Written or Owned in England up to 1200 Containing Music*. Woodbridge: Boydell, 2006.

Ker, N. R. *Catalogue of Manuscripts Containing Anglo-Saxon*. Oxford: Clarendon Press, 1957.

Laistner, M. L. W., with H. H. King. *A Hand-List of Bede Manuscripts*. Ithaca, NY: Cornell University Press, 1943.

Niermeyer, J. F., and C. van de Kieft, rev. J. W. J. Burgers. *Mediae Latinitatis Lexicon Minus*. 2 vols. Leiden: Brill, 2002.

Parker Library on the Web. http://parkerweb.stanford.edu.

Sharpe, Richard. *A Handlist of the Latin Writers of Great Britain and Ireland Before 1540*. Turnhout: Brepols, 1997 (with 2001 supplement).

Skaldic Poetry of the Scandinavian Middle Ages. http://skaldic.arts.usyd.edu.au.

Venezky, Richard L., and Antonette diPaolo Healey. *A Microfiche Concordance to Old English*. Publications of the Dictionary of Old English *1*. University of Toronto Press, 1980.

PRIMARY SOURCES

Auden, W. H. 'In Memory of W. B. Yeats.' In his *Another Time*. New York: Random House, 1940. pp. 93–6.

Bately, Janet (ed.). *The Anglo-Saxon Chronicle: A Collaborative Edition. Vol. 3: MS A*. Cambridge: D. S. Brewer, 1986.

The Old English Orosius. EETS SS 6. 1980.

Borzsák, Stephan (ed.). *Q. Horati Flacci Opera*. Leipzig: Teubner, 1984.

Brehe, S. K. 'Reassembling the *First Worcester Fragment*.' *Speculum* 65 (1990): 521–36.

Campbell, Alistair (ed.). *Æthelwulf: De abbatibus*. Oxford: Clarendon Press, 1967.

The Chronicle of Æthelweard. London: T. Nelson and Sons, 1962.

Frithegodi Monachi Breuiloquium Vitae Beati Wilfredi et Wulfstani Cantoris Narratio Metrica de Sancto Swithuno. Zürich: Artemis-Verlag, 1950.

Clubb, Merrel Dare (ed.). *Christ and Satan: An Old English Poem*. Yale Studies in English 70. New Haven, CT: Yale University Press, 1925.

Colgrave, Bertram (ed.). *The Life of Bishop Wilfrid by Eddius Stephanus*. Cambridge University Press, 1927 (repr. 2007).

Colgrave, Bertram, and R. A. B. Mynors (eds.). *Bede's Ecclesiastical History of the English People*. Oxford: Clarendon Press, 1969.

De Marco, Maria (ed.). *Ars Tatuini*. CCSL 133. 1968. pp. v–141.

Dolbeau, François (ed.). 'Le *Breuiloquium de omnibus sanctis*: Un poème inconnu de Wulfstan chantre de Winchester.' *Analecta Bollandiana* 106 (1988): 35–98.

Dräger, Paul (ed.). *Alcuini Vita sancti Willibrordi/Alkuin: Das Leben des heiligen Willibrord*. Trier: Kliomedia, 2008.

Dreves, Guido Maria, and Clemens Blume (eds.). *Analecta hymnica Medii Aevi*. 55 vols. Leipzig: Reisland, 1886–1922.

Dümmler, Ernst (ed.). *Epistolae Karolini Aevi*. Vol. II. MGH Ep IV. 1895.

Poetae Latini Aevi Carolini. Vol. I. MGH PLAC I. 1881.

Ehwald, Rudolf (ed.). *Aldhelmi Opera*. MGH AA 15. 1919.

Elfassi, Jacques (ed.). *Isidori Hispalensis Episcopi Synonyma*. CCSL IIIB. 2009.

Engelbert, Pius (ed.). *Die Vita Sturmi des Eigil von Fulda*. Veröffentlichungen der Historischen Kommission für Hessen und Waldeck 29. Marburg: N. G. Elwart, 1968.

Finnegan, Robert Emmett (ed.). *Christ and Satan: A Critical Edition*. Waterloo, ON: Wilfred Laurier University Press, 1977.

Fraipont, J. (ed.). *Bedae Venerabilis Opera. Pars IV: Opera rhythmica.* CCSL 122. 1955.

Friedlein, Godofredus (ed.). *Boetii De institutione arithmetica libri duo et de institutione musica libri quinque.* Leipzig: Teubner, 1867.

Fulk, R. D., Robert E. Bjork, and John D. Niles (eds.). *Klaeber's Beowulf: Fourth Edition.* University of Toronto Press, 2008.

Garmonsway, G. N. (ed.). *Ælfric's Colloquy.* Methuen's Old English Library. New York: Appleton-Century-Crofts, 1966.

Gebauer, George John, and Bengt Löfstedt (eds.). *Bonifatii ars metrica.* CCSL 133B. 1980.

Glorie, François (ed.). *Collectiones aenigmatum Merovingicae aetatis.* 2 vols. CCSL 133, 133A. 1968.

Godden, Malcolm, and Susan Irvine (eds.). *The Old English Boethius.* 2 vols. Oxford University Press, 2009.

Godman, Peter (ed.). *Alcuin: The Bishops, Kings, and Saints of York.* Oxford: Clarendon Press, 1982.

Grimm, Jakob (ed.). *Andreas und Elene.* Kassel: Theodor Fischer, 1840.

Guerreau-Jalabert, Anita (ed.). *Abbon de Fleury: Questions grammaticales.* Paris: Société d'Édition 'Les belles lettres', 1982.

Hall, Anthony (ed.). *Commentarii de scriptoribus Britannicis, auctore Johanno Lelando.* 4 vols. Oxford: E theatro Sheldoniano, 1709. (From the HathiTrust Digital Library, http://babel.hathitrust.org; digital version of a copy owned by the University of Michigan Library.)

Hurst, D. (ed.). *Bedae Venerabilis Opera: II. Opera exegetica: 2. In primam partem Samuhelis et In Regum librum XXX quaestiones.* CCSL 119. 1963.

Jaager, Werner (ed.). *Bedas metrische Vita sancti Cuthberti.* Palaestra 198. Leipzig: Mayer & Müller, 1935.

Jones, Christopher A. (ed.). *Old English Shorter Poems. I: Religious and Didactic.* Cambridge, MA: Harvard University Press, 2012.

Jónsson, Guðni (ed.). *Edda Snorra Sturlusonar, Nafnapulur og Skáldatal.* Reykjavík: Íslendingasagnaútgáfan, 1985.

Keeffer, Sarah Larratt (ed.). *Old English Liturgical Verse: A Student Edition.* Peterborough, ON: Broadview Press, 2010.

Keil, Heinrich (ed.). *Grammatici Latini.* 8 vols. Leipzig, 1855–80.

Kendall, C. B. (ed.). *De arte metrica et de schematibus et tropis,* in *Beda Venerabilis: Opera didascalica.* CCSL 123A. 1975. pp. 59–171.

Klaeber, Fr. (ed.). *Beowulf and the Fight at Finnsburg.* 3rd edn. Lexington, MA: D. C. Heath, 1950.

Knowles, David, and Christopher N. L. Brooke (eds.). *The Monastic Constitutions of Lanfranc.* Oxford: Clarendon Press, 2002.

Krapp, George Philip, and E. V. K. Dobbie (eds.). *The Anglo-Saxon Poetic Records.* 6 vols. New York: Columbia University Press, 1931–53.

Kumaniecki, Kazimierz F. (ed.). *M. Tulli Ciceronis scripta quae manserunt omnia 3: De oratore.* Stuttgart: Teubner, 1995.

Laistner, M. L. W. *Bedae Venerabilis Expositio Actuum Apostolorum et Retractatio.* Cambridge, MA: Medieval Academy, 1939.

Lapidge, Michael, and Michael Winterbottom (eds.). *Wulfstan of Winchester: Life of St Æthelwold.* Oxford Medieval Texts. Oxford: Clarendon Press, 1991.

Liebermann, F. *Die Gesetze der Angelsachsen.* 3 vols. Halle: Niemeyer, 1903–16.

Lindsay, W. M. (ed.). *Isidori Hispalensis episcopi etymologiarum siue originum libri XX.* 2 vols. Oxford: Clarendon Press, 1911.

Malone, Kemp (ed.). *Deor.* Rev. edn. University of Exeter Press, 1977.

Miles, Brent. 'The *Carmina Rhythmica* of Æthilwald: Edition, Translation, and Commentary.' *JML* 14 (2004): 73–117.

Miller, Thomas (ed.). *The Old English Version of Bede's Ecclesiastical History of the English People.* 2 vols. in 4. EETS OS 95, 96, 110, 111. 1890–8.

Muir, Bernard J. (ed.). *The Exeter Anthology of Old English Poetry: An Edition of Exeter Dean and Chapter MS 3501.* 2 vols. University of Exeter Press, 1994.

Murison, W. (ed.). *Sir Thomas Browne: Hydriotaphia.* Cambridge University Press, 1933.

Murphy, Gerard. *Early Irish Metrics.* Dublin: Royal Irish Academy, 1961.

Mynors, R. A. B. (ed. and trans.), with R. M. Thomson and M. Winterbottom. *William of Malmesbury: Gesta Regum Anglorum: The History of the English Kings.* Vol. 1. Oxford: Clarendon Press, 1998.

Napier, Arthur (ed.). *Old English Version of the Enlarged Rule of Chrodegang . . .* EETS OS 150. 1916.

O'Brien O'Keeffe, Katherine (ed.). *The Anglo-Saxon Chronicle: A Collaborative Edition. Vol. 5: MS C.* Cambridge: D. S. Brewer, 2001.

O'Donnell, Daniel Paul (ed.). *Cædmon's Hymn: A Multi-media Study, Edition, and Archive.* Cambridge: D. S. Brewer, 2005.

Plummer, Charles (ed.). *Venerabilis Baedae opera historica.* 2 vols. Oxford: Clarendon Press, 1896.

Scragg, D. G. (ed.). *The Battle of Maldon.* Manchester University Press, 1981.

Smith, A. H. (ed.). *Three Northumbrian Poems.* New York: Appleton-Century-Crofts, 1968.

Stevenson, William Henry (ed.). *Asser's Life of King Alfred, together with the Annals of Saint Neots.* Rev. edn. Oxford: Clarendon Press, 1959.

Strecker, Karl (ed.). *Miracula Nynie Episcopi.* MGH PLAC 4, iii. 1923.

Stubbs, William (ed.). *Memorials of Saint Dunstan.* Rolls Series. London: Longman, 1874.

Tangl, Michael (ed.). *Die Briefe des heiligen Bonifatius und Lullus.* MGH ES 1. 1916.

Ure, James M. (ed.). *The Benedictine Office: An Old English Text.* Edinburgh University Press, 1957.

Winterbottom, Michael (ed.). 'An Edition of Faricius, Vita S. Aldhelmi', *JML* 15 (2006): 93–147.

Three Lives of English Saints. Toronto: Pontifical Institute of Medieval Studies, 1972.

Winterbottom, Michael, and R. M. Thomson (eds.). *William of Malmesbury: Gesta Pontificum Anglorum.* 2 vols. Oxford: Clarendon Press, 2007.

Woolf, Rosemary (ed.). *Juliana.* Methuen's Old English Library. London: Methuen, 1955.

Ziolkowski, Jan M. (ed. and trans.). *The Cambridge Songs (Carmina Cantabrigiensia)*. Tempe, AZ: Medieval & Renaissance Texts & Studies, 1998.

Zupitza, Julius (ed.). *Ælfrics Grammatik und Glossar*. Berlin: Weidmann, 1880.

SECONDARY SOURCES

Abels, Richard. 'English Tactics, Strategy and Military Organization in the Late Tenth Century.' In Scragg (ed.), *Battle of Maldon, AD 991*, pp. 143–55.

Abraham, Lenore MacGaffey. 'Cynewulf's *Juliana*: A Case at Law.' *Allegorica* 3 (1978): 172–89; repr. in Bjork (ed.), *Cynewulf Reader*, pp. 171–92.

Amodio, Mark C., and Katherine O'Brien O'Keeffe (eds.). *Unlocking the Wordhord: Anglo-Saxon Studies in Memory of Edward B. Irving, Jr.* University of Toronto Press, 2003.

Andersen, Henning. 'Center and Periphery: Adoption, Diffusion, and Spread.' In Jacek Fisiak (ed.). *Historical Dialectology: Regional and Social*. New York: Mouton de Gruyter, 1988. pp. 39–83.

Anderson, Benedict. *Imagined Communities: Reflections on the Origin and Spread of Nationalism*. Rev. edn. London; New York: Verso, 2006.

Anderson, Diane Warne. 'Medieval Teaching Texts on Syllable Quantities and the Innovations from the School of Alberic of Monte Cassino.' In Carol Dana Lanham (ed.). *Latin Grammar and Rhetoric: From Classical Theory to Medieval Practices*. London: Continuum, 2002. pp. 180–211.

Anderson, Earl R. *Cynewulf: Structure, Style, and Theme in his Poetry*. Rutherford, NJ: Fairleigh Dickinson University Press, 1983.

Anderson, L. F. *The Anglo-Saxon Scop*. University of Toronto Studies, Philological Series 1. Toronto University Library, 1903.

Arendt, Hannah. *Lectures on Kant's Political Philosophy*. Ed. Ronald Beiner. University of Chicago Press, 1982.

Baker, Peter S. 'A Little-Known Variant Text of the Old English Metrical Psalms.' *Speculum* 59 (1984): 263–81.

Bately, Janet M. 'Did King Alfred Actually Translate Anything? The Integrity of the Alfredian Canon Revisited.' *Medium Ævum* 78 (2009): 189–215.

'England and the Continent in the Anglo-Saxon Period.' In Nigel Saul (ed.). *England in Europe: 1066–1453*. New York: St Martin's Press, 1994. pp. 21–35.

'Grimbald of St Bertin's.' *Medium Ævum* 35 (1966): 1–10.

'Old English Prose Before and During the Reign of Alfred.' *ASE* 17 (1988): 93–138.

Bayless, Martha. 'Alcuin's Disputatio Pippini and the Early Medieval Riddle Tradition.' In Guy Halsall (ed.). *Humour, History and Politics in Late Antiquity and the Early Middle Ages*. Cambridge University Press, 2002. pp. 157–78.

Bedingfield, M. Bradford. 'Anglo-Saxons on Fire.' *Journal of Theological Studies* 52 (2001): 658–77.

Biggs, Frederick M., Thomas D. Hill, Paul E. Szarmach, and E. Gordon Whatley (eds.). *Sources of Anglo-Saxon Literary Culture, Volume I*. Kalamazoo, MI: Medieval Institute Publications, 2001.

Bischoff, Bernhard. 'Lorsch im Spiegel seiner Handschriften.' In Friedrich Knöpp (ed.). *Die Reichsabtei Lorsch: Festschrift zum Gedenken an ihre Stiftung 764*. 2 vols. Darmstadt: Hessische Historische Kommission, 1977. Vol. II, pp. 7–125.

Bischoff, Bernhard, and Michael Lapidge (eds.). *Biblical Commentaries from the Canterbury School of Theodore and Hadrian*. CSASE 10. 1994.

Bishop, T. A. M. *English Caroline Minuscule*. Oxford: Clarendon Press, 1971.

Bitterli, Dieter. *Say What I Am Called: The Old English Riddles of the Exeter Book and the Anglo-Latin Riddle Tradition*. University of Toronto Press, 2009.

Bjork, Robert (ed.). *Cynewulf: Basic Readings*. New York: Garland, 1996.

The Cynewulf Reader. New York: Routledge, 2001.

Blair, John. *The Church in Anglo-Saxon Society*. Oxford University Press, 2005.

Blake, N. F. 'The Battle of Maldon.' *Neophilologus* 49 (1965): 332–45.

'The Genesis of *The Battle of Maldon*.' *ASE* 7 (1978): 119–29.

Bloomfield, Morton W. 'Beowulf, Byrhtnoth, and the Judgment of God.' *Speculum* 44 (1969): 545–59.

Bloomfield, Morton W., and Charles W. Dunn. *The Role of the Poet in Early Societies*. Cambridge: D. S. Brewer, 1989.

Bolton, W. F. *A History of Anglo-Latin Literature, 597–1066. Vol. I: 597–740*. Princeton University Press, 1967.

Bonner, Gerald (ed.). *Famulus Christi: Essays in Commemoration of the Thirteenth Centenary of the Birth of the Venerable Bede*. London: SPCK, 1976.

Bonner, Gerald, David Rollason, and Clare Stancliffe (eds.). *St Cuthbert, his Cult and his Community to AD 1200*. Woodbridge: Boydell, 1989.

Boynton, Susan. 'The Didactic Function and Context of Eleventh-Century Glossed Hymnaries.' In Andreas Haug, Christoph März and Lorenz Welker (eds.). *Der lateinische Hymnus im Mittelalter*. Kassel: Bärenreiter, 2004. pp. 301–29.

'The Sources and Significance of the Orpheus Myth in *Musica Enchiriadis* and Regino of Prüm's *Epistola de harmonica institutione*.' *Early Music History* 18 (1999): 47–74.

'Training for the Liturgy as a Form of Monastic Education.' In George Ferzoco and Carolyn Muessig (eds.). *Medieval Monastic Education*. London: Leicester University Press, 2000. pp. 7–20.

Bradley, Henry. 'On Some Poems Ascribed to Aldhelm.' *English Historical Review* 15 (1900): 291–2.

Bredehoft, Thomas A. *Authors, Audiences, and Old English Verse*. University of Toronto Press, 2009.

Early English Metre. University of Toronto Press, 2005.

Textual Histories: Readings in the Anglo-Saxon Chronicle. University of Toronto Press, 2001.

Brehe, S. K. 'Reassembling the *First Worcester Fragment*.' *Speculum* 65 (1990): 521–36.

Brooks, Nicholas. *The Early History of the Church of Canterbury: Christ Church from 597 to 1066*. London: Leicester University Press, 1984.

Brown, Carleton F. 'Cynewulf and Alcuin.' *PMLA* 18 (1903): 308–34.

Brown, George Hardin. *A Companion to Bede*. Woodbridge: Boydell, 2009.

'The Descent-Ascent Motif in *Christ II* of Cynewulf.' *JEGP* 73 (1974): 1–12; repr. in Bjork (ed.), *Cynewulf Reader*, pp. 133–46.

Brown, Michelle P. 'Female Book-Ownership and Production in Anglo-Saxon England: the Evidence of the Ninth-Century Prayerbooks.' In Kay and Sylvester (eds.). *Lexis and Texts*, pp. 45–67.

The Lindisfarne Gospels: Society, Spirituality, and the Scribe. University of Toronto Press, 2003.

Brown, Phyllis Rugg, Georgia Ronan Crampton, and Fred C. Robinson (eds.). *Modes of Interpretation in Old English Literature*. Toronto University Press, 1986.

Budny, Mildred. '"St Dunstan's Classbook" and its Frontispiece: Dunstan's Portrait and Autograph.' In Nigel Ramsay *et al.* (eds.). *St Dunstan: His Life, Times, and Cult*. Woodbridge: Boydell & Brewer, 1992. pp. 103–42.

Bullough, Donald A. *Alcuin: Achievement and Reputation*. Leiden: Brill, 2004.

'Charlemagne's "Men of God": Alcuin, Hildebald, and Arn.' In Joanna Story (ed.). *Charlemagne: Empire and Society*. Manchester University Press, 2005. pp. 136–50.

'The Continental Background of the Reform.' In David Parsons (ed.). *Tenth-Century Studies*. London: Phillimore, 1975. pp. 20–36.

Butler, Sharon E. 'The Cynewulf Question Revived.' *Neuphilologische Mitteilungen* 83 (1982): 15–23.

Caie, Graham D. *A Bibliography of the Junius XI Manuscript: With an Appendix on Cædmon's Hymn*. University of Copenhagen, 1979.

Calder, Daniel G., and Michael J. B. Allen. *Sources and Analogues of Old English Poetry: The Major Latin Texts in Translation*. Cambridge: D. S. Brewer, 1976.

Cameron, M. L. 'The Sources of Medical Knowledge in Anglo-Saxon England.' *ASE* 11 (1983): 135–55.

Campbell, Alistair. *Skaldic Verse and Anglo-Saxon History: The Dorothea Coke Memorial Lecture in Northern Studies*. London: H. K. Lewis for University College London, 1971.

Campbell, James. 'Anglo-Saxon Courts.' In Cubitt (ed.), *Court Culture*, pp. 155–69.

'Elements in the Background to the Life of St Cuthbert and his Early Cult.' In Bonner *et al.* (eds.), *St Cuthbert, his Cult*, pp. 3–19.

'England, c. 991.' In Cooper (ed.), *Battle of Maldon*, pp. 1–17.

Campbell, Lyle, and Martha C. Muntzel. 'The Structural Consequences of Language Death.' In Nancy C. Dorian (ed.). *Investigating Obsolescence: Studies in Language Contraction and Death*. Cambridge University Press, 1989. pp. 181–96.

Carroll, Jayne. 'Concepts of Power in Anglo-Scandinavian Verse.' In Brenda Bolton and Christine Meek (eds.). *Aspects of Power and Authority in the Middle Ages*. Turnhout: Brepols, 2007. pp. 217–33.

Carver, Martin. 'Intellectual Communities in Early Northumbria.' In David Petts and Sam Turner (eds.). *Early Medieval Northumbria: Kingdoms and Communities, AD 450–1100*. Turnhout: Brepols, 2011. pp. 185–206.

Chase, Colin (ed.). *The Dating of Beowulf*. Toronto University Press, 1981 (repr. 1997).

Clemoes, Peter. 'Cynewulf's Image of the Ascension.' In Peter Clemoes and Kathleen Hughes (eds.). *England Before the Conquest*. Cambridge University Press, 1971; repr. in Bjork (ed.), *Cynewulf Reader*, pp. 109–32.

'Style as the Criterion for Dating the Composition of *Beowulf*.' In Chase (ed.), *Dating*, pp. 173–85.

Conner, Patrick W. 'On Dating Cynewulf.' In Bjork (ed.), *Cynewulf: Basic Readings*, pp. 3–22; repr. in Bjork (ed.), *Cynewulf Reader*, pp. 23–56.

Contreni, John J. 'The Pursuit of Knowledge in Carolingian Europe.' In Richard E. Sullivan (ed.). *'The Gentle Voices of Teachers': Aspects of Learning in the Carolingian Age*. Columbus: Ohio State University Press, 1995. pp. 106–41.

Cook, Albert Stanburrough. *The Possible Begetter of the Old English Beowulf and Widsith. Transactions of the Connecticut Academy of Arts and Sciences* 25 (1922): 281–346.

Cooper, Janet (ed.). *The Battle of Maldon: Fiction and Fact*. Rio Grande: Hambledon, 1993.

Cross, J. E. 'Cynewulf's Traditions about the Apostles in *The Fates of the Apostles*.' *ASE* 8 (1979); repr. in Bjork (ed.), *Cynewulf Reader*, pp. 79–93.

Cubitt, Catherine (ed.). *Court Culture in the Early Middle Ages: Proceedings of the First Alcuin Conference*. Turnhout: Brepols, 2003.

Curtius, Ernst Robert. *European Literature and the Latin Middle Ages*. Trans. Willard R. Trask. Bollingen Series 36. Princeton University Press, 1953 (repr. 1990).

Das, Satyendra Kumar. *Cynewulf and the Cynewulf Canon*. Calcutta University Press, 1942.

Davis, Craig R. 'Cultural Historicity in the *Battle of Maldon*.' *Philological Quarterly* 78 (1999): 151–69.

Davíðsdóttir, Sigrún. 'Old Norse Court Poetry: Some Notes on its Purpose, Transmission and Historical Value.' *Gripla* 3 (1979): 186–203.

de Jong, Mayke. *In Samuel's Image: Child Oblation in the Early Medieval West*. New York: Brill, 1996.

DeGregorio, Scott. 'Footsteps of His Own: Bede's Commentary on Ezra-Nehemiah.' In DeGregorio (ed.), *Innovation and Tradition*, pp. 143–68.

(ed.). *The Cambridge Companion to Bede*. Cambridge University Press, 2010.

(ed.). *Innovation and Tradition in the Writings of the Venerable Bede*. Morgantown: West Virginia University Press, 2006.

Deleuze, Gilles. 'The Simulacrum and Ancient Philosophy.' In *The Logic of Sense*, trans. Mark Lester, ed. Constantin V. Boundas. New York: Columbia University Press, 1990. pp. 253–79.

Díaz y Díaz, Manuel C., and José M. Díaz de Bustamante (eds.). *Poesía latina medieval (siglos V–XV)*. Florence: SISMEL, 2005.

Dilkey, M. C., and H. Schneider. 'John Mitchell Kemble and the Brothers Grimm.' *JEGP* 40 (1941): 461–73.

DiNapoli, Robert. 'In The Kingdom of the Blind, the One-Eyed Man is a Seller of Garlic: Depth-Perception and the Poet's Perspective in the Exeter Book Riddles.' *English Studies* 81 (2000): 422–55.

'Poesis and Authority: Traces of an Anglo-Saxon *Agon* in Cynewulf's *Elene.*' *Neophilologus* 82 (1998): 619–30.

Discenza, Nicole Guenther. 'Power, Skill and Virtue in the Old English *Boethius.*' *ASE* 26 (1997): 81–108.

'The Unauthorized Biographies of Anicius Manlius Severinus Boethius.' Given at the first annual symposium of The Alfredian Boethius Project, University of Oxford, July 2003. Retrieved from www.english.ox.ac.uk/boethius/ Symposium2003.html (accessed 6/10/11).

Di Sciacca, Claudia. *Finding the Right Words: Isidore's Synonyma in Anglo-Saxon England.* University of Toronto Press, 2008.

Doane, A. N. '"The Green Street of Paradise": A Note on Lexis and Meaning in Old English Poetry.' *Neuphilologische Mitteilungen* 74 (1973): 456–65.

Doane, A. N., and Carol Braun Pasternack (eds.). *Vox Intexta: Orality and Textuality in the Middle Ages.* Madison: University of Wisconsin Press, 1991.

Dockray-Miller, Mary. *Motherhood and Mothering in Anglo-Saxon England.* New York: St Martin's Press, 2000.

Dodwell, C. R. *Anglo-Saxon Art: A New Perspective.* Manchester University Press, 1982.

Donoghue, Daniel. *Style in Old English Poetry: The Test of the Auxiliary.* New Haven, CT: Yale University Press, 1987.

Drout, Michael D. C. *How Tradition Works: A Meme-Based Cultural Poetics of the Anglo-Saxon Tenth Century.* Medieval and Renaissance Texts and Studies 306. Tempe, AZ: ACMRS, 2006.

Dümmler, Ernst. 'Lorscher Rätsel.' *Zeitschrift für deutsches Altertum und deutsche Literatur* 22 (1878): 258–63.

Dumville, David N. *English Caroline Script and Monastic History.* Woodbridge: Boydell, 1993.

'English Script in the Second Half of the Ninth Century.' In O'Brien O'Keeffe and Orchard (eds.), *Latin Learning*, vol. I, pp. 305–25.

Earl, James W. *Thinking about 'Beowulf'.* Stanford University Press, 1994.

Earle, John. *The Deeds of Beowulf: An English Epic of the Eighth Century, Done into Modern Prose.* Oxford: Clarendon Press, 1892.

Elias, Norbert. *The Court Society.* Trans. Edmund Jephcott. University College Dublin Press, 2006.

What is Sociology? Trans. Stephen Mennell and Grace Morrissey. New York: Columbia University Press, 1978.

Eliason, Norman E. 'The "Improvised Lay" in *Beowulf.*' *Philological Quarterly* 31 (1952): 171–9.

Emms, Richard. 'The Scribe of the Paris Psalter.' *ASE* 28 (1999): 179–83.

Farmer, D. H. 'Saint Wilfrid.' In Kirby (ed.), *Saint Wilfrid at Hexham*, pp. 35–59.

Fassler, Margot E. 'The Office of the Cantor in Early Western Monastic Rules and Customaries: A Preliminary Investigation.' *Early Music History* 5 (1985): 29–51.

Festinger, Leon. 'A Theory of Social Comparison Processes.' *Human Relations* 7 (1954): 117–40.

Finch, Chauncey E. 'Symphosius in Codices Pal. Lat. 1719, 1753 and Reg. Lat. 329, 2078.' *Manuscripta* 13 (1969): 3–11.

Fjalldall, Magnús. *Anglo-Saxon England in Icelandic Medieval Texts*. University of Toronto Press, 2005.

Fleischmann, Suzanne. 'Evaluation in Narrative: The Present Tense in Medieval "Performed Stories".' *Yale French Studies* 70 (1986): 199–251.

Foot, Sarah. *Æthelstan: The First King of England*. New Haven, CT: Yale University Press, 2011.

Fox, Michael, and Manish Sharma (eds.). *Old English Literature and the Old Testament*. University of Toronto Press, 2012.

Frank, Roberta. 'Did Anglo-Saxon Audiences have a Skaldic Tooth?' *Scandinavian Studies* 59 (1987): 338–55.

'The Ideal of Men Dying with their Lord in The Battle of Maldon: Anachronism or Nouvelle vague.' In Ian Wood and Niels Lund (eds.). *People and Places in Northern Europe, 500–1600*. Woodbridge: Boydell, 1991. pp. 95–106.

Old Norse Court Poetry: The Dróttkvaett Stanza. Ithaca, NY: Cornell University Press, 1978.

'The Search for the Anglo-Saxon Oral Poet.' *Bulletin of the John Rylands University Library of Manchester* 75 (1993): 11–36.

'Skaldic Verse and the Date of *Beowulf*.' In Chase (ed.), *Dating*, pp. 121–39.

Frantzen, Allen J. 'The Form and Function of the Preface in the Poetry and Prose of Alfred's Reign.' In Reuter (ed.), *Alfred the Great*, pp. 121–36.

Franzen, Christine. *The Tremulous Hand of Worcester: A Study of Old English in the Thirteenth Century*. Oxford: Clarendon Press, 1991.

Frese, Dolores Warwick. 'The Art of Cynewulf's Runic Signatures.' In Lewis E. Nicholson and Dolores Warwick Frese (eds.). *Anglo-Saxon Poetry: Essays in Appreciation*. University of Notre Dame Press, 1975; repr. in Bjork (ed.), *Cynewulf Reader*, pp. 323–46.

Fulk, R. D. 'Cynewulf: Canon, Dialect, and Date.' In Bjork (ed.), *Cynewulf: Basic Readings*, pp. 23–55; repr. in Bjork (ed.), *Cynewulf Reader*, pp. 3–21.

A History of Old English Meter. Philadelphia: University of Pennsylvania Press, 1992.

'The Origin of the Numbered Sections in *Beowulf* and in Other Old English Poems.' *ASE* 35 (2006): 91–109.

Gade, Kari Ellen. 'Poetry and its Changing Importance in Medieval Icelandic Culture.' In Margaret Clunies Ross (ed.). *Old Icelandic Literature and Society*. Cambridge University Press, 2000. pp. 61–95.

Gameson, Richard. 'The Colophon of the Eadwig Gospels.' *ASE* 31 (2002): 201–22.

The Scribe Speaks? Colophons in Early English Manuscripts. H.M. Chadwick Memorial Lectures 12. Cambridge: Department of Anglo-Saxon, Norse and Celtic, 2002.

Garrison, Mary. 'Alcuin and Tibullus.' In Díaz y Díaz and Díaz de Bustamante (eds.), *Poesía latina medieval*, pp. 749–59.

'The Emergence of Carolingian Latin Literature and the Court of Charlemagne (780–814).' In Rosamond McKitterick (ed.). *Carolingian Culture: Emulation and Innovation*. Cambridge University Press, 1994. pp. 111–40.

'The English and the Irish at the Court of Charlemagne.' In P. Butzer, M. Kerner and W. Oberschelp (eds.). *Karl der Grosse und sein Nachtwirken: 1200 Jahre Kultur und Wissenschaft in Europa. Band I. Wissen und Weltbild.* Turnhout: Brepols, 1997. pp. 97–123.

'The Social World of Alcuin: Nicknames at York and at the Carolingian Court.' In Houwen and MacDonald (eds.), *Alcuin*, pp. 59–79.

Garver, Valerie L. 'Learned Women? Liutberga and the Instruction of Carolingian Women.' In Wormald and Nelson (eds.), *Lay Intellectuals*, pp. 121–38.

Gibson, Margaret, T. A. Heslop, and Richard W. Pfaff (eds.). *The Eadwine Psalter: Text, Image, and Monastic Culture in Twelfth-Century Canterbury.* London: Modern Humanities Research Association, 1992.

Gittos, Helen. 'Is there Any Evidence for the Liturgy of Parish Churches in Late Anglo-Saxon England?' In Francesca Tinti (ed.). *Pastoral Care in Late Anglo-Saxon England.* Woodbridge: Boydell, 2005. pp. 63–82.

Gneuss, Helmut. 'The Battle of Maldon 89: Byrhtnoð's *ofermod* Once Again.' *Studies in Philology* 73 (1976): 117–37.

'Dunstan und Hrabanus Maurus: zur HS Bodleian Auctarium F.4.32.' *Anglia* 96 (1978): 136–48.

Hymnar und Hymnen im Englischen Mittelalter. Tübingen: Niemeyer, 1968.

'King Alfred and the History of Anglo-Saxon Libraries.' In Brown *et al.* (eds.), *Modes of Interpretation*, pp. 29–49.

Lehnbildungen und Lehnbedeutungen im Altenglischen. Berlin: Erich Schmidt, 1955.

Review of J. D. A. Ogilvy, *Books Known to the English, 597–1066. Anglia* 89 (1971): 129–34.

Godden, M. R. 'Did King Alfred Write Anything?' *Medium Ævum* 76 (2007): 1–23.

'Editing Old English and the Problem of Alfred's *Boethius.*' In D. G. Scragg and Paul E. Szarmach (eds.). *The Editing of Old English: Papers from the 1990 Manchester Conference.* Cambridge: D. S. Brewer, 1994. pp. 163–76.

'The Player King: Identification and Self-Representation in King Alfred's Writings.' In Reuter (ed.), *Alfred the Great*, pp. 137–50.

Godman, Peter. 'Alcuin's Poetic Style and the Authenticity of *O mea cella.*' *Studi medievali* 20.2 (1979): 555–83.

'The Anglo-Latin *Opus Geminatum*: From Aldhelm to Alcuin.' *Medium Ævum* 50 (1981): 215–29.

Poets and Emperors: Frankish Politics and Carolingian Poetry. Oxford: Clarendon Press, 1987.

Goffart, Walter. *The Narrators of Barbarian History (AD 500–800): Jordanes, Gregory of Tours, Bede, and Paul the Deacon.* Princeton University Press, 1988.

Gorman, Michael. 'The Codex Amiatinus: A Guide to the Legends and Bibliography.' *Studi medievali* 3rd ser. 44 (2003): 863–910.

Graham, Timothy (ed.). *The Recovery of Old English: Anglo-Saxon Studies in the Sixteenth and Seventeenth Centuries.* Kalamazoo, MI: Medieval Institute Publications, 2000.

Gransden, Antonia. 'Abbo of Fleury's *Passio Sancti Eadmundi.*' *Revue Bénédictine* 105 (1995): 20–78.

Green, Roger P. H. *Latin Epics of the New Testament: Juvencus, Sedulius, Arator.* Oxford University Press, 2006.

Greenblatt, Stephen, and others (eds.). *The Norton Anthology of English Literature.* 8th edn. 2 vols. New York: W. W. Norton, 2006.

Greenfield, Stanley B. 'The Formulaic Expression of the Theme of "Exile" in Anglo-Saxon Poetry.' *Speculum* 30 (1955): 200–6.

Greenfield, Stanley B., and Daniel G. Calder. *A New Critical History of Old English Literature.* New York University Press, 1986.

Gretsch, Mechthild. *The Intellectual Foundations of the English Benedictine Reform.* Cambridge University Press, 1999.

Griffith, Mark. 'The Composition of the Metres.' In *OEB*, vol. 1, pp. 80–134.

'Poetic Language and the Paris Psalter: The Decay of the Old English Tradition.' *ASE* 20 (1991): 167–86.

Groschopp, Friedrich. *Das angelsächsische Gedicht 'Crist und Satan'.* Inaugural dissertation, University of Leipzig. Halle: E. Karras, 1883.

Hansen, Elaine Tuttle. *The Solomon Complex: Reading Wisdom in Old English Poetry.* University of Toronto Press, 1988.

Harris, Stephen J. 'Happiness and the Psalms.' In Fox and Sharma (eds.), *Old Testament*, pp. 292–314.

Hauck, Karl. 'Karolingische Taufpfalzen im Spiegel hofnaher Dichtung: Überlegungen zur Ausmalung von Pfalzkirchen, Pfalzen und Reichsklöstern.' *Nachrichten der Akademie der Wissenschaften in Göttingen: I. Phil.-hist. Klasse* (1985). pp. 1–96.

Heikkinen, Seppo. 'Vergilian Quotations in Bede's *De arte metrica*.' *JML* 17 (2007): 101–9.

Heinzelmann, Martin. '*Studia sanctorum*: éducation, milieux d'instruction et valeurs éducatives dans l'hagiographie en Gaule jusq'à la fin de l'époque mérovingienne.' In Sot (ed.), *Haut Moyen-Age*, pp. 105–38.

Herren, Michael W. 'Scholarly Contacts Between the Irish and the Southern English in the Seventh Century.' *Peritia* 12 (1998): 24–53.

'The Stress Systems in Insular Latin Octosyllabic Verse.' *Cambridge Medieval Celtic Studies* 15 (1988): 63–84.

(ed.). *Insular Latin Studies.* University of Toronto Press, 1981.

Herzog, Reinhart. *Der Bibelepik der lateinischen Spätantike.* Munich: Wilhelm Fink, 1975.

Higham, N. J. *The Convert Kings: Power and Religious Affiliation in Early Anglo-Saxon England.* Manchester University Press, 1997.

Hill, Thomas D. 'Sapiental Structure and Figural Narrative in the Old English *Elene*.' In Bjork (ed.), *Cynewulf Reader*, pp. 207–28.

Hollis, Stephanie. *Anglo-Saxon Women and the Church: Sharing a Common Fate.* Cambridge: Boydell, 1992.

Hollowell, Ida Masters. '*Scop* and *Woðbora* in OE Poetry.' *JEGP* 77 (1978): 317–29.

Hoover, David L. 'Evidence for Primacy of Alliteration in Old English Metre.' *ASE* 14 (1985): 75–96.

Horgan, Dorothy M. 'The Relationship between the OE MSS of King Alfred's Translation of Gregory's Pastoral Care.' *Anglia* 91 (1973): 153–69.

Houwen, L. A. J. R., and A. A. MacDonald (eds.). *Alcuin of York: Scholar at the Carolingian Court.* Germania Latina 3. Groningen: Egbert Forsten, 1998.

Howe, Nicholas. 'Aldhelm's *Enigmata* and Isidorean Etymology.' *ASE* 14 (1985): 37–59.

   Migration and Mythmaking in Anglo-Saxon England. New Haven, CT: Yale University Press, 1989; repr. with new introduction, University of Notre Dame Press, 2001.

Howlett, David. 'Aldhelm and Irish Learning.' *Bulletin du Cange: Archivum Latinitatis Medii Aevi* 52 (1994): 37–75.

   'Seven Studies in Seventh-Century Texts.' *Peritia* 10 (1996): 1–70.

Hutcheson, B. R. *Old English Poetic Metre.* Cambridge: D. S. Brewer, 1995.

Ireland, Colin. 'Aldfrith of Northumbria and the Irish Genealogies.' *Celtica* 22 (1991): 64–78.

   'Aldfrith of Northumbria and the Learning of a *Sapiens*.' In Kathryn A. Klar, Eve E. Sweetser, and Claire Thomas (eds.). *A Celtic Florilegium: Studies in Memory of Brendan O Hehir.* Lawrence, MA: Celtic Studies Publications, 1996. pp. 63–77.

Irvine, Martin. *The Making of Textual Culture: Grammatica and Literary Theory, 350–1100.* Cambridge Studies in Medieval Literature 19. Cambridge University Press, 1994.

Irving, Edward B., Jr. 'Crucifixion Witnessed, or Dramatic Interaction in *The Dream of the Rood*.' In Brown *et al.* (eds.), *Modes of Interpretation*, pp. 101–13.

   'The Heroic Style in *The Battle of Maldon*.' *Studies in Philology* 58 (1961): 457–67.

Isaacs, Neil D. *Structural Principles in Old English Poetry.* Knoxville: University of Tennessee Press, 1968.

Jacobs, Nicolas. 'Anglo-Danish Relations, Poetic Archaism and the Date of *Beowulf*.' *Poetica* 8 (1977): 23–43.

Jarman, A. O. H., and Gwilym Rees Hughes (eds.). *A Guide to Welsh Literature: Volume 1.* 2nd edn. Cardiff: University of Wales Press, 1992.

John, Eric. *Reassessing Anglo-Saxon England.* Manchester University Press, 1996.

Jones, Christopher A. 'Wulfstan's Liturgical Interests.' In Matthew Townend (ed.). *Wulfstan, Archbishop of York.* Turnhout: Brepols, 2004. pp. 325–52.

Kant, Immanuel. *The Critique of Judgement.* Trans. James Creed Meredith. Oxford: Clarendon Press, 1952.

Karkov, Catherine E., and George Hardin Brown (eds.). *Anglo-Saxon Styles.* Albany, NY: SUNY Press, 2003.

Kay, Christian J., and Louise M. Sylvester (eds.). *Lexis and Texts in Early English: Studies Presented to Jane Roberts.* Costerus New Series 133. Amsterdam: Rodopi, 2001.

Keeffer, Sarah Larratt. '"Ic" and "We" in Eleventh-Century Old English Liturgical Verse.' In Amodio and O'Brien O'Keeffe (eds.), *Unlocking the Wordhord*, pp. 123–46.

   'Respect for the Book: A Reconsideration of "Form," "Content," and "Context" in Two Vernacular Poems.' In Keeffer and O'Brien O'Keeffe (eds.), *New Approaches to Editing*, pp. 21–44.

Keeffer, Sarah Larratt and Katherine O'Brien O'Keeffe (eds.). *New Approaches to Editing Old English Verse*. Cambridge: D. S. Brewer, 1998.

Keenan, Hugh T. 'Exodus 312: 'The Green Street of Paradise'.' *Neuphilologische Mitteilungen* 71 (1970): 455–60.

Kemble, John M. 'On Anglo-Saxon Runes.' *Archaeologia* 28 (1840): 327–72.

Kendall, Calvin B. 'Bede and Education.' In DeGregorio (ed.), *Companion to Bede*, pp. 99–112.

The Metrical Grammar of Beowulf. CSASE 5. Cambridge University Press, 1991.

Kerlouegan, François. 'Essai sur la mise en nourriture et l'éducation dans les pays celtiques d'après le témoignage des textes hagiographiques latins.' *Études celtiques* 12 (1969): 101–46.

Keynes, Simon. 'The Cult of King Alfred the Great.' *ASE* 28 (1999): 225–356.

'King Athelstan's Books.' In Lapidge and Gneuss, *Learning and Literature*, pp. 143–201.

Keynes, Simon, and Michael Lapidge. *Alfred the Great: Asser's Life of King Alfred and Other Contemporary Sources*. Harmondsworth: Penguin, 1983.

Kightley, Michael R. 'Communal Interdependence in *The Battle of Maldon*.' *Studia Neophilologica* 82 (2010): 58–68.

Kirby, D. P. 'Bede, Eddius Stephanus, and the "Life of Wilfred".' *English Historical Review* 98 (1983): 101–14.

(ed.). *Saint Wilfrid at Hexham* (Newcastle upon Tyne: Oriel, 1974).

Kleist, Aaron J. (ed.). *The Old English Homily: Precedent, Practice, and Appropriation*. Studies in the Early Middle Ages 17. Turnhout: Brepols, 2007.

Klinck, Anne L. *The Old English Elegies: A Critical Edition and Genre Study*. Montreal: McGill-Queen's University Press, 1992.

Knappe, Gabriele. 'Classical Rhetoric in Anglo-Saxon England.' *ASE* 27 (1998): 5–29.

Traditionen der klassischen Rhetorik im angelsächsischen England. Heidelberg: C. Winter, 1996.

Labov, William. *Language in the Inner City: Studies in the Black English Vernacular*. Philadelphia: University of Pennsylvania Press, 1972.

'The Social Motivation of a Sound Change.' *Word* 19.3 (1963): 273–309.

Sociolinguistic Patterns. Philadelphia: University of Pennsylvania Press, 1972.

Labov, William, and Joshua Waletsky. 'Narrative Analysis: Oral Versions of Personal Experience.' In June Helm (ed.). *Essays on the Verbal and Visual Arts*. Proceedings of the American Ethnological Society. Seattle: University of Washington Press, 1966. pp. 12–44.

Lapidge, Michael. 'Aediluulf and the School of York.' In his *Anglo-Latin Literature, 600–899*, pp. 381–98.

'Aldhelm's Latin Poetry and Old English Verse.' In his *Anglo-Latin Literature, 600–899*, pp. 247–69.

'Anglo-Latin Literature.' In his *Anglo-Latin Literature, 600–899*, pp. 1–35.

Anglo-Latin Literature, 600–899. London: Hambledon Press, 1996.

Anglo-Latin Literature, 900–1066. London: Hambledon Press, 1993.

The Anglo-Saxon Library. Oxford University Press, 2006.

'Autographs of Insular Latin Authors of the Early Middle Ages.' In Paolo Chiesa and Lucia Pinelli (eds.). *Gli autografi medievali: problemi paleografici e filologici.* Spoleto: Centro Italiano di Studi Sull'alto Medioevo, 1994. pp. 103–36.

'Bede the Poet.' In his *Anglo-Latin Literature, 600–899*, pp. 313–38.

'Bede and the Poetic Diction of Vergil.' In Díaz y Díaz and Díaz de Bustamante (eds.), *Poesía latina medieval*, pp. 739–48.

'Bede and the "Versus de die iudicii".' In Bihrer, Andreas, and Elisabeth Stein (eds.). *Nova de veteribus: Mittel- und neulateinische Studien für Paul Gerhard Schmidt.* Munich: KG Saur, 2004. pp. 103–11.

'Bede's Metrical *Vita S. Cuthberti.*' In his *Anglo-Latin Literature, 600–899*, pp. 339–55.

'The Career of Aldhelm.' *ASE* 36 (2007): 15–69.

'The Career of Archbishop Theodore.' In Lapidge (ed.), *Archbishop Theodore*, pp. 1–29.

The Cult of St Swithun. Winchester Studies 4.ii. Oxford: Clarendon Press, 2003.

'Cynewulf and the *Passio S. Iulianae.*' In Amodio and O'Brien O'Keeffe (eds.), *Unlocking the Wordhord*, pp. 147–71.

'The Hermeneutic Style in Tenth-Century Anglo-Latin Literature.' In his *Anglo-Latin Literature, 900–1066*, pp. 105–49.

'Israel the Grammarian in Anglo-Saxon England.' In his *Anglo-Latin Literature, 900–1066*, pp. 87–104.

'Latin Learning in Ninth-Century England.' In his *Anglo-Latin Literature, 600–899*, pp. 409–54.

'The *Life of St Oswald.*' In Scragg (ed.), *Battle of Maldon, AD 991*, pp. 51–8.

'The Present State of Anglo-Latin Studies.' In Herren (ed.), *Insular Latin*, pp. 45–82.

'Rufinus at the School of Canterbury.' In Pierre Lardet (ed.). *La tradition vive: mélanges d'histoire des textes en l'honneur de Louis Holtz.* Manuscripta 20. Turnhout: Brepols, 2003. pp. 119–29.

'A Seventh-Century Insular Latin Debate Poem on Divorce.' *Cambridge Medieval Celtic Studies* 10 (1985): 1–23.

'Some Remnants of Bede's Lost Liber Epigrammatum.' In his *Anglo-Latin Literature, 600–899*, pp. 357–79.

'St Dunstan's Latin Poetry.' In his *Anglo-Latin Literature, 900–1066*, pp. 151–6.

'The Study of Latin Texts in Late Anglo-Saxon England.' In his *Anglo-Latin Literature, 600–899*, pp. 455–98.

'Surviving Booklists from Anglo-Saxon England.' In Lapidge and Gneuss (eds.), *Learning and Literature*, pp. 33–89.

'Theodore and Anglo-Latin Octosyllabic Verse.' In his *Anglo-Latin Literature, 600–899*, pp. 225–45.

'Three Latin Poems from Æthelwold's School at Winchester.' In his *Anglo-Latin Literature, 900–1066*, pp. 225–77.

'Versifying the Bible in the Middle Ages.' In Mann and Nolan (eds.), *Text in the Community*, pp. 11–40.

(ed.). *Archbishop Theodore: Commemorative Studies on his Life and Influence.* CSASE 11. Cambridge University Press, 1995.

Lapidge, Michael, and Helmut Gneuss (eds.). *Learning and Literature in Anglo-Saxon England: Studies Presented to Peter Clemoes on the Occasion of his Sixty-Fifth Birthday.* Cambridge University Press, 1985.

Lapidge, Michael, and Michael Herren. *Aldhelm: The Prose Works.* Cambridge: D. S. Brewer, 1979.

Lapidge, Michael, and James Rosier, with Neil Wright. *Aldhelm: The Poetic Works.* Cambridge: D. S. Brewer, 1985.

Larrington, Carolyne. *A Store of Common Sense: Gnomic Theme and Style in Old Icelandic and Old English Wisdom Poetry.* Oxford: Clarendon Press, 1993.

Law, Vivien. *The Insular Latin Grammarians.* Woodbridge: Boydell, 1982.

Le Page, R. B. 'Alliterative Patterns as a Test of Style in Old English Poetry.' *JEGP* 58 (1959): 434–41.

Lendinara, Patrizia. 'Abbo of Fleury.' In Biggs *et al.* (eds.), *Sources of Anglo-Saxon Literary Culture*, pp. 1–15.

'Gli *Aenigmata Laureshamensia.*' *Pan* 7 (1981): 73–90.

'Instructional Manuscripts in England: the Tenth- and Eleventh-Century Codices and the Early Norman Ones.' In Lendinara *et al.* (eds.), *Form and Content of Instruction*, pp. 59–113.

'Mixed Attitudes to Ovid: The Carolingian Poets and the Glossographers.' In Houwen and MacDonald (eds.), *Alcuin*, pp. 171–213.

'An Old English Gloss to the Scholica graecarum glossarum.' In her *Anglo-Saxon Glosses and Glossaries.* Aldershot: Ashgate Variorum, 1999. pp. 149–56.

'Translating Doomsday: De die iudicii and its Old English Translation (Judgment Day II).' In Hans Sauer and Renate Bauer (eds.). *Beowulf and Beyond.* Frankfurt am Main: Peter Lang, 2007. pp. 17–67.

Lendinara, Patrizia, Loredana Lazzari, and Maria Amalia D'Aronco (eds.). *Form and Content of Instruction in Anglo-Saxon England in the Light of Contemporary Manuscript Evidence.* Textes et études du moyen âge 39. Turnhout: Brepols, 2007.

Lenker, Ursula. 'The Monasteries of the Benedictine Reform and the "Winchester School": Model Cases of Social Networks in Anglo-Saxon England?' *European Journal of English Studies* 4 (2000): 225–38.

Leonhardt, Jürgen. *Dimensio syllabarum: Studien zur lateinischen Prosodie- und Verslehre von der Spätantike bis zur frühen Renaissance.* Göttingen: Vandenhoeck & Ruprecht, 1985.

Lerer, Seth. *Literacy and Power in Anglo-Saxon Literature.* Lincoln: University of Nebraska Press, 1991.

'Old English and its Afterlife.' In David Wallace (ed.). *The Cambridge History of Medieval English Literature.* Cambridge University Press, 1999. pp. 7–34.

'The Riddle and the Book: Exeter Book Riddle 42 in Its Contexts.' *Papers on Language and Literature* 25 (1989): 3–18.

Levison, Wilhelm. 'An Eighth-Century Poem on St. Ninian.' *Antiquity* 14 (1940): 280–91.

Lewis, Ceri W. 'The Court Poets: Their Function, Status, and Craft.' In Jarman and Hughes (eds.), *Guide to Welsh Literature*, pp. 123–56.

Leyser, Karl. 'Die Ottonen und Wessex.' *Frühmittelalterliche Studien* 17 (1983): 73–97.

Liuzza, R. M. (ed.). *Old English Literature: Critical Essays*. New Haven, CT: Yale University Press, 2002.

Lloyd-Jones, J. 'The Court Poets of the Welsh Princes.' *Proceedings of the British Academy* 34 (1948): 167–97.

Locherbie-Cameron, Margaret A. L. 'The Men Named in the Poem.' In Scragg (ed.), *Battle of Maldon, AD 991*, pp. 238–49.

Lockett, Leslie. 'Oswald's *uersus retrogradi*: A Forerunner of Post-Conquest Trends in Hexameter Composition.' In *Latinity and Identity in Anglo-Saxon England* (forthcoming).

Lynch, Joseph H. *Christianizing Kinship: Ritual Sponsorship in Anglo-Saxon England*. Ithaca, NY: Cornell University Press, 1998.

Mac Eoin, Gearóid. 'Poet and Prince in Medieval Ireland.' In Evelyn Mullally and John Thompson (eds.).The Court and Cultural Diversity. Cambridge: D. S. Brewer, 1997. pp. 3–16.

Magennis, Hugh. *Images of Community in Old English Poetry*. CSASE 18. 1996.

Malone, Kemp, and Albert C. Baugh. 'The Old English Period (to 1100).' In Baugh (ed.). *A Literary History of England*. 2nd edn. London: Routledge & Kegan Paul, 1967. pp. 1–105.

Mann, Jill, and Maura Nolan (eds.). *The Text in the Community: Essays on Medieval Works, Manuscripts, Authors, and Readers*. University of Notre Dame Press, 2006.

Marsden, Richard. 'Amiatinus in Italy: The Afterlife of an Anglo-Saxon Book.' In Sauer and Story (eds.), *Anglo-Saxon England*, pp. 217–43.

Masi, Michael. 'Manuscripts Containing the *De musica* of Boethius.' *Manuscripta* 15 (1971): 89–95.

McClure, Judith. 'Bede and the Life of Ceolfrid.' *Peritia* 3 (1984): 71–84.

McCulloh, John M. 'Did Cynewulf Use a Martyrology? Reconsidering the Sources of *The Fates of the Apostles*.' *ASE* 29 (2000): 67–83.

McKinnell, John S. 'On the Date of *The Battle of Maldon*.' *Medium Ævum* 44 (1975): 121–36.

McKitterick, Rosamond. 'Anglo-Saxon Missionaries in Germany: Personal Connections and Local Influences.' In her *Frankish Kings and Culture in the Early Middle Ages*. Aldershot: Ashgate Variorum, 1995. pp. 1–40.

Meyvaert, Paul. 'Bede the Scholar.' In Bonner (ed.), *Famulus Christi*, pp. 40–69.

Miles, Brent. 'The *Carmina Rhythmica* of Æthilwald: Edition, Translation, and Commentary.' *JML* 14 (2004): 73–117.

Milfull, Inge B. *The Hymns of the Anglo-Saxon Church*. CSASE 17. 1996.

Milroy, Lesley. *Language and Social Networks*. 2nd edn. Oxford: Basil Blackwell, 1987.

Mitford, Nancy (ed.). *Noblesse Oblige: An Enquiry into the Identifiable Characteristics of the English Aristocracy*. New York: Harper & Brothers, 1956.

Moisl, Hermann. 'The Bernician Royal Dynasty and the Irish in the Seventh Century.' *Peritia* 2 (1983): 103–26.

Morrish, Jennifer. 'King Alfred's Letter as a Source on Learning in England.' In Paul E. Szarmach (ed.). *Studies in Earlier Old English Prose*. Albany: SUNY Press, 1985. pp. 87–107.

Mostert, Marco. *The Political Theology of Abbo of Fleury: A Study of the Ideas about Society and Law of the Tenth-Century Monastic Reform Movement*. Hilversum: Verloren, 1987.

Muinzer, L. A. 'Maier's Transcript and the Conclusion of Cynewulf's *Fates of the Apostles*.' *JEGP* 56 (1957): 570–87.

Nagel, Thomas. 'What is it Like to be a Bat?' *The Philosophical Review* 83 (1974): 435–50.

Napier, A. 'Collation der altenglischen Gedichte im Vercellibuch.' *Zeitschrift für deutsches Altertum und deutsche Literatur* 33 (1889): 66–73.

Nelson, Janet L. 'Queens as Jezebels: The Careers of Brunhild and Balthild in Merovingian History.' In Derek Baker (ed.). *Medieval Women*. Oxford: Blackwell, 1978. pp. 31–77.

'Was Charlemagne's Court a Courtly Society?' In Cubitt (ed.), *Court Culture*, pp. 39–57.

Newlands, Carole E. 'Alcuin's Poem of Exile: *O mea cella*.' *Mediaevalia* 11 (1985): 19–45.

Newton, Sam. *The Origins of Beowulf and the Pre-Viking Kingdom of East Anglia*. Cambridge: D. S. Brewer, 1993.

Niles, John D. 'The Myth of the Anglo-Saxon Oral Poet.' *Western Folklore* 62 (2003): 7–61.

Old English Enigmatic Poems and the Play of the Texts. Studies in the Early Middle Ages 13. Turnhout: Brepols, 2006.

Old English Heroic Poems and the Social Life of Texts. Studies in the Early Middle Ages 20. Turnhout: Brepols, 2007.

'Skaldic Technique in *Brunanburh*.' *Scandinavian Studies* 59 (1987): 356–66.

Norberg, Dag. *Introduction à l'étude de la versification latine médiéval*. Studia Latina Stockholmiensia 5. Stockholm: Almqvist & Wiksell, 1958.

Nordau, Max. *Degeneration*. With an introduction by George L. Mosse. Lincoln: University of Nebraska Press, 1993.

O'Brien O'Keeffe, Katherine. 'Listening to the Scenes of Reading: King Alfred's Talking Prefaces.' In Mark Chinca and Christopher Young (eds.). *Orality and Literacy in the Middle Ages*. Turnhout: Brepols, 2005. pp. 17–36.

Stealing Obedience: Narratives of Agency and Identity in Later Anglo-Saxon England. University of Toronto Press, 2012.

'The Text of Aldhelm's *Enigma* no. C in Oxford, Bodleian Library, Rawlinson C.697 and Exeter Riddle 40.' *ASE* 14 (1985): 61–73.

Visible Song: Transitional Literacy in Old English Verse. CSASE 4. 1990.

O'Brien O'Keeffe, Katherine, and Alan R. P. Journet. 'Numerical Taxonomy and the Analysis of Manuscript Relationships.' *Manuscripta* 27 (1983): 131–45.

O'Brien O'Keeffe, Katherine, and Andy Orchard (eds.). *Latin Learning and English Lore: Studies in Anglo-Saxon Literature for Michael Lapidge*. 2 vols. University of Toronto Press, 2005.

Ó Carragáin, Éamonn. 'Cynewulf's Epilogue to *Elene* and the Tastes of the Vercelli Compiler: A Paradigm of Meditative Reading.' In Kay and Sylvester (eds.), *Lexis and Texts*, pp. 187–201.

O'Donoghue, Heather. *Old Norse-Icelandic Literature: A Short Introduction*. Oxford: Blackwell, 2004.

O'Neill, Patrick P. 'Another Fragment of the Metrical Psalms in the Eadwine Psalter.' *Notes & Queries* 233 (1988): 434–6.

Ong, Walter J. *Interfaces of the Word: Studies in the Evolution of Consciousness and Culture*. Ithaca, NY: Cornell University Press, 1977.

Opland, Jeff. *Anglo-Saxon Oral Poetry: A Study of the Traditions*. New Haven, CT: Yale University Press, 1980.

   '*Beowulf* on the Poet.' *Mediaeval Studies* 38 (1976): 442–67.

   '*Scop* and *Imbongi*: Anglo-Saxon and Bantu Oral Poets.' *English Studies in Africa* 14 (1971): 161–78.

   '*Scop* and *Imbongi* IV: Reading Prose Poems.' *Comparative Literature* 45 (1993): 97–120.

Orchard, Andy. 'Artful Alliteration in Anglo-Saxon Song and Story.' *Anglia* 113 (1995): 429–63.

   'Both Style and Substance: The Case for Cynewulf.' In Karkov and Brown (eds.), *Anglo-Saxon Styles*, pp. 271–305.

   'Computing Cynewulf: The *Judith*-Connection.' In Mann and Nolan (eds.), *Text in the Community*, pp. 75–106.

   '*The Dream of the Rood*: Cross-References.' In Zacher and Orchard (eds.), *New Readings in the Vercelli Book*, pp. 224–53.

   'Enigma Variations: The Anglo-Saxon Riddle-Tradition.' In O'Brien O'Keeffe and Orchard (eds.), *Latin Learning*, vol. 1, pp. 284–304.

   'Old Sources, New Resources: Finding the Right Formula for Boniface.' *ASE* 30 (2001): 15–38.

   'Oral Tradition.' In Katherine O'Brien O'Keeffe (ed.). *Reading Old English Texts*. Cambridge University Press, 1997. pp. 101–23.

   The Poetic Art of Aldhelm. CSASE 8. 1994.

   'Wish You Were Here: Alcuin's Courtly Poetry and the Boys Back Home.' In Sarah Rees Jones, Richard Marks, and A. J. Minnis (eds.). *Courts and Regions in Medieval Europe*. York Medieval Press, 2000. pp. 21–43.

Orton, Peter. 'The Technique of Object-Personification in *The Dream of the Rood* and a Comparison with the Old English *Riddles*.' *Leeds Studies in English* 11 (1980): 1–18.

O'Sullivan, Sinéad. 'Aldhelm's *De virginitate* – Patristic Pastiche or Innovative Exposition?' *Peritia* 12 (1998): 271–95.

Owen-Crocker, Gale R. 'Hawks and Horse-Trappings: The Insignia of Rank.' In Scragg (ed.), *Battle of Maldon, AD 991*, pp. 220–37.

Page, R. I. 'On the Feasibility of a Corpus of Anglo-Saxon Glosses: The View from the Library.' In R. Derolez (ed.). *Anglo-Saxon Glossography*. Brussels: Paleis der Academiën, 1992. pp. 77–95.

Palmer, James. 'The "Vigorous Rule" of Bishop Lull: Between Bonifatian Mission and Carolingian Church Control.' *Early Medieval Europe* 13 (2005): 249–76.

Parkes, M. B. 'The Manuscript of the Leiden Riddle.' *ASE* 1 (1972): 207–17.

'The Palaeography of the Parker Manuscript of the *Chronicle*, Laws and Sedulius, and Historiography at Winchester in the Late Ninth and Tenth Centuries.' *ASE* 5 (1976): 149–71.

Parkes, Peter. 'Celtic Fosterage: Adoptive Kinship and Clientage in Northwest Europe.' *Comparative Studies in Society and History* 48 (2006): 359–95.

Parks, Ward. 'The Traditional Narrator and the "I heard" Formulas in Old English Poetry.' *ASE* 16 (1987): 45–66.

Pasternack, Carol Braun. 'The Sexual Practices of Virginity and Chastity in Aldhelm's De virginitate.' In Carol Braun Pasternack and Lisa M. C. Wilson (eds.). *Sex and Sexuality in Anglo-Saxon England*. Tempe, AZ: ACMRS, 2004. pp. 93–120.

'Stylistic Disjunctions in *The Dream of the Rood*.' *ASE* 13 (1984): 167–86.

Pfaff, R. W. 'Eadui Basan: Scriptorum Princeps?' In Carola Hicks (ed.). *England in the Eleventh Century*. Stamford: Paul Watkins, 1992. pp. 267–83.

Plumer, Danielle Cunniff. 'The Construction of Structure in the Earliest Editions of Old English Poetry.' In Graham (ed.), *Recovery of Old English*, pp. 243–79.

Plummer, Charles. 'Earle, John (1824–1903)', rev. John D. Haigh. *Oxford Dictionary of National Biography*. Oxford University Press, 2004 (www.oxforddnb.com/view/article/32954, accessed 8 June 2011).

Poole, Russell. 'Skaldic Verse and Anglo-Saxon History: Some Aspects of the Period 1009–1016.' *Speculum* 62 (1987): 265–98.

Pratt, David. 'Problems of Authorship and Audience in the Writings of King Alfred the Great.' In Wormald and Nelson (eds.), *Lay Intellectuals*, pp. 162–91.

Randle, Jonathan T. 'The "Homiletics" of the Vercelli Book Poems: The Case of Homiletic Fragment I.' In Zacher and Orchard (eds.), *New Readings in the Vercelli Book*, pp. 185–224

Rankin, Susan. 'From Memory to Record: Musical Notations in Manuscripts from Exeter.' *ASE* 13 (1984): 97–112.

Raw, Barbara. 'Alfredian Piety: The Book of Nunnaminster.' In Roberts *et al.* (eds.), *Alfred the Wise*, pp. 145–53.

'The Construction of Oxford, Bodleian Library, Junius 11.' *ASE* 13 (1984): 187–207.

Ray, Roger. 'Bede's *Vera Lex Historiae*.' *Speculum* 55 (1980): 1–21.

'Who Did Bede Think He Was?' In DeGregorio (ed.), *Innovation and Tradition*, pp. 11–35.

Remley, Paul G. 'Aldhelm as Old English Poet: *Exodus*, Asser, and the *Dicta Ælfredi*.' In O'Brien O'Keeffe and Orchard (eds.), *Latin Learning*, vol. 1, pp. 90–108.

'*Daniel*, the *Three Youths* Fragment and the Transmission of Old English Verse.' *ASE* 31 (2002): 81–140.

Reuter, Timothy (ed.). *Alfred the Great: Papers from the Eleventh-Century Centenary Conferences.* Aldershot: Ashgate, 2003.

Richards, I. A. *Practical Criticism: A Study of Literary Judgment.* New York: Harcourt, Brace, 1929.

Richards, Mary P. 'Old Wine in a New Bottle: Recycled Instructional Materials in *Seasons for Fasting*.' In Kleist (ed.), *Old English Homily*, pp. 345–64.

Riché, Pierre. *Les écoles et l'enseignement dans l'Occident chrétien.* Paris: Aubier Montaigne, 1979.

Ricoeur, Paul. 'What is a Text?' In David M. Rasmussen (ed.). *Mythic-Symbolic Language and Philosophical Anthropology.* The Hague: Martinus Nijhoff, 1971. pp. 135–50.

Riedinger, Anita. 'The Old English Formula in Context.' *Speculum* 60 (1985): 294–317.

Rigg, A. G., and G. R. Wieland. 'A Canterbury Classbook of the Mid-Eleventh Century (the "Cambridge Songs" Manuscript).' *ASE* 4 (1975): 113–30.

Roberts, Jane, Janet L. Nelson, and Malcolm Godden (eds.). *Alfred the Wise: Studies in Honour of Janet Bately on the Occasion of her Sixty-Fifth Birthday.* Cambridge: D. S. Brewer, 1997.

Roberts, Michael. *Biblical Epic and Rhetorical Paraphrase in Late Antiquity.* Liverpool: Francis Cairns, 1985.

Robinson, Fred C. '"Bede's" Envoi to the Old English *History*: An Experiment in Editing.' *Studies in Philology* 78 (1981): 4–19.

'God, Death, and Loyalty in *The Battle of Maldon*.' In his *Tomb of Beowulf*, pp. 105–21.

'"The Rewards of Piety": Two Old English Poems in Their Manuscript Context.' In P. J. Gallacher and H. Damico (eds.). *Hermeneutics and Medieval Culture.* Albany, NY: SUNY Press, 1989. pp. 193–200.

'Some Aspects of the *Maldon* Poet's Artistry.' In his *Tomb of Beowulf*, pp. 122–37.

'Syntactical Glosses in Latin Manuscripts of Anglo-Saxon Provenance.' *Speculum* 48 (1973): 443–75.

The Tomb of Beowulf: And Other Essays on Old English. Oxford: Blackwell, 1993.

Rogers, H. L. '*The Battle of Maldon*: David Casley's Transcript.' *Notes & Queries* n.s. 32 [230] (1985): 147–55.

Ronalds, Craig, and Margaret Clunies Ross. '*Thureth*: A Neglected Old English Poem and its History in Anglo-Saxon Scholarship.' *Notes & Queries* 246 (2001): 359–70.

Ross, Alan S. C. 'Philological Probability Problems.' *Journal of the Royal Statistical Society, Series B (Methodological)* 12 (1950): 19–59.

'U and Non-U: An Essay in Sociological Linguistics.' In Mitford (ed.), *Noblesse Oblige*, pp. 53–89.

Ross, Margaret Clunies. 'The Skald Sagas as a Genre: Definitions and Typical Features.' In Russell Poole (ed.). *Skaldsagas: Text, Vocation, and Desire in the Icelandic Sagas of Poets.* Berlin: de Gruyter, 2001. pp. 25–49.

Rubenstein, Jay. 'The Life and Writings of Osbern of Canterbury.' In Richard Eales and Richard Sharpe (eds.). *Canterbury and the Norman Conquest.* London: Hambledon, 1995. pp. 27–40.

Ruff, Carin. 'The Place of Metrics in Anglo-Saxon Latin Education: Aldhelm and Bede.' *JEGP* 104 (2005): 149–70.

Rumble, Alexander R. 'Cues and Clues: Palaeographical Aspects of Anglo-Saxon Scholarship.' In Lendinara *et al.* (eds.), *Form and Content of Instruction*, pp. 115–30.

Rushforth, Rebecca. 'The Prodigal Fragment: Cambridge, Gonville and Caius College 734/782a.' *ASE* 30 (2001): 137–44.

Russom, Geoffrey R. 'Artful Avoidance of the Useful Phrase in *Beowulf, The Battle of Maldon*, and *Fates of the Apostles.*' *Studies in Philology* 75 (1978): 371–90.

Old English Meter & Linguistic Theory. Cambridge University Press, 1987.

Samouce, Warren A. 'General Byrhtnoth.' *JEGP* 62 (1963): 129–35.

Sauer, Hans, and Joanna Story, with Gaby Waxenberger (eds.). *Anglo-Saxon England and the Continent*. Tempe, AZ: ACMRS, 2011.

Schaefer, Ursula. 'Hearing From Books: The Rise of Fictionality in Old English Poetry.' In Doane and Pasternack (eds.), *Vox Intexta*, pp. 117–36.

Schaller, Dieter. 'Das Aachener Epos für Karl den Kaiser.' *Frühmittelalterliche Studien* 10 (1976): 134–68; repr. in his *Studien*, pp. 129–63.

Studien zur lateinischen Dichtung des Frühmittelalters. Stuttgart: Anton Hiersemann, 1995.

'Vortrags- und Zirkulardichtung am Hof Karls des Großen.' *Mittellateinisches Jahrbuch* 6 (1970): 14–36; repr. in his *Studien*, pp. 87–109.

Scharer, Anton. 'The Writing of History at King Alfred's Court.' *Early Medieval Europe* 5 (1996): 177–206.

Scheil, Andrew P. *The Footsteps of Israel: Understanding Jews in Anglo-Saxon England*. Ann Arbor: University of Michigan Press, 2004.

Schilling-Estes, Natalie, and Walt Wolfram. 'Alternative Models of Dialect Death: Dissipation vs. Concentration.' *Language* 75 (1999): 486–521.

Schlauch, Margaret. 'The "Dream of the Rood" as Prosopopoeia.' In *Essays and Studies in Honor of Carleton Brown*. New York University Press, 1940. pp. 23–34.

Scragg, Donald. 'The Battle of Maldon.' In his *Battle of Maldon, AD 991*, pp. 15–36.

'*The Battle of Maldon*: Fact or Fiction?' In Cooper (ed.), *Battle of Maldon*, pp. 19–31.

Scragg, Donald (ed.). *The Battle of Maldon, AD 991*. Oxford: Blackwell, 1991.

Shippey, T. A. *Poems of Wisdom and Learning in Old English*. Cambridge: D. S. Brewer, 1976.

Shook, Laurence K. 'Riddles Relating to the Anglo-Saxon Scriptorium.' In J. R. O'Donnell (ed.). *Essays in Honour of Anton Charles Pegis*. University of Toronto Press, 1974. pp. 215–29.

Sims-Williams, Patrick. *Religion and Literature in Western England, 600–800*. CSASE 3. 1990.

Sinisi, Lucia. 'From York to Paris: Reinterpreting Alcuin's Virtual Tour of the Continent.' In Sauer and Story (eds.), *Anglo-Saxon England*, pp. 275–92.

Sisam, Kenneth. 'Cynewulf and his Poetry.' In his *Studies*, pp. 1–28.

Studies in the History of Old English Literature. Oxford: Clarendon Press, 1953.

Sleeth, Charles R. *Studies in Christ and Satan*. University of Toronto Press, 1982.

Sot, Michel (ed.). *Haut Moyen-Age: culture, éducation et société. Études offertes à Pierre Riché*. La Garenne-Colombes: Éditions Européenes Erasme, 1990.

Stafford, Pauline. 'Kinship and Women in the World of *Maldon*: Byrhtnoth and his Family.' In Cooper (ed.), *Battle of Maldon*, pp. 225–35.

Queen Emma and Queen Edith: Queenship and Women's Power in Eleventh-Century England. Oxford: Blackwell, 1997 (repr. 2001).

Unification and Conquest: A Political and Social History of England in the Tenth and Eleventh Centuries. London: Edward Arnold, 1989.

Stanley, E. G. 'The Search for Anglo-Saxon Paganism.' 1975. Repr. in *Imagining the Anglo-Saxon Past*. Cambridge: D. S. Brewer, 2000. pp. 1–110.

Stansbury, Mark. 'Early-Medieval Biblical Commentaries, Their Writers and Readers.' *Frühmittelalterliche Studien* 33 (1999): 49–82.

'Source-Marks in Bede's Biblical Commentaries.' In Jane Hawkes and Susan Mills (eds.). *Northumbria's Golden Age*. Stroud: Sutton, 1999. pp. 383–9.

Steen, Janie. *Verse and Virtuosity: The Adaptation of Latin Rhetoric in Old English Poetry*. University of Toronto Press, 2008.

Stevenson, Jane. 'Altus Prosator.' *Celtica* 23 (1999): 326–68.

'Anglo-Latin Women Poets.' In O'Brien O'Keeffe and Orchard (eds.), *Latin Learning*, vol. II, pp. 86–107.

Stork, Nancy Porter. *Through a Gloss Darkly: Aldhelm's Riddles in the British Library MS Royal 12. C.xxiii*. PIMS Studies and Texts 98. Toronto: Pontifical Institute of Medieval Studies, 1990.

Strecker, Karl. 'Zu den Quellen für das Leben des hl. Ninian.' *Neues Archiv der Gesellschaft für Ältere Deutsche Geschichtskunde zur Beförderung einer Gesamtausgabe der Quellenschriften deutscher Geschichten des Mittelalters* 43 (1922): 1–26.

Szarmach, Paul E. 'Bede on Aldhelm: *Nitidus sermone*.' *American Notes & Queries* 9 (1971): 375–7.

'The (Sub-)Genre of *The Battle of Maldon*.' In Cooper (ed.), *Battle of Maldon*, pp. 43–61.

Ten Brink, Bernhard. *Geschichte der englischen Litteratur*. 2nd edn, rev. Alois Brandl. 2 vols. Strassburg: Trübner, 1899.

Tengvik, Gösta. *Old English Bynames*. Uppsala: Almqvist & Wiksells, 1938.

Thomas, Richard F. *Virgil and the Augustan Reception*. Cambridge University Press, 2001.

Thomson, Rodney M. 'The Norman Conquest and English Libraries.' In Peter Ganz (ed.). *The Role of the Book in Medieval Culture*. 2 vols. Turnhout: Brepols, 1986. vol. II, pp. 27–40.

William of Malmesbury. 2nd edn. Woodbridge: Boydell, 2003.

Thomson, Rodney M., with M. Winterbottom. *William of Malmesbury: Gesta Regum Anglorum: The History of the English Kings: Vol. II. General Introduction and Commentary*. Oxford: Clarendon Press, 1999.

Thornbury, Emily V. 'Æthilwulf *poeta*.' In *Latinity and Identity in Anglo-Saxon England* (forthcoming).

'Aldhelm's Rejection of the Muses and the Mechanics of Poetic Inspiration in Early Anglo-Saxon England.' *ASE* 36 (2007): 71–92.

'Anglo-Saxon Poetics.' Unpublished Ph.D. dissertation. University of Cambridge, 2004.

'*Christ and Satan*: "Healing" Line 7.' *English Studies* 87 (2006): 505–10.

Toswell, M. J. 'The Format of Bibliothèque nationale MS. lat. 8824: The Paris Psalter.' *Notes & Queries* 241 (1996): 130–3.

'The Metrical Psalter and the *Menologium*: Some Observations.' *Neuphilologische Mitteilungen* 94 (1993): 249–57.

Townend, Matthew. 'Contextualizing the *Knútsdrápur*: Skaldic Praise-Poetry at the Court of Cnut.' *ASE* 30 (2001): 145–79.

'Pre-Cnut Praise-Poetry in Viking Age England.' *Review of English Studies* 51 (2000): 349–70.

Trautmann, Moritz. 'Zeit, Heimat und Verfasser der altengl. Rätsel.' *Anglia* 38 (1914): 367–73.

Treharne, Elaine. 'Categorization, Periodization: The Silence of (the) English in the Twelfth Century.' *New Medieval Literatures* 8 (2006): 247–73.

Living Through Conquest: The Politics of Early English, 1020–1220. Oxford University Press, 2012.

Treitler, Leo. 'Oral, Written, and Literate Process in the Transmission of Medieval Music.' *Speculum* 56 (1981): 471–91.

Trilling, Renée R. *The Aesthetics of Nostalgia: Historical Representation in Old English Verse.* University of Toronto Press, 2009.

Trudgill, Peter. 'Contact and Isolation in Linguistic Change.' In Leiv Egil Breivik and Ernst Håkon Jahr (eds.). *Language Change: Contributions to the Study of its Causes.* New York: Mouton de Gruyter, 1989. pp. 227–37.

The Social Differentiation of English in Norwich. Cambridge University Press, 1974.

Tupper, Frederick, Jr (ed.). *The Riddles of the Exeter Book.* Boston: Ginn, 1910.

Turner, Sharon. *The History of the Anglo-Saxons from the Earliest Period to the Norman Conquest.* 6th edn. 2 vols. Philadelphia: Carey and Hart, 1841.

Tyler, Elizabeth M. *Old English Poetics: The Aesthetics of the Familiar in Anglo-Saxon England.* Woodbridge: York Medieval Press, 2006.

Wallach, Luitpold. *Alcuin and Charlemagne: Studies in Carolingian History and Literature.* Ithaca, NY: Cornell University Press, 1959.

Review of J. D. A. Ogilvy, *Books Known to the English, 597–1066. JEGP* 68 (1969): 156–61.

Webber, Teresa. *Scribes and Scholars at Salisbury Cathedral, c. 1075–c. 1125.* Oxford: Clarendon Press, 1992.

Webster, Leslie, and Janet Backhouse (eds.). *The Making of England: Anglo-Saxon Art and Culture, AD 600–900.* University of Toronto Press, 1991.

Whitbread, Leslie. 'The Old English Poem *Aldhelm*.' *English Studies* 57 (1976): 193–7.

'A Study of Bede's *Versus de die iudicii*.' *Philological Quarterly* 23 (1944): 193–221.

White, Peter. '*Amicitia* and the Profession of Poetry in Early Imperial Rome.' *Journal of Roman Studies* 68 (1978): 74–92.

Whitelock, Dorothy. *The Audience of Beowulf.* Oxford: Clarendon Press, 1951.

'The Prose of Alfred's Reign.' In E. G. Stanley (ed.). *Continuations and Beginnings.* London: Nelson, 1966. pp. 67–103.

Whitta, James. 'Ille ego Naso: Modoin of Autun's Eclogues and the *Renouatio* of Ovid.' *Latomus* 61 (2002): 703–31.

Wieland, Gernot R. '*Geminus Stilus*: Studies in Anglo-Latin Hagiography.' In Herren (ed.), *Insular Latin*, pp. 113–33.

'The Glossed Manuscript: Classbook or Library Book?' *ASE* 14 (1985): 153–73.

'A New Look at the Poem Archalis clamare triumuir.' In Gernot R. Wieland, Carin Ruff, and Ross G. Arthur (eds.). *Insignis Sophiae Arcator.* Turnhout: Brepols, 2006. pp. 178–92.

Wilcox, Miranda. 'Vernacular Biblical Epics and the Production of Anglo-Saxon Cultural Exegesis.' Unpublished Ph.D. dissertation. University of Notre Dame, 2006.

Williams, J. E. Caerwyn. 'The Court Poet in Medieval Ireland.' *Proceedings of the British Academy* 57 (1971): 85–135.

Williamson, Craig (ed.). *The Old English Riddles of the Exeter Book.* Chapel Hill: University of North Carolina Press, 1977.

Wilson, R. M. *The Lost Literature of Medieval England.* 2nd edn. London: Methuen, 1970.

Winterbottom, Michael. 'Faricius of Arezzo's Life of St Aldhelm.' In O'Brien O'Keeffe and Orchard (eds.), *Latin Learning*, vol. 1, pp. 109–31.

Wood, Ian. 'The Foundation of Bede's Wearmouth-Jarrow.' In DeGregorio (ed.), *Companion*, pp. 84–96.

Woolf, Rosemary. 'The Ideal of Men Dying with their Lord in the *Germania* and in *The Battle of Maldon*.' *ASE* 5 (1976): 63–81.

Wormald, Patrick. 'Bede and Benedict Biscop.' In Bonner (ed.), *Famulus Christi*, pp. 141–69.

'Bede, *Beowulf*, and the Conversion of the Anglo-Saxon Aristocracy.' In his *Times of Bede*, pp. 30–105.

The Times of Bede: Studies in Early English Christian Society and its Historian. Ed. Stephen Baxter. Oxford: Blackwell, 2006.

Wormald, Patrick, and Janet L. Nelson (eds.). *Lay Intellectuals in the Carolingian World.* Cambridge University Press, 2007.

Wright, Neil. 'Imitation of the Poems of Paulinus of Nola in Early Anglo-Latin Verse.' *Peritia* 4 (1985): 134–51.

'The Metrical Art(s) of Bede.' In O'Brien O'Keeffe and Orchard (eds.), *Latin Learning*, vol. 1, pp. 150–70.

Wright, Thomas. *Womankind in Western Europe, from the Earliest Times to the Seventeenth Century.* London: Groomsbridge & Sons, 1869.

Yorke, Barbara. *The Conversion of Britain: Religion, Politics and Society in Britain, 600–800.* Harlow: Pearson, 2006.

Nunneries and the Anglo-Saxon Royal Houses. London: Continuum, 2003.

Zacher, Samantha. *Preaching the Converted: The Style and Rhetoric of the Vercelli Book Homilies.* University of Toronto Press, 2009.

Zacher, Samantha, and Andy Orchard (eds.). *New Readings in the Vercelli Book.* University of Toronto Press, 2009.

Ziolkowski, Jan M. 'Classical Influences on Medieval Latin Views of Poetic Inspiration.' In Peter Godman and Oswyn Murray (eds.). *Latin Poetry and the Classical Tradition: Essays in Medieval and Renaissance Literature.* Oxford: Clarendon Press, 1990. pp. 15–38.

Nota Bene: Reading Classics and Writing Melodies in the Early Middle Ages. Publications of the Journal of Medieval Latin 7. Turnhout: Brepols, 2007.

Index

CAMBRIDGE STUDIES IN MEDIEVAL LITERATURE

CPSIA information can be obtained
at www.ICGtesting.com
Printed in the USA
LVHW040424020920
664773LV00017B/751

9 781107 643079